Using Machine Learning to Detect Emotions and Predict Human Psychology

Mritunjay Rai
Department of Electrical and Electronics Engineering, Shri Ramswaroop Memorial University, India

Jay Kumar Pandey
Department of Electrical and Electronics Engineering, Shri Ramswaroop Memorial University, India

A volume in the Advances in Psychology, Mental Health, and Behavioral Studies (APMHBS) Book Series

IGI Global
PUBLISHER of TIMELY KNOWLEDGE

Published in the United States of America by
IGI Global
Medical Information Science Reference (an imprint of IGI Global)
701 E. Chocolate Avenue
Hershey PA, USA 17033
Tel: 717-533-8845
Fax: 717-533-8661
E-mail: cust@igi-global.com
Web site: http://www.igi-global.com

Library of Congress Cataloging-in-Publication Data

Names: Rai, Mritunjay, 1985- editor. | Pandey, Jay Kumar, 1987- editor.
Title: Using machine learning to detect emotions and predict human psychology / edited by Mritunjay Rai, Jay Kumar Pandey.
Description: Hershey, PA : Medical Information Science Reference, [2024] | Includes bibliographical references and index. | Summary: "Artificial Intelligence (AI) plays a significant role in the detection and understanding of human emotions. With advancements in machine learning and natural language processing, AI algorithms can analyze various data sources to recognize and interpret emotions accurately"-- Provided by publisher.
Identifiers: LCCN 2023058970 (print) | LCCN 2023058971 (ebook) | ISBN 9798369319109 (hardcover) | ISBN 9798369319116 (ebook)
Subjects: LCSH: Emotions--Data processing. | Machine learning. | Psychology.
Classification: LCC BF531 .U65 2024 (print) | LCC BF531 (ebook) | DDC 152.4--dc23/eng/20240130
LC record available at https://lccn.loc.gov/2023058970
LC ebook record available at https://lccn.loc.gov/2023058971

This book is published in the IGI Global book series Advances in Psychology, Mental Health, and Behavioral Studies (APMHBS) (ISSN: 2475-6660; eISSN: 2475-6679)

British Cataloguing in Publication Data
A Cataloguing in Publication record for this book is available from the British Library.

For electronic access to this publication, please contact: eresources@igi-global.com.

Advances in Psychology, Mental Health, and Behavioral Studies (APMHBS) Book Series

ISSN:2475-6660
EISSN:2475-6679

Editor-in-Chief: Harish C. Chandan, Argosy University, USA

MISSION

The complexity of the human mind has puzzled researchers and physicians for centuries. While widely studied, the brain still remains largely misunderstood.

The **Advances in Psychology, Mental Health, and Behavioral Studies (APMHBS)** book series presents comprehensive research publications focusing on topics relating to the human psyche, cognition, psychiatric care, mental and developmental disorders, as well as human behavior and interaction. Featuring diverse and innovative research, publications within APMHBS are ideally designed for use by mental health professionals, academicians, researchers, and upper-level students.

COVERAGE

- Personality Disorders
- Neurological Disorders
- Counseling & Therapy
- Treatment & Care
- Cognition
- Psychiatry
- Substance Abuse
- Human Behavior
- Socialization
- Trauma & Stress

IGI Global is currently accepting manuscripts for publication within this series. To submit a proposal for a volume in this series, please contact our Acquisition Editors at Acquisitions@igi-global.com or visit: http://www.igi-global.com/publish/.

The Advances in Psychology, Mental Health, and Behavioral Studies (APMHBS) Book Series (ISSN 2475-6660) is published by IGI Global, 701 E. Chocolate Avenue, Hershey, PA 17033-1240, USA, www.igi-global.com. This series is composed of titles available for purchase individually; each title is edited to be contextually exclusive from any other title within the series. For pricing and ordering information please visit http://www.igi-global.com/book-series/advances-psychology-mental-health-behavioral/110200. Postmaster: Send all address changes to above address.

Titles in this Series

For a list of additional titles in this series, please visit:
http://www.igi-global.com/book-series/advances-psychology-mental-health-behavioral/110200

Promoting Mindfulness and Well-Being with Indian Psychology
Anuradha Sathiyaseelan (Christ University, India) and Sathiyaseelan Balasundaram (Christ University, India)
Information Science Reference • © 2024 • 337pp • H/C (ISBN: 9798369326510) • US $245.00

Impact of Climate Change on Mental Health and Well-Being
Debabrata Samanta (Rochester Institute of Technology, Kosovo) and Muskan Garg (Mayo Clinic, USA)
Information Science Reference • © 2024 • 282pp • H/C (ISBN: 9798369321775) • US $245.00

African Womanhood and the Feminist Agenda
Maxwell Constantine Chando Musingafi (National University of Lesotho, Lesotho) and Chipo Hungwe (Midlands State University, Zimbabwe)
Information Science Reference • © 2024 • 280pp • H/C (ISBN: 9798369319994) • US $230.00

Challenges and Opportunities for Women, Parenting, and Child Development
Nava R. Silton (Marymount Manhattan College, USA)
Information Science Reference • © 2024 • 300pp • H/C (ISBN: 9798369312858) • US $230.00

Global Applications of Indian Psychology Therapeutic and Strategic Models
Anuradha Sathiyaseelan (Christ University, India) and Sathiyaseelan Balasundaram (Christ University, India)
Information Science Reference • © 2024 • 325pp • H/C (ISBN: 9781668497784) • US $265.00

Combining Exercise and Psychotherapy to Treat Mental Health
Lara Carneiro (United Arab Emirates University, UAE) and Felipe Schuch (Universidade Federal de Santa Maria, Brazil)
Medical Information Science Reference • © 2024 • 359pp • H/C (ISBN: 9781668460405) • US $325.00

IGI Global
PUBLISHER of TIMELY KNOWLEDGE

701 East Chocolate Avenue, Hershey, PA 17033, USA
Tel: 717-533-8845 x100 • Fax: 717-533-8661
E-Mail: cust@igi-global.com • www.igi-global.com

Table of Contents

Detailed Table of Contents

Artificial emotional intelligence (AEI) is a burgeoning field at the intersection of technology and human emotion, seeking to imbue machines with the capacity to perceive, understand, and respond to human emotions. This chapter encapsulates a comprehensive exploration of AEI, encompassing its foundations, technical intricacies, applications, user perspectives, ethical considerations, challenges, and real-world case studies. The foundations of AEI involve unraveling the complexities of human emotions, from facial expressions and voice tones to physiological signals. Understanding the technical aspects of AEI, including data acquisition, feature extraction, machine learning models, and multi-modal fusion, provides insights into the sophisticated mechanisms driving emotionally intelligent systems. AEI's applications span diverse domains, from virtual health assistants providing mental well-being support to emotionally aware educational platforms adapting to students' learning needs.

Present research is focused on consideration of emotional data. In order to deal with such objective, EEG technique has been applied. Electroencephalography (EEG) is a technique used to measure and record the electrical activity that takes place on the scalp. This recorded activity has been shown to be indicative of the underlying activity occurring in the superficial layer of the brain. Numerous studies have been conducted to investigate the quality of the electroencephalogram (EEG) signal. The major objective of this experiment was to examine the ability to recognize the emotional states shown by individuals. Despite the previous time-consuming nature and lack of accuracy in prior study, a viable solution has been discovered. It can be concluded that the system has a very limited capacity for both adaptation and expansion. Developing a thorough methodology for assessing electroencephalogram (EEG) data is of paramount significance.

In this chapter, the exploration delves into the captivating realm of Emotional Intelligence (EI) and Artificial Emotional Intelligence (AEI) to unravel their profound impact on human-machine harmony. Navigating the tapestry of human emotions and the evolving landscape of technology, the chapter aims to illuminate the synergies and transformative potential these concepts hold. This journey embarks on a captivating exploration into the realms of EI and AEI, investigating how the fusion of these disciplines can redefine the way individuals interact with technology and, fundamentally, with each other. The chapter seeks to dissect the existing divide between EI and AI, elucidating how their integration can revolutionize the prediction of human behavior. Through an understanding and amalgamation of the strengths of both disciplines, the pathway is paved for more intuitive, empathetic, and effective interactions between humans and machines.

Predictive pioneers are bridging the mental health gap in older adults by leveraging advanced digital technologies and user-centric insights. This study explores the potential of machine learning and digital tools in predicting mental health conditions in older adults, facilitating early intervention and support. Through an extensive literature review, user interactions, and healthcare staff interviews, the research aims to bridge gaps in existing knowledge and emphasize real-world application. The research culminates in the creation of highly accurate predictive models for depression in older adults, with valuable insights from user perspectives and healthcare staff guiding future directions. This study contributes innovative methods for mental health prediction and emphasizes the importance of user-centred design, paving the way for effective and accessible mental health interventions for older adults.

This chapter presents a simple and effective approach to designing LSTM networks for the task of emotion recognition. Emotion modelling plays a crucial role in various applications, such as human-computer interaction,

An extremely potent AI solution for animal care is created when Microsoft Custom Vision Service is combined with Azure IoT stack, particularly in hospitals with a shortage of monitoring manpower. The GUI and configuration files for Azure logic apps are unique. Here are various human charity and animal care charity agencies across who need an intelligent solution which can help them in continuous monitoring of animals in the process of their treatments. Human and animal posture detection is an intelligent care solution in India. It is designed using Microsoft technology stack. The whole idea behind the solution is to provide continuous monitoring of humans and animals in the hospital. And in case any improper gestures/postures are detected, then the solution can inform concerned doctors or care takers through mobile alerts. In this chapter, the authors have proposed architecture for hospital monitoring and this system has been implemented in real-time.

This chapter examines the intersection of artificial intelligence (AI) and psychology in healthcare through emotion recognition systems (ERS). By tracing ERS's development, it showcases its crucial role in improving patient care, enhancing mental health treatments, and providing stress management for healthcare workers. It discusses ERS's potential and the challenges it faces, including ensuring accuracy, integrating technology, addressing cultural sensitivity, and managing privacy concerns. The narrative aims to deepen understanding among healthcare professionals, technologists, and ethicists about ERS's nuanced contributions and technical complexities. It highlights the transformative potential of ERS in healthcare, considering both its benefits and the multifaceted issues it presents. Looking ahead, the chapter advocates for progress driven by technological advancements, cross-disciplinary research, and thoughtful policy-making, providing a comprehensive view of how ERS can be effectively integrated into healthcare practices for future enhancements.

Preface

In the realm of Artificial Intelligence (AI), the exploration of human emotions has emerged as a fascinating and consequential domain. We find ourselves at the intersection of technology and psychology, witnessing the transformative power of machine learning in unraveling the intricacies of human sentiment and behavior. This edited reference book, *Using Machine Learning to Detect Emotions and Predict Human Psychology*, represents a collective effort to illuminate the advancements, challenges, and ethical considerations in the field of emotion detection using AI.

The landscape of emotion detection has undergone a paradigm shift, driven by the relentless evolution of AI algorithms, particularly in machine learning and natural language processing. Mritunjay Rai and Jay Kumar Pandey, the esteemed editors of this volume, have curated a comprehensive exploration into the capabilities of AI in discerning and understanding human emotions. As technology continues to progress, we delve into the nuanced aspects of emotion detection, emphasizing the importance of ethical considerations, privacy preservation, and the mitigation of biases in AI systems.

This edited reference book embarks on a multidimensional journey into the captivating realm where Artificial Intelligence intersects with the intricacies of human emotions and psychology. The chapters within this volume serve as a collective exploration, offering profound insights and cutting-edge advancements in the field of emotion detection and predictive psychology using machine learning techniques. From the intricate study of facial expression systems and the burgeoning field of Artificial Emotional Intelligence (AEI) to the innovative applications of Electroencephalography (EEG) for emotion recognition, each chapter unfolds a unique facet of the intricate relationship between technology and human emotions. The narrative extends to the realms of Emotional Intelligence (EI), mental health prediction in older adults, sentiment analysis in digital communication, and the intelligent integration of technology for human and animal care. As the reader navigates through these diverse chapters, a holistic understanding of the transformative potential and ethical considerations in the fusion of AI and psychology emerges, promising to reshape the way we comprehend, predict, and interact with human emotions.

Chapter 1 delves into the intricate world of facial expression systems, focusing on the performance assessment of a deep unified model. The authors meticulously explore the utilization of hybrid models, namely ResNet and DenseNet, within a CNN-based image classification framework for facial expression recognition. The significance of a balanced and representative dataset is emphasized, and the customization of the hybrid ResNet-DenseNet model architecture becomes pivotal. Techniques such as data augmentation, hyperparameter adjustment, and regularization are employed to optimize the model's performance during training. The evaluation metrics include accuracy, precision, recall, F1-score, and a confusion matrix, with a thoughtful consideration of the model's generalization skills using different datasets.

Chapter 2 provides an in-depth exploration of Artificial Emotional Intelligence (AEI), positioning it at the nexus of technology and human emotion. Covering foundations, technical intricacies, applications, user perspectives, ethical considerations, challenges, and real-world case studies, the authors unravel the complexities of AEI. The chapter navigates through various modalities of human expression, including facial expressions, voice tones, and physiological signals. AEI's applications across domains such as virtual health assistants and emotionally aware educational platforms are thoroughly examined, offering a holistic perspective on the transformative potential of emotionally intelligent systems.

Chapter 3 focuses on the consideration of emotional data through the application of Electroencephalography (EEG) techniques. The authors delve into the intricacies of EEG as a tool to measure and record electrical activity on the scalp, revealing its potential in recognizing emotional states. The experiment aims to overcome the time-consuming nature and accuracy challenges of previous studies, presenting a viable solution. The chapter emphasizes the limited capacity for both adaptation and expansion within the system, underlining the paramount significance of developing a thorough methodology for assessing EEG data.

Embarking on a captivating exploration, chapter 4 delves into Emotional Intelligence (EI) and Artificial Emotional Intelligence (AEI), unraveling their profound impact on human-machine harmony. The authors navigate the interplay between human emotions and evolving technology, illustrating how the integration of EI and AI can revolutionize the prediction of human behavior. The chapter advocates for an understanding and amalgamation of the strengths of both disciplines, paving the way for more intuitive, empathetic, and effective interactions between humans and machines.

Chapter 5 explores the potential of machine learning and digital tools in predicting mental health conditions in older adults, aiming for early intervention and support. Through extensive literature review, user interactions, and healthcare staff interviews, the research bridges gaps in existing knowledge. The creation of highly accurate predictive models for depression in older adults is the culmination of this effort, guided by valuable insights from user perspectives and healthcare staff. The study contributes innovative methods for mental health prediction, emphasizing user-centered design and paving the way for effective and accessible mental health interventions for older adults.

Chapter 6 presents a simple yet effective approach to designing Long Short-Term Memory (LSTM) networks for emotion recognition. Focused on applications in human-computer interaction, sentiment analysis, and affective computing, the proposed LSTM architecture captures temporal dependencies and nuances in emotional states. The authors detail the pre-processing of time-series sequences, hyperparameter tuning, and regularization techniques to enhance the network's performance. Benchmark evaluations on emotion datasets showcase the model's capability to accurately predict and classify various emotional states.

Exploring the valuable concept of patterns, chapter 7 delves into pattern analysis, a subfield of artificial intelligence and computer science. Patterns, interpreted in various ways, serve as underlying correlations, regularities, or structures in data streams. The chapter emphasizes the importance of algorithms in uncovering these patterns and their significant role in improving recognition. Through the lens of artificial intelligence, the analysis of patterns in data contributes to anticipating and generating predictions based on fresh information, underscoring its relevance in diverse applications.

Chapter 8 unravels the synergies between facial profiling, machine learning, and emotion detection, shedding light on their impact on human psychology. The meticulous process of facial profiling and its applications in marketing, security, and human-computer interaction are explored. The symbiotic relationship with machine learning advances facial recognition, sentiment analysis, and predictive applications. Ethical considerations and the emphasis on data quality permeate the methodology, serving as a guide for researchers and practitioners navigating the responsible integration of technology into psychology.

In an era dominated by digital communication, chapter 9 explores the profound insights textual data offers into human behavior and emotions. The authors delve into textual sentiment analysis, examining synthetic datasets through advanced techniques such as sentiment analysis, topic modeling, pattern recognition, and emotion detection. The study underscores the potential of textual analysis not only for understanding but also for predicting and addressing mental health challenges in digital communication mediums. The findings reveal that digital textual signs can be effective indicators of mental health conditions.

Chapter 10 presents an intelligent care solution for animal care, combining Microsoft Custom Vision Service with Azure IoT stack. The authors highlight the unique GUI and configuration files for Azure logic apps, emphasizing its potential application in hospitals with limited monitoring manpower. The proposed Human and Animal Posture Detection system aims to continuously monitor humans and animals in hospitals, alerting concerned caregivers in case of improper gestures or postures. The chapter outlines the architecture, implementation in real-time, and the broader implications of this intelligent care solution for both charity and non-charity hospitals.

Chapter 11 explores the intersection of artificial intelligence (AI) and psychology in healthcare through Emotion Recognition Systems (ERS). Tracing the development of ERS, the authors showcase its crucial role in improving patient care, enhancing mental health treatments, and providing stress management for healthcare workers. The narrative delves into ERS's potential, challenges, and technical complexities, addressing accuracy, technology integration, cultural sensitivity, and privacy concerns. Advocating for progress through technological advancements, cross-disciplinary research, and thoughtful policy-making, the chapter provides a comprehensive view of how ERS can be effectively integrated into healthcare practices for future enhancements.

This volume is structured to provide insights into key dimensions of AI's role in emotion detection, spanning various modalities of human expression:

- **Facial Expression Analysis:** Explore the real-time analysis of facial expressions through computer vision techniques, deciphering emotions from subtle cues such as eyebrow movements, eye gaze, lip curvature, and micro-expressions.
- **Speech and Voice Analysis:** Delve into the realm of vocal cues, where AI processes tone, pitch, loudness, speech rate, and language choice to detect a spectrum of emotions in human speech, from joy to anger, sadness to fear.
- **Text Analysis:** Uncover the capabilities of AI in analyzing written content, including social media posts, customer reviews, emails, and chat conversations, to discern emotional tones and sentiments, providing valuable insights for various applications.
- **Biometric Sensing:** Explore the integration of biometric data such as heart rate, skin conductance, and electroencephalography (EEG) signals to infer emotional states, contributing to areas like mental health monitoring, gaming, and human performance analysis.
- **Multimodal Emotion Recognition:** Witness the convergence of data from multiple sources, combining facial expressions, speech, text, and physiological signals, to achieve enhanced accuracy and robustness in emotion recognition.

As editors, we believe that this collaborative endeavor will not only contribute to the scientific community but will also be a valuable resource for researchers, academicians, and professionals in engineering, medicine, healthcare, and psychology.

The book is tailored to be a reference guide for both undergraduate and postgraduate courses, providing a bridge between the evolving fields of AI and psychology. We hope this volume sparks curiosity, fosters interdisciplinary collaboration, and advances our collective understanding of the intricate interplay between artificial intelligence and human emotions.

Editors,

Mritunjay Rai
Department of Electrical and Electronics Engineering, Shri Ramswaroop Memorial University, India

Jay Kumar Pandey
Department of Electrical and Electronics Engineering, Shri Ramswaroop Memorial University, India

Chapter 1
Introduction to Emotion Detection and Predictive Psychology in the Age of Technology

Vaibhav Prakash Vasani
https://orcid.org/0000-0001-6498-553X
Kalinga University, India

Umesh Chandra
CMS Business School, Jain University, India

Gayatri Sahu
Gurukul Kangri University, India

Srinivasulu Boyineni
Malla Reddy Engineering College for Women, India

S. Dhamodaran
Sathyabama Institute of Science and Technology, Chennai, India

Makhan Kumbhkar
ICAR-Indian Institute of Soybean Research, Indore, India

Mritunjay Rai
https://orcid.org/0000-0002-8911-4826
Department of Electrical and Electronics Engineering, Shri Ramswaroop Memorial University, India

Swati Gupta
Vaish College of Engineering, Rohtak, India

ABSTRACT

A performance study of a deep unified model for a facial expression system using hybrid models like ResNet and DenseNet in a CNN-based image classification framework is crucial. Assessing the effectiveness of this complex system that interprets facial expressions to identify emotions is crucial. Data is carefully prepared and separated to produce a balanced and representative dataset. The hybrid ResNet-DenseNet model architecture is crucial. It must be customised for face expression recognition. Data augmentation, hyper parameter adjustment, and regularisation are used to optimise model performance during training. Accuracy, precision, recall, F1-score, and confusion matrix are used to evaluate the model's performance. A different dataset may be used to evaluate its generalisation skills. Comparing the model to others might reveal its performance.

DOI: 10.4018/979-8-3693-1910-9.ch001

1. INTRODUCTION

1.1 Emotion Detection

Emotion detection, a burgeoning field in the realm of artificial intelligence and technology, has made remarkable strides in understanding and interpreting human emotions. Through the utilization of advanced machine learning algorithms and data-driven insights, this technology can discern emotional states by analyzing a variety of cues, including facial expressions, voice tone, and text sentiment. It has found applications in numerous domains, from marketing and customer service to mental health and human-computer interaction. Emotion detection not only aids in gauging customer satisfaction, but also in providing personalized mental health support and improving user experiences in technology interfaces. However, it is essential to address the ethical concerns surrounding privacy and consent, as well as to ensure that the technology is used responsibly and with sensitivity to cultural and individual differences. As emotion detection continues to evolve it holds great potential for enhancing human well-being and understanding, provided it is harnessed conscientiously as shown in fig1.

Figure 1. Emotion detection

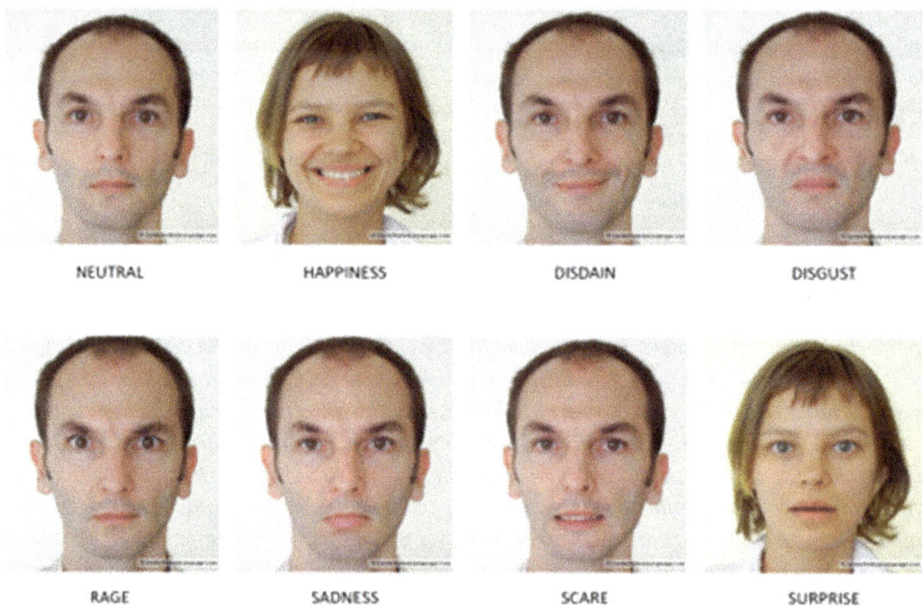

1.2 Predictive Psychology

Predictive psychology is a subfield of psychology that focuses on the development and application of predictive models and data-driven approaches to understand, anticipate, and influence human behavior and mental processes. It leverages a wide range of statistical and computational techniques, such as machine learning and predictive analytics, to make forecasts about future behavior, outcomes, and trends, based on historical data and psychological principles. These predictions can have applications in various domains, including clinical psychology, education, organizational behavior, and consumer behavior, aiming to enhance decision-making, interventions, and strategies to promote positive outcomes and well-being.

1.3 Predictive Psychology in the Age of Technology

Predictive psychology in the age of technology refers to the application of psychological principles and data-driven approaches to make predictions about human behavior and mental processes, often leveraging advanced technology and big data. This field has seen significant developments in recent years due to the proliferation of digital devices, the internet, and the availability of large datasets. Here are some key aspects to consider:

1. **Data Collection and Analysis:** Technology has enabled the collection of vast amounts of data on individuals' online behavior, social interactions, and more. Predictive psychology uses this data to identify patterns and trends in human behavior, helping to predict future actions or preferences.
2. **Machine Learning and AI:** Predictive psychology heavily relies on machine learning and artificial intelligence algorithms to process and analyze data. These algorithms can identify correlations and make predictions based on historical data.
3. **Personalized Recommendations:** In the age of technology, businesses and platforms use predictive psychology to offer personalized recommendations. For example, streaming services suggest content based on your viewing history, and e-commerce sites recommend products based on your previous purchases.
4. **Mental Health Prediction:** Technology is increasingly used to predict mental health conditions. Machine learning models can analyze text or speech to detect signs of depression or anxiety, and wearable devices can monitor physiological data to alert individuals or healthcare professionals to potential issues.
5. **Behavioral Economics:** Technology has allowed psychologists to conduct experiments on a much larger scale. Researchers can study online consumer

behavior, conduct A/B testing, and evaluate the impact of various interventions to predict and influence consumer decisions.

6. **Ethical Concerns:** Predictive psychology raises ethical concerns regarding privacy and the potential for manipulation. The collection of personal data for predictive purposes must be handled with care, and there is a need for regulation to protect individuals.
7. **Bias and Fairness:** Machine learning models used in predictive psychology can inherit biases present in the data they are trained on. Addressing these biases and ensuring fairness in predictions is a critical challenge.
8. **Healthcare and Wellness:** Predictive psychology can play a significant role in healthcare. For example, it can be used to predict disease outbreaks, patient adherence to treatment plans, and the risk of readmission to hospitals.
9. **Education and Learning:** Predictive psychology can be applied in education to identify at-risk students and provide timely interventions. It can also be used to personalize learning experiences based on individual learning styles and needs.
10. **Criminal Justice:** Some predictive systems are used in the criminal justice system to assess the risk of recidivism and inform sentencing decisions. However, this application is controversial due to concerns about fairness and transparency.

In the age of technology, predictive psychology has the potential to transform various aspects of our lives, from marketing and healthcare to education and criminal justice. However, it also brings ethical and privacy challenges that need careful consideration and regulation to ensure responsible and beneficial use.

1.4 Need of Emotion Detection and Predictive Psychology

In this technological era, there has been a revolutionary change in the fields of emotion detection and prediction psychology. Understanding and predicting human emotions has advanced to new heights with the introduction of advanced sensors, large datasets, and robust machine learning algorithms. Today's emotion recognition algorithms are able to read a person's mood from their facial expressions, tone of voice, and even their written words. On the other hand, predictive psychology may take advantage of these developments by using data to predict how people would react emotionally to certain stimuli and scenarios, which has important implications for areas like as advertising, psychology, and computer science. However, there are significant ethical and privacy problems connected to these technologies, which highlights the need of open and honest use of emotion detection and prediction psychology tools in the modern, ever-changing digital environment.

2. LITERATURE REVIEW

Z. Zhang et al. (2023) introduced the cross-modal temporal erase network for weakly supervised detection and prediction of emotion in video. They present a cross-modal temporal erasing network that can weakly-supervisedly find keyframes, context, and audio-related information. Specifically, they use the intra- and inter-modal interaction between the various segments as a starting point for making precise keyframe selections. Then, they delete keyframes in an iterative fashion to train the model to prioritize complimentary information contexts. Our solution outperforms state-of-the-art methods, as shown by extensive testing on three difficult video emotion benchmarks.

L. Stankov et al. (2022) presented life outcome prediction using measures of intelligence and character. This article reviews the psychological tools used in research that draw conflicting results on the predictive validity of personality vs intellect for key outcomes in life. The fine-grained examination of measures used in the evaluation of intellect and personality may explain for at least some contradictory outcomes. Evidence for using the Big Five to predict life outcomes is weak, suggesting that other methods of measuring personality should be investigated. In the future, techniques used in non-experimental research to examine cause-and-effect linkages would be required.

N. Sghir et al. (2023) introduced development in predictive learning analytics. In this study, they looked at the connection between the outcomes that are often predicted and the learning characteristics that were used to make such predictions. They also conducted a comprehensive evaluation of the whole predictive modelling procedure, from data collecting to data preparation to the many kinds of Machine Learning models and how to measure their effectiveness. Finally, they spoke about where they think future research should go and where the gaps in the present literature were. It was hoped that this work will provide interested researchers with a thorough and current resource that would help them rapidly get an understanding of the state of the art in the area of Predictive Learning and Analytics.

S. Pradeshi et al. (2023) focused on the machine learning techniques for emotion analysis in text. Emotion was a mental condition characterized by thoughts and sensations that were directed towards an external stimulus. Expressions of emotion are activities that reveal how they feel about social interactions and external events. Humans can read between the lines of written text and understand its topic and tone. This research focuses on the use of machine learning techniques for emotion detection, and it also examines emotion identification based on textual data.

P. Elosua et al. (2023) provided digital technology in psychological and academic testing. The conventional idea of pencil and paper exams has been expanded with the advent of digital technology in the area of psychological and educational testing and assessment. Opportunities were expanding thanks to new forms of evaluation made possible by the widespread availability of mobile devices, online communities, and computer programmes .

A. C. Edmondson et al. (2023) explained the mature state of psychological security. In this article, they examine the state of the art in psychological safety studies by outlining its many topic areas, evaluating its recent progress, and proposing new avenues for study. They distil the concept of psychological safety down to four overarching themes: efficiency, behavior change, quality of life at work, and leadership. When the globe is shaken by a pandemic, psychological safety becomes even more vital since it allows for organizations to adapt and thrive.

A. L. Cîrneanu et al. (2023) introduced recent advances in emotion detection using neural networks and image analysis. The purpose of this study is to provide a conceptual and historical overview of the development of neural network designs that have shown promising outcomes in the field of FER. This paper advocates for the use of CNN-based architectures over other types of neural network architectures, such as recurrent neural networks or generative adversarial networks, by comparing and contrasting their key features and performance, as well as the benefits and drawbacks of the proposed models in the papers that were analyzed. This study also provides an overview of the existing datasets that were presently used for emotion identification from facial expressions and micro-expressions. The many applications of FER systems are discussed, including those in the fields of medicine, teaching, security, and social IoT.

N. Ahmed et al. (2023) looked in-depth analysis of how learning algorithms might be used to multimodal emotion identification. Emotion recognition was the study of recognizing and reacting to a wide range of human emotions, from joy to fear to embarrassment. The COVID- 19 pandemic has injected much-needed fresh energy into the field of emotion identification. People's mental health in the COVID-19 epidemic was reflected in the flood of emotions and ideas that were shared and uploaded on social media. This paper provides a summary of many publicly accessible; high-accuracy emotion acquisition methods to help readers better grasp the current ecosystem of applied emotion detection. The most popular emotion recognition datasets were also compared.

K Anusha et al. (2023) provided methodology for constructing and cleaning a multilingual text corpus for mood analysis. There have been a lot of discoveries in the previous several years. However, these preexisting methods have not been successful in addressing two fundamental issues. First, the text corpus accessible from different sources was written in different languages, which might make it more difficult to extract the proper emotions throughout the emotion extraction process. Second, the rising use of emojis in text corpora has complicated the difficulty of emotion extraction since they are frequently used to convey sarcasm, and sarcasm detection was notoriously difficult. This paper, thus, presents a framework for the automatic development of a sentiment extraction procedure, included a pre-processing of the text corpus for normalization of the text with respect to emojis, sarcasm, and numerous local language effects.

L. Zhou et al. (2022) provided network analysis using a concept of flourishing via connections as a predictor of nursing students' mental health. Nursing students' mental health was profoundly impacted by their sense of psychological well-being, which in turn influences their choices to remain in the nursing profession, especially in the wake of the recent COVID-19 epidemic. Despite the undeniable connection between intimate relationships and psychological health, the particular routes via which these interactions were connected to one another and which were most strongly associated to the mental health of nursing students remain unclear. The purpose of this study is to investigate a relationship-based model of flourishing by examined the network structure, core and bridge variables, and predictors among well-being characteristics.

S. T. Chavali et al. (2022) presented intelligent facial expression analysis that could guess your age and gender. In this study, they suggest a method for determining a person's emotional state based on their facial expression, and they provide two techniques for doing the same for their age and gender. The gender and age-related effects on human face expressions were also the focus of this study. Anger, disgust, happiness, fear, sadness, surprise, and a neutral state were the seven emotions the model can presently identify from a person's facial data. There were three parts to the proposed system: 3. recognized an individual's emotional state. The first model was developed using the KNN and SVM algorithms. Model correctness in the Recognition system is shown by the evaluation metrics.

W. Qi et al. (2022) introduced recognize and predict college students' emotions and mental states using a deep neural network. According to the findings, pupils' mental health impacts their academic performance. Students should make an effort to maintain a healthy mental state, gain insight into their emotions, and control their thoughts. The emotional well-being of pupils relies heavily on the example set by their leaders. Students and institutions must take on the responsibility of emotional leadership. To foster a peaceful learning environment, it was in everyone's best interest for schools and students to work together to develop kids' emotional literacy and self-regulation skills. Student frustration with interpersonal communication stems from a mismatch between the nuanced demands of successful social interaction and the more straightforward nature of the average student. Students' mental health issues stem mostly from three factors: a lack of public speaking confidence, poor interpersonal skills, and an obsession with and anxiety over the outcomes of extracurricular activities.

3. PROBLEM STATEMENT

One of the central challenges in the age of technology lies in the ethical and privacy concerns surrounding emotion detection and predictive psychology. As these technologies advance, they increasingly raise questions about the collection and utilization of personal and emotional data without informed consent, potentially infringing upon individuals' privacy. Moreover, the potential for biases and misinterpretations in emotion detection algorithms underscores the risk of perpetuating societal inequalities. Predictive psychology, while promising in its applications, also sparks apprehension regarding the manipulation and exploitation of individuals' emotional vulnerabilities, especially in marketing and advertising. Therefore, striking a balance between harnessing the benefits of these technologies and ensuring responsible, transparent, and equitable use is a pressing concern as they become more integrated into our lives.

4. PROPOSED WORK

The current study has been pre-processed first using many different noise-reduction techniques. Noise levels were evaluated to determine the overall image quality. A CNN model, trained using Hybrid models, is given the images to analyze. Figure 2 presents the proposed research methodology in which flow of work is expressed.

Figure 2. Proposed research methodology

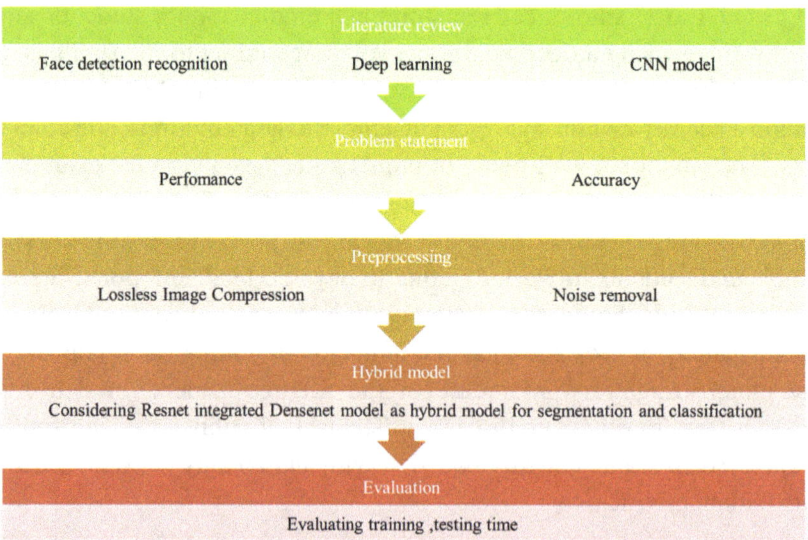

The purpose of this simulation experiment is to compare the performance of numerous CNN models using filtered simulations of real-world data. A hybrid model that combines ResNet and DenseNet has been created to further improve performance. Fig2 depicts the results of an analysis of validation, training, and testing effectiveness and error rates, and Figure 3 explains the architecture. The facial recognition dataset is being investigated for use in the training process. The dataset is currently undergoing preprocessing to have the pictures resized and compressed. Once the first processing is done, the photographs are clustered together. Taking into account both the DensNet model and the ResNet50 model is recommended in order to get a more precise result, as shown by the development of a hybrid ensemble model. These studies did help improve accuracy, but there's room for growth in how quickly training, testing, and validation can be done.

Figure 3. Proposed work model

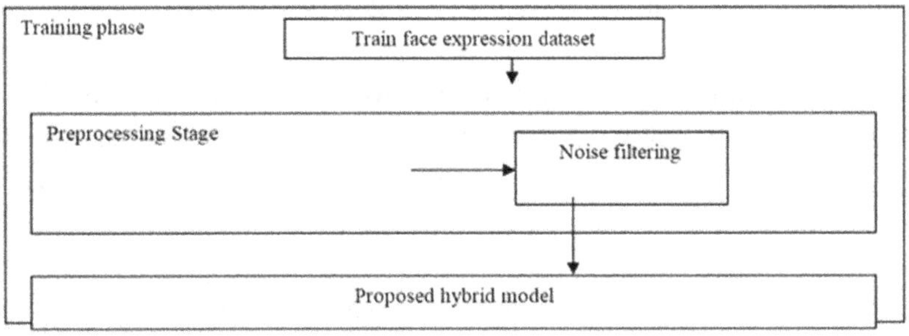

5. RESULT AND DISCUSSION

The LFW dataset is used to build a deep learning model that is used in the face recognition system. In the area of computer vision, it is standard practice to use the LFW dataset to train a deep learning model for face identification. Many facial recognition systems use the LFW dataset as a standard for performance. It includes over 13,000 tagged facial photos gathered from throughout the web. During simulation, the model takes batch sizes of 16 and 25 epochs into account. Eighty percent of the dataset was evaluated during training, ten percent was utilized for validation, and the remaining ten percent was used for testing. Fig4 depicts the photos utilized in the simulation.

Using the LFW (Labelled Faces in the Wild) dataset to train a deep learning model for face recognition takes use of a tried-and-true tool in the area of computer vision. LFW is a significant dataset for training and assessing face recognition

Figure 4. Sample images of the LFW dataset

algorithms, since it contains over 13,000 labelled facial photos acquired from the internet. Variations of lighting, stance, and facial expressions are all indicative of the wide range of situations shown here. In order to fully use the LFW dataset, it is common practise to subject the images to stringent preprocessing in order to achieve size and quality uniformity. Because of their superior capacity to recognise subtleties in face data, deep learning models, and in particular CNNs, have become the go-to option for feature extraction. In order for the model to learn to extract discriminative features from faces, the LFW dataset is divided into training and validation sets throughout the training phase. After the model has been trained, it is tested against an extremely reliable face recognition benchmark: the remaining data in the dataset. While the LFW dataset is a good starting point, it is important to note that other data sources and methods may be needed to address the full range of challenges faced in real-world applications of face recognition, such as demographic and environmental variations.

Confusion Matrix Have Been Obtained During Testing That is Shown Below for Four Models

Table 1 shows the confusion matrix for CNN model in which there are four different categories those are anger, normal, fear, happy with its true label and predicted label.

Predicted Label

Table 2 shows the confusion matrix for hybrid model in which there are four different categories those are anger, normal, fear, happy with its true label and predicted label.

Table 1. Confusion matrix for CNN model

Confusion matrix					
True Label	**Anger**	1897	40	24	28
	Normal	21	1920	31	19
	Fear	39	18	1926	17
	Happy	43	22	19	1936
		Anger	**Normal**	**Fear**	**Happy**

TP: 7679
Overall Accuracy: 95.99%

Table 2. Confusion matrix for hybrid model

Confusion matrix					
True Label	**Anger**	1930	24	13	17
	Normal	12	1952	20	11
	Fear	26	9	1956	9
	Happy	32	15	11	1963
		Anger	**Normal**	**Fear**	**Happy**

TP: 7801
Overall Accuracy: 97.51%

Predicted Label

Table 3 presents comparative analysis of overall accuracy those are calculated by exploring the confusion matrix for CNN and Hybrid model considering Table 1 and Table 2.

Fig5 plotted by considering the value calculated in table 3 and compared then in graphically format.

Table 4 expresses comparison of time taken at training time in second.

Fig6 shows the time taken in graphically at training time in second for CNN model and hybrid model.

Table 3. Comparison of accuracy

CNN Model	Hybrid Model
95.99%	97.51%

Figure 5. Comparison of accuracy

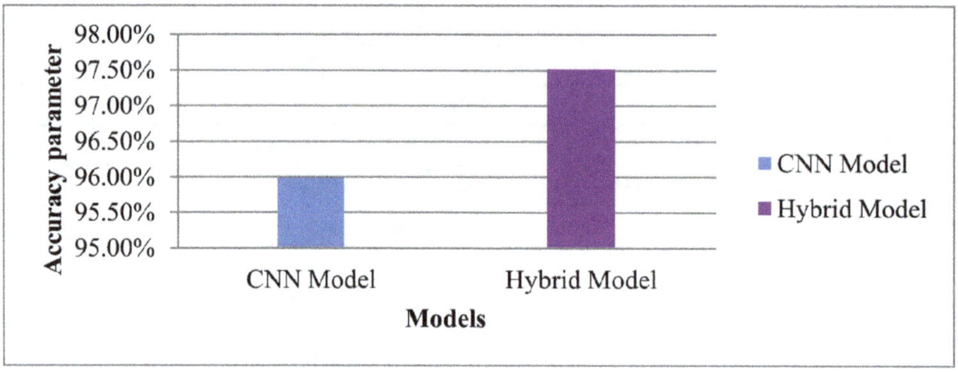

Table 4. Comparison of training time in second

CNN Model	Hybrid Model
148	127

Figure 6. Comparison of time consumption to present performance of proposed work

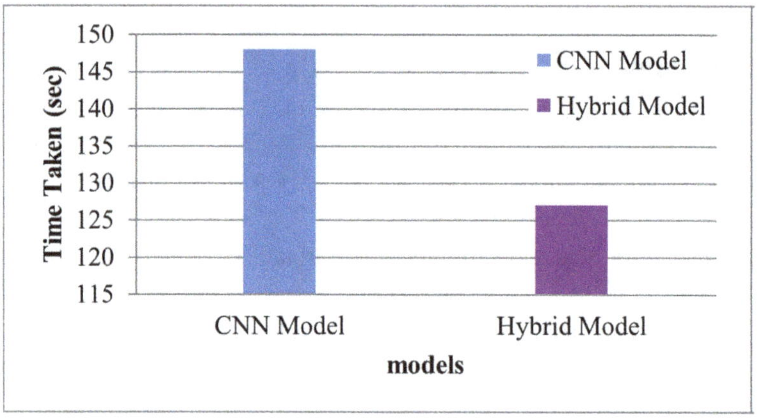

6. CONCLUSION

The current trend in research is to reduce picture size during preprocessing in order to increase performance. As the group size decreased, so did the amount of time needed for training. Based on the simulation findings, we can say that the suggested hybrid model outperforms the regular CNN model. The suggested work is also more precise than previous methods. The hybrid design of the ResNet-DenseNet model is essential. It is necessary to tailor it specifically for facial expression recognition. Data augmentation, hyperparameter tuning, and regularization techniques are used to enhance the performance of the model throughout the training process. The model's performance is evaluated using metrics like as accuracy, precision, recall, F1-score, and confusion matrix. An alternative dataset may be used to assess its ability to generalize. Assessing the model in relation to others might unveil its performance. Examining the model's predictions on sample images helps in discerning its capabilities and limitations. Take into account the ongoing process of optimizing, refining, and making modifications based on real-world conditions to enhance the performance of the model. It is of utmost importance to guarantee fairness in models, rectify biases, and uphold ethical standards in facial expression identification. Ablation studies investigate the impact of architectural modifications on model performance. Data and insights from performance analysis are meticulously documented and made available to the public. The study starts by providing a thorough examination of the capabilities of the Deep Unified Model, as well as proposing potential avenues for further research and improvements. Face emotion identification deep learning algorithms are inherently dynamic, necessitating iterative refinement for optimal performance.

7. FUTURE SCOPE

Emotional analysis and predictive psychology in the modern day contain tremendous potential. Improved accuracy and granularity in emotion recognition, enabled by the ongoing development of AI and machine learning algorithms, will pave the way for novel uses in fields as diverse as mental health, personalised user experiences, and human-robot interaction. And with the help of predictive psychology, we can now anticipate how people will feel in reaction to certain stimuli, which has far-reaching implications for fields like advertising and mental health care. Nonetheless, the ethical and regulatory aspects will become increasingly important, with ongoing research focusing on ensuring responsible use, mitigating biases, and safeguarding privacy, shaping a future where technology becomes an essential tool in understanding, supporting, and enhancing human emotions.

REFERENCES

Ahmed, N., Al Aghbari, Z., & Girija, S. (2023). A systematic survey on multimodal emotion recognition using learning algorithms. Intell. Syst. with Appl., 17. doi:10.1016/j.iswa.2022.200171

Anusha, K. (2023). A Framework To Build And Clean Multi- Language Text Corpus For Emotion Detection 101. Research Gate.

Pandey, B. (2022). Effective and Secure Transmission of Health Information Using Advanced Morphological Component Analysis and Image Hiding. *Artificial Intelligence on Medical Data.* Springer Nature Singapore. . doi:10.1007/978-981-19-0151-5_19

Bhattacharya, S., Agarwala, A., & Roy, S. (2022). Mood detection and prediction using conventional machine learning techniques on COVID19 data. *Social Network Analysis and Mining, 12*(1), 1–23. doi:10.1007/s13278-022-00957-x PMID:36161249

Cîrneanu, A. L., Popescu, D., & Iordache, D. (2023). New Trends in Emotion Recognition Using Image Analysis by Neural Networks, A Systematic Review. *Sensors (Basel), 23*(16), 7092. doi:10.3390/s23167092 PMID:37631629

Dhingra, M., Dhabliya, D., Dubey, M. K., Gupta, A., & Reddy, D. H. (2022). A Review on Comparison of Machine Learning Algorithms for Text Classification. *2022 5th International Conference on Contemporary Computing and Informatics (IC3I),* Uttar Pradesh, India. 10.1109/IC3I56241.2022.10072502

Edmondson, A. C., & Bransby, D. P. (2023). Psychological Safety Comes of Age: Observed Themes in an Established Literature. *Annual Review of Organizational Psychology and Organizational Behavior, 10*(1), 55–78. doi:10.1146/annurev-orgpsych-120920-055217

Elosua, P., Aguado, D., Fonseca-Pedrero, E., Abad, F. J., & Santamaría, P. (2023). New Trends in Digital Technology-Based Psychological and Educational Assessment. *Psicothema, 35*(1), 50–57. doi:10.7334/psicothema2022.241 PMID:36695850

Gupta, A. (2019). Script classification at word level for a Multilingual Document. *IJAST, 28*(20), 1247–1252.

Gupta, A. (2020). An Analysis of Digital Image Compression Technique in Image Processing. *IJAST, 28*(20), 1261–1265.

Gupta, A., Kaushik, D., Garg, M., & Verma, A. (2020). Machine Learning model for Breast Cancer Prediction. *2020 Fourth International Conference on I-SMAC (IoT in Social, Mobile, Analytics and Cloud) (I-SMAC).* IEEE. 10.1109/I-SMAC49090.2020.9243323

Jain, V., Beram, S. M., Talukdar, V., Patil, T., Dhabliya, D., & Gupta, A. (2022). Accuracy Enhancement in Machine Learning During Blockchain Based Transaction Classification. *2022 Seventh International Conference on Parallel, Distributed and Grid Computing (PDGC)*, Solan, Himachal Pradesh, India. 10.1109/PDGC56933.2022.10053213

Khan, A. R. (2022). Facial Emotion Recognition Using Conventional Machine Learning and Deep Learning Methods: Current Achievements, Analysis and Remaining Challenges. *Information (Basel)*, *13*(6), 268. doi:10.3390/info13060268

Kshirsagar, P. R., Reddy, D. H., Dhingra, M., Dhabliya, D., & Gupta, A. (2022). *Detection of Liver Disease Using Machine Learning Approach*. 2022 5th International Conference on Contemporary Computing and Informatics (IC3I), Uttar Pradesh, India. 10.1109/IC3I56241.2022.10073425

Kshirsagar, P. R., Reddy, D. H., Dhingra, M., Dhabliya, D., & Gupta, A. (2023). *A Scalable Platform to Collect, Store, Visualize and Analyze Big Data in Real-Time*. 2023 3rd International Conference on Innovative Practices in Technology and Management (ICIPTM), Uttar Pradesh, India. 10.1109/ICIPTM57143.2023.10118183

Lalitha Kumari, P. (2023). *Methodology for Classifying Objects in High-Resolution Optical Images Using Deep Learning Techniques*. Lecture Notes in Electrical Engineering. Springer Nature Singapore., doi:10.1007/978-981-19-8865-3_55

LatifS.AliH. S.UsamaM.RanaR.SchullerB.QadirJ. (2022). *AI-Based Emotion Recognition: Promise, Peril, and Prescriptions for Prosocial Path*. arXiv. http://arxiv.org/abs/2211.07290

Mandal, D., Shukla, A., Ghosh, A., Gupta, A., & Dhabliya, D. (2022). Molecular Dynamics Simulation for Serial and Parallel Computation Using Leaf Frog Algorithm. *2022 Seventh International Conference on Parallel, Distributed and Grid Computing (PDGC)*, Solan, Himachal Pradesh, India. 10.1109/PDGC56933.2022.10053161

Pradeshi, S., & Patil, J. "Study on Emotion Analysis of Text using Machine Learning Approaches," SSRN *Electron. J.*, 2023, doi:10.2139/ssrn.4361140

Qi, W., & Li, Y. (2022). Research on Emotion Recognition and Mental State Prediction of College Students Based on Deep Neural Network. *Mobile Information Systems, 2022*, 1–8. doi:10.1155/2022/1607177

Sghir, N., Adadi, A., & Lahmer, M. (2023). Recent advances in Predictive Learning Analytics: A decade systematic review (2012–2022). Springer. doi:10.1007/s10639-022-11536-0

Stankov, L. (2016). vs. Zisman and Ganzach (2022) Debate. *Journal of Intelligence, 11*(5), 2023. doi:10.3390/jintelligence11050095 PMID:37233344

Teja Chavali, S., Tej Kandavalli, C., Sugash, T. M., & Subramani, R. (2022). Smart Facial Emotion Recognition with Gender and Age Factor Estimation. Procedia Comput. Sci., 218, 113–123. doi:10.1016/j.procs.2022.12.407

Veeraiah, V., Ahamad, G. P. S., Talukdar, S. B., Gupta, A., & Talukdar, V. (2022). Enhancement of Meta Verse Capabilities by IoT Integration. *2022 2nd International Conference on Advance Computing and Innovative Technologies in Engineering (ICACITE),* (pp. 1493-1498). IEEE. 10.1109/ICACITE53722.2022.9823766

Veeraiah, V., Khan, H., Kumar, A., Ahamad, S., Mahajan, A., & Gupta, A. (2022). Integration of PSO and Deep Learning for Trend Analysis of Meta-Verse. *2022 2nd International Conference on Advance Computing and Innovative Technologies in Engineering (ICACITE).* IEEE. 10.1109/ICACITE53722.2022.9823883

Zhang, Z., Wang, L., & Yang, J. (2023). *Weakly Supervised Video Emotion Detection and Prediction via Cross-Modal Temporal Erasing Network* (Vol. 1)., doi:10.1109/CVPR52729.2023.01811

Zhou, L., Sukpasjaroen, K., Wu, Y. M., Wang, L., Chankoson, T., & Cai, E. L. (2022). Predicting nursing students' psychological well-being: Network analysis based on a model of thriving through relationships. *BMC Medical Education, 22*(1), 1–11. doi:10.1186/s12909-022-03517-1 PMID:35710399

Chapter 2
Unraveling the World of Artificial Emotional Intelligence

Mohammed Belghachi
https://orcid.org/0009-0009-7067-4493
Tahri Mohamed University of Bechar, Algeria

ABSTRACT

Artificial emotional intelligence (AEI) is a burgeoning field at the intersection of technology and human emotion, seeking to imbue machines with the capacity to perceive, understand, and respond to human emotions. This chapter encapsulates a comprehensive exploration of AEI, encompassing its foundations, technical intricacies, applications, user perspectives, ethical considerations, challenges, and real-world case studies. The foundations of AEI involve unraveling the complexities of human emotions, from facial expressions and voice tones to physiological signals. Understanding the technical aspects of AEI, including data acquisition, feature extraction, machine learning models, and multi-modal fusion, provides insights into the sophisticated mechanisms driving emotionally intelligent systems. AEI's applications span diverse domains, from virtual health assistants providing mental well-being support to emotionally aware educational platforms adapting to students' learning needs.

INTRODUCTION

In the dynamic realm of artificial intelligence (AI), the infusion of emotional intelligence marks a pivotal juncture, redefining the boundaries of human-machine interaction. This exploration delves deep into the multifaceted landscape of Artificial Emotional Intelligence (AEI), where algorithms are not only processing data but

DOI: 10.4018/979-8-3693-1910-9.ch002

also deciphering and responding to human emotions (figure 1). As we stand at the intersection of technology and empathy, this introduction seeks to provide a nuanced understanding of the historical roots, technical intricacies, societal impacts, and ethical considerations that characterize the integration of emotional intelligence into AI systems.

Figure 1. Emotional intelligence

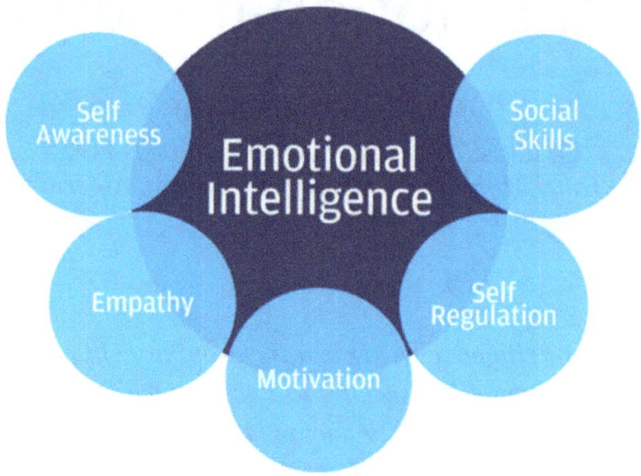

The chapter, "Unraveling the World of Artificial Emotional Intelligence," makes a significant contribution in terms of conceptual depth, novelty, and technical insights. Conceptually, it lays a solid foundation by exploring the fundamental principles of emotional intelligence and tracing the evolution of Artificial Emotional Intelligence (AEI). The chapter introduces interdisciplinary perspectives, bridging psychology, computer science, and ethics to provide a comprehensive understanding of AEI.

In terms of novelty, the chapter stands out by incorporating ethical considerations as a substantial component. It emphasizes privacy concerns, bias mitigation, and responsible deployment, recognizing the importance of ethical guidelines in the development and application of AEI. The chapter's consideration of cultural sensitivity is a novel aspect, acknowledging the need for AEI systems to adapt to and respect diverse cultural norms in emotional expressions. On the technical front, the chapter delves into the foundations of AEI, providing insights into the algorithms, models, and methodologies used for recognizing and responding to human emotions. It explores the real-time processing challenges in AEI, highlighting the technical intricacies involved in ensuring timely responses to emotional cues. The focus on explainability underscores the technical aspects of making AEI systems transparent and understandable.

In summary, the chapter's conceptual contributions provide a holistic view of AEI, its evolution, and its interdisciplinary nature. The incorporation of ethical considerations and a focus on cultural sensitivity bring novelty to the discussion, while the technical aspects provide a detailed exploration of the algorithms and challenges in implementing AEI. Together, these elements contribute to a comprehensive and insightful examination of Artificial Emotional Intelligence.

Background and Significance

In recent years, the intersection of artificial intelligence and emotional intelligence has given rise to a burgeoning field known as AEI. The background of AEI lies in the recognition of the pivotal role emotions play in human interactions and experiences. Traditional artificial intelligence systems, while adept at tasks requiring logical reasoning, lacked the capacity to comprehend and respond to human emotions. This gap prompted researchers to delve into the intricate realm of emotions, seeking to imbue machines with the ability to recognize, interpret, and appropriately respond to the diverse spectrum of human feelings.

The significance of unraveling the world of AEI is profound, encompassing a wide range of applications with transformative potential. In human-computer interactions, AEI holds the promise of creating more intuitive, personalized, and empathetic interfaces. Virtual assistants, educational platforms, and customer service chatbots equipped with AEI capabilities can adapt to users' emotional states, fostering more meaningful and responsive engagements. Moreover, in healthcare, AEI can play a pivotal role in mental well-being support, offering timely interventions based on emotional cues.

Ethical considerations within the realm of AEI are equally significant. As systems become more adept at understanding and responding to emotions, ensuring user privacy, addressing biases, and promoting transparent practices become paramount. The background and significance of unraveling AEI lie not only in technological advancements but also in the ethical and societal implications of introducing emotionally intelligent systems into our daily lives. This exploration seeks to provide a comprehensive understanding of AEI, acknowledging both its transformative potential and the ethical considerations essential for responsible development and deployment.

Objectives of the Study

The study on AEI aims to achieve several key objectives that contribute to a comprehensive understanding of this burgeoning field. Firstly, the study seeks to elucidate the foundational principles of AEI, delving into the intricate mechanisms that underlie the recognition and interpretation of human emotions by artificial systems. By exploring the technical aspects of data acquisition, feature extraction, and machine learning models, the study aims to provide insights into the sophisticated processes driving emotionally intelligent systems.

Secondly, the study endeavors to unravel the diverse applications of AEI across various domains. From virtual health assistants supporting mental well-being to emotionally aware educational platforms adapting to individual learning needs, the objectives include showcasing the practical implementations and real-world impact of AEI. Understanding how AEI can enhance user experiences, facilitate learning, and improve customer interactions forms a pivotal aspect of the study's objectives.

Furthermore, the study has a user-centric focus, aiming to capture the diverse perspectives and expectations regarding AEI. User perspectives play a crucial role in shaping the acceptance and ethical considerations associated with emotionally intelligent systems. By exploring how users perceive and interact with AEI technologies, the study seeks to provide valuable insights into the nuanced interplay between enhanced experiences, privacy concerns, and ethical expectations.

Ethical considerations constitute a significant dimension of the study's objectives. As AEI technologies evolve, ensuring responsible development and deployment practices becomes imperative. The study aims to delineate the ethical considerations surrounding privacy, fairness, transparency, and user empowerment in the context of AEI, thereby contributing to the establishment of ethical guidelines and industry standards.

Lastly, the study on AEI aims to address the challenges and future directions within the field. By identifying current challenges, such as accuracy in emotion recognition and cross-cultural adaptation, the study aims to pave the way for future advancements. The objectives include providing insights into the ongoing research efforts, potential solutions to existing challenges, and guiding principles for the responsible evolution of AEI.

In summary, the objectives of this study are multifaceted, encompassing a thorough exploration of foundational principles, practical applications, user perspectives, ethical considerations, and the future trajectory of AEI. Through these objectives, the study aims to contribute to the holistic understanding and responsible development of AEI technologies.

FOUNDATIONS OF EMOTIONAL INTELLIGENCE

The integration of Emotional Intelligence (EI) into artificial intelligence (AI) systems marks a profound shift in the way machines understand and respond to human emotions (figure 2). In examining the foundations of Emotional Intelligence

Figure 2. Foundations of emotional intelligence

in AI, we navigate through the intricate web of technologies and methodologies that enable machines to interpret and engage with emotions, mirroring the complexity inherent in human emotional processing (Barrett, L. F. (2019)) (Prentice et al., 2020) (Kambur, 2021) (Krar Muhsin Thajil & Hadi AL-Abrrow, 2023) (Zhu et al., 2022).

Defining Emotional Intelligence

Emotional Intelligence (EI) represents a multifaceted construct encompassing the ability to recognize, comprehend, and regulate emotions in oneself and others. In the context of artificial intelligence (AI), defining Emotional Intelligence becomes a nuanced endeavor that involves translating these human capabilities into algorithms and computational models.

- **Recognition of Emotions:**

At its core, EI involves the accurate identification of emotions, both in oneself and in others. In the realm of AI, this translates to developing algorithms capable of discerning subtle emotional cues, be it from facial expressions, voice intonations, or written text. Machine learning models are trained to recognize patterns associated with various emotions, allowing AI systems to categorize and understand the emotional states of individuals.

- **Understanding Emotional Context:**

Beyond mere recognition, true emotional intelligence involves an understanding of the context surrounding emotions. In AI, this extends to comprehending the situational cues that influence emotional responses. Advanced natural language processing (NLP) techniques enable machines to grasp the subtleties of language, tone, and context, contributing to a more nuanced understanding of the emotional landscape.

- **Regulation and Response:**

An essential facet of human emotional intelligence is the ability to regulate emotions and respond appropriately. In the AI domain, this manifests as developing algorithms capable of generating contextually relevant and emotionally appropriate responses. This involves not only understanding emotions but also tailoring AI interactions to align with the emotional needs and expectations of users.

- **Incorporating Cultural Sensitivity:**

Cultural nuances significantly impact the expression and interpretation of emotions. Defining emotional intelligence in AI requires consideration of cultural diversity. Machine learning models must be trained on diverse datasets that encompass various cultural contexts, ensuring that AI systems exhibit sensitivity to cultural differences in emotional expression.

In essence, defining Emotional Intelligence in the context of AI involves creating computational models that emulate the cognitive processes related to emotion in humans. From recognizing emotional cues to understanding their context and generating appropriate responses, these foundational aspects lay the groundwork for machines to navigate the intricate world of human emotions in a meaningful and responsive manner.

Human Emotional Cues

Understanding human emotional cues is a pivotal aspect of infusing Emotional Intelligence (EI) into artificial intelligence (AI) systems. Human communication is rich with non-verbal expressions, and deciphering these cues is crucial for machines to engage in emotionally intelligent interactions.

- **Facial Expressions:**

Facial expressions are powerful indicators of emotional states. In the realm of AI, recognizing and interpreting facial cues involves leveraging computer vision technologies. Algorithms are trained on diverse datasets to discern subtle changes in facial features, enabling machines to identify emotions such as joy, sadness, anger, and surprise. The nuanced analysis of microexpressions further refines the AI system's ability to capture fleeting emotional states.

- **Tone of Voice:**

Beyond words, the tone of voice carries significant emotional information. In the AI landscape, natural language processing (NLP) algorithms are employed to analyze not just the words spoken but also the intonation, pitch, and rhythm of speech. This allows machines to detect emotions such as enthusiasm, frustration, or sadness, enhancing their capacity to understand the emotional nuances embedded in verbal communication.

- **Body Language:**

Human gestures and body language offer additional layers of emotional cues. AI systems can be trained to recognize and interpret these non-verbal signals, incorporating machine learning techniques to grasp the emotional context of physical movements. Understanding gestures, posture, and other bodily expressions enables machines to align their responses with the emotional dynamics of a given interaction.

- **Written Text and Textual Cues:**

In digital communication, written text becomes a primary medium for expressing emotions. AI systems equipped with EI capabilities employ natural language processing algorithms to analyze textual content. This involves detecting sentiment, understanding contextual clues, and identifying linguistic patterns that convey emotional undertones. By deciphering the emotional cues in written communication, machines can respond more appropriately in text-based interactions.

- **Multi-Modal Integration:**

A holistic approach to recognizing human emotional cues involves the integration of multiple modalities. Combining insights from facial expressions, tone of voice, body language, and textual analysis enables AI systems to form a comprehensive understanding of the user's emotional state. This multi-modal integration enhances the accuracy and richness of emotional intelligence in machines.

In summary, decoding human emotional cues for AI involves a sophisticated interplay of computer vision, natural language processing, and machine learning techniques. By comprehensively analyzing facial expressions, tone of voice, body language, and written text, AI systems can emulate a nuanced understanding of emotions, paving the way for more empathetic and contextually aware interactions with users.

Relevance to AI

The integration of Emotional Intelligence (EI) into artificial intelligence (AI) is not merely a theoretical pursuit; it holds profound significance in shaping the functionality and impact of AI systems. Understanding the relevance of EI to AI involves exploring its practical applications and implications across various domains.

- **Humanizing Interactions:**

Emotional intelligence in AI contributes to humanizing interactions between machines and users. By recognizing and responding to human emotions, AI systems can simulate a more empathetic and human-like engagement. This is particularly relevant in applications such as virtual assistants, where a more emotionally aware interaction enhances user experience and fosters a sense of connection.

- **Virtual Assistants and Customer Service:**

One of the tangible applications of EI in AI is evident in virtual assistants and customer service applications. An emotionally intelligent virtual assistant can gauge user frustration, satisfaction, or urgency through tone of voice and language cues. This enables the system to tailor responses, offering not just solutions but also emotional support, thereby enhancing the overall user experience.

- **Mental Health Support Systems:**

In the domain of mental health, EI-equipped AI systems hold promise. These systems can detect subtle changes in user behavior, vocal patterns, or written expressions that may indicate emotional distress. By identifying these cues, AI can potentially offer timely interventions, provide support, or connect users with appropriate mental health resources.

- **User Experience Enhancement:**

Emotional intelligence contributes significantly to the enhancement of user experiences across various applications. Whether in gaming, education, or entertainment, AI systems that understand and respond to user emotions can tailor their interactions, content recommendations, or challenges to align with individual emotional states, creating a more personalized and engaging experience.

- **Ethical Considerations:**

The relevance of EI in AI extends to ethical considerations. As machines become more integrated into human lives, the ethical implications of emotionally intelligent AI systems become crucial. Ensuring that these systems respect user privacy, avoid emotional manipulation, and address biases in emotional recognition is a critical aspect of responsible AI development.

In essence, the relevance of Emotional Intelligence to AI lies in its capacity to elevate interactions, enhance user experiences, and address ethical considerations. As AI systems increasingly permeate diverse aspects of human life, the infusion of emotional intelligence becomes not just a technical advancement but a fundamental element in shaping the societal impact of intelligent machines.

As we delve into the foundations of Emotional Intelligence in AI, the synthesis of psychological insights, technological innovation, and ethical considerations becomes paramount. This section sets the stage for a deeper exploration of how machines, equipped with emotional awareness, can navigate the intricacies of human emotions, ultimately transforming the nature of human-AI interactions.

EVOLUTION OF ARTIFICIAL EMOTIONAL INTELLIGENCE

The journey of AEI spans from theoretical conceptualizations to the practical integration of emotional awareness into artificial intelligence (AI) systems. This exploration delves into key milestones and developments, tracing the evolution of AEI from its nascent stages to its current prominence (Budhwar et al., 2022) (Igboyi et al., 2023) (Bhardwaj et al., 2023) (Kavyashree M. B. & Anupama Sundar D., 2023) (Prentice, 2023).

Theoretical Foundations

The theoretical foundations of AEI lie in the intersection of psychology, cognitive science, and the early conceptualizations of machine intelligence. This section explores the intellectual origins that paved the way for the development of AEI, highlighting key theories and early models.

- **Emotion Theories in Psychology:**

The theoretical underpinnings of AEI draw heavily from psychological models of emotion. Early theories, such as James-Lange's theory and Cannon-Bard's theory, offered insights into the physiological and cognitive aspects of emotions. Psychologists like Paul Ekman, through his work on universal facial expressions, provided a basis for the identification of emotional cues that could potentially be translated into machine-readable data.

- **Emotional Intelligence Models:**

The concept of emotional intelligence, popularized by psychologists like Daniel Goleman and Howard Gardner, introduced the idea that emotional skills are crucial for successful human interaction. These models proposed that emotional intelligence involves not only recognizing and understanding one's emotions but also effectively managing them. The transferability of these principles to machines formed the theoretical foundation for endowing AI with emotional awareness.

- **Early AI and Cognitive Science:**

In the nascent days of AI, researchers explored the emulation of cognitive processes, including aspects related to emotion. The work of pioneers like Alan Turing and Marvin Minsky laid the groundwork for the theoretical understanding of machine intelligence. However, it wasn't until later that researchers explicitly began considering the integration of emotional aspects into AI.

- **Computational Models of Emotion:**

Theoretical frameworks, such as the OCC model (Ortony, Clore, and Collins) and the Somatic Marker Hypothesis by Antonio Damasio, introduced computational models of emotion. These models attempted to formalize the mechanisms underlying emotional processes in humans. Such models provided a basis for envisioning how machines could be programmed to simulate aspects of emotional understanding and response.

- **Social Robotics and Human-Computer Interaction:**

Theoretical explorations gained momentum with the rise of social robotics and human-computer interaction research. Scholars began investigating the role of emotions in fostering more natural and intuitive interactions between humans and machines. Theoretical frameworks in these domains aimed to conceptualize how machines could perceive, interpret, and respond to human emotions in a socially acceptable manner.

- **Cognitive Computing Paradigms:**

The advent of cognitive computing paradigms, emphasizing machine learning and neural network approaches, further enriched the theoretical foundations of AEI. The realization that machines could learn and adapt to emotional cues through data-driven processes marked a paradigm shift, opening up new possibilities for the practical realization of emotionally intelligent machines.

In summary, the theoretical foundations of AEI emerged from a confluence of psychological theories, models of emotional intelligence, early AI research, computational models of emotion, and the evolving landscape of social robotics and human-computer interaction. These theoretical underpinnings provided the intellectual scaffolding for the subsequent development and implementation of emotional intelligence in artificial intelligence systems.

Early Experiments and Prototypes

The emergence of AEI was marked by pioneering experiments and prototypes that sought to translate theoretical concepts into practical applications. This section delves into the early endeavors that laid the groundwork for the development of AEI technologies.

- **Early Emotion Recognition Systems:**

The initial phase of AEI witnessed experimental efforts to develop emotion recognition systems. Researchers began exploring methods to teach machines to recognize and interpret facial expressions, vocal tones, and other physiological indicators of emotion. Early systems focused on basic emotion categories, such as happiness, sadness, anger, and surprise.

- **Text-Based Analysis Prototypes:**

Beyond facial expressions and vocal cues, early prototypes delved into text-based emotion analysis. Researchers aimed to develop algorithms capable of discerning emotional nuances in written text. These prototypes explored the use of natural language processing (NLP) techniques to identify sentiment, emotional tone, and contextual clues within textual content.

- **Affective Computing Initiatives:**

The term "affective computing," coined by Rosalind Picard in the 1990s, marked a significant milestone. Affective computing initiatives focused on imbuing machines with the ability to recognize and respond to human emotions. Early projects, such as the MIT Media Lab's "Galvactivator" and "Facial Action Coding System (FACS)" by Paul Ekman, exemplified pioneering efforts in developing technology capable of capturing emotional signals.

- **Prototypes in Human-Computer Interaction:**

Early experiments extended into the realm of human-computer interaction (HCI). Prototypes sought to enhance user experiences by incorporating emotional awareness into interfaces. These experiments aimed to create more intuitive and responsive systems, exploring how emotional cues could be utilized to tailor interactions and improve user engagement.

- **Limitations and Challenges:**

The early experiments highlighted challenges in AEI development. Limited computing power, sparse datasets, and the complexity of human emotions posed significant obstacles. The prototypes often struggled with accuracy and lacked the sophistication seen in contemporary AEI systems. Nonetheless, these challenges paved the way for iterative improvements and refined approaches in subsequent research.

- **Influence on Subsequent Research:**

Despite limitations, early experiments played a crucial role in shaping the trajectory of AEI research. They provided valuable insights into the technical challenges, ethical considerations, and potential applications of emotionally intelligent systems. The lessons learned from these early prototypes informed subsequent research endeavors, fostering a continuous evolution in the field.

In summary, the era of early experiments and prototypes in AEI laid the foundation for subsequent advancements. These pioneering initiatives explored the feasibility of imbuing machines with emotional awareness, identified challenges, and set the stage for a more refined and sophisticated exploration of emotional intelligence in artificial intelligence systems.

Rise of Affective Computing

The "Rise of Affective Computing" marked a pivotal era in the development of AEI. This section explores the key developments and initiatives that characterized this period, with a focus on affective computing and its profound impact on the integration of emotional awareness into artificial intelligence.

- **Rosalind Picard's Pioneering Work:**

The term "Affective Computing" was coined by Rosalind Picard in the mid-1990s. Her seminal book, "Affective Computing," laid the theoretical foundation for a new paradigm in AI. Picard emphasized the significance of incorporating emotional intelligence into machines, advocating for systems that could recognize, interpret, and respond to human emotions.

- **The Emoti-Chair and Wearable Devices:**

Picard's research group at the MIT Media Lab introduced the Emoti-Chair, an early example of affective computing. This chair utilized sensors to detect physiological signals such as heart rate and skin conductance, providing insights into the user's emotional state. Additionally, wearable devices, such as affective wristbands, were developed to capture real-time emotional data, contributing to the nascent field of physiological computing.

- **Expansion of Emotion Recognition Technologies:**

Affective computing saw a significant expansion of emotion recognition technologies. Researchers began exploring computer vision techniques for facial expression analysis, voice sentiment analysis, and gesture recognition. These technologies aimed to enhance the accuracy and breadth of emotional cues that AI systems could recognize, paving the way for more sophisticated emotionally intelligent applications.

- **Development of Databases and Benchmarks:**

To advance research in affective computing, efforts were made to create comprehensive databases and benchmarks for emotion recognition. Datasets, such as the Affectiva-MIT Facial Expression Dataset and the Emotional Speech Synthesis Database, provided standardized resources for training and evaluating emotion recognition algorithms. These initiatives facilitated collaboration and benchmarking within the research community.

- **Commercial Applications and Industry Adoption:**

The rise of affective computing coincided with an increasing interest from industry. Companies began recognizing the potential of emotionally intelligent systems for improving user experiences. Commercial applications emerged in fields such as marketing, user interface design, and virtual customer service, reflecting a growing acknowledgment of the practical value of affective computing.

- **Ethical Considerations in Affective Computing:**

As affective computing gained prominence, ethical considerations came to the forefront. Privacy concerns, the responsible use of emotional data, and potential biases in emotion recognition algorithms became focal points of discussion. Researchers and practitioners began addressing these ethical challenges to ensure the responsible deployment of affective computing technologies.

In summary, the rise of affective computing was characterized by groundbreaking research, technological advancements, and a growing recognition of the practical applications of emotional intelligence in AI. This period set the stage for the integration of affective computing into mainstream AI applications, laying the groundwork for the emotionally aware systems we encounter in various aspects of our lives today.

Machine Learning Advancements

The evolution of AEI has been profoundly influenced by advancements in machine learning. This section delves into the key developments in machine learning that contributed to the enhancement of AEI, allowing algorithms to better understand and respond to human emotions.

- **Transition to Deep Learning:**

A significant leap in AEI came with the widespread adoption of deep learning techniques. Deep neural networks, with their ability to learn complex hierarchical representations, brought a paradigm shift. This transition enabled AEI models to automatically extract intricate patterns from large datasets, leading to improved accuracy in emotion recognition tasks.

- **Convolutional Neural Networks (CNNs) for Image Analysis:**

In the domain of computer vision, Convolutional Neural Networks (CNNs) played a pivotal role. CNNs proved highly effective in analyzing visual data, making them particularly suited for tasks such as facial expression recognition. Their hierarchical feature extraction capabilities allowed AEI systems to discern nuanced facial cues with greater precision.

- **Recurrent Neural Networks (RNNs) for Temporal Sequences:**

Recognizing the temporal nature of emotional expressions, Recurrent Neural Networks (RNNs) became instrumental. RNNs and their variants, such as Long Short-Term Memory (LSTM) networks, excelled in capturing sequential dependencies in data. This made them well-suited for analyzing dynamic aspects of emotional expressions, such as changes in facial expressions over time or shifts in vocal tones.

- **Transfer Learning and Pre-trained Models:**

Machine learning advancements in transfer learning allowed AEI models to benefit from pre-trained models on vast datasets. Models pre-trained on general tasks, such as image recognition or natural language processing, were fine-tuned for specific AEI tasks. This approach proved efficient, especially when dealing with limited labeled emotional data.

- **Ensemble Learning and Fusion Techniques:**

Ensemble learning techniques, combining predictions from multiple models, gained prominence in AEI. Ensemble methods, such as bagging and boosting, were employed to improve robustness and generalization. Fusion techniques, integrating information from various modalities like facial expressions, voice, and text, further enhanced the comprehensiveness of emotional understanding.

- **Explainability and Interpretability:**

As machine learning models became more complex, the need for explainability and interpretability in AEI systems grew. Techniques such as attention mechanisms and model interpretability tools were developed to provide insights into how models made predictions. This not only addressed concerns about the "black-box" nature of deep learning but also increased trust in AEI technologies.

In summary, machine learning advancements propelled AEI into a new era of accuracy and sophistication. The shift to deep learning, the use of specialized neural network architectures, and the incorporation of transfer learning techniques played pivotal roles in improving the capabilities of AEI systems, making them more adept at understanding and responding to the complexities of human emotions.

Integration into Mainstream Applications

The integration of AEI into mainstream applications represents a transformative phase where theoretical concepts evolved into practical implementations. This section explores the key developments and applications that brought AEI technologies into various facets of our daily lives.

- **Virtual Assistants and Chatbots:**

The widespread adoption of AEI is evident in virtual assistants and chatbots. Virtual assistants like Siri, Alexa, and Google Assistant have integrated emotional intelligence to better understand user queries and respond with appropriate tones and expressions. Chatbots in customer service applications leverage AEI to enhance interactions, providing more empathetic and personalized responses.

- **Emotionally Aware User Interfaces:**

User interfaces across digital platforms began incorporating AEI to create emotionally aware designs. Websites, applications, and interactive systems adapt their interfaces based on user emotions, offering tailored content, recommendations, or support. This application of AEI enhances user engagement and satisfaction.

- **Gaming and Entertainment:**

AEI has found its way into the gaming and entertainment industry. Game developers use emotional intelligence to create characters that respond dynamically to players' emotions, enhancing the immersive experience. Similarly, streaming platforms leverage AEI to recommend content based on users' emotional preferences and reactions.

- **Mental Health Applications:**

AEI plays a significant role in mental health applications. These applications analyze user inputs, such as text or voice, to detect emotional states and provide supportive interventions. AEI technologies contribute to the development of mental health chatbots, emotion-tracking apps, and virtual therapy platforms.

- **Marketing and Advertising:**

In the realm of marketing and advertising, AEI is employed to gauge consumer reactions. Advertisements and marketing campaigns are designed with an understanding of emotional responses, aiming to evoke specific feelings. AEI technologies analyze consumer sentiments to optimize advertising strategies and tailor content to resonate with target audiences.

- **Automotive Systems:**

Automotive systems have integrated AEI for improved driver safety and comfort. Emotion-aware technologies can monitor drivers' emotional states, detecting signs of fatigue or distraction. These systems may adjust ambient lighting, music, or provide alerts to enhance the overall driving experience and safety.

- **Educational Platforms:**

AEI has been applied to educational platforms to create more personalized learning experiences. Systems can adapt content and teaching styles based on students' emotional engagement and comprehension levels. This approach aims to enhance the effectiveness of educational materials and foster a positive learning environment.

- **Accessibility Technologies:**

AEI contributes to accessibility technologies, making digital interfaces more inclusive. Emotion-aware systems assist individuals with different emotional needs or conditions, ensuring a more supportive and adaptive interaction experience. This inclusivity extends to interfaces for people with neurodivergent conditions.

In summary, the integration of AEI into mainstream applications reflects its diverse and impactful applications across industries. From enhancing user interfaces to revolutionizing customer service, mental health support, gaming, and beyond, AEI technologies have become integral components of numerous digital experiences, shaping the way we interact with technology on a daily basis.

Ethical and Societal Considerations

The integration of AEI into various applications has raised important ethical and societal considerations. This section explores the key dimensions of these considerations, addressing the challenges and implications associated with the deployment of emotionally intelligent systems.

- **Privacy Concerns:**

The collection and analysis of emotional data raise privacy concerns. AEI systems often rely on capturing sensitive information related to users' emotions, which may include facial expressions, voice tones, or physiological signals. Ensuring the privacy and security of this emotional data becomes crucial, necessitating robust data protection measures and transparent privacy policies.

- **Informed Consent:**

Obtaining informed consent from users becomes a critical ethical consideration. Users should be aware of how their emotional data will be used and have the option to opt in or opt out of emotional tracking. Transparent communication about the purpose, duration, and scope of emotional data collection is essential to uphold principles of autonomy and informed decision-making.

- **Emotional Manipulation:**

The potential for emotional manipulation is a significant ethical concern. AEI systems, if misused, could manipulate users' emotions for commercial or political purposes. Striking a balance between personalized experiences and avoiding manipulation requires clear ethical guidelines, responsible design practices, and regulatory frameworks that govern the ethical use of emotionally intelligent technologies.

- **Bias and Fairness:**

Emotion recognition systems may exhibit biases, leading to differential treatment based on factors such as race, gender, or cultural background. Ensuring fairness and mitigating biases in AEI models are imperative to prevent discriminatory outcomes. Ethical considerations include thorough testing for biases, diverse training datasets, and ongoing efforts to address and rectify any identified biases.

- **Emotional Well-Being and Mental Health:**

While AEI applications in mental health support are promising, there are ethical considerations regarding their impact on emotional well-being. Ensuring that AEI interventions are supportive, accurate, and align with mental health best practices becomes crucial. Ethical guidelines must prioritize user well-being and avoid potential harm.

- **Transparency and Explainability:**

The opacity of some AEI models poses challenges to transparency and explainability. Users may not understand how decisions about their emotions are made, leading to concerns about accountability and trust. Developing transparent and interpretable AEI systems is essential to address these ethical considerations and foster user trust.

- **Accessibility and Inclusivity:**

Ethical considerations extend to ensuring that AEI technologies are accessible and inclusive. Designing systems that accommodate diverse emotional expressions and needs, including those of neurodivergent individuals, is essential. Ethical guidelines should prioritize creating technology that enhances inclusivity and does not inadvertently exclude certain user groups.

- **Regulatory Frameworks:**

The development and deployment of AEI technologies necessitate robust regulatory frameworks. Ethical guidelines and legal standards must be established to govern the responsible use of emotionally intelligent systems. Regulatory oversight can help prevent misuse, protect user rights, and ensure that AEI technologies align with societal values.

In summary, addressing the ethical and societal considerations associated with AEI requires a multifaceted approach. This includes transparent data practices, informed consent, mitigation of biases, prioritizing user well-being, promoting inclusivity, and establishing regulatory frameworks that balance innovation with ethical safeguards.

Balancing the potential benefits of AEI with ethical considerations is crucial for the responsible and sustainable development of emotionally intelligent technologies.

In summary, the evolution of AEI reflects a progression from theoretical musings to practical applications, driven by advancements in affective computing, machine learning, and ethical considerations. This journey continues to unfold as AEI technologies become more ingrained in our daily interactions with intelligent systems.

TECHNICAL ASPECTS OF AEI

(AEI involves a complex interplay of technical components to enable machines to perceive, understand, and respond to human emotions. This detailed exploration delves into the key technical aspects that constitute the foundation of AEI systems (Prentice, 2023).

- **Data Acquisition and Preprocessing:**

AEI's technical development relies on data acquisition and preprocessing processes. Data acquisition involves collecting diverse datasets, such as facial expressions and voice tones, to capture emotional expressions. Preprocessing refines this data through noise reduction, feature extraction, and data augmentation, ensuring technical accuracy and ethical considerations in handling emotional data.

- **Feature Extraction:**

Feature extraction is a crucial stage in Artificial Emotion Intelligence (AEI), transforming raw data into meaningful patterns for understanding human emotions. It involves identifying key features from facial expressions, voice tones, and physiological signals to create a comprehensive understanding of emotional states. The chosen features balance the richness of emotional expressions with computational efficiency, forming the basis for training models.

- **Machine Learning Models:**

Machine Learning models are crucial in AEI systems, transforming data insights into actionable emotion recognition. They use features from facial expressions, voice tones, and physiological signals to discern and generalize emotional states. Supervised learning approaches train models using annotated datasets. Continuous advancements in machine learning techniques improve accuracy, reduce biases, and enhance generalization across diverse demographic groups.

- **Multi-Modal Fusion**:

Multi-Modal Fusion is a crucial aspect of AEI, integrating information from various sources to enhance emotion recognition. It uses facial expressions, voice tones, and physiological signals to provide a comprehensive understanding of human emotions. This technique, used early or late, creates a unified representation of emotional cues, enhancing the overall emotional intelligence of AEI systems.

- **Real-Time Processing:**

Real-Time Processing is a crucial aspect of AEI, enabling swift analysis and response to emotional cues with minimal latency. It involves data acquisition, preprocessing, feature extraction, and machine learning model inference, enhancing responsiveness and adaptability in applications like virtual assistants and chatbots.

- **Explainability and Interpretability:**

Explainability and interpretability are crucial in AEI technical architecture, ensuring transparency and understanding in decision-making processes. They provide clarity, insight into the model's internal workings, and are essential in applications requiring trust and understanding. Balancing accuracy with transparency promotes responsible deployment, user trust, and ethical use in various domains.

- **Cross-Cultural Considerations:**

Cross-cultural considerations are crucial in AEI technical implementation, as emotions are influenced by cultural norms, values, and communication styles. Customizing models to account for cultural nuances in facial expressions ensures a universal understanding of emotions. This approach enhances the robustness and generalizability of AEI systems.

- **Ethical AI Practices:**

Ethical AI practices are crucial in the development of artificial intelligence (AEI), focusing on fairness, transparency, privacy, and accountability. These practices involve obtaining informed consent, safeguarding user privacy, and addressing biases. Transparent communication, diverse perspectives, and ethical excellence contribute to the long-term acceptance and positive societal impact of AI systems.

In summary, the technical aspects of AEI involve a sophisticated combination of data acquisition, feature extraction, machine learning models, multi-modal fusion, real-time processing, explainability, cross-cultural considerations, and adherence to ethical AI practices. This holistic approach contributes to the development of effective, responsible, and culturally sensitive AEI systems.

APPLICATIONS OF AEI

AEI finds diverse applications across various domains, enhancing user experiences, enabling more natural interactions, and contributing to the development of emotionally aware systems. This detailed exploration provides insights into the specific applications of AEI and their implications (Doğru, 2022) (Winstinindah Sandroto & Fransiska, 2021) (Amorim et al., 2019) (Mellouk et al., 2020) (Singh et al., 2022).

- **Virtual Assistants and Chatbots**:

AEI is revolutionizing human-computer interactions through virtual assistants and chatbots. These tools use voice tones and natural language processing to understand user emotions, enabling personalized responses. Chatbots, used in customer service and online platforms, also benefit from AEI, addressing user sentiments and enhancing interaction quality. As applications advance, AEI continues to shape emotionally intelligent virtual assistants and chatbots.

- **Mental Health Support**:

AEI technologies are being used in mental health support to monitor and understand individuals' emotional well-being. These applications use facial expression analysis and voice tone recognition to gauge users' emotional states. They can identify signs of stress, anxiety, or depression, and offer personalized interventions. Real-time emotional monitoring enhances self-awareness and provides additional support alongside traditional services. AEI technologies offer innovative solutions for emotional well-being.

- **Gaming and Entertainment**:

AEI technology is revolutionizing gaming and entertainment by analyzing players' emotional cues, allowing games to adapt in real-time. This enhances engagement and personalized experiences. In the entertainment industry, AEI technologies are used to gauge audience reactions during live performances or virtual events. This real-time feedback allows content creators to tailor productions based on emotional responses, blurring the lines between virtual and real-world interactions.

- **Human-Computer Interaction:**

AEI technologies significantly improve Human-Computer Interaction (HCI) by enabling real-time emotional responses. They use facial expression analysis and voice tone recognition to understand users' emotions, enabling empathetic interfaces. This allows computers to adapt responses and behaviors based on users' emotions, such as in virtual assistants and smart devices. As AEI evolves, it promises to redefine human-computer interactions.

- **Automotive Systems:**

AEI technologies are revolutionizing the automotive industry by incorporating emotional awareness into driving experiences. By analyzing cues like facial expressions and voice tones, these technologies enhance safety, comfort, and overall well-being. AEI can also create adaptive driving environments, such as adjusting driving modes based on stress or fatigue, and adapting lighting, music, and climate control based on emotional states.

- **Marketing and Advertising**

AEI technologies offer transformative potential in marketing and advertising by analyzing emotional cues like facial expressions and voice tones. They enable marketers to gauge audience responses, inform content creation, and tailor content based on emotional engagement. This approach aims to create personalized campaigns and foster deeper connections between brands and consumers, revolutionizing the way businesses understand and leverage emotional responses.

- **Accessibility Technologies:**

AEI is transforming accessibility technologies by enhancing user experience for individuals with diverse abilities. Technologies like facial expression analysis and voice tone recognition create intuitive interfaces for disabled users. These adaptive technologies interpret and respond to users' emotions, fostering a more inclusive and emotionally intelligent digital environment.

- **Robotics and Social Robots:**

AEI technologies are revolutionizing robotics by enabling social robots to interact with humans in emotionally intelligent ways. These robots, using facial expression analysis and voice tone recognition, can adapt their behaviors based on users' emotions, creating engaging and empathetic interactions. Applications include healthcare, education, and companion robotics, offering emotional support for individuals with challenges or the elderly.

- **Security and Authentication:**

AEI technologies, like facial expression analysis and voice tone recognition, enhance security and authentication by utilizing emotional cues to improve accuracy and reliability. These systems can adapt to variations in users' appearances or conditions, providing a more robust and user-friendly solution. As technology advances, AEI holds the potential to contribute to more sophisticate and reliable user authentication methods.

- **Human Resources and Recruitment:**

AEI technologies, such as facial expression analysis and voice tone recognition, can improve HR and recruitment processes by assessing candidates' emotional intelligence and interpersonal skills. They contribute to employee well-being and workplace satisfaction, and can be used in video interviews to evaluate candidates based on cultural fit and qualifications. As technology advances, AEI could revolutionize talent management strategies.

These applications showcase the versatility and impact of AEI across different sectors, contributing to more emotionally intelligent and responsive technologies in our daily lives. As AEI continues to evolve, its applications are likely to expand, influencing how we interact with technology and each other.

USER PERSPECTIVES

Understanding the user perspectives on AEI is crucial for evaluating its impact and acceptance. Users may have varied responses and expectations regarding the integration of emotional intelligence into technology. Some key user perspectives include (Mitocaru et al., 2022) (Alshahrani et al., 2023) (Rodrigues & Cardoso, 2023) (Du et al., 2023) (Cardoso et al., 2023):

- **Emotional Engagement:**

Users may appreciate AEI for its ability to create emotionally engaging experiences, such as more empathetic virtual assistants or personalized content in entertainment. Positive emotional engagement can contribute to user satisfaction and loyalty.

- **Privacy Concerns:**

Users may express concerns about the privacy implications of AEI, especially when it involves the analysis of facial expressions or voice tones. Clear communication and transparent practices in handling emotional data are essential to address these concerns.

- **Efficacy and Accuracy:**

Users are likely to assess the effectiveness and accuracy of AEI applications. If these technologies can accurately recognize and respond to their emotions, users may find value in the personalized and adaptive features offered.

- **Ethical Considerations:**

User perspectives may encompass ethical considerations, such as the fair and unbiased treatment of diverse emotions and the avoidance of manipulation through emotional insights. Users may expect AEI systems to adhere to ethical standards in their design and use.

- **Acceptance in Different Contexts:**

User acceptance may vary across different contexts of AEI application. For instance, users may embrace emotional support features in mental health applications but approach emotional recognition in security contexts with caution.

- **User Education:**

Users may express the need for clear communication and education about how AEI works, what data is being used, and how their emotions contribute to the functioning of these systems. Transparent communication can build trust and acceptance.

- **Customization and Control:**

Users may value the ability to customize and control how AEI systems interact with their emotions. Preferences for adjusting sensitivity levels or opting out of emotion tracking in certain contexts may vary among users.

- **Cultural Sensitivity:**

User perspectives may highlight the importance of cultural sensitivity in AEI, recognizing and respecting diverse cultural expressions of emotions. AEI systems should be designed to accommodate cultural variations.

Gathering and incorporating user perspectives in the development and deployment of AEI technologies is essential for ensuring that these systems align with user expectations, values, and preferences. It also fosters a user-centric approach, enhancing the overall acceptance and success of AEI applications.

In summary, user perspectives on AEI reflect a nuanced interplay of positive reception, concerns about privacy and ethics, and expectations for applications across diverse domains. Addressing user concerns, ensuring transparency, and prioritizing ethical considerations contribute to building user trust and acceptance of AEI technologies.

ETHICAL CONSIDERATIONS

The integration of AEI raises a spectrum of ethical considerations that demand careful attention to ensure responsible and equitable deployment. Some key ethical considerations in the development and use of AEI include (Li et al., 2023) (Dosso et al., 2023) (Yang et al., 2022):

- **Privacy Concerns:**

AEI often involves the analysis of personal emotional data, such as facial expressions and voice tones. Ensuring robust privacy measures, obtaining informed consent, and providing users with control over their emotional data are imperative to address privacy concerns.

- **Bias and Fairness:**

The potential for bias in AEI algorithms, including cultural biases in emotion recognition, poses ethical challenges. Developers must strive to mitigate biases in training data and algorithms to ensure fair treatment across diverse demographic groups.

- **Transparency and Explainability:**

The opacity of AI algorithms can be a source of ethical concern. Ensuring transparency and explainability in AEI systems allows users to understand how their emotional data is being used, fostering trust and accountability.

- **Informed Consent:**

Users should be adequately informed about the collection, processing, and utilization of their emotional data. Obtaining informed consent ensures that users understand and agree to the terms of emotional data use in AEI applications.

- **Security Risks:**

AEI systems may become targets for malicious activities, leading to potential security breaches. Implementing robust cybersecurity measures is essential to safeguard emotional data and prevent unauthorized access.

- **Mitigating Unintended Consequences:**

Developers should anticipate and address unintended consequences of AEI, such as emotional manipulation or the exacerbation of mental health issues. Ethical considerations involve actively working to mitigate these risks.

- **Cultural Sensitivity:**

Cultural variations in the expression and interpretation of emotions require careful consideration. AEI systems should be designed to recognize and respect diverse cultural norms, avoiding cultural biases in emotion recognition.

- **Ensuring User Autonomy:**

Users should have control over their interaction with AEI systems. Providing options for customization, such as adjusting sensitivity levels or opting out of emotional tracking, ensures that users maintain autonomy over their emotional data.

- **Long-term Impact on Well-being:**

The potential long-term impact of AEI on individual and societal well-being is an ethical consideration. Continuous monitoring of emotional states and the emotional influence of technology should be conducted responsibly.

- **Accessibility and Inclusivity:**

Ethical considerations include ensuring that AEI technologies are accessible and inclusive, catering to individuals with diverse abilities and avoiding the creation of emotional experiences that may exclude certain groups.

Addressing these ethical considerations requires collaboration among developers, researchers, policymakers, and users. Establishing ethical guidelines, industry standards, and ongoing ethical assessments are essential to navigate the complex ethical landscape of AEI and foster its responsible and beneficial integration into society.

CHALLENGES AND FUTURE DIRECTIONS

The development and implementation of AEI bring forth challenges that need to be addressed, along with opportunities for future advancements. Some notable challenges and potential directions for the future include (Shahraki & Nafchi, 2022) (Fang et al., 2022) (Govindasamy et al., 2023):

Challenges:

- **Ethical Concerns:**

Ethical considerations, such as privacy issues, biases, and the responsible use of emotional data, pose ongoing challenges. Future developments should prioritize ethical guidelines to ensure the responsible deployment of AEI technologies.

- **Bias and Fairness:**

Addressing biases in emotion recognition algorithms is a persistent challenge. Ongoing efforts to diversify training datasets and implement bias mitigation strategies are essential to enhance fairness across diverse populations.

- **Interdisciplinary Collaboration:**

AEI development requires collaboration across disciplines, including psychology, computer science, and ethics. Bridging these interdisciplinary gaps is crucial for a comprehensive understanding of human emotions and the ethical implications of AEI.

- **User Understanding and Trust:**

Users may find it challenging to understand how AEI systems work, leading to concerns and hesitancy. Future directions should include initiatives to educate users, enhance transparency, and build trust in AEI technologies.

- **Cultural Variations:**

Recognizing and accommodating cultural variations in emotional expressions remain challenging. Future AEI systems should aim for cultural sensitivity and customization to ensure accurate emotion recognition across diverse cultures.

- **Data Security:**

The security of emotional data is a critical concern. Protecting emotional data from unauthorized access and ensuring robust cybersecurity measures are essential to prevent breaches and maintain user trust.

Future Directions:

- **Explainable AI:**

Advancements in explainable AI can contribute to addressing the transparency challenge in AEI. Future systems should prioritize explainability to help users understand how emotional insights are derived and used.

- **Personalized AEI:**

Tailoring AEI experiences to individual users can enhance personalization and user satisfaction. Future developments should explore ways to customize AEI systems based on user preferences and sensitivities.

- **Continual Bias Mitigation:**

Ongoing efforts to mitigate biases in AEI algorithms should be a focus. Regular updates, diverse dataset curation, and continuous evaluation can contribute to reducing and preventing biases in emotion recognition.

- **Cross-disciplinary Research:**

Increased collaboration between researchers from psychology, neuroscience, and AI is essential. Future AEI development should draw insights from multiple disciplines to achieve a deeper understanding of human emotions.

- **Integration with Mental Health Care:**

AEI technologies can play a significant role in mental health support. Future directions should explore the integration of AEI into mental health applications, providing valuable insights and interventions for emotional well-being.

- **Standardization and Regulation:**

Establishing industry standards and regulations for AEI can contribute to ethical and responsible development. Future efforts should focus on creating frameworks that guide the ethical deployment and use of AEI technologies.

- **User-centric Design:**

Prioritizing user-centric design principles can address usability challenges. Future AEI systems should be designed with user needs, preferences, and expectations at the forefront to enhance overall user experience.

- **Long-term Impact Assessment:**

Anticipating and studying the long-term impact of AEI on individuals and society is crucial. Future research should involve longitudinal studies to assess the sustained effects of continuous emotional monitoring and interaction with AEI systems.

Navigating these challenges and embracing future directions with a commitment to ethics, transparency, and user well-being will shape the trajectory of AEI, contributing to its responsible integration into various aspects of human life.

CASE STUDIES

Examining real-world case studies provides valuable insights into the practical applications, successes, and challenges of AEI. Here are a few illustrative case studies (Gautam et al., 2023) (Grobelny et al., 2021) (Wang et al., 2023):

- **Affectiva's Emotion AI in Market Research:**

Affectiva, a pioneer in Emotion AI, has collaborated with market researchers to analyze consumers' emotional responses to advertisements. Using facial expression analysis, the technology measures emotional engagement and helps marketers optimize campaigns based on audience reactions.

- **Kokoro Care and Emotional Support Robots:**

Kokoro Care developed robots equipped with AEI capabilities to provide emotional support, particularly in healthcare settings. These robots, such as Paro, a therapeutic seal robot, use AEI to respond to users' emotional states and provide comfort, especially for individuals in hospitals or nursing homes.

- **Amazon's Alexa Emotion Recognition:**

Amazon has explored incorporating emotion recognition capabilities into its voice-activated assistant, Alexa. This involves analyzing users' vocal patterns to infer emotional states. The goal is to create a more personalized and emotionally responsive interaction between users and the virtual assistant.

- **Microsoft's Seeing AI for Accessibility:**

Microsoft's Seeing AI, an app designed for individuals with visual impairments, utilizes AEI features. The app can describe people's emotions based on facial expressions, assisting users in understanding social cues and emotional states in their surroundings.

- **Emotion AI in Education - Riiid Labs:**

Riiid Labs has explored the use of Emotion AI in education technology. By analyzing students' facial expressions and engagement levels during online learning sessions, the system provides insights into learners' emotional states, allowing for adaptive and personalized learning experiences.

- **Sony's Aibo Companion Robot:**

Sony's Aibo, an AI-powered robotic dog, incorporates AEI to respond to users' emotions. The robot can express emotions through its movements and responses, creating a more interactive and emotionally engaging experience for users.

These case studies highlight the diverse applications of AEI across industries, from market research and healthcare to virtual assistants and education. While showcasing the potential benefits, they also underscore the need for ethical considerations, user acceptance, and ongoing advancements in technology for more effective and responsible deployment of AEI.

CONCLUSION

In conclusion, AEI represents a transformative field with the potential to revolutionize human-computer interactions across various domains. The exploration of AEI involves understanding and harnessing the complex interplay of emotions, technology, and ethical considerations.

Throughout this detailed examination, we've delved into the foundations, technical aspects, applications, user perspectives, ethical considerations, challenges, and case studies associated with AEI. From the intricate processes of emotion recognition to the deployment of emotionally intelligent systems in virtual health assistants, educational platforms, customer service chatbots, and socially interactive robots, the impact of AEI is diverse and far-reaching. The user perspective on AEI reflects a nuanced balance between enhanced user experiences, concerns about privacy and ethical implications, and expectations for responsible and inclusive applications. Ethical considerations play a central role, addressing issues of privacy, fairness, transparency, and user empowerment. Challenges in AEI, including accuracy in emotion recognition, cross-cultural adaptation, privacy concerns, and biases, highlight the need for ongoing research and development. As AEI continues to evolve, it is crucial to prioritize ethical guidelines, user-centric design, and cross-disciplinary collaboration to ensure responsible innovation. The case studies presented showcase real-world implementations of AEI, demonstrating its potential to positively impact mental well-being, education, customer service, content recommendations, and human-robot interactions. These examples provide valuable insights into both the successes and challenges associated with integrating AEI into diverse applications. Looking ahead, the future directions for AEI involve addressing challenges, refining accuracy, advancing cross-cultural adaptability, ensuring privacy, and establishing clear ethical frameworks. The ongoing pursuit of responsible and inclusive development, guided by user feedback and ethical considerations, will shape the trajectory of AEI, fostering a more emotionally intelligent and user-friendly technological landscape. As AEI continues to progress, it is poised to play a pivotal role in shaping the future of human-machine interactions, enriching our digital experiences with emotional awareness and understanding.

REFERENCES

Alshahrani, H. M., Yaseen, I., & Drar, S. (2023). Textual Emotion Analysis-based Disabled People Talking Using Improved Metaheuristics with Deep Learning Techniques for Intelligent Systems. *Journal of Disability Research, 2*(3). doi:10.57197/JDR-2023-0034

Amorim, M., Cohen, Y., Reis, J., & Rodrigues, M. (2019). Exploring opportunities for artificial emotional intelligence in service production systems. *IFAC-PapersOnLine, 52*(13), 1145–1149. doi:10.1016/j.ifacol.2019.11.350

Bapat, G. S., Ayedee, N., Bhalerao, K., Kumar, A., & Singh, S. (2023). From Natural to Artificial and Now to Emotional Intelligence. *Advances in Communication. Devices and Networking, 1037*, 321–333. doi:10.1007/978-981-99-1983-3_31

Barrett, L. F., Adolphs, R., Marsella, S., Martinez, A. M., & Pollak, S. D. (2019). Emotional expressions reconsidered: Challenges to inferring emotion from human facial movements. *Psychological Science in the Public Interest, 20*(1), 1–68. doi:10.1177/1529100619832930 PMID:31313636

Bhardwaj, B., Sharma, D., & Dhiman, M. C. (2023). AI and Emotional Intelligence for Modern Business Management. *Advances in Logistics, Operations, and Management Science, 1*, 13. doi:10.4018/979-8-3693-0418-1

Budhwar, P., Malik, A., De Silva, M. T. T., & Thevisuthan, P. (2022). Artificial intelligence – challenges and opportunities for international HRM: A review and research agenda. *International Journal of Human Resource Management, 33*(6), 1065–1097. doi:10.1080/09585192.2022.2035161

Pedro J. S. Cardoso, João M. F. Rodrigues, Rui Novais. (2023). Multimodal Emotion Classification Supported in the Aggregation of Pre-trained Classification Models. *Computational Science – ICCS 2023, 10477*, 433.

Doğru, Ç. (2022). A Meta-Analysis of the Relationships Between Emotional Intelligence and Employee Outcomes. *Frontiers in Psychology*, 13. PMID:35548499

Dosso, J. A., Kailley, J. N., Guerra, G. K., & Robillard, J. M. (2023). Older adult perspectives on emotion and stigma in social robots. *Frontiers in Psychiatry, 13*, 13. doi:10.3389/fpsyt.2022.1051750 PMID:36713914

Kavyashree, M. B., & Anupama Sundar, D. (2023). Emotional Intelligence on Job Attitudes of Employees. *International Journal of Engineering Technology and Management Sciences, 7*(4), 362–375. doi:10.46647/ijetms.2023.v07i04.050

Du, Y., Zhang, K., & Trovato, G. (2023). Composite Emotion Recognition and Feedback of Social Assistive Robot for Elderly People. *Lecture Notes in Computer Science, 14051*, 220–231. doi:10.1007/978-3-031-35894-4_16

Fang, Z., Liu, Z., Hung, C.-C., Sekhavat, Y. A., Liu, T., & Wang, X. (2022). Learning coordinated emotion representation between voice and face. *Applied Intelligence.*

Govindasamy, P., Sankar Ganesh, R., & Ramesh, R. (2023). Redefining the Performance Management using Emotional Artificial Intelligence. *2023 International Conference on Applied Intelligence and Sustainable Computing (ICAISC)*, (pp. 1-8). IEEE. 10.1109/ICAISC58445.2023.10200202

Grobelny, J., Radke, P., & Maczka, D. P. (2021). Emotional intelligence and job performance: A meta-analysis. *International Journal of Work Organisation and Emotion, 12*(1), 115620. doi:10.1504/IJWOE.2021.115620

Igboyi, E. M., Asenge, E. L., & Iortyom, D. K. (2023). Emotional Intelligence and Employee Productivity in Benue Internal Revenue Service. *Journal of Production. Operations Management and Economics, 41*, 34–44.

Kambur, E. (2021). Emotional Intelligence or Artificial Intelligence?: Emotional Artificial Intelligence. *Florya Chronicles of Political Economy, 7*(2), 147–168.

Li, Q., Liu, T., Liu, Z., & Chai, Y. (2023). Emotionally intelligent virtual tour guide in handling group conflicts: Effect on user outcomes. *Computer Animation and Virtual Worlds, 34*(3-4), e2153. doi:10.1002/cav.2153

Mellouk, W., & Handouzi, W. (2020). Facial emotion recognition using deep learning: Review and insights. *Procedia Computer Science, 175*, 689–694. doi:10.1016/j.procs.2020.07.101

Mitocaru, A., Poboroniuc, M. S., Irimia, D. C., Placinta, S., & Baciu, A. (2022). Brain-Computer Interface Based Control for a Humanoid Robot. *2022 International Conference and Exposition on Electrical And Power Engineering (EPE)*, (pp. 714-718). IEEE. 10.1109/EPE56121.2022.9959801

Prentice, C. (2023). Leveraging Emotional and Artificial Intelligence for Organisational Performance. *Leveraging Emotional and Artificial Intelligence for Organisational Performance, 87*, 103. doi:10.1007/978-981-99-1865-2

Prentice, C. (2023). Leveraging Emotional and Artificial Intelligence for Organisational Performance. *Leveraging Emotional and Artificial Intelligence for Organisational Performance, 25*, 40. doi:10.1007/978-981-99-1865-2

Prentice, C., Lopes, S. D., & Wang, X. (2020). Emotional intelligence or artificial intelligence– an employee perspective. *Journal of Hospitality Marketing & Management, 29*(4), 377–403. doi:10.1080/19368623.2019.1647124

Rodrigues, J. M. F., & Cardoso, P. J. S. (2023). Body-Focused Expression Analysis: A Conceptual Framework. *Universal Access in Human-Computer Interaction, 14021*, 596.

Sandroto, C. W., & Fransiska, J. (2021). The importance of emotional intelligence for the sales associates profession as a mediation between job stress and job satisfaction. *International Journal of Management and Economics, 57*(4), 331–342. doi:10.2478/ijme-2021-0012

Singh, R., Gehlot, A., & Joshi, A. (2022). Study on Facial Recognition to Detect Mood and Suggest Songs. *2022 International Interdisciplinary Humanitarian Conference for Sustainability (IIHC)*, (pp. 1078-1084). IEEE. 10.1109/IIHC55949.2022.10060265

Thajil, K. M., & AL-Abrrow, H. (2023). The effect of the bright triad on positive innovation in the healthcare sector: The mediating role of emotional intelligence. *International Journal of Healthcare Management, 0*(0), 1–12. doi:10.1080/20479700.2023.2177608

Wang, W., Kofler, L., Lindgren, C., Lobel, M., Murphy, A., Tong, Q., & Pickering, K. (2023). AI for Psychometrics: Validating Machine Learning Models in Measuring Emotional Intelligence with Eye-Tracking Techniques. *Journal of Intelligence, 11*(9), 170. doi:10.3390/jintelligence11090170 PMID:37754899

Yang, M., Wang, Z., Xu, Q., Li, C., & Xu, R. (2022). Leveraging hierarchical semantic-emotional memory in emotional conversation generation. *CAAI Transactions on Intelligence Technology.*

Zhu, D., Doan, T., Kanjanakan, P., & Kim, P. B. (2022). The impact of emotional intelligence on hospitality employees' work outcomes: A systematic and meta-analytical review. *Journal of Hospitality Marketing & Management, 31*(3), 326–347. doi:10.1080/19368623.2021.1978914

Chapter 3
Ethical Considerations in Emotion Data Collection and IoT Integration

Dharmesh Dhabliya
https://orcid.org/0000-0002-6340-2993
Vishwakarma Institute of Information Technology, Pune, India

Rahul Sharma
Auricle Global Society of Education and Research, India

Sukhvinder Singh Dari
https://orcid.org/0000-0002-6218-6600
Symbiosis Law School, Symbiosis International University, Pune, India

Busani Sravani
Malla Reddy Engineering College for Women, India

Sanjiv Kumar Jain
https://orcid.org/0000-0001-8942-7681
Medi-Caps University, Indore, India

Ritika Dhabliya
Yashika Journal Publications Pvt. Ltd., India

Jay Kumar Pandey
https://orcid.org/0000-0003-4086-5730
Shri Ramswaroop Memorial University, India

Ankur Gupta
https://orcid.org/0000-0002-4651-5830
Vaish College of Engineering, Rohtak, India

ABSTRACT

Present research is focused on consideration of emotional data. In order to deal with such objective, EEG technique has been applied. Electroencephalography (EEG) is a technique used to measure and record the electrical activity that takes place on the scalp. This recorded activity has been shown to be indicative of the underlying activity occurring in the superficial layer of the brain. Numerous studies have been conducted to investigate the quality of the electroencephalogram (EEG) signal. The major objective of this experiment was to examine the ability to recognize the emotional states shown by individuals. Despite the previous time-consuming nature and lack of accuracy in prior study, a viable solution has been discovered. It can be concluded that the system has a very limited capacity for both adaptation and expansion. Developing a thorough methodology for assessing electroencephalogram (EEG) data is of paramount significance.

DOI: 10.4018/979-8-3693-1910-9.ch003

1. INTRODUCTION

The integration of Emotion Data Collection, particularly through EEG (Electroencephalogram) technology, with Internet of Things (IoT) devices for emotion detection and classification using Long Short-Term Memory (LSTM) networks raises important ethical considerations. Below are key ethical considerations that researchers and practitioners should carefully address:

1. **Informed Consent and Privacy:** Obtaining informed consent from participants is critical when collecting emotion data using EEG devices. Participants should be fully informed about the nature of the data collected, the purpose of the study, and how their data will be used. Additionally, researchers should ensure that participants have the option to withdraw from the study at any time. The integration of IoT devices introduces the risk of data being collected without individuals' explicit consent, making it essential to implement robust consent mechanisms.
2. **Data Security and Confidentiality:** Given the sensitive nature of emotion data, ensuring robust data security and confidentiality is paramount. Researchers must implement encryption and secure storage practices to protect the collected EEG data from unauthorized access or breaches. Clear guidelines on data sharing and storage limitations should be established to prevent the misuse of personal information.
3. **Bias and Fairness in Emotion Detection:** Ethical concerns arise when implementing emotion detection algorithms that may exhibit bias, leading to unfair treatment or misinterpretation of emotions. It is crucial to evaluate and address biases in the training data used for LSTM networks to ensure fair and unbiased emotion classification. Transparent reporting of algorithmic decisions and continuous monitoring for biases are necessary ethical practices.
4. **Data Ownership and Control:** Establishing clear guidelines on data ownership and control is essential. Participants should have control over their emotion data, including the ability to access, modify, or delete it. The integration of IoT devices may involve data being transmitted to centralized servers, necessitating transparent policies on data ownership and control throughout the data lifecycle.
5. **Consent for IoT Integration:** When integrating emotion data collection with IoT devices, participants should explicitly consent to the incorporation of their data into an IoT ecosystem. Transparency regarding the types of devices involved, the purpose of integration, and any potential sharing of data with third-party applications or services is crucial.
6. **Minimization of Harm:** Researchers must take measures to minimize potential harm to participants. This includes avoiding invasive data collection practices,

ensuring that the emotional content of the data is handled with care, and providing adequate psychological support for participants who may experience distress during or after the study.

7. **Transparency and Openness:** Maintaining transparency throughout the research process is vital. Researchers should openly communicate the goals, methods, and potential implications of the study to participants and the broader public. This includes being transparent about the limitations of emotion detection technologies and the potential impact on individuals' privacy.
8. **Continual Ethical Review:** Regular ethical reviews should be conducted to assess the ongoing implications of the research. As technologies evolve, researchers must stay vigilant to emerging ethical challenges and update their practices accordingly. This includes considering the ethical implications of new IoT devices and updated emotion detection algorithms.

By addressing these ethical considerations, researchers can promote responsible and ethical practices in emotion data collection, IoT integration, and the development of emotion detection models using technologies like EEG and LSTM networks. This ensures that advancements in these technologies are aligned with ethical principles, respect participants' rights, and contribute positively to the well-being of individuals involved in such studies.

1.1 Ethical Considerations

Responsible decision-making relies heavily on ethical concerns in many fields, including science, medicine, business, and research. Fairness, openness, privacy, and regard for human rights are all important factors to think about [1]. Ethical concerns generally revolve on problems like data privacy, algorithmic prejudice, and the potential for abuse in the context of technology and data-driven sectors like artificial intelligence and big data. New ethical concerns are raised by technological advancements on a regular basis, calling for constant discussion and the creation of solid ethical frameworks to deal with these issues as they arise. If technical progress is to benefit society as a whole and not cause unintended damage to specific people or groups, then ethical issues must be given top priority.

1.2 Emotion Data Collection

Emotion data collection, a field at the intersection of psychology, technology, and data science, involves the systematic gathering and analysis of emotional states and expressions in individuals. This process often employs a variety of techniques and technologies, including facial recognition software, physiological sensors,

Figure 1. Ethical considerations

voice analysis, and wearable devices, to capture and quantify emotions such as happiness, sadness, anger, and more. Emotion data collection holds great promise in diverse applications, ranging from mental health monitoring and market research to human-computer interaction and personalized user experiences. However, this burgeoning field also raises significant ethical and privacy concerns, as it necessitates the handling of highly sensitive personal information. Striking a balance between harnessing the potential insights from emotion data and safeguarding individual rights and privacy is an ongoing challenge that requires careful attention in both research and practical implementation.

1.3 Ethical Considerations in Emotion Data Collection

Ethical considerations in emotion data collection are of paramount importance in today's digital age, where technology enables the capture and analysis of individuals' emotional states. These considerations encompass issues like informed consent, privacy, and data security. When collecting emotional data, it is crucial to ensure that individuals willingly provide their information and understand how it will be used. Additionally, safeguarding their privacy and protecting sensitive emotional information from unauthorized access or misuse is imperative. Moreover, the potential for bias in emotion-detection algorithms and the ethical use of this data in various applications must be carefully monitored. Striking a balance between harnessing the insights gained from emotion data and respecting individuals' rights and well-being is central to ensuring that technology improves our lives without compromising ethical standards. Ethical considerations in emotion data collection, therefore, serve as a critical compass guiding the responsible development and utilization of this evolving technology.

1.4 Need of Ethical Considerations in Emotion Data Collection and IoT

Ethical considerations in emotion data collection and its integration with IoT raise important questions about privacy, consent, and the responsible use of sensitive emotional information in a connected world. Collecting and analyzing emotional data through IoT devices can offer valuable insights into human behavior and well-being. However, this also comes with the risk of infringing upon personal privacy, potentially without informed consent. Providing people with choice and transparency about the use of their emotional data is essential. essential. Moreover, addressing the potential for biases in emotion-detection algorithms and safeguarding against misuse, such as emotional surveillance or manipulative advertising, is crucial. Striking a balance between technological innovation and protecting individuals' rights and well-being remains a core challenge in the ethical integration of emotion data into IoT. Ethical guidelines and responsible practices are vital to navigate this complex landscape and harness the potential of these technologies for the betterment of society while respecting fundamental ethical principles.

2. LITERATURE REVIEW

There have been different researches in area of emotion detection where Deep learning mechanisms are applied.

H. Alam et al. (2023) introduced smart baby monitoring system that uses machine learning to recognise emotions and the internet of things. Using a machine learning model, the technology can also determine how infants in the database were feeling. The external web camera allows parents to keep tabs on their kid in real time, while the mobile app alerts them when their infant is crying and allows them to remotely rock the baby cradle. Additionally, they had access to the room's current temperature and humidity. The baby monitoring device was a boon for working parents everywhere since it allows them to keep an eye on their children even when they had to split their attention between the office and the nursery.

T. Y. R. Destyanto et al. (2023) reviewed emotion detection considers the role of data, classification, and experimental techniques. They were tasked with conducting a thorough evaluation of emotion detection research undertaken in Southeast Asia, paying special attention to the types of physiological data used, the methods of classification used, and the number and duration of participants in each study. PRISMA criteria were applied to 22 articles from journals and conferences that are indexed by SCOPUS. Heart rate and skin conductivity were found to be the most often obtained physiological data employing wristbands, from a range of around 5-31 persons. Classification analysis included a wide variety of approaches. Participants were either sat or standing for the bulk of the examinations, depending on whether they were designed to assess fundamental or applied skills.

A. P. Plageras et al. (2023) connected health and therapy for the mind and body. In a nearby computer system, a "Smart Healthcare-Room" has just been established. Data sent between the hospital and the patient throughout treatment and hospital stay is very secure because to this network's design. The installation of a "Emotion Care System" allows for the "Data Learning" strategy to be managed across all operations and sensor communication. The information will be sent through a network to a programme built on top of the IoT framework, which will then alert the appropriate medical personnel as to the patient's physical and mental health.

B. Struminskaya et al. (2023) reviewed problems and solutions with using third-party data in surveys from an ethical perspective. In this literature review, they revisit ethical issues and empirical evidence on the effects of participants' privacy concerns on their willingness to take part in studies that gather these new data sources to augment surveys. They also talk about ways to reassure participants by protecting their privacy throughout data collection and distribution. They wrap off by raising some unanswered issues and point out some potential future lines of inquiry.

A. Wexler et al. (2023) did research on the low-risk gadgets raises ethical questions for scientists. This remark offers a summary of ethical issues that should be taken into account by scientists designing and testing low-risk gadgets that interface with humans. Examples include electronic wearables and biological sensors. They describe the steps involved in an independent review, making it clear that there were many degrees of scrutiny that may be applied to a study based on its methodology and the degree of danger it poses. They illustrate key ethical issues for using such low-risk gadgets in research using real-world examples.

M. Behnke et al. (2022) presented ethical issues and a checklist for conducting wearable emotional research. They also offered some potential methods for lowering danger. They talked with ethics committee members and appropriate researchers to develop the new rules. The judges (N = 26) liked our strategies and gave us constructive criticism that helped us improve our instructions. Finally, they provided a checklist summary of our ideas for ease of use by future studies. Their recommendations help safeguard the interests of researchers and study participants in the future.

S. Chamishka et al. (2022) introduced a real-time method for identifying emotions from a person's speech using feature modelling driven by recurrent neural networks. This study presents a novel approach to feature extraction for chatting audio data based on the use of BoAW based feature embeddings. To that aim, they provide a cutting-edge, RNN-based emotion detection model capable of making instantaneous, categorical emotion predictions that factor in both the conversation context and the moods of the individual speakers. It was determined how well the proposed method and model performed using an empirical evaluation of real-time prediction capabilities and two benchmark datasets. With a weighted accuracy of 60.87 percent and an unweighted accuracy of 60.97 percent on the IEMOCAP dataset, the proposed technique significantly surpassed state-of-the-art models.

M. Fadda et al. (2022) focused on the privacy and confidentiality arise when collecting, storing, and analyzed geo-referenced tweets for studies on mental health. The goal of this paper is to examine the current regulations for geo-referenced tweets used in mental health research, and to weigh the benefits and drawbacks of each. They contribute to the ongoing conversation on the ethical implications of big data research and provide guidance to researchers and stakeholders on how to handle them, with a focus on the use of spatially referenced data in the area of mental health research. There is a growing awareness of data privacy and confidentiality issues, making it imperative to establish professional standards of conduct in order to ensure that research conducted with health-related social media data is conducted ethically and can be easily assessed.

M. Hosseini et al. (2022) introduced ethics challenges presented by big data analysis in the social sciences. This study examines the moral implications of using massive datasets in SSR. They begin by bringing to light the informational chasm separating big data ethics, SSR, and research ethics. Then, we spoke about three aspects of large-scale SSR that, from a research ethics standpoint, need special attention: A lack of regulatory oversight and ethical recommendations for safeguarding subjects and societies in big data SSR; (2) the interpretive nature of both SSR and big data; (3) difficulty in foreseeing & controlling risks associated with the publication and reuse of big data SSR.

F. V. S. Jothiraj et al. (2022) presented IoT and ML for individualized emotion recognition. In this study, they introduce a wearable IoT device for monitoring patient emotions, with a focus on people on the autistic spectrum. Individuals' perspiration and heart rates were tracked and analyzed for the impact of emotional states using a small number of inexpensive sensors and cloud computing services. The suggested method uses machine learning algorithms to correctly identify an individual's emotional state with an accuracy of up to 92% while the person was at rest. The suggested method yields results that were on par with those of cutting-edge medical IoT systems.

S. M. Mohammad et al. (2022) provided ethics guide for sentiment analysis and automatic emotion recognition. This article presents fifty ethical issues for AER based on a synthesis and organisation of work on AI ethics and emotion recognition. Importantly, this ethics sheet elaborates on hidden assumptions in the typical framing of AER, as well as in the typical selections made with regards to data, procedure, and assessment.

J. Navarro-Alamán et al. (2022) presented EmotIoT was an IoT platform designed to enhance end-user happiness. In this, where user detection was important, they offer an approach that may aid in the rapid design of IoT systems. To put the offered technique to the test, they develop a prototype IoT smart recommender system called EmotIoT using the suggested steps. Using data from IoT devices, the system can project how a user would feel in the future. To help the user reach their goal, it suggests further steps they might do.

3. PROBLEM STATEMENT

Emotion data collection and its integration with the IoT presents a number of ethical difficulties, including those relating to privacy, informed permission, data security, and the potential for exploitation of sensitive emotional information. Responsible use of IoT requires taking precautions to avoid endangering people's privacy, safety, and security by doing things like fixing problems with bias and accuracy in emotion-detection technologies and preventing the data from being used in exploitative or manipulative ways. The dependability of EEG signals has been the subject of a great deal of research. Objective of the researchers in conducting this study was to enhance their proficiency in seeing and interpreting individuals' emotional states. Notwithstanding the protracted duration and flawed outcomes of the first inquiry, a resolution has ultimately been attained. Nevertheless, the aforementioned probes exhibited limitations in terms of their range and flexibility. In order to effectively analyse EEG data, it is necessary to have an advanced system that is capable of accurately distinguishing emotions. Another strategy that might enhance accuracy and efficiency is eliminating superfluous data.

4. RESEARCH METHODOLOGY

The proposed research encompasses emotional detection, overhead processing, and EEG signal processing using LSTM techniques. Researchers are now focusing their efforts on the examination of emotional detecting aspects in order to enhance their understanding of consumer behaviour.

Figure 2. Proposed research methodology

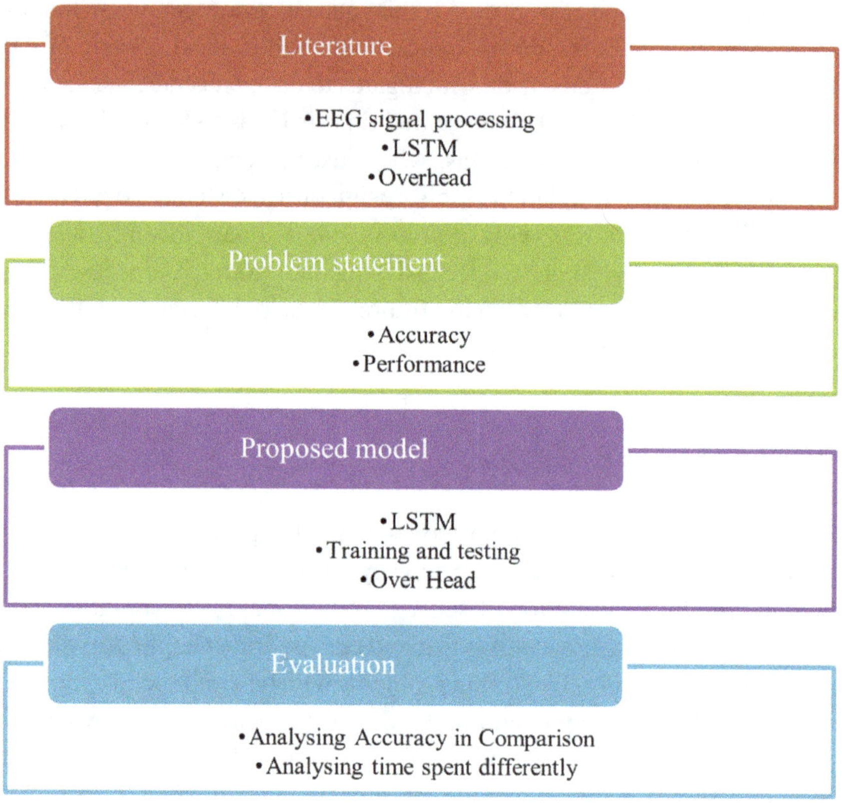

The proposed research addresses a range of challenges, including scalability, variables influencing impact, reliability, and adaptability. Researchers are using LSTM techniques to assess the validity of the null hypothesis. The Emotion recognition system will be used, using the DEAP dataset. The primary objectives of this endeavour are achieving scalability and flexibility via the use of LSTM in identification of emotional states. The integration of LSTM algorithms allows a unique approach that combines emotion detection and behaviour analysis. The last suggested phase in the workflow is to gather data prior to its filtration and utilisation in LTSM processes. Table1 shows the comparison between conventional and proposed approach.

Table 1. Comparison between conventional and proposed approach

Parameters	Conventional approach	Proposed work
Epoch	18	18
Batch size	64	64
Optimization	Not applied	PSO
Classification model	LSTM	Hybrid LSTM
Learning rate	0.001	0.001
Accuracy	96%	98%
Performance	15 Minute per epoch	14 Minute per epoch

5. PROPOSED WORK

The proposed study has used a LSTM model in conjunction with a data filtering strategy. In contrast, the usual approach employed decision tree, SVM, & KNN algorithms without any pre-filtering procedure. The usual technique was limited in terms of both time consumption and accuracy. The suggested effort uses the Matlab software as the simulation platform. Various aspects that exert influence on the accuracy and performance of simulations are taken into consideration.

- **LSTM layer:** The LSTM layer is being used in our research, using deep learning and feedback connection, in order to train the network. The proposed model employs LSTM networks for the purpose of classification. This is achieved via the use of HL, DL, fully linked layers, and classification layers. The EEG data provided has undergone processing and predictions have been generated using LSTM approach.
- **Dropout layer:** The use of a dropout layer allows for the detection of overfitting during the plotting step via the examination of the validation loss. As the model undergoes more training iterations, its idiosyncrasies become increasingly evident. After a given duration, the training process gradually diminishes its capacity to efficiently integrate new data. The provided data may potentially include a representative sample of the population or a particular subgroup. Overfitting occurs when a model demonstrates a high degree of accuracy in fitting both training data & validation data.
- **Fully connected layer:** Completely connected layer refers to the process of multiplying an input by a weight matrix in a layer where all neurons are connected to each other. Subsequently, an additional component in the form of a bias vector is included. The completely Connected Layer (output size) function may be used to obtain the completely connected layer of the proposed task, which is defined by the Output Size parameter.

Figure 3. Process flow of proposed work

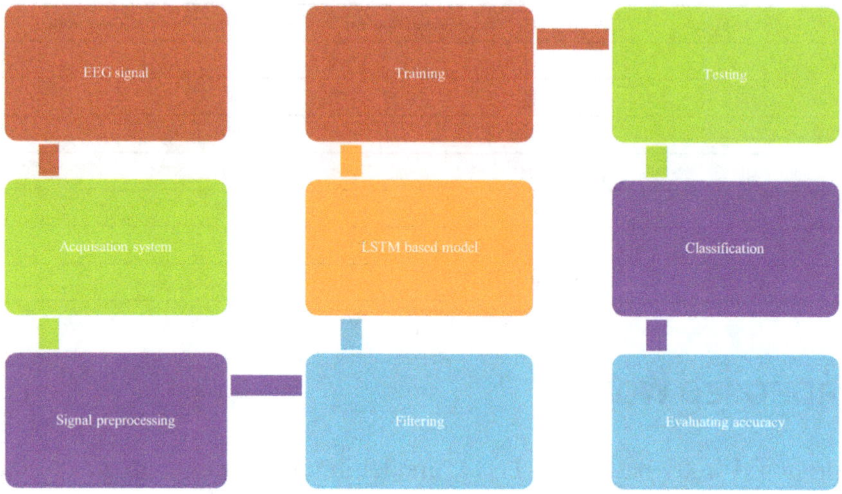

- **Softmax:** In a neural network, the last hidden layer is activated by a softmax layer. An alternate activation function is employed in place of ReLU, the sigmoid, or tanh. The addition of the Softmax layer is required due to the transition of the output from the previous layer into the input of NN. The softmax function is frequently executed at the output layer of a neural network, and this layer often provides assistance. This layer's number of nodes should mirror that of the output layer.
- **Classification layer:** The classification layer is generally recognised as the primary focus of research and application in the field of neural networks. The process of categorising large datasets into different groups for the purpose of creating a set of rules is a crucial aspect of classification. Classification plays a crucial role in facilitating decision-making, pattern detection, dimensionality reduction, and data mining. In the suggested study, the use of classification techniques has facilitated the segregation of the dataset, hence enabling the generation of rules that can be employed to train the model for the purpose of EEG signal categorization. Decisions have been made based on the rules generated throughout the testing process.
- **Batch size:** The batch size has been regarded as a hyperparameter. The process involves determining the number of samples needs to be collected prior to making adjustments to the parameters inside the internal model. Batch programming is well recognised as a kind of loop structure. The process involves iterating through several samples in order to do a prediction

Figure 4. Process flow for proposed work for EEG classification using LSTM

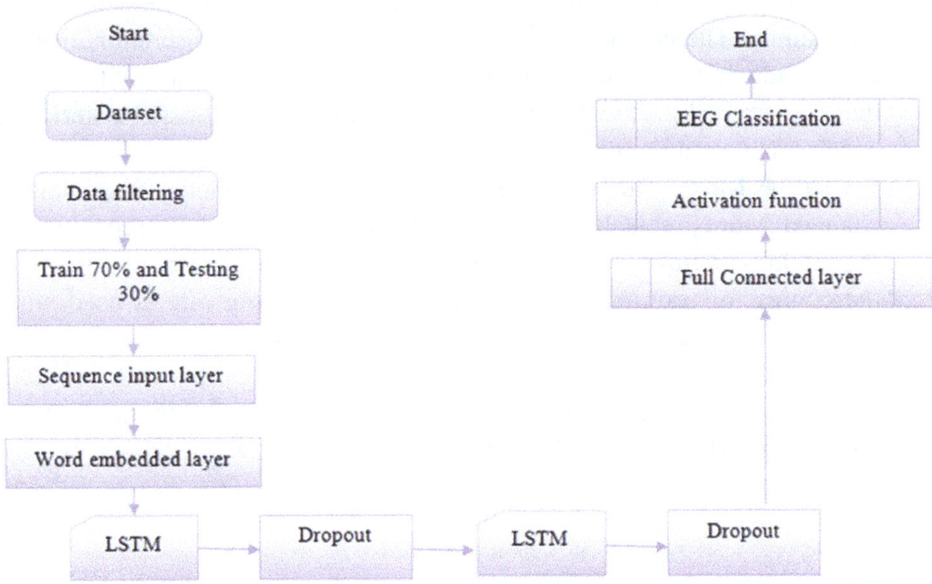

operation. Predictions are compared to expected output variables and error is found in the batch.

- **Gradient threshold:** The gradient threshold is defined by a pair of parameters that are separated by commas. This consists of both the Gradient Threshold and a positive scalar. The Gradient Threshold Approach involves the clipping of the gradient if its magnitude exceeds the predetermined threshold value.
- **Epoch:** Several epochs are regarded as hyperparameters in the context of this study. These concepts serve to establish the measurement of time. This particular time count is associated with a learning method. The time clock reflects the duration required for a learning algorithm to operate on a comprehensive dataset used for training objectives. The concept of an epoch entails the use of each sample within a dataset for the purpose of training, hence facilitating the modification of parameters within an internal model. An epoch refers to the aggregation of either several or single batches. An epoch that consists of a single batch is referred to as the batch gradient descent learning method.
- **Batch v/s Epoch:** The comparison between batch size and epoch involves the consideration of the amount of samples. The aforementioned samples undergo processing prior to any modifications being made to the model. The practise of counting epochs refers to the tallying of the total number of

iterations that occur during the training of a dataset. The size of the batch should be more than or equal to the number of samples in the dataset used for training. The enumeration of epochs is defined as a discrete numerical number ranging from one to infinity. The operator has the ability to operate the programme based on their own needs and terminate it using criteria and epoch count as supporting mechanisms.

- **Learning Rate:** The learning rate is a hyperparameter that may be changed. More precisely, it pertains to the regulation of the extent to which the model is adjusted considering the estimated level of imprecision. In the context of training neural networks, the learning rate is used when there are minuscule positive values accessible. The interval of positive integers under consideration starts at zero and concludes at one. The challenges associated with model adaption are influenced by the learning rate. Within the framework of the suggested study, the learning rate has been determined to be 0.001.

6. RESULT AND DISCUSSION

6.1 Training and Testing

The evaluation of proposed hybrid LSTM model includes the consideration of training accuracy and test accuracy for SVM, NAÏVE, LSTM, and the proposed hybrid LSTM model.

Figure 5. Comparison of training, testing, validation accuracy and loss for SVM, NAÏVE, LSTM and Proposed hybrid LSTM model

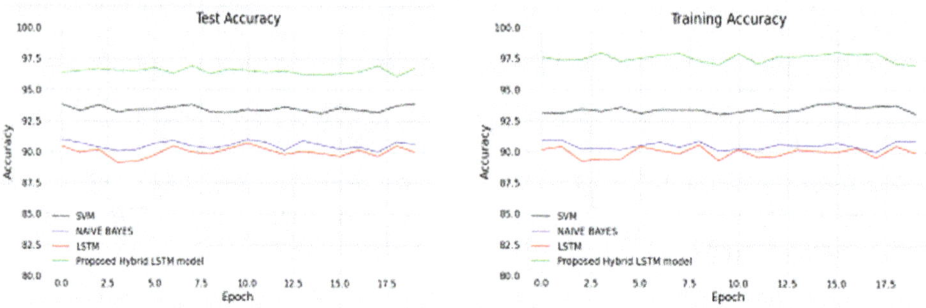

6.2 Confusion Matrix in Case of Conventional LSTM Model

A typical LSTM model was used to conduct a testing operation, where 1000 signals were taken into account for each class. The confusion matrix for standard LSTM model is shown in Table2.

Table 2. Confusion matrix in case of conventional LSTM model

Class	Class 1	Class 2	Class 3
Class 1	959	24	21
Class 2	24	957	16
Class 3	17	19	963

The presented format here provides an overview of the accuracy; recall, precision, and F1 score, as shown in Table3.

Results

TP: 2879

Overall Accuracy: 95.97%

Table 3. Accuracy parameters for conventional work

Class	Accuracy	Precision	Recall	F1 Score
1	97.13%	0.96	0.96	0.96
2	97.23%	0.96	0.96	0.96
3	97.57%	0.96	0.96	0.96

6.3 Confusion Matrix in Case of Proposed LSTM Model

The suggested hybrid LSTM model was used to conduct a testing operation, with a total of 1000 signals being investigated for each class. The recommended hybrid LSTM model's confusion matrix is shown in Table4.

Presented format here provides overview of accuracy; recall, precision, and F1 score, as shown in Table5.

Table 4. Confusion matrix in case of proposed LSTM model

Class	Class 1	Class 2	Class 3
Class 1	977	9	14
Class 2	9	974	15
Class 3	14	17	971

Table 5. Accuracy parameters for proposed work

Class	Accuracy	Precision	Recall	F1 Score
1	98.47%	0.98	0.98	0.98
2	98.33%	0.98	0.97	0.97
3	98%	0.97	0.97	0.97

6.3.1 Results

TP: 2922
Overall Accuracy: 97.4%

6.4 Comparison Analysis of Accuracy

6.4.1. Accuracy

Considering table3 and table5, accuracy, precision, recall, F1-score have table have been obtained

Considering table6 which shows comparison of accuracy has been made for conventional and proposed work.

Table 6. Comparison of Accuracy

Class	Conventional work	Proposed work
1	97.13%	98.47%
2	97.23%	98.33%
3	97.57%	98%

Figure 6. Comparison of accuracy

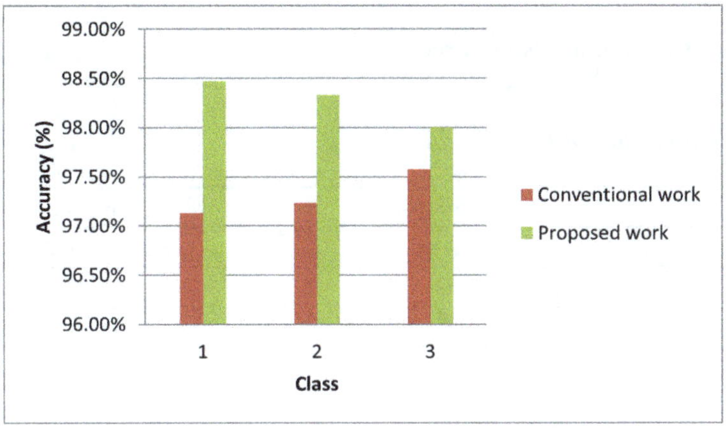

6.4.2. Precision

Table7 shows the comparison of precision.

Table 7. Comparison of Precision

Class	Conventional work	Proposed work
1	0.96	0.98
2	0.96	0.98
3	0.96	0.97

Figure 7. Comparison of precision

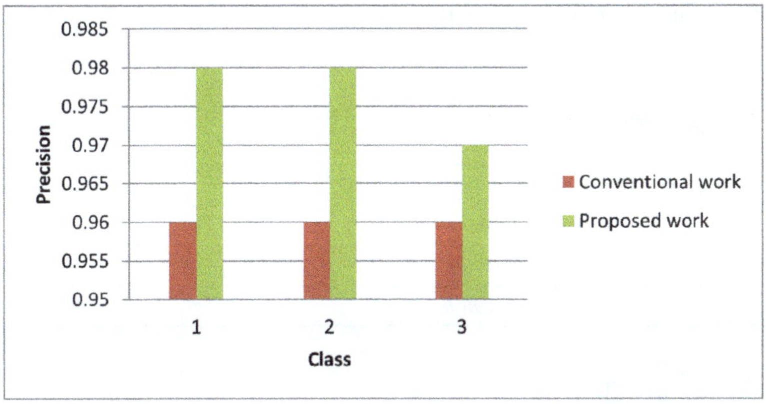

6.4.3. Recall value

Table8 shows the comparison of recall value.

Table 8. Comparison of Recall value

Class	Conventional work	Proposed work
1	0.96	0.98
2	0.96	0.97
3	0.96	0.97

Figure 8. Comparison of recall value

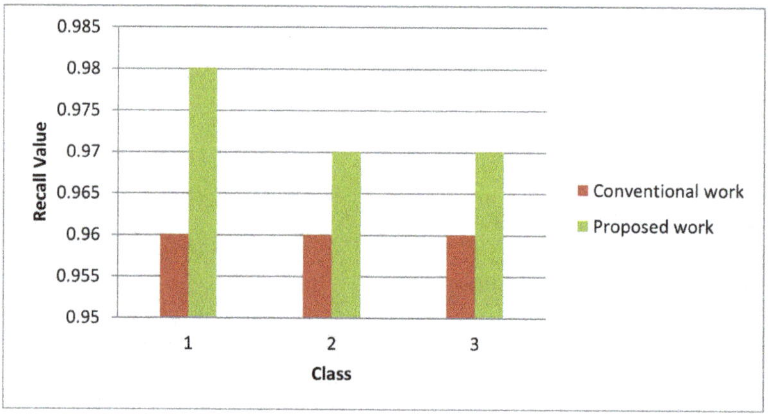

6.4.4. F1-Score

Table9 shows the comparison of F1-score.

Table 9. Comparison of F1-score

Class	Conventional work	Proposed work
1	0.96	0.98
2	0.96	0.97
3	0.96	0.97

Figure 9. Comparison of F1-score

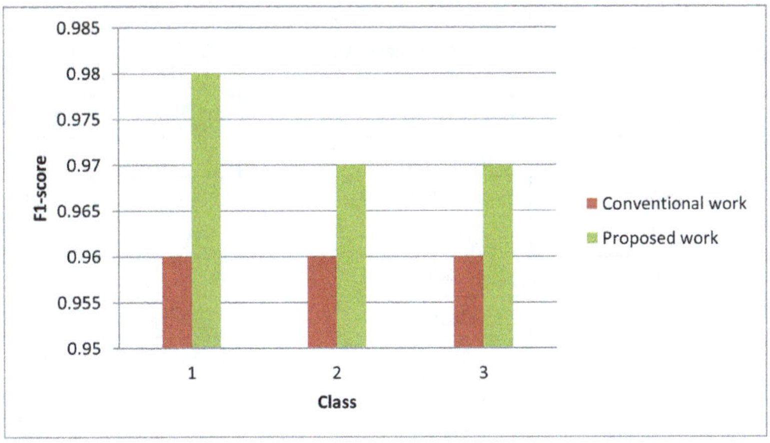

6.5 Comparative Analysis of Performance

In order to assure the performance of proposed work, testing time taken by different model has been considered. Following data is presenting comparative analysis of testing time by different emotion detection and classification approaches where as Table10 shows the comparative analysis of time consumption.

Considering above simulation, time consumption in case of proposed work in comparison of conventional approaches has been presented in following figure

7. CONCLUSION

By addressing ethical considerations, researchers can promote responsible and ethical practices in emotion data collection, IoT integration, and the development of emotion detection models using technologies like EEG and LSTM networks. This ensures that advancements in these technologies are aligned with ethical principles, respect participants' rights, and contribute positively to the well-being of individuals involved in such studies. EEG shows that the electrical activity at the scalp is reflective of that at the brain's surface. Several studies have examined the validity of EEG data. The study's major objective was to learn about the participants' subjective perceptions. There is a path ahead, despite the fact that previous research has been inconsistent and erroneous. Information suggests a limited capacity for growth and adaptation inside the system. Emotional state identification with EEG requires complex analytic processes. Deleting old or irrelevant data may also make your database safer and faster. Primary research interests include EEG signal processing, LSTM overhead, and

Table 10. Comparative analysis of time consumption

Epoch	SVM	NAÏVE BAYES	LSTM	Proposed Hybrid LSTM model
1	15.25785	14.75269066	14.57264	14.24672
2	15.3823	15.03733902	14.35064	13.37596
3	15.79672	15.40668746	15.10544	14.42056
4	15.81084	15.52033706	14.89504	14.21212
5	15.0479	14.50336221	13.55147	13.01667
6	15.89166	15.85485919	15.06015	14.72462
7	15.01367	14.31979971	14.26154	14.23352
8	15.2102	15.05431565	14.24074	13.31301
9	15.64983	15.55276686	15.02351	14.22195
10	15.1468	14.34066048	13.83215	13.05366
11	15.0084	14.98875904	14.70828	14.05617
12	15.99336	15.01602923	14.90731	14.73472
13	15.24357	14.40193155	14.20365	13.97738
14	15.02577	14.80619548	14.57863	14.11233
15	15.19035	14.61105998	14.23541	13.30996
16	15.41125	14.55119007	14.42433	14.05201
17	15.79901	15.2695863	15.15966	14.74905
18	15.46332	14.9670383	14.429	13.73171

emotion identification. Researchers can't get a handle on emotion detection without first understanding its predecessor. Overhead should be included using specialised LSTM algorithms to improve performance without sacrificing accuracy. Accuracy and productivity may be measured by contrasting the original plan with the actual results. Proposed hybrid LSTM model has been compared to convention classification mechanism such as SVM, Naïve bayes, LSTM. Simulation results conclude that accuracy and performance of proposed work is better than conventional approaches. Convention LSTM approach is yielding about 96 percentage of accuracy, where as proposed model is yielding 98% accuracy.

8. FUTURE SCOPE

Emotion data collecting and Internet of Things integration are two areas where ethical issues are likely to become more important in the future as technology develops. The

Figure 10. Time comparison in case of conventional and proposed work

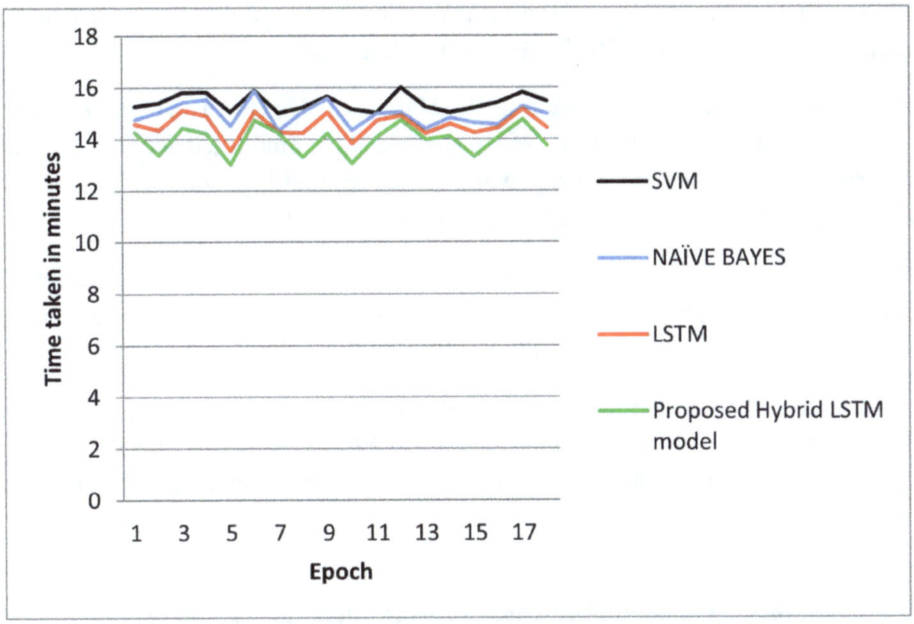

possibilities for collecting, analysing, and using emotional data rise dramatically as the Internet of Things penetrates more and more areas of everyday life. Privacy and permission of people must be protected, biases in emotion-detection algorithms must be reduced, and abuse must be prevented, all of which provide ongoing issues for researchers and legislators. Responsible and fair integration of emotion data into IoT will be greatly aided by the creation of thorough ethical frameworks, which will encourage innovations that improve well-being without compromising core ethical principles and human rights. In the more networked world of the future, this area is expected to remain active and important.

REFERENCES

Alam, H., Burhan, M., Gillani, A., Haq, I., Arshed, M. A., Shafi, M., & Ahmad, S. (2023). IoT Based Smart Baby Monitoring System with Emotion Recognition Using Machine Learning. *Wireless Communications and Mobile Computing*, *2023*, 1–11. doi:10.1155/2023/1175450

Bansal, R., Gupta, A., Singh, R., & Nassa, V. K. (2021). Role and Impact of Digital Technologies in E-Learning amidst COVID-19 Pandemic. *2021 Fourth International Conference on Computational Intelligence and Communication Technologies (CCICT)*. IEEE. . http://dx.doi.org/10.1109/CCICT53244.2021.00046

Behnke, M., Saganowski, S., Kunc, D., & Kazienko, P. (2022). Ethical Considerations and Checklist for Affective Research with Wearables. *IEEE Transactions on Affective Computing*, 1–14. doi:10.1109/TAFFC.2022.3222524

Chamishka, S., Madhavi, I., Nawaratne, R., Alahakoon, D., De Silva, D., Chilamkurti, N., & Nanayakkara, V. (2022). A voice-based real-time emotion detection technique using recurrent neural network empowered feature modelling. *Multimedia Tools and Applications*, *81*(24), 35173–35194. doi:10.1007/s11042-022-13363-4

Destyanto, T. Y. R. (2023). Emotion Detection Research: A Systematic Review Focuses on Data Type, Classifier Algorithm, and Experimental Methods. *Int. J. Ind. Eng. Eng. Manag.*, *5*(1), 31–43. doi:10.24002/ijieem.v5i1.7077

Fadda, M., Sykora, M., Elayan, S., Puhan, M. A., Naslund, J. A., Mooney, S. J., Albanese, E., Morese, R., & Gruebner, O. (2022). Ethical issues of collecting, storing, and analyzing geo-referenced tweets for mental health research. *Digital Health*, *8*. doi:10.1177/20552076221092539 PMID:35433020

Fleming, J., & Zegwaard, K. E. (2018). Methodologies, methods and ethical considerations for conducting research in work-integrated learning. *Int. J. Work. Learn.*, *19*(3), 205–213.

Gupta, A., Kaushik, D., Garg, M., & Verma, A. (2020). Machine Learning model for Breast Cancer Prediction. *2020 Fourth International Conference on I-SMAC (IoT in Social, Mobile, Analytics and Cloud) (I-SMAC)*. IEEE.10.1109/I-SMAC49090.2020.9243323

Gupta, A., Singh, R., Nassa, V. K., Bansal, R., Sharma, P., & Koti, K. (2021). Investigating Application and Challenges of Big Data Analytics with Clustering. *2021 International Conference on Advancements in Electrical, Electronics, Communication, Computing and Automation (ICAECA)*. IEEE. http://dx.doi.org/10.1109/ICAECA52838.2021.9675483

Hosseini, M., Wieczorek, M., & Gordijn, B. (2022). Ethical Issues in Social Science Research Employing Big Data. *Science and Engineering Ethics*, *28*(3), 1–21. doi:10.1007/s11948-022-00380-7 PMID:35705883

Jarwar, M. A., & Chong, I. (2017). Exploiting IoT services by integrating emotion recognition in Web of Objects. *Int. Conf. Inf. Netw*. IEEE. 10.1109/ICOIN.2017.7899474

JothirajF. V. S.MashhadiA. (2022). Personalized Emotion Detection using IoT and Machine Learning. arXiv. https://arxiv.org/abs/2209.06464v1

Dushyant, K., Muskan, G., Gupta, A., & Pramanik, S. (2022). *Utilizing Machine Learning and Deep Learning in Cybesecurity: An Innovative Approach.* Cyber Security and Digital Forensics. Wiley. . http://dx.doi.org/ doi:10.1002/9781119795667.ch12

Kshirsagar, P. R., Reddy, D. H., Dhingra, M., Dhabliya, D., & Gupta, A. (2022). A Review on Comparative study of 4G, 5G and 6G Networks. *2022 5th International Conference on Contemporary Computing and Informatics (IC3I).* IEEE. . http:// dx.doi.org/10.1109/IC3I56241.2022.10073385

Kshirsagar, P. R., Reddy, D. H., Dhingra, M., Dhabliya, D., & Gupta, A. (2023). A Scalable Platform to Collect, Store, Visualize and Analyze Big Data in Real- Time. *2023 3rd International Conference on Innovative Practices in Technology and Management (ICIPTM).* IEEE. . http://dx.doi.org/10.1109/ICIPTM57143.2023.10118183

Mohammad, S. M. (2022). Ethics Sheet for Automatic Emotion Recognition and Sentiment Analysis. *Computational Linguistics, 48*(2), 239–278. doi:10.1162/ coli_a_00433

Navarro-Alamán, J., Lacuesta, R., García-Magariño, I., & Lloret, J. (2022). EmotIoT: An IoT System to Improve Users' Wellbeing. *Applied Sciences (Basel, Switzerland), 12*(12), 5804. Advance online publication. doi:10.3390/app12125804

Pandey B. (2022). Effective and Secure Transmission of Health Information Using Advanced Morphological Component Analysis and Image Hiding. *Artificial Intelligence on Medical Data.* Springer Nature Singapore. doi:10.1007/978-981-19-0151-5_19

Pathania, V. (2022). A Database Application of Monitoring COVID-19 in India. *Artificial Intelligence on Medical Data.* Springer Nature Singapore. . http://dx.doi.org/ doi:10.1007/978-981-19-0151-5_23

Plageras, A. P., & Psannis, K. E. (2023). IoT-based health and emotion care system. *ICT Express, 9*(1), 112–115. doi:10.1016/j.icte.2022.03.008

Struminskaya, B., & Sakshaug, J. W. (2023). Ethical Considerations for Augmenting Surveys with Auxiliary Data Sources. *Public Opinion Quarterly, 87*(S1, no. S1), 619–633. doi:10.1093/poq/nfad030 PMID:37705919

Veeraiah, V. G. P, S. Ahamad, S. B. Talukdar, A. Gupta, and V. Talukdar, "Enhancement of Meta Verse Capabilities by IoT Integration," 2022 2nd International Conference on Advance Computing and Innovative Technologies in Engineering (ICACITE). IEEE, Apr. 28, 2022. . Available: http://dx.doi.org/10.1109/ICACITE53722.2022.9823766

Veeraiah, V., Khan, H., Kumar, A., Ahamad, S., Mahajan, A., & Gupta, A. (2022). Integration of PSO and Deep Learning for Trend Analysis of Meta-Verse. *2022 2nd International Conference on Advance Computing and Innovative Technologies in Engineering (ICACITE).* IEEE.10.1109/ICACITE53722.2022.9823883

Veeraiah, V., Kumar, K. R., Lalitha Kumari, P., Ahamad, S., Bansal, R., & Gupta, A. (2022). Application of Biometric System to Enhance the Security in Virtual World. *2022 2nd International Conference on Advance Computing and Innovative Technologies in Engineering (ICACITE).* IEEE.10.1109/ICACITE53722.2022.9823850

Veeraiah, V., Rajaboina, N. B., Rao, G. N., Ahamad, S., Gupta, A., & Suri, C. S. (2022). Securing Online Web Application for IoT Management. 2022 2nd International Conference on Advance Computing and Innovative Technologies in Engineering (ICACITE). IEEE. http://dx.doi.org/10.1109/ICACITE53722.2022.9823733

Wexler, A., & Largent, E. (2023). Ethical considerations for researchers developing and testing minimal-risk devices. *Nature Communications, 14*(1), 1–5. doi:10.1038/s41467-023-38068-6 PMID:37087446

Chapter 4
Bridging the Gap:
Emotional Intelligence, AEI, and Predicting Human Behavior

Zainab Khan
Aligarh Muslim University, India

S. Reshma Jamal
Aligarh Muslim University, India

ABSTRACT

In this chapter, the exploration delves into the captivating realm of Emotional Intelligence (EI) and Artificial Emotional Intelligence (AEI) to unravel their profound impact on human-machine harmony. Navigating the tapestry of human emotions and the evolving landscape of technology, the chapter aims to illuminate the synergies and transformative potential these concepts hold. This journey embarks on a captivating exploration into the realms of EI and AEI, investigating how the fusion of these disciplines can redefine the way individuals interact with technology and, fundamentally, with each other. The chapter seeks to dissect the existing divide between EI and AI, elucidating how their integration can revolutionize the prediction of human behavior. Through an understanding and amalgamation of the strengths of both disciplines, the pathway is paved for more intuitive, empathetic, and effective interactions between humans and machines.

1. INTRODUCTION

"Illuminating the tapestry of Human-machine harmony", opening with a thought-provoking quote or scenario that captures the essence of emotional intelligence and its intersection with artificial intelligence, we set the stage for an exploration into the evolving relationship between humans and machines. As we navigate the evolving landscape of Emotional Intelligence and Artificial Emotional Intelligence,

DOI: 10.4018/979-8-3693-1910-9.ch004

one cannot help but wonder about the profound implications awaiting us in the future. How will the synthesis of human emotions and machine intelligence redefine the very fabric of our society? Can we envision a world where machines not only understand our feelings but also contribute to our emotional growth? The journey into the realms of AEI prompts us to ponder: What new horizons of empathy and understanding will emerge as we continue to bridge the gap between the emotional intricacies of humanity and the computational prowess of machines? The answers to these questions may shape a future where our interactions with technology not only reflect our emotions but also elevate the human experience to unprecedented heights.

The chapter challenges traditional notions, questioning whether the right to emotions is exclusive to humans or if machines can also possess a form of emotional intelligence. In the grand symphony of human emotion and artificial intelligence, the union of Emotional Intelligence (EI) and Artificial Emotional Intelligence (AEI) emerges as a promising crescendo. As we embark on this journey to bridge the gap between human and artificial emotional understanding, it is imperative to remember that our goal is not to replace, but to enhance. To create machines that complement our innate empathy, not supplant it. This integration is not just about technological advancement, but about enriching our human experience. It is about forging a profound connection between us and the technology that surrounds us. As we move forward, let us be guided by the wisdom that understanding and embracing our emotions, and those of others, is the cornerstone of meaningful interactions. Together, we venture into a future where machines resonate with the cadence of our hearts, making our interactions more intuitive, empathetic, and profoundly human.

The distinct emphases of EI on emotions and human interactions, and Artificial Intelligence (AI) on data-driven analysis and decision-making, provide complementary strengths. By integrating the emotional understanding and interpersonal skills of EI with AI's data-processing capabilities, we can create more emotionally intelligent machines that can understand and respond to human emotions in a more nuanced and effective manner. This integration opens up new possibilities for enhancing human-computer interaction across various domains. Integrating AI with Emotional Intelligence extends beyond traditional problem-solving capabilities. It allows machines to understand, interpret, and respond to human emotions, creating a more empathetic and intuitive interaction. This not only enhances efficiency but also fosters a deeper connection between technology and humans.

1.1. Emotional Intelligence: Definition and History

The study of people's emotional reactions was spurred by developments in psychology in the early 20th century. People became more comfortable expressing their emotions in the 1960s. The first step towards developing emotional intelligence is the capacity for comfortable emotional expression. Emotional intelligence (EI) includes assessing and controlling one's emotions and those of others. People with strong emotional intelligence (EI) can regulate these feelings and alter their emotional states.

Table 1. Definitions of Emotional Intelligence (Srinivasan, P. 2013)

Authors	Definition of Emotional Intelligence
Salovey and Mayer (1990)	Emotional intelligence, a component of social intelligence, is defined as the capacity to identify and discriminate between one's own and other people's feelings and emotions as well as the application of knowledge to guide one's decisions and actions
Dr Reuven Bar-On (1997)	The range of emotional, social, and personal skills that affect a person's total capacity to manage pressures and demands in the environment is known as emotional intelligence.
Bechara, Tranel & Damasiio (2000)	Distinct from cognitive intelligence or intelligence quotient, emotional intelligence is a compilation of emotional skills.
David Caruso (2000)	Being emotionally intelligent means knowing how to use your feelings to solve issues and lead a more productive life. A solution only consists of parts, whether it be intelligence without emotional intelligence or emotional intelligence without intelligence. Working from the head to the heart is the whole remedy.
Geetu Bharwaney (2001)	The ability to recognize, comprehend, and respond appropriately to emotions is a necessary component of emotional intelligence.
Zeidner, Roberts, and Matthews, (2002)	The ability to recognize, feel, and integrate emotions into ideas, as well as control one's own and other people's good and negative emotions, is known as emotional intelligence.
Esther Orioli - Creator of the EQ Map	The capacity to perceive, comprehend, and use emotions as a source of energy effectively is known as emotional intelligence.
Radon Green - Founder of Feeling Mind Institute	The recognition that thoughts and emotions are two continuous processes rather than two distinct entities is essential to emotional intelligence. Emotionally intelligent people understand the "whole self," which includes each person's head, heart, and gut. To be emotionally intelligent, one must be self-aware when interacting with others.
Dalip Singh - An Indian perspective	The capacity to successfully and appropriately react to a wide range of emotional cues that are evoked from one's immediate surroundings and inner self is known as emotional intelligence. The three psychological aspects that make up emotional intelligence are emotional competency, emotional maturity, and emotional sensitivity. These dimensions encourage people to accurately perceive, understand, and manage the dynamics of human behavior.
Hein (2007)	The ability to naturally experience, use, communicate, identify, retain, learn from, regulate, and comprehend emotions is known as emotional intelligence. Emotional sensitivity, emotional memory, emotional processing, problem-solving ability, and emotional learning ability are the four components of emotional intelligence that each kid possesses to a different extent when they are born. The foundation of an individual's emotional intelligence consists of these four innate elements.

Table 1. brings together definitions of Emotional Intelligence (EI) from several authors, each contributing their interpretation of the term.

1.1.1 Historical Context

Edward Thorndike defined "social intelligence" in the 1930s as the capacity to get along with others. In the 1970s and 1980s, the phrase "Emotional Intelligence" started to take shape. The concept of multiple intelligences, which encompassed intrapersonal and interpersonal intelligence, was first proposed by psychologists like Howard Gardner. These psychologists also touched on topics that eventually found their way into the framework for emotional intelligence (J M Official, 2023). The term "alexithymia" (derived from Greek, where "a" means absence, "lexis" means word, and "thymos" represents feelings) was first used in 1973 by Peter Sifneos to describe the lack of words for feelings. It would be most accurate to characterize this state as emotional intelligence's counterpart. The subject of "Why is it that some people achieve overall emotional health and well-being while others don't?" was first investigated by clinical psychologist Reuven Bar-On in 1980. Using the Emotional Quotient Inventory (EQ-i), he conducted direct work on evaluating emotional intelligence. He first used the term "emotional quotient" in 1985. John D. Mayer and Peter Salovey coined the term "emotional intelligence" in 1990 (Golis, 2023). 'Emotional Intelligence: Why it can matter more than IQ?' by Daniel Goleman was published in 1995. He made emotional intelligence a more widely accepted idea (Srinivasan, 2013).

1.2. Artificial Emotional Intelligence: Concept, Definition & History

The proliferation of gadgets and systems has been facilitated by the technological revolution, which has helped address the problems encountered in day-to-day living. Troubleshooting has been the primary goal of the majority of these systems. Most of these systems have been focused on solving problems. According to Makridakis (2017), "the impact of digital and industrial revolutions has a great impact on every aspect of life, society, companies, and employment". Artificial intelligence (AI) technology is one of the most significant innovations of the technological revolution. AI is described as a computer-based system created to carry out tasks created by humans (Simon, 1980). As stated by Norvig and Russell (2009), AI is "a technology that thinks like a human, acts like a human, thinks rationally and acts rationally". "Can machines do what people do?" Since the 1950s, artificial intelligence (AI) has advanced quickly, which gave rise to the question. AI systems use a variety of programs to carry out basic, restricted tasks that will simplify life and work. Today, though, it's advanced to the point where it can recognize emotions. AI can identify emotions from voice and facial expressions. For instance, certain AI systems may require vocal input to interpret users' feelings. AI occasionally can detect emotions by examining minute changes in facial expressions. Is it still true that emotional intelligence is what separates humans from machines? Artificial intelligence scientists have recently introduced the concept of Artificial Emotional Intelligence, which challenges the notion that the capacity for feeling emotions is exclusive to humans and other biological beings.

Andrew McStay (2018) 'artificial emotional intelligence' can be understood as the 'capacity to see, read, listen, feel, classify and learn about emotional life (Kambur, 2021). The ability to feel emotions, or emotional intelligence, sets humans apart from other species. Artificial emotional intelligence is the study of how to give computers the capacity to mimic human conduct, which includes the understanding and demonstration of emotions in addition to logic. Things are shifting quickly and continuously. In this emerging field, a lot of research is being conducted. It is anticipated that artificial emotional intelligence will be recognized as a fully functional technological advancement. As the name implies, artificial emotional intelligence integrates emotion into artificial intelligence to create a system that can identify, decipher, analyze, and mimic feelings of emotion or affect. It can be stated categorically that the merging of artificial intelligence and emotional intelligence is about to take a significant turn for the better. This is a technology that will have a profound effect on not only the workforce and business but also on society and human existence in general (Dasgupta, 2019). According to Barnard Marr "When computers can read emotions by analyzing data, including facial expressions, gestures, tone of voice, force of keystrokes, and more to determine a person's emotional state and then react to it, we call this artificial emotional intelligence" (Marr, B. 2021).

Artificial Emotional Intelligence involves the integration of emotion recognition technologies into artificial intelligence systems, enabling machines to understand and respond to human emotions. It refers to the capability of artificial intelligence systems to be emotionally aware, recognizing and comprehending human emotions through various cues such as facial expressions, tone of voice, and other non-verbal signals. AEI is concerned with making machines more emotionally intelligent, enhancing their ability to understand and respond to human emotions.

A subset of artificial intelligence called "artificial emotional intelligence" is concerned with remembering, identifying, and responding to human emotions. Artificial Emotional Intelligence (Amorim et al., 2019) is essentially a computing system based on human-machine interaction that can distinguish emotions automatically from speech and audio-visual data by detecting facial expressions. As humans typically do, artificial emotional intelligence enables a variety of methods and strategies to be applied to the gathered and processed data to identify emotions from many paths.

1.2.1. Background of Artificial Emotional Intelligence

Rosalind W. Picard of the MIT Media Lab first used the phrase "affective computing" in her groundbreaking book in 1995. On the other hand, the idea was there somewhat earlier; John D. Williamson, for instance, filed the first patent for automatic speech emotion recognition in 1978. Janet E. Cahn, also of the MIT Media Lab, wrote "The Generation of Affect in synthesized speech" in 1989. Fumio Hara and Hiroshi Kobayashi published their research on neural networks that automatically recognize the six basic facial expressions in 1992. The first real-time system that can identify user emotion and produce customized agent output in a 2D audiovisual input-output chain for emotionally intelligent dialogues was made possible by the European SEMAINE project, which concluded in 2010. This study focused on depicting emotion in the face. Similar initiatives include ARIA-VALUSPA (Artificial Retrieval of Information Assistants-Virtual Agents with Linguistic Understanding, Social Skills, and Personalised Aspects), which started in 2015, and SimSensei, a project started in 2011 at the University of Southern California. Established in 2004, the Human-Machine Interaction Network on Emotion (HUMAINE) ceased operations in 2007 and transitioned into a non-funded network. In 2014, under the presidency of co-author Björn Schuller, it became the Association for the Advancement of Affective Computing (AAAC), based in the United Kingdom. The International Conference on Affective Computing and Intelligent Interaction (ACII) was initiated in 2005 and has since been conducted every two years. Published since its debut in 2010, IEEE Transactions on Affective Computing is still the primary publication on the subject. Björn Schuller was the initiator and co-organizer of the Interspeech 2009 Emotion Recognition Challenge, which was the first open competition event in the field. In 2011, Schuller expanded on this concept with the first Audio/Visual Emotion Challenge (AVEC). In addition to events for text analysis connected to sentiment and emotion, several challenges of a similar nature have emerged, such as the OMG Emotion Challenge, FERA, MEC, and EmotiW. AVEC hosted the first physiology-based contest in 2015. Among the commercial start-ups specializing in human emotion recognition are Affectiva (2009), which focuses on physiology and video; audEERING (2012), which focuses on audio; and RealEyes (2007), which focuses on video. In an industry that is expanding quickly, these have grown into multimillion-dollar enterprises with an increasing number of peers. However, the public still knows very little about consumer products (Schuller, & Schuller, 2018).

These historical developments have laid the foundation for the advancement of emotion recognition technologies and the integration of Emotional Intelligence (EI) and Artificial Intelligence (AI) in predicting human behavior and emotions. The progress in affective computing, including the recognition of facial expressions, speech emotion, and real-time emotion recognition systems, has contributed to the potential of AI to understand and respond to human emotions in various contexts.

When it comes to feeling emotions, humans have always been able to assert superiority over robots. However, it won't continue to be the case. The people who work in the subject of artificial emotional intelligence, also known as affective computing or emotion AI, are confident in the possibility that machines will be able to understand and interact with emotions, despite the doubts of some. Artificial emotional intelligence is the ability of computers to analyze a variety of data, such as gestures, tone of voice, force of keystrokes, and facial expressions, to identify and interpret an individual's emotional state. With the help of this capability, human-machine interaction will be much more natural and akin to human-to-human interaction.

1.2.2. What is the Mechanism of Artificial Emotional Intelligence?

Artificial emotional intelligence systems gather data, assess it, compare it to other data points, and identify significant emotions like joy and fear using a range of technologies, including computer vision, sensors and cameras, a massive amount of real-world data, speech science, and deep learning algorithms. After the system has determined which feeling is appropriate, it deduces the meaning of the emotion for each situation. The algorithms improve in their ability to discern the subtleties of human speech as the emotion database expands.

Example: With its product Affdex for Market Research, emotion detection software provider Affectiva assists marketers and advertisers in capturing real-time facial emotions while watching videos. Realeyes is another startup that offers artificial emotional intelligence solutions to marketers for market research. The artificial emotional intelligence of Cogito assists in determining the caller's mood and modifies the agent's approach in real time. Technology with artificial emotional intelligence can potentially help identify mental health issues. A mental health monitoring tool called CompanionMx can spot symptoms of anxiety and mood swings when someone speaks into their phone (Marr, 2021).

On the other hand, artificial emotional intelligence (AEI) has long since established itself in films and television. Think of the HAL 9000 computer in 2001: A Space Odyssey (1968), which showed the first signs of socioemotional intelligence, and the highly emotional personal AI device Samantha in 2013's Her. Another early example is the AI-equipped vehicle KITT, which recognizes that its driver is in "a slightly irritable mood caused by fatigue" in the 1982 Knight Rider series pilot. In movies, AI also frequently falls in love. For example, in Electric Dreams (1984), a user and a personal computer battle it out for the affection of the same woman, and in Wall-E (2008), the title robot develops feelings for another robot. There is an infinite number of examples. However, these hypothetical human-computer conversations differ greatly from dealing with the real AI of today, like Alexa, Cortana, Siri, or even lower-end AI like IBM's Watson, which is primarily devoid of emotional intelligence. Due to this enthusiasm with AEI, other fields have emerged, including Affective computing, Social and Behavioral computing, and Emotion augmented machine learning.

Even more nuanced and sophisticated human characteristics, like sympathy, are currently being taught to AI helpers. Koko, a spin-off of the MIT Media Lab, has created a system that makes AI assistants appear to have empathy. For example, the Koko system doesn't respond with a pre-programmed message like "I'm sorry to hear that" if a user is having a rough day. Alternatively, it might inquire further before guiding to assist the client in viewing his problems differently. Koko would advise him to view tension as a positive feeling that could be used to motivate him to take action, for instance, if he were experiencing stress. (Wilson, & Daugherty, 2018).

As stated by Kumar et al. (2018), emotion recognition systems have a variety of applications in human-machine interaction, including business management, advertising campaigns, social survey administration, product feedback analysis, and health monitoring. These include driving assistance, cyber security, fraud detection, e-learning, identification-driven social robots, human resource management, patient counseling, and more. To identify changes in emotions, researchers have employed a range of algorithms and techniques; the accuracy rate varies depending on whether advanced deep learning algorithms (Spiers, 2016) such as neural network algorithms and natural language processing algorithms (Sekhon & Agarwal, 2015) or traditional emotion recognition (Kim, 2016) are used. The shape, landmarks, and facial features of a general image taken by cameras, sensors, signals, or any other electrophysical device can be used to recognize facial images (Kumar et al., 2018) (Kumar, & Martin, 2023).

Picard (1998) argues that computers need to be able to synthesize and generate emotions if they are to ever display or experience any emotions. He lists five elements that make up the human emotional system; an affective computer system needs to have all or some of these elements. These comprise the following: 1) emotional behavior; 2) fast primary emotions; 3) emotions produced cognitively; 4) emotional experience, encompassing subjective feelings, physiological awareness, and cognitive awareness; and 5) interactions between the body and mind (Baillie, 2002).

1.2.3. Comparative Analysis: Emotional Intelligence vs Artificial Emotional Intelligence.

Artificial intelligence is rapidly advancing to the point that it can perform many "human" tasks well, such as language translation, illness diagnosis, and customer

Table 2. What separates AEI from EI?

Emotional Intelligence (EI)	Artificial Emotional Intelligence (AEI)
Rooted in psychology and human behavior.	A branch of artificial intelligence focused on technology.
Centered around emotions, human relationships, and interactions.	Rooted in logic and machinery, emphasizing data analysis.
Focuses on emotional awareness and regulation in humans.	Concerned with enabling machines to understand human emotions.
More innate, rooted in personal qualities, with a complex learning process.	Can be taught and programmed through algorithms.
Pertains to natural human engagement and social skills.	Concerned with replicating and enhancing interactions with technology.
Involves continuous development of emotional skills through experiences.	Requires algorithms to learn and adapt to emotional expressions in human communication.
Applied in personal development, leadership, and relationships.	Applied in technology interfaces, chatbots, and virtual assistants to enhance user experience.

Table 2. outlines the differences between Artificial Emotional Intelligence (AEI) and Emotional Intelligence (EI). It serves as a comprehensive guide, illustrating the contrasting aspects of these two fields and their respective applications in human and technological contexts.

service. This is giving rise to justifiable worries that human employment may eventually be completely replaced by AI in the economy. However, that isn't the most likely or even the inevitable result. AI cannot address human empathy, which is a basic aspect of emotional intelligence. Empathy is the capacity to not only understand another person's feelings but also to respond to them thoughtfully and compassionately. Because AI lacks personal feelings and experiences, it is unable to fully understand the emotional exchange that is based on shared experiences.

The debate of Emotional Intelligence vs. Artificial Intelligence isn't about choosing one over the other. Instead, it's about understanding the strengths and limitations of both and leveraging them effectively. AI can automate tasks, analyze data, and make our lives more convenient. However, it can't replace the unique human ability to connect emotionally with others, to understand the depth of human experiences, or to respond with genuine empathy.

In a world where the digital revolution is a reality, embracing both AI and EI is essential. A successful future will be one where AI enhances our lives and work while emotional intelligence keeps us grounded in the uniquely human capacity for understanding and empathy. It's not a battle of AI vs. EI but rather an interdependent relationship where both coexist, each complementing and enhancing the other's capabilities.

1.3. Identifying Common Goals

Emotional Intelligence (EI) and Artificial Emotional Intelligence (AEI) share a common objective of advancing emotional understanding and interactions, albeit in distinct contexts. EI, deeply rooted in psychology and human behavior, focuses on elevating emotional awareness in human-to-human interactions. A crucial component of creating and maintaining deep human connections is emotional intelligence. Throughout multiple investigations, Schutte et al. (2001) discovered a substantial correlation between higher emotional intelligence (EI) and more successful relationships with others (Housten, 2019). It strives to foster empathy, effective communication, and positive relationships, contributing to improved mental well-being and satisfaction in personal and professional spheres. On the other hand, AEI, as a facet of artificial intelligence, aims to extend these goals to human-to-machine interactions. Its purpose is to create technology interfaces that recognize and appropriately respond to human emotions, enhancing user experiences and reducing friction in interactions with machines.

EI and AEI together have the potential to positively impact society. Making AI more human-like through emotional understanding, can lead to advancements in various sectors, fostering better human-machine relationships and offering new possibilities for equal treatment. One of the primary goals is to reduce barriers between humans and machines. Artificial Emotional Intelligence seeks to create a more natural and empathetic interaction, fostering acceptance and collaboration in various domains.

In essence, both EI and AEI converge in their pursuit of leveraging emotional intelligence to enrich the quality of interactions, whether they be among humans or between humans and machines.

1.4. Integrating EI and AEI

Emotional intelligence and artificial intelligence are combined to create artificial emotional intelligence. Being emotionally intelligent means being able to identify one's own and other people's emotions, controlling and differentiating between emotions, and using our emotions as a guide for our actions and thoughts. It is the most fundamental characteristic that defines what it is to be human. Even though artificial intelligence is a technology designed to help people accomplish things more efficiently, it still lacks some cognitive abilities. But shortly, artificial intelligence (AI) solutions will proliferate, and their worth and appeal will be primarily driven by emotional intelligence.

The integration of Emotional Intelligence and Artificial Intelligence represents a significant advancement in the development of more human-centric and empathetic technologies, with the potential to revolutionize the way humans interact with machines. Integrating emotional understanding into AI systems enables machines to interpret and respond to human emotions, making interactions more nuanced and empathetic. It also enhances human-computer interaction by making technology more intuitive and user-friendly. It also allows machines to demonstrate a form of empathy, understanding, and responding to user emotions. Empathetic AI can be particularly beneficial in healthcare, mental health support, and other sensitive domains where understanding and responding to human emotions are critical.

The ultimate goal is to create seamless and enriching experiences for users, where technology complements and enhances human capabilities rather than creating barriers. This integration reduces the learning curve for users and makes technology a more integral and natural part of everyday life.

The demands of customers are ever-evolving, and technology is forced to keep improving. Businesses can greatly benefit from the integration of AI and EI in their sales and customer service departments. The customer experience can be enhanced with chatbots and mobile apps that can identify and react to people's emotional responses, such as frustration, impatience, and anger. Additionally, artificial emotional intelligence can help doctors and nurses provide better care, enhance workplace productivity, and tailor the educational experience for students. Artificial emotional intelligence (EI) systems are anticipated to collaborate with humans and operate similarly to them, hence enhancing conversational and relational aspects of contact (Joshi, 2017).

1.4.1. The Integration of Emotional Intelligence (EI) and Artificial Intelligence (AI) Has Several Benefits

Firstly, it can encourage human-machine cooperation, allowing robots to complement human abilities and relieve workers from tedious work so they can focus on more important, strategic, and creative projects (Rossi, 2023).

Secondly, it can enhance customer experience by enabling brands to better understand and respond to customer needs, improve customer satisfaction, and increase employee productivity (Clark, 2023).

Thirdly, emotional intelligence continues to be an undeniable advantage that improves our communication, leadership, and decision-making by allowing us to deeply connect, empathize, and work collectively (Reece, 2023).

Overall, the integration of EI with AI can lead to more empathetic and human-centric technologies that complement and enhance human capabilities, rather than creating barriers.

1.4.2. Integrating AI And Emotional Intelligence Can Present Several Challenges

- Authenticity: The authenticity of true human emotions will never be replaced by artificial intelligence, even though AI is getting better at identifying and reacting to human emotions. Genuine human connections will always hold a special place in our hearts, and AI should be seen as a complementary tool rather than a replacement.
- Technical challenges: Integrating emotional intelligence into AI systems requires advanced technology and complex algorithms that can interpret and respond to human emotions accurately (Pahlavan, 2023). This can be a challenging task, as emotions are complex and multifaceted.
- Ensuring user safety: The greatest risk is not the AI itself, but the humans behind AI teaching AI agents to exploit emotional tipping points to influence human actions. To avoid AI systems being utilized in unwanted ways, it is imperative to make sure they are developed and deployed ethically.
- Adapting to human needs: Emotion recognition in AI needs to be sophisticated enough to adapt to the wide range of human emotions and cultural differences (Muhammad, 2023). This can be a challenging task, as emotions can be subtle and context-dependent.
- Advancement of human-machine cooperation: The workplace may undergo major changes as a result of the integration of AI into different corporate processes, thus it's critical to make sure that technology is used to enhance rather than replace human talents (Rossi, 2023). This requires a shift in mindset and organizational culture.
- Improving client satisfaction: Chatbots and tailored recommendations are just two examples of how AI may dramatically change customer interactions. However, it is crucial to ensure that AI systems are designed to provide a positive customer experience and not hinder human-AI interactions.

1.5. Case Studies: AI and Emotional Intelligence in Action

1.5.1 Case Study: Transforming Healthcare With AI and Emotional Intelligence

In 2021, a global healthcare provider faced challenges in administrative workflows, patient communication, and diagnostics. To address these issues, the organization embraced AI and Emotional Intelligence (EI). Key implementations included AI-powered virtual nurse assistants, 24/7 patient support through chatbots and apps,

Table 3. Future Frontiers: AEI's evolution and influence across diverse sectors (Joshi, N. 2017).

Artificial intelligence: what is it?	What are the potential benefits of integrating EI and AI?	For artificial emotional intelligence, what does the future hold?
Combining artificial and emotional intelligence results in artificial emotional intelligence. Emotional intelligence includes the following skills: recognizing and identifying one's own and other people's emotions; controlling and differentiating between emotions; and using emotions to influence our actions and thought processes.	For businesses looking to improve their sales and customer service divisions, EI and AI integration is very advantageous. Mobile apps and chatbots can better serve customers by identifying and responding to people's emotional states, such as irritation, dissatisfaction, and anger. They will also be utilized to help doctors and nurses provide care, enhance workplace productivity, and customize the educational experiences of learners.	The market research, automotive, and healthcare industries are expected to undergo a total transformation as AEI expands into a multibillion-dollar industry during the next five years. Multimodal emotion identification and an emotion chip are two ideas included in the AEI's future road map that will let organizations use emotion analytics to make decisions.

Table 3. illustrates the significant development and impact of Artificial Emotional Intelligence (AEI) in various sectors. It sheds light on the complementary nature of artificial and emotional intelligence and forecasts the critical role that AEI will play in transforming sectors including sales, customer service, market research, the automobile industry, and healthcare.

streamlined administrative tasks using AI and automation, and the use of AI for error detection in patient self-administration.

The organization explored AI-enabled robots for surgeries, fraud detection, and integrated technologies like natural language processing and speech recognition. To improve communication, specific efforts were made to enhance interactions between healthcare providers and patients. AI was also employed for diagnoses, aiming to reduce costs and improve health outcomes.

The integration of AI and Emotional Intelligence revolutionized healthcare. Virtual nurse assistants, AI-powered diagnostics, and improved communication channels enhanced patient experiences and operational efficiency. Looking ahead, ethical considerations and regulatory governance are crucial for responsible AI use in healthcare. The organization plans to explore more AI applications in diagnostics, treatment planning, and personalized medicine, emphasizing a commitment to ethical standards.

1.5.2 Case Study: AI in Healthcare for Face Attractiveness Prediction

This case study focuses on predicting facial attractiveness using AI, specifically deep learning and multi-task learning. The SCUT-FBP5500 database, containing 5,500 face frontal photos, was utilized. Elham Vahdati suggested a deep convolutional neural network (CNN) that has been pre-trained on a substantial face dataset. The multi-task learning scheme extended the model to facial attribute recognition tasks.

Experiments conducted on the SCUT-FBP5500 dataset revealed noteworthy advancements in facial beauty assessment, gender recognition, and face recognition tasks. The study showcases AI's potential to understand and predict human aesthetic preferences. The success of the deep learning and multi-task learning scheme highlights AI's versatility in various applications, influencing industries like cosmetics, entertainment, and social media.

In summary, these case studies exemplify the transformative impact of AI and Emotional Intelligence in healthcare and aesthetic assessments. The advancements highlight the potential for continued innovation in these fields, emphasizing the importance of ethical considerations and regulatory governance in shaping the responsible use of AI technologies.

1.6. Ethical Consideration in Integrating AEI and EI

The integration of Artificial Emotional Intelligence (AEI) and Emotional Intelligence (EI) presents a transformative shift in human-computer interaction, offering unprecedented opportunities and capabilities. However, the ethical implications of this integration must be carefully considered to ensure responsible and beneficial outcomes. Several key ethical considerations arise in the process:

- Informed Consent: The power to give informed consent for the gathering and use of personal emotional data should be granted to users. Ethical integration necessitates transparent communication about how emotional intelligence features will be applied and obtaining explicit consent from users.
- Ethical considerations should prioritize empowering users rather than exploiting emotional vulnerabilities. AEI and EI technologies should be designed to enhance users' emotional well-being, providing them with valuable insights and support rather than diminishing their autonomy.
- Bias Mitigation: Like any form of artificial intelligence, AEI, and EI systems are susceptible to bias, which can lead to unfair outcomes or reinforce existing societal prejudices. Ethical integration requires proactive measures to identify and address biases in emotional intelligence algorithms. Numerous initiatives provide tools for fairness, ethical AI, and bias reduction, such as the FAT ML and XAI community, Google, Microsoft, and Facebook.
- Guarding against Manipulations: AEI and EI have the potential to influence human emotions and behaviors. Ethical considerations mandate safeguards against intentional or unintentional manipulation of individuals' emotions

through technology. Developers must prioritize designing systems that empower users rather than manipulate them, fostering emotional well-being and genuine human-computer interaction.

- Privacy Concerns: It is crucial to establish robust privacy safeguards, ensuring that emotional data is treated with the utmost confidentiality and that individuals have control over the use and sharing of their emotional insights.
- Public engagement and education: They are critical ethical considerations. Ensuring that the public is informed about the capabilities, limitations, and ethical implications of AEI and EI technologies promotes transparency, trust, and responsible use.
- Age-appropriate Design: Consideration should be given to age-appropriate design, particularly when implementing AEI and EI in applications used by children or vulnerable populations. Ethical guidelines should prevent emotional manipulation and ensure the well-being of users, especially those who may be more susceptible to emotional influence.
- Long-term impact on Mental health: Continuous exposure to emotionally intelligent systems may have long-term effects on users' mental health. Ethical considerations should include monitoring and addressing any negative impact on emotional well-being and providing resources for users to manage their emotional engagement with technology.

The analysis reveals that accountability, explainability, privacy, justice, robustness, and safety are the most frequently mentioned ethical aspects in AI guidelines. Technical fixes have been developed or are under development for these aspects, indicating a strong focus on operationalizing ethics through mathematical and technical solutions. (Hagendorff, 2020).

- The AI4People framework outlines the five ethical AI framework principles: beneficence, non-maleficence, autonomy, fairness, and explicability (Floridi et al., 2018). Using the five principles, we may look into how AI affects meaningful work. The first principle is beneficence or the advantages AI may offer in terms of advancing human welfare and upholding human dignity in a manner that is sustainable for the environment. Making sure AI doesn't hurt people is the goal of non-maleficence; this involves protecting people's privacy and keeping AI systems safe and secure. Allowing humans to control AI decisions is the essence of autonomy. The goal of justice is to maintain societal cohesiveness and unity while equitably allocating the advantages and disadvantages of AI use. In conclusion, explicability refers to making sure AI functions in a way that is understandable and accountable, allowing us to demand accountability from those who use it. (Bankins, & Formosa, 2023).

As we venture into a future increasingly shaped by AI, addressing these ethical considerations not only ensures the trustworthy and equitable deployment of technology but also safeguards human well-being. Responsible AI development demands a commitment to transparency, fairness, and respect for individual autonomy. By integrating these ethical principles into the fabric of AI initiatives, we pave the way for a future where technology aligns with human values, fostering a society that benefits from the transformative potential of AI without compromising fundamental ethical standards.

1.7. Integrating Psychological Insights: The Vital Role of Psychology in Bridging EI and AEI

The synergy of psychological insights holds a pivotal role in harmonizing Emotional Intelligence (EI) and Artificial Emotional Intelligence (AEI), providing profound insights into human emotions and enhancing emotional intelligence in both humans and machines. Psychology, as the scientific exploration of human behavior and mind, contributes valuable insights into the intricacies of emotions, forming the foundation for understanding emotional intelligence. It plays a vital role in bridging emotional intelligence (EI) and artificial emotional intelligence (AEI). Psychologists, understanding human emotions and behavior, contribute to developing more empathetic and effective AI systems. For instance, leveraging natural language processing (NLP) and speech recognition technologies allows AI systems to analyze the tone and sentiment of human speech, responding in an appropriate and empathetic manner. Additionally, psychologists play a crucial role in ensuring that AI systems are designed ethically, addressing concerns like bias, transparency, and privacy issues.

This psychological foundation is integral to the development of AEI algorithms, ensuring accurate perception and response to a diverse array of human emotions. By incorporating insights from affective computing, cognitive psychology, and behavioral psychology, AEI algorithms can achieve a more sophisticated understanding of emotions. This integration enables AEI to interpret emotions contextually, consider cultural nuances, and respond empathetically, effectively bridging the gap between human and artificial emotional intelligence. The infusion of psychological insights aligns with James Gross's Process Model of Emotion Regulation, guiding the refinement of AEI algorithms for a nuanced understanding of emotion regulation strategies. By incorporating Gross's model, AEI systems can surpass mere recognition, actively adapting responses to align with users' unique emotional regulation tendencies, resulting in more effective and ethical AI systems that better serve human needs.

Psychology and the philosophy of mind that stems from it are important in the advancement of artificial intelligence and are either directly or indirectly regarded as one of the theories that drive AI. According to Miller (2019), the current AI theory of reinforcement learning is influenced by behaviorist psychology. It describes how organisms form expectations of stimuli in response to rewards or punishments in their environment, which results in habitual behaviors for maximum benefit. Advances in psychology are essential to addressing the problems facing the AI community, especially concerning the emotional reaction of artificially intelligent machines and decision-making in unclear situations. The study of advanced mental processes in cognitive psychology sets humans apart from computers by producing subjective emotional orientations like love, hate, contentment, and discontent through the processing of external stimuli. By monitoring subjective emotional changes and upgrading internal knowledge structures, artificial intelligence (AI) retrains robots to comprehend human attitudes and preferences with the help of human cognitive psychology (Kriegeskorte and Douglas, 2018; Pradhan et al., 2020).

To imitate human psychological behaviors, artificial intelligence integrates psychology, brain science, and computer science. This promotes mutual integration and the development of more universal and independent AI. This interdisciplinary approach enhances human-computer interaction and elevates social intelligence levels. Artificial intelligence products infiltrate psychology fields as psychology advances, leading to innovations such as big data-driven public opinion analyses, intelligent medical image grading, intelligent surveillance management systems, facial expression-based emotion recognition systems, and suicide early warning systems. This reciprocal relationship promotes both psychology and AI, shortening research cycles and accelerating progress (Branch, 2019).

The "society of mind" theory was put forth by artificial intelligence pioneer Marvin Minsky in 1985 in an effort to combine computational theory, artificial intelligence, and the fields of developmental, dynamic, and cognitive psychology. This ground-breaking notion sparked a wave of study into giving computers emotional intelligence and the capacity to recognize and communicate emotions. In 2020, Taylor improved the interpretability, equity, and transparency of machine learning by integrating cognitive psychology into explainable artificial intelligence (XAI) (Zhao, Wu, Zhou, Wang, & Jia, 2022).

In conclusion, the synthesis of AI and psychology signifies not just technical evolution but a holistic approach, promising a future where AI resonates with human emotions and upholds ethical considerations, fostering a harmonious coexistence between humans and machines.

1.8. Navigating the Pitfalls: Considerations in Integrating AEI and EI

- Emotional Complexity: Human emotions are complex and multifaceted. Teaching AI systems to interpret and respond appropriately to a wide range of emotions, considering cultural nuances and individual differences, poses a significant challenge.
- It's crucial to have robust cybersecurity safeguards in place and to protect sensitive data from unwanted access. Because it is so delicate, emotional data must adhere to strict security guidelines to avoid breaches.
- Assessing and managing the impact of AEI on human-machine interactions is a multifaceted challenge. Striking a balance between enhancing user experience and avoiding unintended consequences is essential for positive outcomes.
- The introduction of AEI in various industries may lead to the automation of tasks that traditionally rely on emotional intelligence. Jobs requiring interpersonal skills, empathy, and emotional understanding, such as customer service representatives or certain roles in healthcare, could be at risk of automation.
- AI's incapacity for genuine emotional experience poses a significant pitfall. While it can recognize and respond to emotions based on patterns, AI lacks the subjective depth and personal context that human emotions entail.
- Unequal access to AI-driven emotional intelligence tools may exacerbate social inequalities. Considerations must be given to ensure equitable access and prevent the technology from widening existing societal gaps.
- The use of AEI for persuasive purposes or emotional manipulation raises ethical concerns. Without proper safeguards, there is a risk that AI systems could exploit emotional vulnerabilities or manipulate individuals for various purposes, including commercial gains.
- AEI systems may inadvertently perpetuate and amplify existing biases present in training data. Biases in the training data could be replicated by the AI, which could potentially make them worse, producing unfair and discriminatory results.

Navigating the pitfalls and embracing the promise

As we navigate the intricate terrain of integrating Artificial Emotional Intelligence (AEI) and Emotional Intelligence (EI), proactive consideration and resolution of challenges become paramount. From the complexities of emotional interpretation to ethical concerns and the risk of automation, addressing these issues ensures the responsible development of AI systems. Now, let's explore how overcoming these challenges can lead to a promising future, where AEI transforms our world and fosters seamless human-machine collaboration.

1.9. Future Trends

The combination of Emotional Intelligence (EI) and Artificial Intelligence (AI) is poised to bring about transformative changes across various industries. It has the potential to revolutionize various industries.

Figure 1. Future trends that highlight the potential impacts of integration of EI and AI

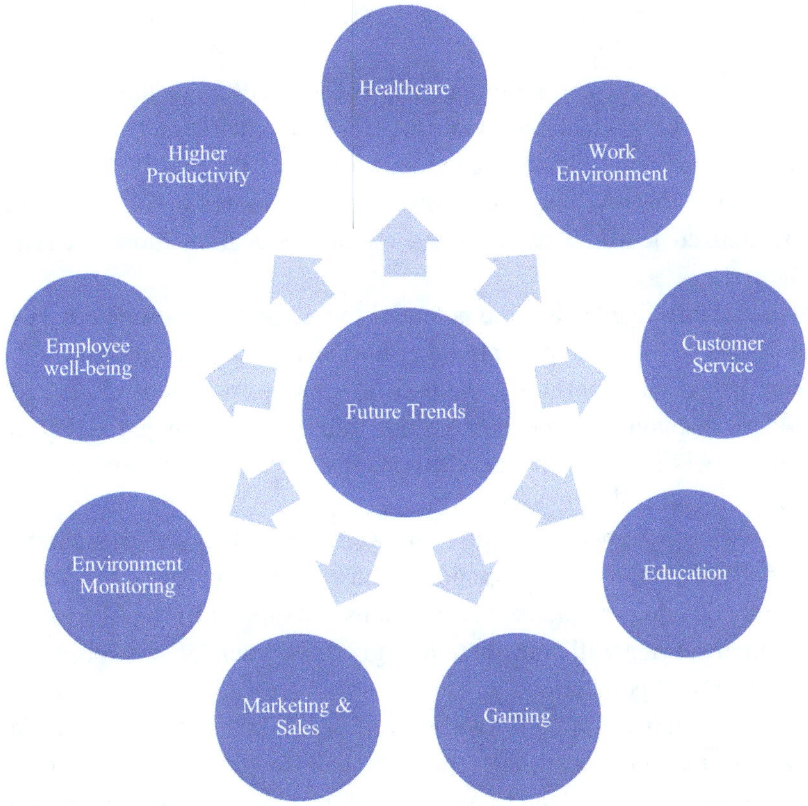

- Healthcare: Virtual nurses and therapists powered by AI will augment human healthcare providers, ensuring more comprehensive and personalized care. AI-powered tools will play a crucial role in identifying and providing support for mental health concerns, enabling early intervention and continuous monitoring.

- Early Intervention and Continuous Monitoring: AI systems will examine behavioural and emotional data to anticipate possible health problems, allowing for early detection and preventative actions. Also, wearable devices and other technologies will be integrated with AI to monitor emotional states, providing real-time insights for proactive healthcare.
- Work environment: Emotionally intelligent AI will help create more inclusive and supportive work environments, assisting in stress management, conflict resolution, and employee motivation, ultimately leading to higher productivity.
- Customer service: Artificial intelligence (AI) and emotional intelligence (EI)-powered chatbots and mobile apps can identify and handle people's emotional reactions, like discomfort, irritability, and anger, enhancing the user experience.
- Education: Artificial emotional intelligence will personalize the learning experience of students, providing tailored feedback and support. AI will play a significant role in education, with tools for grading student exams, automating the process, and saving time for teachers. AI will also help in personalized learning experiences, making education more accessible and efficient.
- Artificial intelligence has the potential to mitigate discrimination by treating all people equally and programming it to be emotionally neutral.
- Gaming: AI will continue to be used in gaming, with non-player characters (NPCs) displaying more human-like traits, improving gameplay and risk analysis. AI in gaming will also help in creating more immersive and engaging experiences for players.
- Enhanced Customer Service: AI-powered customer service chatbots will better understand and respond to customer emotions, providing more empathetic and personalized interactions. The integration of EI in AI-driven customer service will contribute to higher customer satisfaction, loyalty, and positive brand perception.
- Marketing and Sales: AI-powered tools will become more sophisticated, enabling marketers and sales professionals to better understand customer behavior, preferences, and trends. i.e. Companies can boost sales conversions, enhance client engagement, and optimize their marketing strategies with the support of AI.
- Environment Monitoring: AI will play a crucial role in monitoring and preserving the environment, detecting signs of environmental degradation, and identifying potential solutions for environmental problems. AI can analyze vast amounts of data collected from sensors and satellite imagery to

provide insights into climate change, deforestation, and other environmental issues.

- Employee Well-being Programs: AI can contribute to the design and implementation of employee well-being programs by identifying trends in emotional states and recommending initiatives to address specific needs. Through continuous monitoring, AI can detect early signs of burnout or declining mental health, prompting the implementation of preventive measures to support employee well-being.
- The current generation is experiencing a rise in mental disorders, which pose a threat to human life due to their erratic patterns. The incapacity to regulate one's thoughts or emotions might impair one's effectiveness in carrying out routine tasks, which can affect other people. To help the person, an emotionally intelligent agent is able to recognize trends, examine facts, and offer precise remedies.
- Higher Productivity and Employee Motivation: AI can analyze emotional data to identify bottlenecks or inefficiencies in workflows and suggest optimizations that align with individual and team strengths. AI can create personalized motivation plans for employees based on their emotional preferences, work styles, and career aspirations.

These future trends demonstrate the potential of EI and AI to revolutionize various industries by enhancing emotional understanding and interactions, fostering better human-machine relationships, and offering new possibilities for equal treatment.

2. DISCUSSION

The convergence of Artificial Intelligence (AI) and Emotional Intelligence (EI) was explored in this chapter, highlighting their mutual objective of improving human-machine interactions. There are several potential problems associated with the integration of AI and EI. While developments in customer service, education, healthcare, and other fields demonstrate the potential advantages, the complexity of this integration is brought to light by ethical issues, potential biases, and the requirement for strong cybersecurity. The significance of comprehending human emotions is emphasized by psychology's pivotal role in bridging EI and AEI. It becomes clear as we avoid the traps that responsible AI development is crucial, with an emphasis on openness, equity, and user welfare. Future trends point to revolutionary shifts in a variety of industries and a peaceful coexistence of humans and robots.

3. CONCLUSION

In conclusion, the impact of Artificial Intelligence (AI) is transforming our world, offering innovative solutions and paving the way for future advancements. By imbuing machines with human-like traits, we've not only improved performance but also revolutionized risk analysis across diverse sectors. A standout contributor to this transformation is Emotional Artificial Intelligence (AEI), making significant strides in various occupational fields. AEI addresses underlying global challenges, promoting accessibility and ensuring equitable outcomes. With its intelligence, AEI has the potential to redefine our existing norms and open new avenues for coexistence. Presently, AEI's effectiveness is evident in healthcare, aiding in cancer classification; in consultation services, facilitating easy interactions and offering emotional state suggestions through virtual assistance; and in business, where virtual chatbots enhance efficiency, ensure quality assurance, and fortify security features in the automobile industry. The current landscape of Emotional Artificial Intelligence not only signifies heightened efficiency but also points toward a promising future characterized by technological innovation and seamless human-machine collaboration.

REFERENCES

Amorim, M., Cohen, Y., Reis, J., & Rodrigues, M. (2019). Exploring opportunities for artificial emotional intelligence in service production systems. *IFAC-PapersOnLine*, *52*(13), 1145–1149. doi:10.1016/j.ifacol.2019.11.350

Baillie, P. (2002). *The synthesis of emotions in artificial intelligences: an affective agent architecture for intuitive reasoning in artificial intelligences* [Doctoral dissertation, University of Southern Queensland].

Bankins, S., & Formosa, P. (2023). The ethical implications of artificial intelligence (AI) for meaningful work. *Journal of Business Ethics*, *185*(4), 1–16. doi:10.1007/s10551-023-05339-7

Bar-On, R. (1997). BarOn emotional quotient inventory (Vol. 40). *Multi-health systems*.

Bechara, A., Tranel, D., & Damasio, H. (2000). Characterization of the decision-making deficit of patients with ventromedial prefrontal cortex lesions. *Brain*, *123*(11), 2189–2202. doi:10.1093/brain/123.11.2189 PMID:11050020

Clark, S. (2023). *AI Gets Empathetic: Advances in Emotional Intelligent AI.* CMSWire. https://www.cmswire.com/digital-experience/ai-gets-empathetic-advances-in-emotionally-intelligent-ai/

Dasgupta, R. (2019). *Artificial Emotional Intelligence – A New Skyline.* IUJ Journal of Management.

Golis, C. (2023). *A Brief History of Emotional Intelligence.* Emotional Intelligence Course. https://www.emotionalintelligencecourse.com/history-of-eq/

Hagendorff, T. (2020). The ethics of AI ethics: An evaluation of guidelines. *Minds and Machines, 30*(1), 99–120. doi:10.1007/s11023-020-09517-8

Housten, E. (2019). *The importance of Emotional Intelligence.* Positive Psychology. https://positivepsychology.com/importance-of-emotional-intelligence

Joshi, N. (2017). *Artificial Emotional Intelligence: The future of AI.* Allerin. https://www.allerin.com/blog/artificial-emotional-intelligence-the-future-of-ai

Kambur, E. (2021). Emotional Intelligence or Artificial Intelligence?: Emotional Artificial Intelligence. *Florya Chronicles of Political Economy, 7*(2), 147–168. doi:10.17932/IAU.FCPE.2015.010/fcpe_v07i2004

Khaldun, S. A. (2023). *Emotional Intelligence vs. Artificial Intelligence: The Human Touch in a Digital World.* Linkedin. https://www.linkedin.com/pulse/emotional-intelligence-vs-artificial-human-touch-s-a-al-khaldi

Kriegeskorte, N., & Douglas, P. K. (2018). Cognitive computational neuroscience. *Nature Neuroscience, 21*(9), 1148–1160. doi:10.1038/s41593-018-0210-5 PMID:30127428

Kumar, H., & Martin, A. (2023). Artificial Emotional Intelligence: Conventional and deep learning approach. *Expert Systems with Applications, 212*, 118651. doi:10.1016/j.eswa.2022.118651

Makridakis, S. (2017). The forthcoming Artificial Intelligence (AI) revolution: Its impact on society and firms. *Futures, 90*, 46–60. doi:10.1016/j.futures.2017.03.006

Marr, B. (2021). *What Is Artificial Emotional Intelligence?* Bernard Marr. https://bernardmarr.com/what-is-artificial-emotional-intelligence/

Muhammad, Z. (2023). *Human Emotions Integration. Can It Be A Challenge for AI?* Read write. https://readwrite.com/human-emotions-integration-can-it-be-a-challenge-for-ai/

Official, J. M. (2023). *Historical Background and Evolution of Emotional Intelligence*. Linkedin. https://www.linkedin.com/pulse/historical-background-evolution-emotional-intelligence-jm-official

Pahlavan, B. (2023). *Why is Emotional Intelligence In AI Important and Challenging?* AiThority. https://aithority.com/machine-learning/why-is-emotional-intelligence-in-ai-important-and-challenging/

Reece, A. D. (2023). *The Truth About Emotional Intelligence and AI: Thriving in an AI-Powered Era*. Linkedin. https://www.linkedin.com/pulse/truth-emotional-intelligence-ai-thriving-ai-powered-d-reece-pcc

Rossi, D. (2023). *The Indispensable Role of Emotional Intelligence for Leaders in the Age of AI*. Workplace Peace Institute. https://www.workplacepeaceinstitute.com/post/the-indispensable-role-of-emotional-intelligence-for-leaders-in-the-age-of-ai

Russell, S. J., & Norvig, P. (2010). *Artificial intelligence a modern approach*.

Salovey, P., & Mayer, J. D. (1990). Emotional intelligence. *Imagination, Cognition and Personality*, *9*(3), 185–211. doi:10.2190/DUGG-P24E-52WK-6CDG

Schuller, D., & Schuller, B. W. (2018). The age of artificial emotional intelligence. *Computer*, *51*(9), 38–46. doi:10.1109/MC.2018.3620963

Srinivasan, P. (2013). *Practical Emotional Intelligence*. Neelkamal publications Pvt. Ltd.

Wilson, H. J., & Daugherty, P. R. (2018). *Humans and AI are Joining Forces. Harvard Business Review*. HBR. https://hbr.org/2018/07/collaborative-intelligence-humans-and-ai-are-joining-forces

Zeidner, M., Roberts, R. D., & Matthews, G. (2002). Can emotional intelligence be schooled? A critical review. *Educational Psychologist*, *37*(4), 215–231. doi:10.1207/S15326985EP3704_2

Zhao, J., Wu, M., Zhou, L., Wang, X., & Jia, J. (2022). Cognitive psychology-based artificial intelligence review. *Frontiers in Neuroscience*, *16*, 1024316. doi:10.3389/fnins.2022.1024316 PMID:36278021

Chapter 5
Predictive Pioneers:
Bridging the Mental Health Gap in Older Adults Through Advanced Digital Technologies

Rita Komalasari
https://orcid.org/0000-0001-9963-2363
Yarsi University, Indonesia

ABSTRACT

Predictive pioneers are bridging the mental health gap in older adults by leveraging advanced digital technologies and user-centric insights. This study explores the potential of machine learning and digital tools in predicting mental health conditions in older adults, facilitating early intervention and support. Through an extensive literature review, user interactions, and healthcare staff interviews, the research aims to bridge gaps in existing knowledge and emphasize real-world application. The research culminates in the creation of highly accurate predictive models for depression in older adults, with valuable insights from user perspectives and healthcare staff guiding future directions. This study contributes innovative methods for mental health prediction and emphasizes the importance of user-centred design, paving the way for effective and accessible mental health interventions for older adults.

1. INTRODUCTION

In recent years, the intersection of mental health, digital technology, and predictive analytics has paved the way for innovative solutions in healthcare (Koutsouleris et al., 2022). The statistics are both staggering and disconcerting, a significant portion of the elderly population grapples with melancholy and anxiety. What compounds the

DOI: 10.4018/979-8-3693-1910-9.ch005

issue is the tendency for individuals to defer seeking therapy until crisis strikes, often driven by a complex interplay of shame and misinformation (Karatas et al., 2022). Against this backdrop, the imperative for early intervention and support becomes paramount. In order to assist older folks with early intervention and support, this chapter explores a ground-breaking method that uses digital technology and machine learning to forecast their anxiety and depression conditions in the future (Biswas, 2022). To understand the landscape comprehensively, this chapter thoroughly explores existing literature. The background is laid via a narrative review. These provide a detailed grasp of the possibilities and difficulties of employing digital technology to forecast mental health issues in older persons (Buenaventura et al., 2020). Central to this study are the predictive models developed, which exhibit notably high accuracy in contrast to prior research outlined in the review (Kadylak & Cotten, 2020). An essential revelation surfaced during this process: the nuances of predicting anxiety status proved to be more complex than anticipated, shedding light on the need for careful consideration of input data. This chapter delves into the human aspect of technology implementation. Important usability and motivational concerns were highlighted during interactive sessions with older persons. Understanding their perspectives is pivotal in designing effective, user-friendly digital mental health monitoring and management tools. Incorporating the viewpoint of healthcare staff is integral to any implementation strategy. The present research uses in-depth interviews to investigate current procedures and past encounters with technology in community healthcare contexts. These insights provide valuable guidance for seamless integration into existing healthcare frameworks. Quantitatively, the efficacy of digital mental health tools in predicting anxiety and depression is underscored by the potential to significantly enhance the determination of depression presence and severity in the elderly. Machine learning algorithms, particularly adept at processing self-reported mood data, emerge as a powerful tool in this endeavor. The notable predictive power exhibited by these models lends credence to the viability of the prediction strategy, laying the foundation for a data-driven paradigm shift in mental health diagnostics. Qualitatively, the chapter advocates for a nuanced approach to policymaking and practitioner integration. Beyond the mere introduction of digital tools, the emphasis lies on tailoring applications to the unique needs of the elderly population. This creative and practical strategy bridges the gap between theoretical advancements and practical implementation, offering a more personalized and effective mental health care experience.

This work makes significant contributions to the field. First, it shows that a novel approach to forecasting anxiety and depression in the elderly has promise. Additionally, the study considers how the suggested method might be implemented, connecting the gap between academic research and practical application. This section explores the exciting field of using AI and digital technologies to foretell the onset of mental health issues in the elderly. A more comprehensive and efficient strategy for supporting mental health in the elderly may be achieved by attending to both the technological and human elements and implementation considerations. The various stakeholders can leverage the knowledge and information generated by this research to bring about meaningful changes and improvements in the present situation. The key individuals and groups, including General practitioners, psychiatrists, and mental health professionals, can utilize the insights to enhance their diagnostic and intervention strategies for older adults. The predictive models may assist in early identification and targeted interventions. Community healthcare organizations and clinics can benefit from the research findings to integrate digital technology effectively into their practices. Understanding the challenges and opportunities highlighted in the study can guide the implementation of mental health monitoring tools. Policymakers in healthcare and aging-related domains can use the research to advocate for policy changes that support the integration of digital mental health tools into existing frameworks. This may involve considerations for funding, training, and infrastructure development. Developers of digital health tools can gain valuable insights into the usability challenges and motivational factors identified through interactive sessions with older adults. This information may guide the development of exciting and accessible apps for the elderly. The research outcomes empower older adults and their families with knowledge about the potential benefits of digital technology in monitoring mood and managing mental health. This awareness can reduce stigma, encourage proactive engagement, and prompt discussions with healthcare providers. The suggested approach for predicting anxiety and depression in the elderly may be further upon by the academic community. Researchers may look at the broader implications of incorporating technology into mental healthcare for the elderly, do longitudinal research, and explore potential improvements. Public health organizations may utilize the study results to create educational programs and awareness campaigns on mental health in older individuals. This has the potential to promote proactive treatment-seeking and lessen the societal stigma of mental health concerns. Insurance companies can use the research to assess the potential cost-effectiveness of early interventions facilitated by digital technology. As a result, insurance plans that encourage or pay for the use of these devices to track the mental health of the elderly may emerge. By disseminating the knowledge gained from this research to these diverse stakeholders, the potential for positive change and improvement in the mental health landscape for older adults can be maximized.

1.1 Background

In the landscape of mental health, the elderly population often faces barriers to seeking timely treatment for depression and anxiety (Reynolds et al., 2022).

Over 264 million people throughout the world suffer from depression, with a disproportionate number of those affected being those aged 65 and over (Monroe & Harkness, 2023). A study by Curran et al. (2020) emphasizes that the prevalence of depression and anxiety tends to increase with age, impacting overall mental health in older populations. Research by Zenebe et al. (2021) highlights that older adults are often underdiagnosed and undertreated for mental health conditions due to factors such as stigma and age-related misconceptions. According to research published in the Journal of Frontiers in Psychiatry, a mere 10% of older persons suffering from mental health concerns obtain the assistance they need (Seifert et al., 2019). Previous study underscores the potential of digital interventions in improving mental health outcomes, particularly in older adults. According to Jecker (2021), 73% of those 65 and above use the Internet, which shows that this age group is becoming more comfortable with technology. Previous research examines the promising role of machine learning in predicting mental health issues. According to research published in World Psychiatry, the accuracy of psychiatric outcome predictions may be improved using machine learning algorithms. Individuals suffering from anxiety and depression might greatly benefit from beginning treatment as soon as possible, according to a meta-analysis conducted by Chekroud et al. (2021). An article published in the Journal of Geriatric Care and Research sheds light on the importance of identifying and addressing mental health concerns in older persons early to avoid worsening (Girdhar et al., 2020). Innovative techniques are urgently needed due to the rising incidence of mental health concerns in older persons, as well as the difficulties associated with underdiagnosis and undertreatment (Hamm et al., 2020). Leveraging digital technology, as highlighted in contemporary research, particularly using machine learning models, aligns with the evolving landscape of healthcare. As supported by relevant studies, early intervention can significantly improve older adults' well-being (Lee et al., 2020). This emphasizes the significance of the study's proposed innovative approach to forecasting anxiety and depression in this susceptible group. In this chapter, the author will look at a revolutionary approach to this problem using digital tools and machine learning. Predicting whether or not older persons may have depression or anxiety in the future is crucial for providing them with early intervention and assistance. The findings could have far-reaching consequences for healthcare systems and mental health services, particularly for the elderly. Using machine learning to improve mental health has reached a new level by creating very accurate depression prediction models for the elderly. This establishes a standard for future studies in mental health prediction and adds to the methodological improvement of predictive models. This understanding can guide researchers and practitioners in optimizing models for more nuanced mental health conditions. Interactive sessions with older adults offer crucial insights into usability and motivational factors. This knowledge can guide the design of digital mental health tools, emphasizing a user-centered approach. Improving the user experience enhances the adoption and effectiveness of these tools in real-world settings. Exploring healthcare staff perspectives on technology implementation in community healthcare settings provides a roadmap for integrating digital tools into routine practices. This can catalyze a shift in healthcare delivery, fostering a more technology-inclusive mental health monitoring and intervention approach. The research fosters a comprehensive view of mental health in the aging population by combining prediction algorithms and the opinions of older persons and healthcare workers. This comprehensive approach is essential in providing all-encompassing treatments that tackle the complex nature of mental health. An important addition is the research considering implementing the suggested strategy. The study empowers older adults by acknowledging their views on digital technology for mood monitoring and mental health management. This acknowledgment reduces the stigma associated with mental health issues in older populations and encourages active participation in their mental well-being. The results of this research may help shape rules and standards for the use of digital technology in mental healthcare, which is of great interest to lawmakers and professional groups. Potentially, this will contribute to our understanding of the norms, best practices, and ethical concerns surrounding mental health technologies. The study's many contributions include comprehensive knowledge of mental health in older persons, user experience, implementation factors, and predictive modeling. By addressing these dimensions, the research has the potential to shape the future of mental healthcare for older populations, setting a precedent for more effective, user-friendly, and integrated approaches. Using both secondary and primary data, this project will attempt to discover how machine learning technologies might be used to address the real-world problem of predicting the occurrence of anxiety and depression in the elderly. It goes even further by exploring how the old utilize technology to monitor and treat mental health concerns and how doctors feel about the idea of using technology to predict when the elderly would feel sad or anxious.

1.2 Method

This chapter methodically examines the existing literature using a narrative review. The subtleties of the area can be fully grasped with this level of methodological depth. Academic rigor and accuracy are cornerstones of this ground-breaking work, and rigorous analysis is the bedrock upon which predictive models are built. According to the literature analysis that looks at prior methodologies, there has not been much research on using machine learning to predict anxiety and depression. The following figure 1 illustrates the specific method.

Figure 1. The specific method

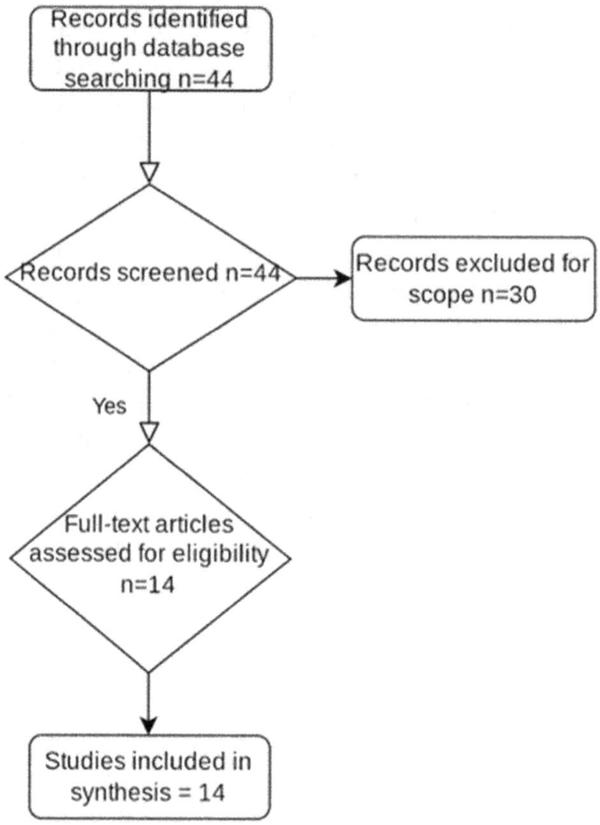

2. THE MENTAL HEALTH GAP IN OLDER ADULTS

This section discusses the possibility of using modern tech to identify cases of anxiety and depression in the elderly (Rajawat et al., 2021). Not only did staff members have expertise with telehealth equipment, but there are also avenues in community healthcare that may be used to establish a predictive strategy (Krokstad et al., 2022). Despite the benefits of employing predictive technology for depression and anxiety, staff noticed many difficulties, including the likelihood that staff may avoid participation in new practices, which would increase future pressure (Dhimolea et al., 2022). This chapter summarises the work, places it in the context of previous research, discusses its merits and flaws, and suggests areas for further study. Digital technologies, particularly smartphones and tablets, are increasingly utilized in healthcare to improve mental health outcomes for older adults. In order to circumvent the limitations of one-time appointments in detecting and diagnosing mental health issues like anxiety and depression, these technologies enable the collection of health data, which in turn allows patients to self-report these subjective states. Between 2019 and 2023, there was an 11.11% rise in the percentage of 65+ individuals in the UK who owned a smartphone and a 14.29% increase in the percentage of 65+ adults who used a tablet to access the Internet (Milte et al., 2023). According to this, people in the UK who are nearing retirement age are actively embracing new digital technology.

As part of the broader idea of telehealth, including telemonitoring, patients may have their vitals monitored more often without physically visiting a healthcare facility. Telemonitoring tracks vitals like blood pressure and glucose levels and shows promise for tracking mental health metrics like subjective mood states collected by self-report methods. Machine learning has shown potential in healthcare, among other areas where it has been used. Several fields, including medical imaging, genetics and genomics, disease detection and diagnosis (including mental health issues), and medical imaging, have begun to use machine learning methods in their quest for answers. Data that might be used in this way is becoming more accessible due to the broad, expanding, and voluntary usage of digital technology, which includes older persons (Mannheim et al., 2019). Medical professionals may use these tools to learn more about their elderly patients' mental health care needs and better address them. Due to the low adoption of applications and websites with supporting evidence for mental health, digital technology use in healthcare might be problematic (Pirhonen et al., 2020). In order to avoid healthcare problems and save money, it is crucial to intervene early for older persons suffering from anxiety and depression. Anxiety and depression in the elderly can be better predicted with the help of machine learning, which is finding more and more uses in healthcare. This may lead to earlier interventions, which would be suitable for society. When developing new healthcare services, it is essential to consider including this technology (Xie et al., 2021). Failing to do so can lead to poor adoption or even abandonment of the services altogether. To ensure a smooth rollout, addressing healthcare workers' lack of engagement at all levels, the dispersal of knowledge on new technologies and clinicians' need for more buy-in is crucial.

Current research on the use of technology in mental health treatment indicates that short staff training is not enough to maintain practice benefits over time. Regular monitoring by skilled and experienced professionals may facilitate professionals' behavior modification. According to Hülür and Macdonald (2020), human support for technology systems is often disregarded when developing novel solutions. By surveying their administrative leadership, Chen et al. (2021) determined the barriers prohibiting US-based community behavioral healthcare agencies from embracing technology in behavioral healthcare. Concerns about privacy, expense, organizational resources, and the availability of high-quality Internet on a local level were among the obstacles. When designing new technological interventions, ensuring their value and cost-effectiveness is essential (Miller, 2020). Then, when considering how to incorporate these interventions into current healthcare pathways, it is essential to consider implementation early on, including involving end users and healthcare staff in the design process.

In this research review, we look at how machine learning may be used to forecast the onset of anxiety and depression in the elderly. Finding research gaps and describing the existing literature are the goals of the review. The word 'elderly' was used to develop search phrases for the review from relevant publications and keywords in the study topic. Since the study aimed to identify and classify current approaches to the relevant topics, it did not evaluate the quality of the retrieved papers. The selected search phrases were discussed and expanded upon by experts, who recommended that critical, well-known publications be located via the searches. Since they brought back already-known things, prediction and prediction became part of the final set of terms. Searches should also include the phrase "neural networks," according to experts. Research had to be published in English, use machine learning methods, and discuss how to forecast when these circumstances may appear in the future to be considered for the review. Future prediction, anxiety or depression emphasis, human data, and an empirical investigation were all deemed ineligible.In order to find the best papers on anxiety and depression, a systematic mapping review was carried out. Titles and abstracts that were unclear were sifted through in the review process. Next, machine learning techniques like clustering and random forests were applied to the remaining publications in the final collection. Next, the condition that was anticipated (depression/anxiety) was named, followed by the factors that were used as inputs and outputs, the design of the research, and the capacity to predict.A total of 245 articles were included in the research. However, 191 of those were excluded for various reasons. Among them were the following: a lack of attention to forecasting emotional features or depression tendencies, a lack of use of machine learning, a lack of peer review, and the omission of any discussion of depression or anxiety. A comprehensive paper sift was also included in the review; there are still 19 articles that need to be included in the information extraction step. Some machine learning technologies used were the hidden Markov Model, Viterbi pathcounting, a training technique based on Stochastic Variational Inference, and Naïve Bayes support vector machine. Both prospective and retrospective investigations were a part of the research design, and the predictive ability measure was also evaluated. Using machine learning techniques to forecast instances of anxiety and depression has been the focus of several studies. While SVMs and logistic regression get the most attention, other techniques, including LASSO, elastic nets, neural networks, and Bayesian methods, are also used in other research (Das et al., 2022).

Depression, anxiety, and other mental health issues, as well as behavioral and emotional difficulties, have found relief via the use of these methods. Using the sensitivity and specificity, accuracy, and area under the curve (AUC) of these models, researchers have investigated the impact of several factors on anxiety and depression. A case in point is that logistic regression and support vector machines emerged victorious in research involving 89,840 TBI patients when it came to predicting the onset of depression (Ramos et al., 2020). Among 1,397 white women surveyed for postpartum depression, a high socioeconomic position, a personal or family history of depression, and the Eysenck Personality Inventory were identified as substantial predictors in another research supported by the Spanish government. Research including 1,793 people with diabetes indicated that random forest, multi-layer perceptron, logistic regression with ridge parameter, and support vector machine were the most effective models for predicting depressed symptoms (Nagaraj et al., 2022). Previous research has used machine learning approaches to forecast the onset of anxiety and depression. Two of the most popular are SVMs and logistic regression. This study delves into the use of machine learning techniques to predict future anxiety and depression, shedding light on different approaches and highlighting knowledge gaps in the current literature. Few studies used self-report measures or neurological signs like MRI data; most relied on patients' medical histories (Nemesure et al., 2021). Most studies used self-report measures of depression and anxiety as their end variables, with just a small number using clinical diagnoses. Several techniques assessed the ability to predict, including ROC curve analysis, sensitivity, specificity, precision, recall, and accuracy. Most research used retrospective designs, whereas only four used future designs (Priya et al., 2020). The lack of interest in a sample that solely includes seniors is noteworthy since people's mood trajectories vary with age. Suicide is associated with depression, which is more frequent among the elderly than dementia. Prediction methods that look at static, short-term metrics acquired over less than a day tend to concentrate on finding high-risk situations. Research on medical record-based prediction presupposes elderly persons have consistent and frequent interactions with healthcare providers. Research into methods of data collecting that include continuous monitoring over many days is necessary, as are further prospective studies to evaluate models built in hindsight (Richter et al., 2020). A lack of interest in anticipating future worry or a bias favoring publishing research that predicts depression may explain the enormous discrepancy between the two. These recommendations need more study to explore and guide future initiatives fully.While machine learning has shown promise in predicting the occurrence of anxiety and depression in younger groups, studies examining its use with older adults are few (van Mens et al., 2020). It is unclear from the available literature if the under-investigation in anxiety is due to its perceived difficulty in prediction or some other factor. More prospective research is needed to understand how various techniques may operate in practice, as retrospective studies are overrepresented.While there have been some experiments with using machine learning to forecast mental health issues, none of these methods has been shown to apply to the large-scale monitoring of seniors' mental health. One more realistic way to find mental health issues in this group would be to use self-reporting technologies that work across platforms. Predicting the occurrence of future mental health disorders using a mix of self-report data and a machine learning algorithm might pave the way for early intervention and the avoidance of crises (Andersson et al., 2021). Dissimilarities in purpose, methodology, and culture characterize the primary ways statistical inference and machine learning vary. Machine learning seeks to generate accurate predictions about the world, whereas statistical inference seeks to discover what is true. After a model has been trained, machine learning reduces the number of tests used to determine its assumptions and forecast accuracy, allowing it to perform well even when statistical inference methods would otherwise fail. Because of the cultural norms that have long governed mental health research, models in this field often use statistical inference techniques (Portugal et al., 2019). This, however, is starting to change as more and more studies show that there is a growing interest in using machine learning for mental health research, specifically in predicting future cases of depression and anxiety.The frequency of mental health concerns like depression and anxiety varies greatly across different settings, but they are common among older persons overall. Mood swings, a lack of interest in or enjoyment from life, altered eating habits, disturbed sleep, slowed or accelerated activity, extreme fatigue, guilt, and thoughts of suicide are all symptoms of major depressive disorder. Suicide, medical mortality, cognitive decline, physical disability, increased healthcare resource use, and somatic symptoms are more likely among elderly individuals suffering from depression (Zhang et al., 2021). At least one person in seven will suffer from depression over their lifetime. Research on the frequency of depression among the elderly varies greatly, but the consensus is that this demographic has a lower depression prevalence than the whole population. Mild depressive symptoms are widespread in this demographic, and older persons suffer from depression at a higher rate than dementia. Estimates put the percentage of community-based persons over 65 years old afflicted with anxiety disorders at between 13.1%, highlighting the prevalence of anxiety disorders among the elderly (Roderburg et al., 2023). Anxiety symptoms include a lack of calm, excessive worrying, agitation, difficulty focusing, impatience, disturbed sleep, and tense muscles. Those who suffer from anxiety disorders are more likely to engage in self-injurious or suicidal behaviors.Medications, cognitive therapies, and behavioral approaches abound for the treatment of depression and anxiety. When it comes to anxiety and depression, the National Institute for Health and Care Excellence has published some suggestions on what to do (Kajdy et al., 2020). Instruction and close supervision of complex psychosocial and pharmaceutical treatments are two examples of the things included in these severity-based recommendations.Experiencing physical health issues or going through a difficult life transition are two things that might put you at risk for developing depression and anxiety later in life. Longer hospital stays and higher healthcare expenditures might be the result of older persons' increasing usage of physical healthcare due to the existence of mental health issues. One potential strategy to alleviate strain on mental health services and other healthcare systems is the early detection of mental health issues in the elderly. Nevertheless, there are obstacles to identification and diagnosis, such as the fact that primary care doctors fail to notice signs of poor mental health in older persons, the stigma associated with mental health issues, and the dread of dementia. Modern methods of diagnosing and treating mental health issues are being made possible by advancements in digital technology (Wu et al., 2021). Patients may use their smartphones to do self-evaluations, have remote videoconferences with therapists, access professional information, play games that reward good behavior, and engage with a virtual coach to modify their habits for the better. Many groups are looking at how digital technology may work with mental health therapies already in place or even better. Despite the abundance of apps claiming to alleviate mental health issues ailments or enhance coping skills, there is little credible research to back their claims of effectiveness. According to a literature review, there are many more mental health apps without an evidence base than with one. Similarly, it is unclear what, if any, long-term consequences apps with mental health claims may have.New data-driven approaches are needed for mental health monitoring and management in digital platforms. They may find apps like Buddy, Wellhappy, and Five Ways to Well-being that support emotional and mental health (Robinson, 2022). Further research is needed to learn how successful these applications are and how long their benefits stay. Improving the detection and treatment of mental health concerns in the elderly is greatly facilitated by advancements in digital technology. By reducing diagnostic and care barriers, digital technologies may improve the quality of life for the elderly.Potentially undiagnosed mental health issues in the elderly population might be better detected with the use of modern technology. Stigmatization of mental health issues may explain why many seniors avoid talking about or seeing a doctor when they are depressed or anxious. As the number of people using smartphones and other digital devices continues to climb among the elderly, this might be a great tool for helping them keep track of their emotions and get help before problems escalate. This early intervention might be in the form of self-care instructions provided by digital technology or in the form of alerts to healthcare providers about the user's potential mental health decline. It would suggest that older folks like utilizing technology since it allows them to do tasks more swiftly or opens new opportunities. Some older adults may lack the motivation to use technology for various reasons (Collado et al., 2021). They could think it is too demanding on their bodies and minds to learn how to use new gadgets, that it is too pricey, too big, or too complicated, or that they like the tried-and-true ways of doing things the old-fashioned way. Some factors that can impact the long-term use of technology by older adults include how reliable the device is, difficulties with memory and learning new functions, the fact that family and friends are too busy, impatient, or quick-witted to instruct older adults in the proper use of technology properly, and the belief that older adults can handle daily tasks independently or would rather rely on family support than rely on assistive technology. The following table 1 illustrates the comparison chart.

Table 1. Comparison of work with existing work

Aspect	Current Chapter	Existing Work
Focus on Technology in Mental Health	Envisions the use of digital technology to predict anxiety and depression in older adults	Prior studies, such as Rajawat et al. (2021), have explored the potential of modern tech for identifying mental health issues, but the focus on predicting in older adults may be distinct
Community Healthcare Integration	Advocates for integrating digital mental health tools into existing healthcare frameworks	Krokstad et al. (2022) identify avenues in community healthcare for establishing predictive strategies, indicating some parallel in focus
Challenges and Difficulties Acknowledged	Recognizes difficulties, including staff resistance, which may impede the adoption of predictive technology	Dhimolea et al. (2022) also note challenges, including staff resistance, emphasizing potential barriers to the implementation of new practices
Technological Trends in Older Adults	Highlights the increasing use of smartphones and tablets among older adults in the UK	Milte et al. (2023) similarly report a rise in technology adoption among older individuals, indicating a trend in digital technology acceptance
Machine Learning in Healthcare	Emphasizes the potential of machine learning in predicting anxiety and depression	Aligns with broader trends where machine learning is increasingly used in healthcare, as highlighted in several studies, including Mannheim et al. (2019)
Research Gap Identification	Explicitly identifies areas for further exploration, such as refining machine learning applications and investigating long-term effectiveness	Aligns with the emphasis on future research directions in various studies, such as Richter et al. (2020) and Nemesure et al. (2021)
Evaluation of Existing Literature	Conducts a research review to identify gaps and describe existing literature	Similar systematic approaches, like Chen et al. (2021), evaluate barriers to technology adoption in community behavioral healthcare agencies
Integration of Self-Report Data and Machine Learning	Proposes the use of self-report data and machine learning for predicting mental health issues	Previous studies (Andersson et al., 2021) suggest integrating self-report data with machine learning for early detection and prevention of mental health issues
Attention to Implementation Challenges	Recognizes the importance of addressing healthcare workers' lack of engagement and involving end users in the design process	Aligns with recommendations in literature (Miller, 2020), emphasizing the importance of considering implementation challenges early on

3. DEPRESSION PREDICTION MODELS

For the development of more accurate depression prediction models, the results of this research have significant methodological consequences for the future of geriatric mental health prediction. Recent articles, such as those by Su et al. (2020) and Bzdok and Meyer-Lindenberg, have emphasized the potential of machine learning in predicting mental health illnesses. It must be acknowledged, however, that the uniqueness of these models as they pertain to older persons is often unexplored (Cho et al., 2019). A more excellent average sadness score was associated with subsequent positive depression status in both models, according to the data. One of the models also has lethargy, which could be a reflection of the individuals' actual energy levels. The DSM-5 states that major depressive disorder is characterized by a low mood and an inability to muster the energy to confront daily tasks (Park et al., 2023). These findings suggest that individuals in this community may be able to detect the onset of depression symptoms with the use of a daily self-report. This study adds to the growing body of data suggesting machine learning might be helpful in the diagnosis and prognosis of mental health disorders. While the LASSO has been used to predict the likelihood of depression in the past, no study has specifically examined this group in its senior years. Another change from the current method of depression prediction is the use of daily self-report data collected for machine learning. The research contains drawbacks, even if the LASSO technique has virtues.

Given that the study's final model was trained on a small sample size of 37 people from only two locations in the UK, its potential use in clinical settings is questionable (Ma et al., 2023). However, it is well-known that repeated 5-fold cross-validation may provide conservative findings while also helping to alleviate the over-fitting issue. The study addresses this gap by crafting predictive models that exhibit a level of accuracy surpassing that of counterparts presented in the mapping review. This signifies a methodological advancement and underscores the robustness and applicability of these models in the intricate landscape of mental health prediction for older adults. The superior performance of these models positions them as a noteworthy contribution to the evolving field, providing a foundation for more targeted and effective interventions in geriatric mental health. An intricate grasp of the difficulties of modeling mental health disorders is shown by the study's investigation of using machine learning to forecast anxiety levels. The observation that the generated model lacked utility aligns with the recognition, emphasized by Roush et al. (2020), that mental health conditions are inherently heterogeneous and multifaceted. This nuanced insight is a valuable contribution to the ongoing refinement of machine learning applications in mental health. It underscores the complexity of predicting anxiety status, necessitating a more tailored and nuanced approach to modeling. As the field advances, the importance of adapting models to specific conditions and demographic groups becomes increasingly evident. This recognition is pivotal for future research endeavors seeking to enhance the precision and effectiveness of machine learning applications in the nuanced landscape of mental health prediction, particularly for anxiety in older adults.

The interactive sessions with older adults constitute compelling evidence of the critical intersection of usability and motivation, aligning seamlessly with user-centered design principles. In line with broader conclusions in digital health research, the usability issues and motivating factors discussed in these sessions highlight the critical significance of user experience in promoting technology adoption (Pywell et al., 2020). This evidence is a poignant reminder of the imperative to design digital mental health tools with a profound understanding of older adults' unique needs and preferences. The resonance between identified challenges and broader digital health research findings underscores the universality of the importance of user-centered design. As the study advocates, tailoring interventions to align with the lived experiences of older adults is not just a recommendation but a foundational requirement for the successful implementation and sustained use of digital mental health tools in this demographic. The valuable insights extracted from in-depth interviews with healthcare staff substantiate the compelling case for seamlessly integrating digital tools into routine healthcare practices. The current tendency to incorporate technology into conventional healthcare systems is in perfect harmony with the recognition of established practices and previous technological implementations in community healthcare settings (Lattie et al., 2022). This evidence is a robust foundation for advocating the feasibility and practical considerations of implementing digital mental health tools in real-world healthcare contexts. The alignment of the study's findings with the ongoing evolution toward technology integration in healthcare further emphasizes the potential for digital tools to become an intrinsic and practical facet of routine healthcare practices, particularly in mental health interventions for older adults. The study's deliberate inclusion of predictive models and qualitative insights from user and healthcare staff perspectives underscores a steadfast commitment to cultivating a holistic understanding of mental health in older adults. This approach aligns seamlessly with the principles that Graham et al. (2020) advocated, highlighting the significance of considering psychological, social, and environmental factors in addressing mental health issues among older populations (Wilson et al., 2021). The findings from the research greatly aid in developing a more comprehensive knowledge of mental health by acknowledging and embracing its intrinsically complicated nature. Researchers have been able to comprehend better prediction models and the many interrelated factors that make up older individuals' mental health by combining quantitative and qualitative methods. This holistic approach lays the groundwork for more inclusive and effective interventions that resonate with the complexity of mental health in this demographic. Bolstering the connection between theoretical research and real-world application, the study purposefully includes a component that focuses on implementing the recommended strategy. All of the recommendations by Wisniewski and Torous (2020) are fully compatible with this strategic addition. Liberati et al. (2021) are calling for a change in thinking and more concrete actions to tackle the underdiagnosis and undertreatment of mental health issues in the elderly. The evidence presented in this section underscores the study's practical relevance and potential to make a tangible impact on improving patient care. By acknowledging and addressing the critical transition from research findings to practical application, the study contributes valuable insights to the academic discourse and positions itself as a catalyst for positive change within healthcare practice and patient outcomes. This commitment to implementation bridges the crucial divide between theory and practice, fostering a trajectory toward more effective, patient-centered mental health interventions for older adults.

The study's intentional acknowledgment and exploration of older adults' perspectives on utilizing digital technology for mental health management stand as robust evidence of an empowering approach. This methodology aligns seamlessly with the fundamental principles of patient-centered care, a concept underscored in Di Carlo et al.'s (2021) systematic review, emphasizing the positive impact of involving patients in decisions about their care. The evidence presented in this section affirms the paramount importance of considering older adults not merely as recipients of mental health interventions but as active participants in their mental health journey. By incorporating their views and preferences, the study fosters a sense of empowerment among older adults, recognizing their agency in decisions related to their mental well-being. This patient-centered perspective respects the autonomy of older individuals and contributes to more effective and sustainable mental health management strategies tailored to their unique needs and preferences. The findings and contributions of the study serve as compelling evidence that can significantly inform the development of policies and guidelines about integrating digital technology in mental healthcare. This aligns strategically with the imperative call for evidence-based policymaking in healthcare, as consistently advocated by various reputable public health organizations Thieme et al., (2020). The presented evidence substantiates the study's potential to influence the establishment of standards and ethical considerations for the judicious leveraging of digital technology in mental health. By providing nuanced insights into the practicalities, challenges, and benefits associated with incorporating technology into mental healthcare for older adults, the study contributes a vital layer of knowledge essential for the formulation of policies that are not only informed by evidence but also considerate of the unique needs and contexts of older populations. This evidence, thus, positions the study as a valuable resource for policymakers endeavoring to shape guidelines that propel the responsible and effective integration of digital tools into mental health frameworks.

The chapter makes a significant contribution to the field of mental health therapy for older adults in terms of concept, novelty, and technical aspects: The central conceptual contribution lies in the exploration of the transformative potential of digital technology in predicting anxiety and depression among older adults. This conceptualization acknowledges the pressing need for innovative approaches to address mental health issues in this demographic. The chapter introduces a novel perspective by emphasizing the importance of bridging the gap between theoretical advancements and real-world policy solutions. The call for comprehensive integration of digital mental health tools into existing healthcare frameworks, along with tailored applications for the elderly, adds a novel layer of practicality and creativity to the discourse. The technical contribution of the chapter is evident in its exploration of machine learning algorithms for predicting anxiety and depression in older adults. The acknowledgment of machine learning's suitability for processing self-reported mood data and its relatively good prediction power represents a technical breakthrough in the application of data-driven strategies for mental health diagnostics in the elderly. In summary, the chapter's contributions lie in its innovative conceptualization, practical recommendations for integration, technical exploration of machine learning applications, and a forward-looking perspective that charts a course for sustained progress in the field of digital mental health for older adults.

4. SOLUTIONS AND RECOMMENDATIONS

Based on the study's findings, there is a pressing need for policymakers to embrace and support the integration of digital mental health tools into existing healthcare frameworks. Developing policies incentivizing healthcare organizations to adopt and implement such tools can enhance the overall mental health infrastructure. Furthermore, the creation of guidelines ensuring ethical use, data privacy, and the seamless integration of these technologies into routine care should be prioritized. This study has contributed significantly to advancing mental health prediction in older adults through innovative digital technology and machine learning applications. The development of highly accurate predictive models for depression, coupled with a nuanced understanding of the challenges in predicting anxiety status, underscores the methodological progression achieved. User-centered design principles, gleaned from interactive sessions, offer crucial insights into usability and motivation, emphasizing the importance of tailoring digital mental health tools to the unique needs of older adults. Integrating digital technology into routine healthcare practices, as explored through healthcare staff interviews, reveals the feasibility and practical considerations essential for successful implementation. By combining quantitative and qualitative methods, this study examines mental health in the elderly from every angle, recognizing the multifaceted character of these problems. With the use of innovative digital technology and machine learning, this project intends to predict when anxiety and depression may strike the elderly so that early intervention can be made possible. The study's overarching goal is to provide mental health assistance for older people by creating reliable prediction models and user-centered design principles and understanding the obstacles to implementation.

5. FUTURE RESEARCH DIRECTIONS

An avenue for future research may be a longitudinal study to evaluate the suggested prediction models' efficacy in real-world circumstances over the long run. Additionally, further investigation into refining machine learning applications for predicting anxiety status in older adults is warranted, addressing the identified challenges. Exploring the scalability of user-centered digital tools in diverse healthcare settings and populations would provide valuable insights for widespread implementation. Finally, a more complete picture of the benefits of digital technology integration into mental health treatment for older persons might be provided by studies that concentrate on the effects of these treatments on healthcare expenditures and health outcomes.

6. CONCLUSION

By enabling the prediction of anxiety and depression in older adults, digital technology has the potential to alter the field of mental health therapy radically. However, to truly harness the potential of this approach, it is crucial to extend beyond theoretical advancements and offer comprehensive real-world policy solutions. Advocating for integrating digital mental health tools into existing healthcare frameworks should accompany tangible recommendations for policymakers and practitioners. Making applications tailored to the needs of the elderly is one creative and practical way to close the gap between theory and practice in mental health care, which might lead to better results from digital technologies. Moreover, highlighting potential research directions is vital for the continual progress of the field. Explicitly identifying areas where further exploration is warranted, such as refining machine learning applications for predicting anxiety in older adults or investigating the long-term effectiveness of predictive models, provides a roadmap for future research endeavors. This ensures that the momentum gained from the current study is sustained and that the evolving landscape of digital mental health in older populations continues to be explored. Determining the presence and severity of depression in the elderly might be significantly improved with the use of machine learning algorithms. Machine learning is a good fit for data on self-reported mood, and the models' relatively good prediction power lends credence to the prediction strategy.

REFERENCES

Andersson, S., Bathula, D. R., Iliadis, S. I., Walter, M., & Skalkidou, A. (2021). Predicting women with depressive symptoms postpartum with machine learning methods. *Scientific Reports*, *11*(1), 7877. doi:10.1038/s41598-021-86368-y PMID:33846362

Biswas, R. (2022). Outlining big data analytics in health sector with special reference to Covid-19. *Wireless Personal Communications*, *124*(3), 2097–2108. doi:10.1007/s11277-021-09446-4 PMID:34873378

Buenaventura, R. D., Ho, J. B., & Lapid, M. I. (2020). COVID-19 and mental health of older adults in the Philippines: A perspective from a developing country. *International Psychogeriatrics*, *32*(10), 1129–1133. doi:10.1017/S1041610220000757 PMID:32349826

Chekroud, A. M., Bondar, J., Delgadillo, J., Doherty, G., Wasil, A., Fokkema, M., Cohen, Z., Belgrave, D., DeRubeis, R., Iniesta, R., Dwyer, D., & Choi, K. (2021). The promise of machine learning in predicting treatment outcomes in psychiatry. *World Psychiatry; Official Journal of the World Psychiatric Association (WPA)*, *20*(2), 154–170. doi:10.1002/wps.20882 PMID:34002503

Chen, A. T., Ge, S., Cho, S., Teng, A. K., Chu, F., Demiris, G., & Zaslavsky, O. (2021). Reactions to COVID-19, information and technology use, and social connectedness among older adults with pre-frailty and frailty. *Geriatric Nursing*, *42*(1), 188–195. doi:10.1016/j.gerinurse.2020.08.001 PMID:32863038

Cho, G., Yim, J., Choi, Y., Ko, J., & Lee, S. H. (2019). Review of machine learning algorithms for diagnosing mental illness. *Psychiatry Investigation*, *16*(4), 262–269. doi:10.30773/pi.2018.12.21.2 PMID:30947496

Collado-Mateo, D., Lavín-Pérez, A. M., Peñacoba, C., Del Coso, J., Leyton-Román, M., Luque-Casado, A., Gasque, P., Fernández-del-Olmo, M. Á., & Amado-Alonso, D. (2021). Key factors associated with adherence to physical exercise in patients with chronic diseases and older adults: An umbrella review. *International Journal of Environmental Research and Public Health*, *18*(4), 2023. doi:10.3390/ijerph18042023 PMID:33669679

Cui, X., Xiao, R., Liu, X., Qiao, H., Zheng, X., Zhang, Y., & Du, J. (2021). Adaptive LASSO logistic regression based on particle swarm optimization for Alzheimer's disease early diagnosis. *Chemometrics and Intelligent Laboratory Systems*, *215*, 104316. doi:10.1016/j.chemolab.2021.104316

Curran, E., Rosato, M., Ferry, F., & Leavey, G. (2020). Prevalence and factors associated with anxiety and depression in older adults: Gender differences in psychosocial indicators. *Journal of Affective Disorders*, *267*, 114–122. doi:10.1016/j.jad.2020.02.018 PMID:32063562

Das, B., Murgaonkar, D., Navyashree, S., & Kumar, P. (2022). Novel combination artificial neural network models could not outperform individual models for weather-based cashew yield prediction. *International Journal of Biometeorology*, *66*(8), 1627–1638. doi:10.1007/s00484-022-02306-1 PMID:35641796

Dhimolea, T. K., Kaplan-Rakowski, R., & Lin, L. (2022). Supporting Social and Emotional Well-Being with Artificial Intelligence. In *Bridging Human Intelligence and Artificial Intelligence* (pp. 125–138). Springer International Publishing., doi:10.1007/978-3-030-84729-6_8

Di Carlo, F., Sociali, A., Picutti, E., Pettorruso, M., Vellante, F., Verrastro, V., Martinotti, G., & di Giannantonio, M. (2021). Telepsychiatry and other cutting-edge technologies in COVID-19 pandemic: Bridging the distance in mental health assistance. *International Journal of Clinical Practice*, *75*(1), ijcp.13716. doi:10.1111/ijcp.13716 PMID:32946641

Girdhar, R., Srivastava, V., & Sethi, S. (2020). Managing mental health issues among elderly during COVID-19 pandemic. *Journal of Geriatric Care and Research*, *7*(1), 32–35.

Graham, S. A., Lee, E. E., Jeste, D. V., Van Patten, R., Twamley, E. W., Nebeker, C., Yamada, Y., Kim, H.-C., & Depp, C. A. (2020). Artificial intelligence approaches to predicting and detecting cognitive decline in older adults: A conceptual review. *Psychiatry Research*, *284*, 112732. doi:10.1016/j.psychres.2019.112732 PMID:31978628

Hamm, M. E., Brown, P. J., Karp, J. F., Lenard, E., Cameron, F., Dawdani, A., Lavretsky, H., Miller, J. P., Mulsant, B. H., Pham, V. T., Reynolds, C. F., Roose, S. P., & Lenze, E. J. (2020). Experiences of American older adults with pre-existing depression during the beginnings of the COVID-19 pandemic: A multicity, mixed-methods study. *The American Journal of Geriatric Psychiatry*, *28*(9), 924–932. doi:10.1016/j.jagp.2020.06.013 PMID:32682619

Hülür, G., & Macdonald, B. (2020). Rethinking social relationships in old age: Digitalization and the social lives of older adults. *The American Psychologist, 75*(4), 554–566. doi:10.1037/amp0000604 PMID:32378949

Jecker, N. S. (2021). Nothing to be ashamed of: Sex robots for older adults with disabilities. *Journal of Medical Ethics, 47*(1), 26–32. doi:10.1136/medethics-2020-106645 PMID:33199655

Kadylak, T., & Cotten, S. R. (2020). United States older adults' willingness to use emerging technologies. *Information Communication and Society, 23*(5), 736–750. doi:10.1080/1369118X.2020.1713848

Kajdy, A., Feduniw, S., Ajdacka, U., Modzelewski, J., Baranowska, B., Sys, D., Pokropek, A., Pawlicka, P., Kaźmierczak, M., Rabijewski, M., Jasiak, H., Lewandowska, R., Borowski, D., Kwiatkowski, S., & Poon, L. C. (2020). Risk factors for anxiety and depression among pregnant women during the COVID-19 pandemic: A web-based cross-sectional survey. *Medicine, 99*(30), e21279. doi:10.1097/MD.0000000000021279 PMID:32791708

Karatas, M., Eriskin, L., Deveci, M., Pamucar, D., & Garg, H. (2022). Big Data for Healthcare Industry 4.0: Applications, challenges and future perspectives. *Expert Systems with Applications, 200*, 116912. doi:10.1016/j.eswa.2022.116912

Koutsouleris, N., Hauser, T. U., Skvortsova, V., & De Choudhury, M. (2022). From promise to practice: Towards the realisation of AI-informed mental health care. *The Lancet. Digital Health, 4*(11), e829–e840. doi:10.1016/S2589-7500(22)00153-4 PMID:36229346

Krokstad, S., Weiss, D. A., Krokstad, M. A., Rangul, V., Kvaløy, K., Ingul, J. M., Bjerkeset, O., Twenge, J., & Sund, E. R. (2022). Divergent decennial trends in mental health according to age reveal poorer mental health for young people: Repeated cross-sectional population-based surveys from the HUNT Study, Norway. *BMJ Open, 12*(5), e057654. doi:10.1136/bmjopen-2021-057654 PMID:35584877

Lattie, E. G., Stiles-Shields, C., & Graham, A. K. (2022). An overview of and recommendations for more accessible digital mental health services. *Nature Reviews Psychology, 1*(2), 87–100. doi:10.1038/s44159-021-00003-1

Lee, K., Jeong, G. C., & Yim, J. (2020). Consideration of the psychological and mental health of the elderly during COVID-19: A theoretical review. *International Journal of Environmental Research and Public Health, 17*(21), 8098. doi:10.3390/ijerph17218098 PMID:33153074

Liberati, E., Richards, N., Willars, J., Scott, D., Boydell, N., Parker, J., Pinfold, V., Martin, G., Dixon-Woods, M., & Jones, P. B. (2021). A qualitative study of experiences of NHS mental healthcare workers during the Covid-19 pandemic. *BMC Psychiatry, 21*(1), 250. doi:10.1186/s12888-021-03261-8 PMID:33980215

Ma, J., Dhiman, P., Qi, C., Bullock, G., van Smeden, M., Riley, R. D., & Collins, G. S. (2023). Poor handling of continuous predictors in clinical prediction models using logistic regression: A systematic review. *Journal of Clinical Epidemiology, 161*, 140–151. Advance online publication. doi:10.1016/j.jclinepi.2023.07.017 PMID:37536504

Mannheim, I., Schwartz, E., Xi, W., Buttigieg, S. C., McDonnell-Naughton, M., Wouters, E. J., & Van Zaalen, Y. (2019). Inclusion of older adults in the research and design of digital technology. *International Journal of Environmental Research and Public Health, 16*(19), 3718. doi:10.3390/ijerph16193718 PMID:31581632

Miller, E. A. (2020). Protecting and improving the lives of older adults in the COVID-19 era. *Journal of Aging & Social Policy, 32*(4-5), 297–309. doi:10.1080/08959420.2020.1780104 PMID:32583751

Milte, R., Jemere, D., Lay, K., Hutchinson, C., Thomas, J., Murray, J., & Ratcliffe, J. (2023). A scoping review of the use of visual tools and adapted easy-read approaches in Quality-of-Life instruments for adults. *Quality of Life Research: An International Journal of Quality of Life Aspects of Treatment, Care and Rehabilitation, 32*(12), 1–18. doi:10.1007/s11136-023-03450-w PMID:37344727

Monroe, S. M., & Harkness, K. L. (2023). Why Recurrent Depression Should Be Reconceptualized and Redefined. *Current Directions in Psychological Science, 32*(3), 204–211. doi:10.1177/09637214221143045

Nagaraj, P., Muneeswaran, V., & Deshik, G. (2022, August). Ensemble Machine Learning (Grid Search & Random Forest) based Enhanced Medical Expert Recommendation System for Diabetes Mellitus Prediction. In *2022 3rd International Conference on Electronics and Sustainable Communication Systems* (ICESC) (pp. 757-765). IEEE.

Nemesure, M. D., Heinz, M. V., Huang, R., & Jacobson, N. C. (2021). Predictive modeling of depression and anxiety using electronic health records and a novel machine learning approach with artificial intelligence. *Scientific Reports, 11*(1), 1980. doi:10.1038/s41598-021-81368-4 PMID:33479383

Park, D., Lim, S., Choi, Y., & Oh, H. (2023). *Depression Emotion Multi-Label Classification Using Everytime Platform with DSM-5 Diagnostic Criteria*. IEEE. doi:10.1109/ACCESS.2023.3305477

Pirhonen, J., Lolich, L., Tuominen, K., Jolanki, O., & Timonen, V. (2020). "These devices have not been made for older people's needs"-Older adults' perceptions of digital technologies in Finland and Ireland. *Technology in Society*, *62*, 101287. doi:10.1016/j.techsoc.2020.101287

Portugal, L. C., Schrouff, J., Stiffler, R., Bertocci, M., Bebko, G., Chase, H., Lockovitch, J., Aslam, H., Graur, S., Greenberg, T., Pereira, M., Oliveira, L., Phillips, M., & Mourão-Miranda, J. (2019). Predicting anxiety from wholebrain activity patterns to emotional faces in young adults: A machine learning approach. *NeuroImage. Clinical*, *23*, 101813. doi:10.1016/j.nicl.2019.101813 PMID:31082774

Priya, A., Garg, S., & Tigga, N. P. (2020). Predicting anxiety, depression and stress in modern life using machine learning algorithms. *Procedia Computer Science*, *167*, 1258–1267. doi:10.1016/j.procs.2020.03.442

Pywell, J., Vijaykumar, S., Dodd, A., & Coventry, L. (2020). Barriers to older adults' uptake of mobile-based mental health interventions. *Digital Health*, *6*, 2055207620905422. doi:10.1177/2055207620905422 PMID:32110429

Rajawat, A. S., Rawat, R., Barhanpurkar, K., Shaw, R. N., & Ghosh, A. (2021). Depression detection for elderly people using AI robotic systems leveraging the Nelder-Mead Method. In *Artificial Intelligence for Future Generation Robotics* (pp. 55–70). Elsevier. doi:10.1016/B978-0-323-85498-6.00006-X

Ramos-Lima, L. F., Waikamp, V., Antonelli-Salgado, T., Passos, I. C., & Freitas, L. H. M. (2020). The use of machine learning techniques in trauma-related disorders: A systematic review. *Journal of Psychiatric Research*, *121*, 159–172. doi:10.1016/j.jpsychires.2019.12.001 PMID:31830722

Reynolds, C. F. III, Jeste, D. V., Sachdev, P. S., & Blazer, D. G. (2022). Mental health care for older adults: Recent advances and new directions in clinical practice and research. *World Psychiatry; Official Journal of the World Psychiatric Association (WPA)*, *21*(3), 336–363. doi:10.1002/wps.20996 PMID:36073714

Richter, T., Fishbain, B., Markus, A., Richter-Levin, G., & Okon-Singer, H. (2020). Using machine learning-based analysis for behavioral differentiation between anxiety and depression. *Scientific Reports*, *10*(1), 16381. doi:10.1038/s41598-020-72289-9 PMID:33009424

Robinson, S. (2022). 15 Promoting health in the National Health Service. *Principles and Practice of Health Promotion and Public Health*, *382*, 382–408. doi:10.4324/9780367823696-19

Roderburg, C., Yaqubi, K., Konrad, M., May, P., Luedde, T., Kostev, K., & Loosen, S. H. (2023). Association between inflammatory bowel disease and subsequent depression or anxiety disorders-A retrospective cohort study of 31,728 outpatients. *Journal of Psychiatric Research.* Advance online publication. doi:10.1016/j.jpsychires.2023.11.026 PMID:38048672

Roush, J. F., O'Brien, K. M., & Ruha, A. L. (2020). Evaluating a recovery-oriented intensive outpatient program for veterans at risk for suicide. *Crisis*. doi:10.1027/0227-5910/a000703 PMID:32781902

Seifert, A., Reinwand, D. A., & Schlomann, A. (2019). Designing and using digital mental health interventions for older adults: Being aware of digital inequality. *Frontiers in Psychiatry*, *10*, 568. doi:10.3389/fpsyt.2019.00568 PMID:31447716

Su, C., Xu, Z., Pathak, J., & Wang, F. (2020). Deep learning in mental health outcome research: A scoping review. *Translational Psychiatry*, *10*(1), 116. doi:10.1038/s41398-020-0780-3 PMID:32532967

Thieme, A., Belgrave, D., & Doherty, G. (2020). Machine learning in mental health: A systematic review of the HCI literature to support the development of effective and implementable ML systems. [TOCHI]. *ACM Transactions on Computer-Human Interaction*, *27*(5), 1–53. doi:10.1145/3398069

van Mens, K., de Schepper, C. W. M., Wijnen, B., Koldijk, S. J., Schnack, H., de Looff, P., Lokkerbol, J., Wetherall, K., Cleare, S., C O'Connor, R., & De Beurs, D. (2020). Predicting future suicidal behaviour in young adults, with different machine learning techniques: A population-based longitudinal study. *Journal of Affective Disorders*, *271*, 169–177. doi:10.1016/j.jad.2020.03.081 PMID:32479313

Wilson, J., Heinsch, M., Betts, D., Booth, D., & Kay-Lambkin, F. (2021). Barriers and facilitators to the use of e-health by older adults: A scoping review. *BMC Public Health*, *21*(1), 1–12. doi:10.1186/s12889-021-11623-w PMID:34399716

Wisniewski, H., & Torous, J. (2020). Digital navigators to implement smartphone and digital tools in care. *Acta Psychiatrica Scandinavica*, *141*(4), 350–355. doi:10.1111/acps.13149 PMID:31930477

Wu, Y., Levis, B., Sun, Y., He, C., Krishnan, A., Neupane, D., & Thombs, B. D. (2021). Accuracy of the Hospital Anxiety and Depression Scale Depression subscale (HADS-D) to screen for major depression: systematic review and individual participant data meta-analysis. *bmj*, *373*. doi:10.1136/bmj.n972

XieB.CharnessN.FingermanK.KayeJ.KimM. T.KhurshidA. (2021). When going digital becomes a necessity: Ensuring older adults' needs for information, services, and social inclusion during COVID-19. In *Older Adults and COVID-19* (pp. 181-191). Routledge. doi:10.2196/preprints.19117

Zenebe, Y., & Akele, B., W/Selassie, M., & Necho, M. (. (2021). Prevalence and determinants of depression among old age: A systematic review and meta-analysis. *Annals of General Psychiatry, 20*(1), 55. doi:10.1186/s12991-021-00375-x PMID:34922595

Zhang, Y., Wang, S., Hermann, A., Joly, R., & Pathak, J. (2021). Development and validation of a machine learning algorithm for predicting the risk of postpartum depression among pregnant women. *Journal of Affective Disorders, 279*, 1–8. doi:10.1016/j.jad.2020.09.113 PMID:33035748

ADDITIONAL READINGS

Komalasari, R. (2022). A Social Ecological Model (SEM) to Manage Methadone Programmes in Prisons. In Handbook of Research on Mathematical Modeling for Smart Healthcare Systems (pp. 374-382). IGI Global. doi:10.4018/978-1-6684-4580-8.ch020

Komalasari, R. (2023). The Relationship Between Cybersecurity and Public Health. In *Handbook of Research on Current Trends in Cybersecurity and Educational Technology* (pp. 78–91). IGI Global. doi:10.4018/978-1-6684-6092-4.ch005

Komalasari, R. (2023). Postnatal Mental Distress: Exploring the Experiences of Mothers Navigating the Healthcare System. In Perspectives and Considerations on Navigating the Mental Healthcare System (pp. 159-181). IGI Global. doi:10.4018/978-1-6684-5049-9.ch007

Komalasari, R. (2023). Designing Health Systems for Better, Faster, and Less Expensive Treatment. In *Exploring the Convergence of Computer and Medical Science Through Cloud Healthcare* (pp. 1–13). IGI Global. doi:10.4018/978-1-6684-5260-8.ch001

Komalasari, R. (2023). The Ethical Consideration of Using Artificial Intelligence (AI) in Medicine. In Advanced Bioinspiration Methods for Healthcare Standards, Policies, and Reform (pp. 1-16). IGI Global. doi:10.4018/978-1-6684-5656-9.ch001

Komalasari, R. (2023). Healthcare for the Elderly With Digital Twins. In Digital Twins and Healthcare: Trends, Techniques, and Challenges (pp. 145-156). IGI Global. doi:10.4018/978-1-6684-5925-6.ch010

Komalasari, R. (2023). Cloud Computing's Usage in Healthcare. In Recent Advancements in Smart Remote Patient Monitoring, Wearable Devices, and Diagnostics Systems (pp. 183-194). IGI Global. doi:10.4018/978-1-6684-6434-2.ch009

Komalasari, R. (2023). History and Legislative Changes Governing Medical Cannabis in Indonesia. In Medical Cannabis and the Effects of Cannabinoids on Fighting Cancer, Multiple Sclerosis, Epilepsy, Parkinson's, and Other Neurodegenerative Diseases (pp. 274-284). IGI Global. doi:10.4018/978-1-6684-5652-1.ch012

Komalasari, R. (2023). Ambient Assisted Living (AAL) Systems to Help Older People. In Exploring Future Opportunities of Brain-Inspired Artificial Intelligence (pp. 84-99). IGI Global. doi:10.4018/978-1-6684-6980-4.ch006

Komalasari, R. (2023). Telemedicine in Pandemic Times in Indonesia: Healthcare Professional's Perspective. In Health Informatics and Patient Safety in Times of Crisis (pp. 138-153). IGI Global. doi:10.4018/978-1-6684-5499-2.ch008

Komalasari, R. (2023). Cloud Computing's Usage in Healthcare. In Recent Advancements in Smart Remote Patient Monitoring, Wearable Devices, and Diagnostics Systems (pp. 183-194). IGI Global. doi:10.4018/978-1-6684-6434-2.ch009

Komalasari, R. (2023). The Relationship Between Cybersecurity and Public Health. In *Handbook of Research on Current Trends in Cybersecurity and Educational Technology* (pp. 78–91). IGI Global. doi:10.4018/978-1-6684-6092-4.ch005

Komalasari, R. (2023). Treatment of Menstrual Discomfort in Young Women and a Cognitive Behavior Therapy (CBT) Program. In Perspectives on Coping Strategies for Menstrual and Premenstrual Distress (pp. 194-211). IGI Global. doi:10.4018/978-1-6684-5088-8.ch011

Komalasari, R. (2023). Healthcare for the Elderly With Digital Twins. In Digital Twins and Healthcare: Trends, Techniques, and Challenges (pp. 145-156). IGI Global. doi:10.4018/978-1-6684-5925-6.ch010

Komalasari, R. (2023). Telemedicine in Pandemic Times in Indonesia: Healthcare Professional's Perspective. In Health Informatics and Patient Safety in Times of Crisis (pp. 138-153). IGI Global. doi:10.4018/978-1-6684-5499-2.ch008

Komalasari, R. (2023). Regulatory Shift Healthcare Applications in Industry 5.0. In Advanced Research and Real-World Applications of Industry 5.0 (pp. 149-165). IGI Global. doi:10.4018/978-1-7998-8805-5.ch008

Komalasari, R. (2023). Exploring Pedagogies Of Affect In Secondary School Physical Education For Enhanced Emotional Well-Being. *Pedagogik: Jurnal Pendidikan Guru Sekolah Dasar, 11*(2), 117–127. doi:10.33558/pedagogik.v11i2.7374

Komalasari, R. (2023). Integrating sport education model and the athletics challenges approach for transformative physical education in Indonesian Middle Schools. *Motion: Jurnal Riset Physical Education, 13*(2), 118–135. doi:10.33558/motion.v13i2.7372

Komalasari, R. (2023). Efek Ganja Medis pada Pasien Parkinson: A Literature Review of Clinical Evidence. *Journal of Islamic Pharmacy, 8*(1), 44–48. doi:10.18860/jip.v8i1.17832

Komalasari, R. (2023). Rancangan Program Bagi Keberhasilan Gerakan Mencuci Tangan Yang Sehat Bagi Para Ibu Dan Anak. *Sulolipu: Media Komunikasi Sivitas Akademika dan Masyarakat, 23*(1), 55-60. doi:10.32382/sulolipu.v23i1.3103

Komalasari, R. (2024). Unravelling the Veil: Exploring the Nexus of Insecure Attachment and Functional Somatic Disorders in Adults. In *Discourses, Inquiries, and Case Studies in Healthcare, Social Sciences, and Technology*. IGI Global.

Komalasari, R. (2024). Advancing Healthcare: Economic Implications of Immediate MRI in Suspected Scaphoid Fractures - A Comprehensive Exploration. In *Future of AI in Medical Imaging*. IGI Global.

Komalasari, R. (2024). Women's perceptions of midlife mothering during perimenopause: the impact on health and well-being through life's transitions. In *Utilizing AI Techniques for the Perimenopause to Menopause Transition*. IGI Global.

Komalasari, R. (2024). Machine Learning in Health Information Security: Unraveling Patterns, Concealing Secrets, and Mitigating Vulnerabilities. In *Enhancing Steganography Through Deep Learning Approaches*. IGI Global.

Komalasari, R. (2024). Navigating Complexity: Unraveling the IVHM Requirements Puzzle in Unmanned Aerial Systems Through Innovative IVHM-RD Methodology and Rigorous Data Analysis. In *Ubiquitous Computing and Technological Innovation for Universal Healthcare*. IGI Global.

Komalasari, R. (2024). Trust Dynamics in Remote Patient-Expert Communication: Unraveling the Role of ICT in Indonesia's Private Healthcare Sector. In *Improving Security, Privacy, and Connectivity Among Telemedicine Platforms*. IGI Global.

Komalasari, R. (2024). Cyberbullying in the Health Care Workplace: How to Find Your Way Through the Digital Maze. In *Workplace Cyberbullying and Behavior in Health Professions*. IGI Global. doi:10.4018/979-8-3693-1139-4.ch004

Komalasari, R. (2024). Harmonizing Minds and Machines: A Transformative AI-Based Mental Health Care Framework in Medical Tourism. In *Impact of AI and Robotics on the Medical Tourism Industry*. IGI Global.

Komalasari, R. (2024). Navigating the Future of Healthcare: A User-Centric Approach to Designing Lucrative Business Models for the IoMT. In *Lightweight Digital Trust Architectures in the Internet of Medical Things (IoMT)*. IGI Global.

Komalasari, R. (2024). Biospheric Reverie: Unraveling Indoor Air Quality through Bio-Inspired Textiles, Awareness, and Decision-Making. In *Intelligent Decision Making Through Bio-Inspired Optimization*. IGI Global.

Komalasari, R. (2024). An Integrated Approach to Next-Generation Telemedicine and Health Advice Systems through AI Applications in Disease Diagnosis. In *AI-Driven Innovations in Digital Healthcare: Emerging Trends, Challenges, and Applications*. IGI Global.

Komalasari, R. (2024). Transformative Insights: Harnessing Artificial Intelligence for Enhanced Ovarian Cancer Prediction and Prognosis. In *Biomedical Research Developments for Improved Healthcare*. IGI Global.

Komalasari, R. (2024). Bridging the Gap: Theory of Change Guided Digital Health Implementation in Indonesian Primary Care. In *Analyzing Current Digital Healthcare Trends Using Social Networks*. IGI Global.

Komalasari, R. (2024). Navigating the Digital Frontier: A Socio-Technical Review of Indonesia's NHS E-Health Strategy and the Path to Seamless Healthcare Transformation. In *Inclusivity and Accessibility in Digital Health*. IGI Global.

Komalasari, R. (2024). *Pursuit of Excellence: A Comprehensive Framework for Ensuring Quality in Digital Health Apps. In Multi-Sector Analysis of the Digital Healthcare Industry*. IGI Global.

Komalasari, R. (2024). Fostering Transparency in AI for Disease Detection: Exploring Meaningful Explanations and Interactive Modalities in Healthcare. In *Federated Learning and Privacy-Preserving in Healthcare AI*. IGI Global.

Komalasari, R. (2024). Predictive Pioneers: Bridging the Mental Health Gap in Older Adults through Advanced Digital Technologies. In *Using Machine Learning to Detect Emotions and Predict Human Psychology*. IGI Global.

Komalasari, R. (2024). Unravelling the Veil: Exploring the Nexus of Insecure Attachment and Functional Somatic Disorders in Adults. In *Discourses, Inquiries, and Case Studies in Healthcare, Social Sciences, and Technology*. IGI Global.

Komalasari, R. (2024). Cyberbullying in the Health Care Workplace: How to Find Your Way Through the Digital Maze. In *Workplace Cyberbullying and Behavior in Health Professions*. IGI Global. doi:10.4018/979-8-3693-1139-4.ch004

Komalasari, R. (2024). Navigating Mental Health Crises: Understanding Pivotal Phases, Health Campaigns, and Community Resilience for Recovery and Reform. In *The Role of Health Literacy in Major Healthcare Crises*. IGI Global.

Komalasari, R. (2024). Decoding the Genomic and Proteomic Landscape: Dissemination and Mechanisms of Antibiotic Resistance in Environmental Staphylococci. In *Contemporary Approaches to Mitigating Antibacterial Drug Resistance*. IGI Global.

Komalasari, R. (2024). Unveiling the Future: Blockchain-Powered Digital Twins for Personalized Privacy Preservation in Metaverse Healthcare Data Management. In *Examining the Metaverse in Healthcare: Opportunities, Challenges, and Future Directions*. IGI Global. doi:10.4018/979-8-3693-1906-2.ch017

Komalasari, R. (2024). Safeguarding the Future: Cutting-Edge Time-Stamping Services and Blockchain Technologies for Maintaining EHR Data Integrity Over the Long Term. In *Blockchain and IoT Approaches for Secure Electronic Health Records (EHR)*. IGI Global.

Komalasari, R. (2024). Empowering Informed Healthcare Choices in Rural Areas: SIKDA - A Novel Model for Enhancing Patient Access to Reliable Consumer Health Information in Indonesia. In *Emerging Technologies for Health Literacy and Medical Practice*. IGI Global.

Komalasari, R. (2024). Advancing Trauma Care: Contemporary Cranio-Maxillo-Facial Surgery in Indonesia and Beyond. In *Contemporary Cranio-Maxillo-Facial Surgery: From Trauma to Reconstruction*. IGI Global.

Komalasari, R. (2024). Innovations in Neurodegenerative Disease Diagnosis: Unraveling the Transformative Potential of Deep Learning and MRI Integration. In *Deep Learning Approaches for Early Diagnosis of Neurodegenerative Diseases*. IGI Global.

Komalasari, R. (2024). Secure and privacy-preserving federated learning with explainable artificial intelligence for smart healthcare systems. In *Federated Learning and AI for Healthcare 5.0*. IGI Global.

Komalasari, R. (2024) Optimizing Prostate Cancer Radiotherapy: Advanced Machine Learning in Virtual Patient-Specific Plan Verification. *Indonesian Journal of Cancer.*

Komalasari, R. (2024). Bridging Uncertainties: Exploring the Lived Experiences of Pediatric Long-COVID-19 Through ME/CFS Caregiver Narratives. In G. Rao & S. Dhamdhere-Rao (Eds.), *Clinical Practice and Post-Infection Care for COVID-19 Patients* (pp. 207–227). IGI Global. doi:10.4018/978-1-6684-6855-5.ch009

Komalasari, R., & Mustafa, C. (2023). Combating International Cyber Conflict: A Healthy Just War and International Law Analysis of NATO and Indonesian Policies. Jurnal Pertahanan: Media Informasi tentang Kajian & Strategi Pertahanan yang Mengedepankan Identity. *Nasionalism & Integrity*, *9*(3), 559–570. doi:10.33172/jp.v9i2.16794

Komalasari, R., & Mustafa, C. (2023). Analysis Of The Propulsion And Maneuvering Characteristics Of Autonomous Underwater Vehicles And Their Strategic Defense. *Propeller Jurnal Permesinan, 1*(2).

Komalasari, R., & Mustafa, C. (2023). Amphibious Forces in the Total War Age: Exploring Indonesia's Multifaceted Contributions to Statecraft in the Asia-Pacific Region. *Jurnal Strategi Pertahanan Laut*, *9*(2), 62–77. doi:10.33172/spl.v9i2.12606

Komalasari, R., & Mustafa, C. (2023). The Evolution and Institutionalization of the Naval Partnership between Indonesia and ASEAN. *Jurnal Strategi Pertahanan Laut*, *9*(2), 1–18. doi:10.33172/spl.v9i2.12576

Komalasari, R., & Mustafa, C. (2023). A Healthy Game-Theoretic Evaluation of NATO and Indonesia's Policies in the Context of International Law. *Jurnal Pertahanan: Media Informasi tentang Kajian & Strategi Pertahanan yang Mengedepankan Identity. Nasionalism & Integrity*, *9*(2), 333–349. doi:10.33172/jp.v9i2.16794

Komalasari, R., Nurhayati, N., & Mustafa, C. (2022). Enhancing the Online Learning Environment for Medical Education: Lessons From COVID-19. In Policies and procedures for the implementation of safe and healthy educational environments: Post-COVID-19 perspectives (pp. 138-154). IGI Global. doi:10.4018/978-1-7998-9297-7.ch009

Komalasari, R., Nurhayati, N., & Mustafa, C. (2022). Insider/outsider issues: Reflections on qualitative research. *The Qualitative Report*, *27*(3), 744–751. doi:10.46743/2160-3715/2022.5259

Komalasari, R., Nurhayati, N., & Mustafa, C. (2022). Professional Education and Training in Indonesia. In *Public Affairs Education and Training in the 21st Century* (pp. 125–138). IGI Global. doi:10.4018/978-1-7998-8243-5.ch008

Komalasari, R., Nurhayati, N., & Mustafa, C. (2022). Professional Education and Training in Indonesia. In *Public Affairs Education and Training in the 21st Century* (pp. 125–138). IGI Global. doi:10.4018/978-1-7998-8243-5.ch008

Komalasari, R., Wilson, S., & Haw, S. (2021). A systematic review of qualitative evidence on barriers to and facilitators of the implementation of opioid agonist treatment (OAT) programmes in prisons. *The International Journal on Drug Policy*, *87*, 102978. doi:10.1016/j.drugpo.2020.102978 PMID:33129135

Komalasari, R., Wilson, S., & Haw, S. (2021). A social ecological model (SEM) to exploring barriers of and facilitators to the implementation of opioid agonist treatment (OAT) programmes in prisons. *International Journal of Prisoner Health*, *17*(4), 477–496. doi:10.1108/IJPH-04-2020-0020

Komalasari, R., Wilson, S., Nasir, S., & Haw, S. (2020). Multiple burdens of stigma for prisoners participating in Opioid Antagonist Treatment (OAT) programmes in Indonesian prisons: A qualitative study. *International Journal of Prisoner Health*, *17*(2), 156–170. doi:10.1108/IJPH-03-2020-0018

Mustafa, C. (2020). The influence of sunni islamic values on rehabilitation as judicial decision for minor drug users in Indonesian court. *Ijtihad: Jurnal Wacana Hukum Islam dan Kemanusiaan*, *20*(1), 79-96. doi:10.18326/ijtihad.v20i1.79-96

Mustafa, C. (2021). Qualitative Method Used in Researching the Judiciary: Quality Assurance Steps to Enhance the Validity and Reliability of the Findings. *The Qualitative Report*, *26*(1), 176–185. doi:10.46743/2160-3715/2021.4319

Mustafa, C. (2021). Key Finding: Result of a Qualitative Study of Judicial Perspectives on the Sentencing of Minor Drug Offenders in Indonesia: Structural Inequality. *The Qualitative Report*, *26*(5), 1678–1692. doi:10.46743/2160-3715/2021.4436

Mustafa, C. (2021). The view of judicial activism and public legitimacy. *Crime, Law, and Social Change*, *76*(1), 23–34. doi:10.1007/s10611-021-09955-0

Mustafa, C. (2021). The News Media Representation of Acts of Mass Violence in Indonesia. In *Mitigating Mass Violence and Managing Threats in Contemporary Society* (pp. 127–140). IGI Global., doi:10.4018/978-1-7998-4957-5.ch008

Mustafa, C. (2021). The Challenges to Improving Public Services and Judicial Operations: A unique balance between pursuing justice and public service in Indonesia. In Handbook of research on global challenges for improving public services and government operations (pp. 117-132). IGI Global. doi:10.4018/978-1-7998-4978-0.ch007

Mustafa, C., Malloch, M., & Hamilton Smith, N. (2020). Judicial perspectives on the sentencing of minor drug offenders in Indonesia: Discretionary practice and compassionate approaches. *Crime, Law, and Social Change*, *74*(3), 297–313. doi:10.1007/s10611-020-09896-0

Suhariyanto, B. (2023). Contradiction Over The Application Of Corporate Liability In Corruption Court Decisions In Indonesia. *Indonesia Law Review*, *13*(1), 8.

Suhariyanto, B., Mustafa, C., & Santoso, T. (2021). Liability incorporate between transnational corruption cases Indonesia and the United States of America. *J. Legal Ethical & Regul. Isses*, *24*, 1.

KEY TERMS AND DEFINITIONS

Ageing: Physical, mental, and social changes are expected outcomes of ageing, defined as the standard and progressive process of becoming older. It includes changes in a person's physical, mental, and social selves accompanying ageing.

Anxiety: A continuous and uncontrolled fear of the unknown is the physical and mental manifestation of anxiety. As a typical emotional response to stress, it may range from mild to severe and significantly impact people's day-to-day functioning.

Depression: Symptoms of depression include a lack of interest in once enjoyable activities, a pervasive feeling of hopelessness, and an inability to improve one's spirits. It could significantly affect a person's emotional, mental, and physical well-being, making it hard for them to carry out their daily activities.

Digital technology: refers to the systems, networks, and applications that process and transmit information using binary code. It consists of the internet, smartphones, and computers, all of which collaborate to facilitate data storage and communication, among other things.

Machine learning: Artificial intelligence, known as machine learning, focuses on teaching computers new skills by exposing them to data and analyzing it statistically. The main goal is to build systems that can improve with time and do not need to be programmed to do anything.

Chapter 6
Designing LSTM Networks for Emotion Modelling

Kiran Sree Pokkuluri
https://orcid.org/0000-0001-8601-4304
Shri Vishnu Engineering College for Women, India

S. S. S. N. Usha Devi N.
https://orcid.org/0000-0002-2292-7494
UCEK-JNTUK, India

Alex Khang
GRITEx SCEDEX, AIoCF, USA

ABSTRACT

This chapter presents a simple and effective approach to designing LSTM networks for the task of emotion recognition. Emotion modelling plays a crucial role in various applications, such as human-computer interaction, sentiment analysis, and affective computing. The proposed LSTM architecture incorporates sequential information inherent in emotional expressions, allowing the model to capture temporal dependencies and nuances in emotional states. The input data, typically in the form of time-series sequences, is pre-processed to extract relevant features and fed into the LSTM network. The model is trained on labelled emotion datasets, enabling it to learn patterns and relationships between input features and corresponding emotional states. To enhance the network's performance, hyper parameter tuning, and regularization techniques are employed. The model's effectiveness is evaluated on benchmark emotion datasets, demonstrating its capability to accurately predict and classify various emotional states.

DOI: 10.4018/979-8-3693-1910-9.ch006

1.INTRODUCTION

The study of human emotions has gained considerable focus in the domains of machine learning and artificial intelligence. The capacity to recognise and analyse human emotional states known as emotion modelling has profound effects on a variety of fields, including affective computing, sentiment analysis, and human-computer interaction. Using deep learning methods, especially LSTM (Zhang et al., 2020) networks, to capture the dynamic and temporal aspect of emotional expressions is one well-known strategy in this field. Emotions have a complex and multifaceted pattern that changes over time and are essential to human behaviour and communication (Jiang, Jiao, Wang, Zhang, & Wu, 2021). The temporal connections and delicate transitions seen in emotional states are frequently too nuanced for traditional emotion modelling techniques to accurately represent. The capacity of deep learning to handle sequential data efficiently offers an alluring path towards enhancing the precision and level of detail in emotion modelling (Ma et al., 2019).

The construction and use of LSTM networks for emotion modelling are explored in this research. Recurrent neural networks (RNNs) (Du et al., 2020) of the long-term dependency (LSTM) type were developed especially to tackle the problem of encoding long-term dependencies in sequential input. They can selectively store and recover information over long periods of time thanks to the memory cells and gates included in its architecture. Our goal is to better comprehend human affect by disentangling the intricacies of emotional expressions through the integration of LSTMs into emotion modelling (Zhao et al., 2019).

Developing artificial intelligence systems that are more sensitive and empathic requires an understanding of and modelling of emotions. The user experience in human-computer interaction can be greatly improved by computers' capacity to identify and respond to users' emotional states (Yin et al., 2021). A type of emotion modelling called sentiment analysis is essential for analysing social media sentiment, product evaluations, and public opinion. The foundation of affective computing, an interdisciplinary field that involves creating computers that can perceive, understand, and react to human emotions, is emotion modelling. Conventional methods for modelling emotions, which depend on manually created features and rule-based frameworks, are inadequate for expressing the complexity and nuance of human emotions. With its data-driven methodology, deep learning presents a viable answer by enabling models to automatically derive hierarchical representations from unprocessed data. As an RNN variation, LSTMs are especially well-suited for jobs that need sequential data, which makes them a prime choice for emotion modelling (Pokkuluri & Usha Devi Nedunuri, 2020).

The temporal dynamics of emotional manifestations is one of the main challenges in emotion modelling. Emotions are dynamic; they change throughout time and are frequently impacted by internal or external factors. These temporal connections are difficult for traditional machine learning models to grasp, which results in a loss of important details and subtlety in the depiction of emotions (Xie et al., 2019). LSTMs are a good option for situations where the evolution of emotions is a crucial component because they are specifically developed to solve this problem and perform exceptionally well in modelling long-range dependencies.

The vanishing gradient issue that conventional RNNs encountered was particularly addressed by Hochreiter and Schmidhuber when they introduced LSTMs in 1997 (Pokkuluri & Nedunuri, 2022). The vanishing gradient issue makes it more difficult for the network to learn and spread knowledge across lengthy sequences. By adding memory cells and gating mechanisms, which let them to selectively store and discard information, LSTMs help to reduce this problem. Because of this architecture, LSTMs (Yu & Kim, 2020) can capture dependencies over long periods of time, which makes them ideal for jobs that need sequential pattern modelling, like language modelling, emotion modelling, and speech recognition. There are numerous important steps in the creation of an LSTM network for emotion modelling. The input data, often in the form of time-series sequences depicting emotional expressions, undergoes preprocessing to extract significant features. The LSTM network, which has been trained on labelled emotion datasets, is then fed these features. In order to accurately capture the complex link between features and emotions, the network must learn to associate patterns in the input data with corresponding emotional states during training.

Tuning the hyperparameters of the LSTM network becomes essential to improving its performance (Pokkuluri & Usha, 2021). The number of LSTM units, dropout rates, and learning rate are some of the parameters that greatly influence the model's learning capacity. Regularisation strategies like dropout are used to improve the model's generalisation on unknown inputs and avoid overfitting. For emotion modelling, the suggested LSTM architecture strikes a compromise between practicality and efficacy (Vijayvergia & Kumar, 2021). Its capacity to function successfully even with constrained processing resources emphasises its applicability for real-world scenarios. Because of this, it is a desirable option in situations when implementing sophisticated models is not feasible. Through testing on benchmark emotion datasets, the resilience of the constructed LSTM network is assessed. The model's practical deployment across multiple domains is demonstrated by its capacity to reliably anticipate and classify distinct emotional states, as demonstrated by the results (Babu et al., 2023). In addition to making implementation easier, the architecture's simplicity offers insights into the model's interpretability, which is vital in real-world applications where transparency is essential.

The paper is structured as follows: Section 1 introduces and discusses the significance of emotional modelling using LSTM; Section 2 shows the comprehensive literature survey with conclusions at the end of the section; Section 3 provides the general methods and architecture design of the proposed architecture; Section 4 presents the experimental results and compares them to the current baseline methods; the paper concludes with a conclusion and future extension.

2. LITERATURE SURVEY

Recently, there has been a growing interest in computational modelling and understanding of human emotions due to the goal of creating artificial intelligence systems that are more sympathetic. The use of (Senthilkumar et al., 2022) networks has become one of the most effective methods for capturing the subtleties and temporal dynamics of emotional expressions. This review of the literature examines significant discoveries, approaches, and developments in the field of emotion modeling-related LSTM network design, providing insight into the field's development and suggesting directions for future research.

A breakthrough in the capture of sequential dependencies was brought about by the introduction of deep learning, specifically RNNs. RNNs showed potential in language modelling and speech recognition applications using time-series data. But obstacles like the vanishing gradient problem made it difficult for them to accurately capture long-term connections. The shortcomings of conventional RNNs were solved by Hochreiter and Schmidhuber's 1997 invention of LSTMs (Sakalle et al., 2021). With their gating mechanisms and memory cells, LSTMs have shown themselves to be effective in capturing long-range dependencies in sequential data. Because of this architectural advancement, temporal dynamics may be modelled more effectively, which is why LSTMs are a good choice for modelling emotions.

Random Forest (RF) and Decision Tree (DT) are popular machine learning algorithms employed for emotion modeling. In emotion recognition tasks, the input features are typically textual or audio data, and the goal is to predict the emotional state associated with that input. In emotion modeling, both RF (Noroozi et al., 2017) and DT (Sun et al., 2019) can capture complex relationships between input features and emotions. While Decision Trees may be prone to overfitting, Random Forest's ensemble approach enhances generalization and robustness. Choosing between them depends on the dataset size, complexity, and the balance between interpretability and predictive performance in the context of emotion modeling tasks.

Promising outcomes in improving human-computer interaction have been observed when using LSTM networks for emotion modelling. Interfaces that are more engaging and responsive can be produced by systems that are capable of adjusting their replies according to the emotional states of their users. LSTM

(Geng, 2023) networks are particularly good at collecting subtle sentiments from text data in sentiment analysis, a subset of emotion modelling. Sentiment predictions in dynamic environments can be made more accurately by capturing temporal dependencies and contextual data. LSTM-based emotion models (Liu et al., 2023) have played a major role in the field of affective computing (Deng et al., 2021), which aims to develop systems with emotional intelligence. Applications that are personalised and emotionally intelligent can now be developed thanks to these systems' real-time ability to detect and react to user emotions. Labelled emotional expressions from benchmark datasets are employed frequently in the assessment of LSTM networks for emotion modelling. Popular datasets for rigorous model assessment are AffectNet, CK+, and EmoReact, which offer a wide variety of emotional settings.

Like other deep learning models, LSTM networks are effective, but they are not always interpretable. It is important to comprehend how these models get at particular predictions, particularly in applications where openness is critical. Potential avenues for future research could include improving the LSTM-based emotion models' (Pokkuluri et al., 2022) interpretability. There are other ways to convey emotions, such as through voice, body language, and facial expressions. Adding data from several modalities to LSTM networks may result in emotion models that are more precise and thorough. Future investigation into multimodal emotion modelling research is an attractive prospect.Long short-term memory networks (LSTM networks) have shown promise in offline operations, but real-time applications continue to be a barrier for them. Improving LSTM-based emotion models' effectiveness and speed can increase their usefulness, particularly in interactive.

The literature on LSTM network architecture for emotion modelling shows how rule-based systems of the past were gradually replaced by deep learning systems of the present. Since LSTMs can capture temporal dynamics (Kumbhar & Bhandari, 2019), they have emerged as a key component in the creation of increasingly complex and precise emotion models. The relevance of this research field is highlighted by its useful applications in sentiment analysis, emotional computing, and human-computer interaction (Raju et al., 2023). LSTM-based emotion modelling will continue to evolve as long as issues like interpretability are resolved, multimodal techniques are investigated, and real-time capabilities are enhanced. The potential for deep learning and human emotion comprehension to work together is enormous, pointing to a time when AI systems will be able to not only identify but also fully understand and react to the whole range of human emotions (Jiang, Jiao, Wang, Zhang, & Wu, 2021).

3. DESIGN OF LSTM NETWORKS FOR EMOTION MODELLING

The architecture of LSTM networks for emotion modelling involves a hierarchical structure of interconnected layers designed to capture and process sequential information effectively. The key components of the architecture are shown in figure 1.

3.1 Input Layer and Embedding Layer

The input layer receives sequential data representing emotional expressions, such as time-series features extracted from facial expressions, physiological signals, or text.Each element of the sequence is treated as a time step, and the input layer processes the information accordingly. In the case of textual input, an embedding layer may be employed to convert discrete words or tokens into continuous vector representations. This layer helps in capturing semantic relationships and improving the model's ability to understand contextual information.

3.2 LSTM Layers

Stacked LSTM layers form the core of the architecture. Each LSTM layer contains memory cells, gates, and hidden states that enable the network to capture short-term and long-term dependencies in sequential data.The memory cells store and retrieve information over time, allowing the model to learn patterns and context in emotional expressions.The gates, including the input, output, and forget gates, regulate the flow of information within the network, controlling what information is stored or discarded.

The International Survey on Emotion Antecedents and Reactions (ISEAR) dataset is a collection of texts describing emotional experiences. This dataset is used in the field of natural language processing and sentiment analysis for critical emotion classification tasks. It consists of sentences or short paragraphs, each labeled with the corresponding emotion expressed in the text.The ISEAR dataset typically includes the following emotions Angry, Relief, Bored, Happy, Hate, Fun, Love, Surprise, Enthusiasm and the distribution is shown in table 1.

Table 1. Data distribution

Classes	Angry	Relief	Bored	Happy	Hate	Fun	Love	Surprise	Enthusiasm
Size	78953	25982	32589	21555	258974	369845	98235	5698	26998

3.3 Dropout Layer and Dense (Fully Connected) Output Layer

To prevent overfitting and enhance generalization, a dropout layer may be added between LSTM layers. Dropout randomly deactivates a fraction of the neurons during training, encouraging the network to learn more robust and generalized representations. The output layer receives the final representation from the LSTM layers and produces predictions for emotional states.Activation functions such as softmax are commonly used to convert the network's output into probability distributions over different emotion classes.

3.4 Loss Function and Optimizer and Hyper Parameters

The choice of an appropriate loss function, such as categorical cross-entropy for multi-class classification tasks, guides the network during training by quantifying the difference between predicted and actual emotional labels.An optimizer, like Adam or RMSprop, is employed to minimize the loss function during training. It adjusts the weights of the network based on gradients calculated through backpropagation. Critical hyper parameters include the learning rate, batch size, and the number of LSTM units and layers. These parameters are fine-tuned to optimize the network's performance.

Figure 1. Data distribution

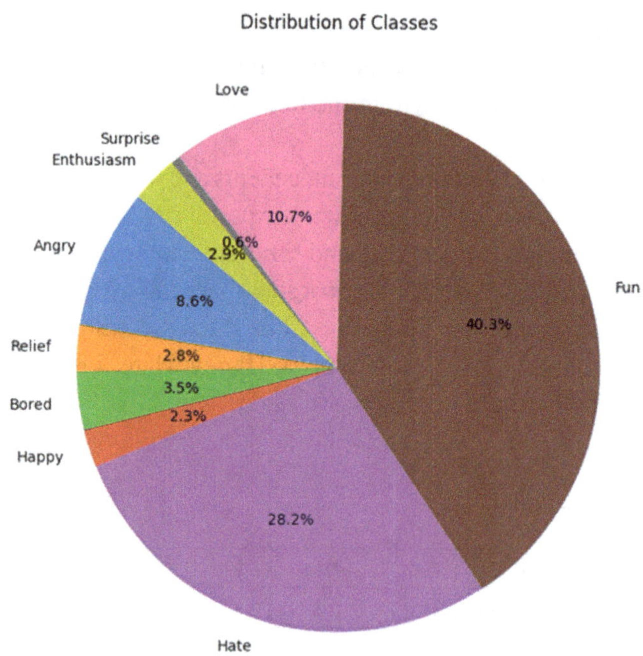

Figure 2. Design of LSTM for emotion detection

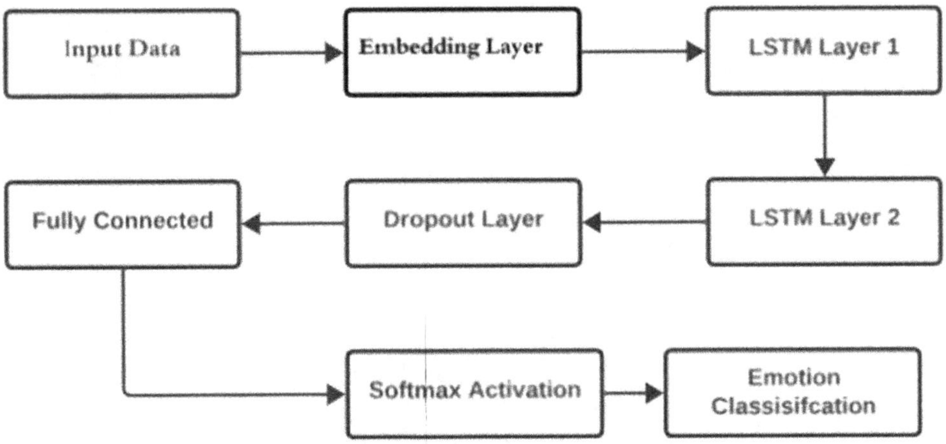

4. EXPERIMENTAL RESULTS AND COMPARISON

We have collected a ISEAR -The International Survey on Emotion Antecedents and Reactions dataset for this experimentation as discussed in the section 3. We have used 75% datasets for training and 25% for testing. The major technique used in this paper to avoid overfitting during training is dropout technology. Every LSTM layer employs dropout. In each training batch, it ignores half of the features in order to primarily detect the units. A specific percentage of neurons' activation value ceases functioning when the feature detection unit's contact decreases. This allows the model to be generalised and independent of certain local factors. The parameters in the ILSTM that must be established batch size (Batchsize), iteration duration (Iterations), training termination condition (Patience), and cross-validation times (Kfold) are among the model parameters in this work. The model performance that is obtained exhibits significant variation based on the parameter values. %e accuracy rate is the evaluation index utilised in this paper to identify the parameters of the best model. The accuracy rate is calculated by dividing the total number of samples by the sum of the positive sentiment data that was recognised as positive and the negative sentiment data that was identified as negative. As our most generally used indicator, the accuracy rate cannot accurately reflect the classification capabilities of the model when the sample is unbalanced. In the test dataset, for instance, there are 10% of negative samples and 90% of positive samples. The accuracy rate is over 90% if all of the model's classification results are positive samples. The higher outcomes of LSTM can be attributed to its capacity to grasp sequential relationships in emotional expressions, as demonstrated in Figure 3. Because of its superior ability

Figure 3. Confusion matrix for RF, DT, and LSTM

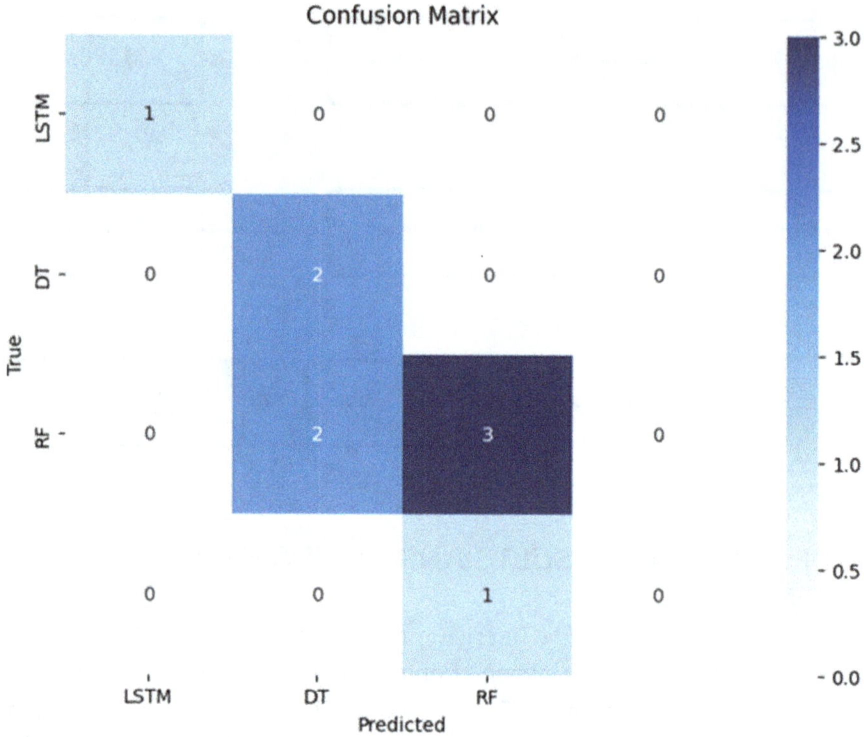

to comprehend subtle patterns and context within a sequence, LSTM is a good choice for jobs involving temporal dependencies, including text or speech-based emotion recognition. When compared to more conventional ensemble techniques like Random Forest (RF) and Decision Tree (DT) in this particular situation, LSTM performs better overall and is able to distinguish small emotional nuances more accurately.

Common metrics used in binary and multiclass classification tasks are recall (sensitivity) and F1 score. This is a quick mathematical breakdown of these measurements.

1. Sensitivity to Recall: A model's recall quantifies its capacity to identify every pertinent case. It is computed as the ratio of true positives, or positive cases that the model correctly predicted, to the total of false negatives, or positive instances that the model missed.

Recall: Genuine AdvantagesPositive Aspects Plus False NegativesTrue Positives + False Negatives = RecallReal Advantages

2. F1 Score: The harmonic mean of recall and precision is the F1 Score. It offers a harmony between recall and precision. Precision—the ratio of true positives to the total of true positives and false positives—and recall are used to compute it.

F1 Score=2 Accuracy + RecallAccuracy plus RecallF1 Score = 2×Recall + PrecisionAccurate Memory

The calculation of precision is as

Precision is computed as follows: precision is the ratio of true positives to the total of false positives and true positives.

Accuracy = Real GainsPositives Both Real and FalseTrue Positives plus False Positives equals precision.Real Gains

In Figure 4, LSTM performs better in terms of F1 Score and Recall than Random Forest (RF) and Decision Tree (DT). Because LSTM is recurrent, it can record complex temporal connections that are essential to comprehending emotional context. It is quite good at picking up on subtle patterns, which results in greater Recall (reducing false negatives) and an excellent F1 Score that strikes a balance between recall and precision. Although DT and RF offer strong ensemble techniques, LSTM has an advantage because it can extract sequential information from emotional expressions. This ensures a more complete representation of emotions and improves performance metrics, especially when temporal context is critical for accurate classification.

Figure 4. Recall and F1 score comparison for RF, DT, and LSTM

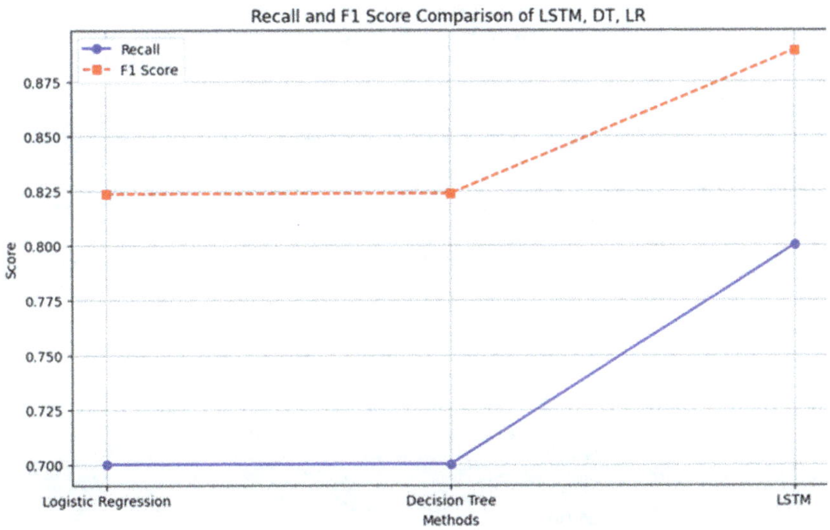

In Figure 5,6 LSTM exhibits superior accuracy and precision compared to Random Forest (RF) and Decision Tree (DT). LSTM's recurrent architecture excels in capturing nuanced temporal patterns inherent in emotional sequences. This leads to higher accuracy by minimizing misclassifications and higher precision by reducing

Figure 5. Accuracy and precision comparison for RF, DT, and LSTM

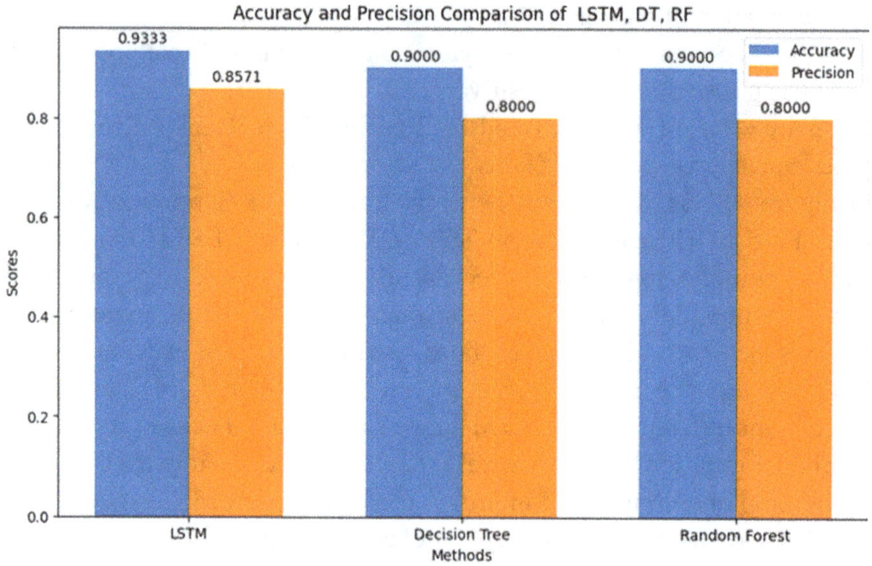

Figure 6. Scatter plot RF, DT, and LSTM

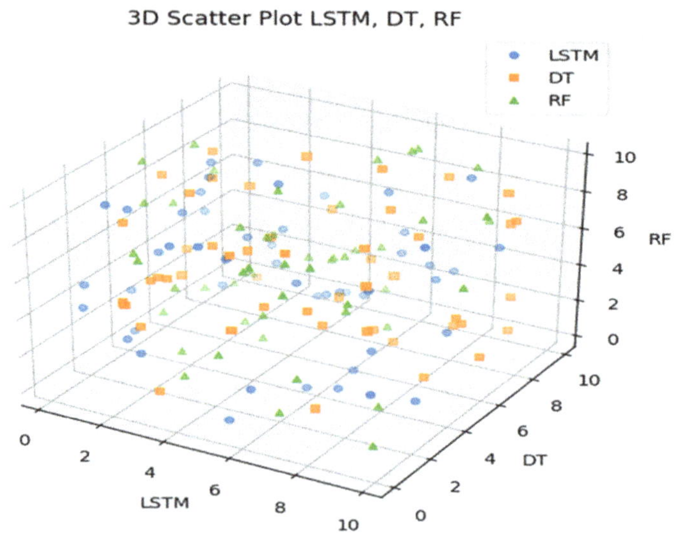

false positives. While RF and DT offer robust ensemble methods, LSTM's strength lies in understanding intricate temporal dependencies, allowing it to better discern emotional nuances. As a result, LSTM tends to achieve a more accurate and precise representation of emotions, making it particularly effective in scenarios where temporal context plays a crucial role in classification accuracy.

The LSTM hyperparameters show a batch size of 32, a learning rate of 0.9, and 16 LSTM units. These results point to a strong configuration that may effectively capture complex temporal patterns in emotional data. A greater learning rate speeds convergence, while a modest number of LSTM units balances model complexity. The model is more sensitive to temporal subtleties because of the smaller batch size. By contrast, the Random Forest (RF) and Decision Tree (DT) hyperparameters show bigger tree-related parameters and lower learning rates. This suggests that for emotion recognition tasks, the LSTM design performs better because it is more adapted to capture subtle temporal connections as shown in table 2. Execution time for LSTM can be influenced by the number of layers, the number of units in each layer, and the sequence length of input data, the average execution line is 0.6ms. RF is an ensemble method consisting of multiple decision trees. The parallel training of individual trees makes RF suitable for parallel computing, resulting in faster training times, the average execution time is 0.55 ms. Decision Trees are relatively fast to train since they involve recursive binary splitting of the data based on feature thresholds, the average execution time is 0.65ms

Table 2. Hypermeters comparison with baseline methods

Hyper Parameters Methods	Learning Rate	Batch Size	Number of LSTM Units
LSTM	0.9	16	32
RF	0.001	32	64
DT	0.01	64	128

5. CONCLUSION

Our work shows that LSTM networks are a useful tool for modelling emotions. The results demonstrate the capacity of LSTM to capture subtle temporal patterns in emotional expressions. This configuration with a learning rate of 0.9, 16 LSTM units, and a batch size of 32 produces these kinds of results. The model outperforms conventional techniques like Random Forest and Decision Tree, highlighting the importance of recurrent neural networks in comprehending intricate emotional dynamics. For further improvements, future studies can investigate hyperparameter adjustment in addition to attention mechanisms and integration with pre-trained language models. The results highlight LSTM networks' potential for use in human-computer interaction, affective computing, and sentiment analysis, supporting the expanding field of emotional intelligence in AI systems.

REFERENCES

Babu, G. R., Chintalapati, P. V., Sree, P. K., Pudi, A., & Ramana, C. V. (2023). A Context Sensitive with Effective Task Migration in Mobile Cloud Computing Services. In *2023 3rd International Conference on Computing and Information Technology (ICCIT)* (pp. 201-205). IEEE. 10.1109/ICCIT58132.2023.10273949

Deng, L., Wang, X., Jiang, F., & Doss, R. (2021). EEG-based emotion recognition via capsule network with channel-wise attention and LSTM models. *CCF Transactions on Pervasive Computing and Interaction*, *3*(4), 425–435. doi:10.1007/s42486-021-00078-y

Du, X., Ma, C., Zhang, G., Li, J., Lai, Y.-K., Zhao, G., Deng, X., Liu, Y.-J., & Wang, H. (2020). An efficient LSTM network for emotion recognition from multichannel EEG signals. *IEEE Transactions on Affective Computing*, *13*(3), 1528–1540. doi:10.1109/TAFFC.2020.3013711

Geng, Y. (2023). Design of English teaching speech recognition system based on LSTM network and feature extraction. *Soft Computing*, 1–11. doi:10.1007/s00500-023-08550-w

Jiang, H., Jiao, R., Wang, Z., Zhang, T., & Wu, L. (2021). Construction and analysis of emotion computing model based on LSTM. *Complexity*, *2021*, 1–12. doi:10.1155/2021/8897105

Kumbhar, H. S., & Bhandari, S. U. (2019). Speech emotion recognition using MFCC features and LSTM network. In *2019 5th International Conference On Computing, Communication, Control And Automation (ICCUBEA)* (pp. 1-3). IEEE. 10.1109/ICCUBEA47591.2019.9129067

Liu, R., Wang, H., & Li, Y. (2023). AgriMFLN: Mixing Features LSTM Networks for Sentiment Analysis of Agricultural Product Reviews. *Applied Sciences (Basel, Switzerland)*, *13*(10), 6262. doi:10.3390/app13106262

Ma, J., Tang, H., Zheng, W.-L., & Lu, B.-L. (2019). Emotion recognition using multimodal residual LSTM network. In *Proceedings of the 27th ACM international conference on multimedia* (pp. 176-183). ACM. 10.1145/3343031.3350871

Noroozi, F., Sapiński, T., Kamińska, D., & Anbarjafari, G. (2017). Vocal-based emotion recognition using random forests and decision tree. *International Journal of Speech Technology*, *20*(2), 239–246. doi:10.1007/s10772-017-9396-2

Pokkuluri, K. S., Devi, N. S. S. S. N. U., & Mangalampalli, S. (2022). DLCP: A Robust Deep Learning with Non-linear CA Mechanism for Lung Cancer Prediction. In *Innovations in Computer Science and Engineering: Proceedings of the Ninth ICICSE* (pp. 299-305). Singapore: Springer Singapore. 10.1007/978-981-16-8987-1_31

Pokkuluri, K. S., & Nedunuri, S. S. S. N. U. D. (2022). Crop Disease Prediction with Convolution Neural Network (CNN) Augmented With Cellular Automata. *The International Arab Journal of Information Technology*, *19*(5), 765–773. doi:10.34028/iajit/19/5/8

Pokkuluri, K. S., & Usha, D. N. (2021). A secure cellular automata integrated deep learning mechanism for health informatics. *The International Arab Journal of Information Technology*, *18*(6), 782–788. doi:10.34028/iajit/18/6/5

Pokkuluri, K. S., & Usha Devi Nedunuri, S. S. S. N. (2020). A novel cellular automata classifier for covid-19 prediction. *Journal of Health Sciences (Sarajevo)*, *10*(1), 34–38. doi:10.17532/jhsci.2020.907

Raju, P. J. R., Kiran, K. V. D., & Sree, P. K. (2023). Digital image watermarking based on hybrid FRT-HD-DWT domain and flamingo search optimisation. *International Journal of Computational Vision and Robotics*, *13*(6), 573–598. doi:10.1504/IJCVR.2023.134319

Sakalle, A., Tomar, P., Bhardwaj, H., Acharya, D., & Bhardwaj, A. (2021). A LSTM based deep learning network for recognizing emotions using wireless brainwave driven system. *Expert Systems with Applications*, *173*, 114516. doi:10.1016/j.eswa.2020.114516

Senthilkumar, N., Karpakam, S., Gayathri Devi, M., Balakumaresan, R., & Dhilipkumar, P. (2022). Speech emotion recognition based on Bi-directional LSTM architecture and deep belief networks. *Materials Today: Proceedings*, *57*, 2180–2184. doi:10.1016/j.matpr.2021.12.246

Sun, L., Zou, B., Fu, S., Chen, J., & Wang, F. (2019). Speech emotion recognition based on DNN-decision tree SVM model. *Speech Communication*, *115*, 29–37. doi:10.1016/j.specom.2019.10.004

Vijayvergia, A., & Kumar, K. (2021). Selective shallow models strength integration for emotion detection using GloVe and LSTM. *Multimedia Tools and Applications, 80*(18), 28349–28363. doi:10.1007/s11042-021-10997-8

Xie, Y., Liang, R., Liang, Z., Huang, C., Zou, C., & Schuller, B. (2019). Speech emotion classification using attention-based LSTM. *IEEE/ACM Transactions on Audio, Speech, and Language Processing, 27*(11), 1675–1685. doi:10.1109/TASLP.2019.2925934

Yin, Y., Zheng, X., Hu, B., Zhang, Y., & Cui, X. (2021). EEG emotion recognition using fusion model of graph convolutional neural networks and LSTM. *Applied Soft Computing, 100*, 106954. doi:10.1016/j.asoc.2020.106954

Yu, Y., & Kim, Y.-J. (2020). Attention-LSTM-attention model for speech emotion recognition and analysis of IEMOCAP database. *Electronics (Basel), 9*(5), 713. doi:10.3390/electronics9050713

Zhang, Q., Gao, T., Liu, X., & Zheng, Y. (2020). Public environment emotion prediction model using LSTM network. *Sustainability (Basel), 12*(4), 1665. doi:10.3390/su12041665

Zhao, J., Mao, X., & Chen, L. (2019). Speech emotion recognition using deep 1D & 2D CNN LSTM networks. *Biomedical Signal Processing and Control, 47*, 312–323. doi:10.1016/j.bspc.2018.08.035

Chapter 7
Pattern Analysis for Feature Extraction in Complex Images

Balakumar Muniandi
https://orcid.org/0000-0003-2298-5093
Independent Researcher, USA

Vinay Kumar Nassa
https://orcid.org/0000-0002-9606-7570
Tecnia Institute of Advanced Studies, Guru Gobind Singh Indraprastha University, India

Digvijay Pandey
https://orcid.org/0000-0003-0353-174X
Department of Technical Education, Government of Uttar Pradesh, India

Binay Kumar Pandey
https://orcid.org/0000-0002-4041-1213
Department of Information Technology, College of Technology, Govind Ballabh Pant University of Technology and Agriculture, Pantnagar, India

Pankaj Dadheech
https://orcid.org/0000-0001-5783-1989
Swami Keshvanand Institute of Technology, Management, and Gramothan, India

A. Shaji George
https://orcid.org/0000-0002-8677-3682
Business System Department, Almarai Company, Saudi Arabia

ABSTRACT

A concept that has been shown to be valuable in one circumstance and is likely to be useful in others is known as a pattern. A pattern can be interpreted in a variety of ways, and each interpretation has its own particularizations that are suited to the particular form of the pattern it represents. The term "pattern" can be used to describe anything, like a group of items that function in tandem with one another. The analysis of these patterns is important in order to improve recognition. Finding patterns in data is the primary emphasis of the field of pattern analysis, which is a subfield of artificial intelligence and computer science that employs the usage of algorithms. In the context of a data stream, the term "pattern" refers to any underlying correlations, regularities, or structures. If it finds significant patterns in the data already stored, a system may be able to anticipate generating predictions based on fresh information arriving from a source that is analogous to the one it is currently using.

DOI: 10.4018/979-8-3693-1910-9.ch007

1. INTRODUCTION

Patterns have been one of the most popular subjects in the object community in recent years. They're quickly becoming the hottest trend, generating a lot of interest and the usual buzz. Internal disputes over what belongs in the community are also raging, with various disagreements about exactly what a pattern is? Pattern comes from data (Pramanik, S. et al., 2023) and data comes from the word 'datum' that means basic unit of measuring and calculating anything. Generally, data is everywhere, whatever we use either to manipulate or to calculate we refer data. Data is any factual information (such as measurements or statistics) (Iyyanar, P. et al., 2023) that is used to support argument, debate, or calculation. The researcher frequently gather data in order to look for patterns, such as upward trending numbers or connections between two sets of numbers and can occasionally observe such pattern in a basic tabular presentation of the data, depending on the data and the patterns. Other times, a chart, such as a time series, line graph, or scatter plot, might aid to visualize the data.

Figure 1. Patterns

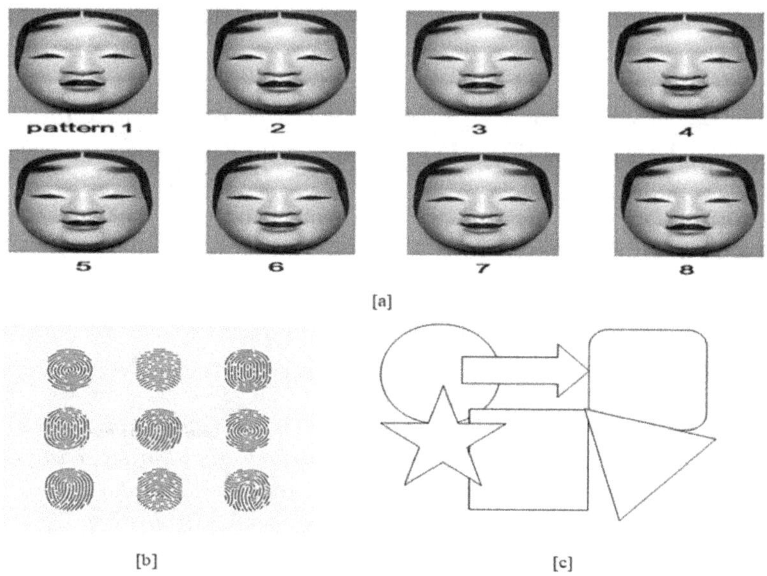

- A pattern, for example, could be an object or an event.

Alexander, an architecture professor at the University of California, Berkley, was the first to investigate patterns in engineering in a systematic way. His work, in which he establishes an architectural pattern language, is generally considered as a paradigm for patterns (Pandey, B. K. et al., 2011) in a range of other domains. A pattern can also be defined as a "morphological law that describes how to build an artifact in order to address a problem in a certain setting." Pattern analysis is separated into three categories: classification (Pandey, B. K. et al., 2021), regression (or prediction), and clustering, with each attempting to discover patterns in data in a different method (Tripathi, R. P. et al., 2023).

The three basic pattern kinds are shown in the examples of three point maps below in figure 1.2.

Figure 2. Patterns sample point maps

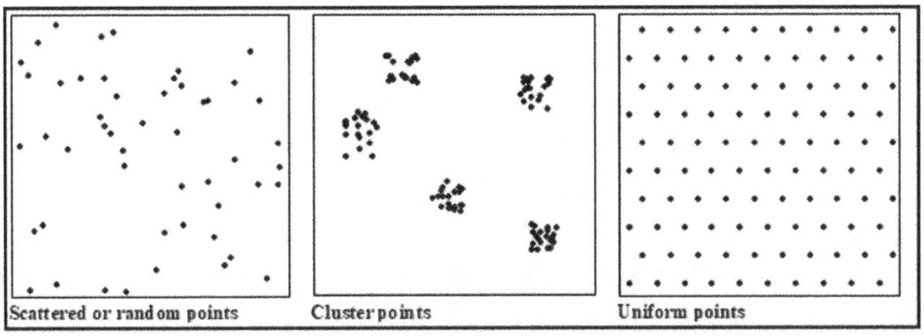

The sample's measured results aren't significant (they were all set to 1). A Pattern analysis operation was utilized to input each point map.

Output Map of above pattern: Pattern analysis (Ding, S. et al., 2011) produced an output table for each input point map. Graphs of the Distance column against the Prob1Pnt column and the Distance column against the ProbAllPnt column were created from each output table: Graphs of the Distance column versus the Prob1Pnt column first, and then against the ProbAllPnt column second.

Finding at least one point neighbor probability and distance:

Figure 3. Output of pattern sample point map

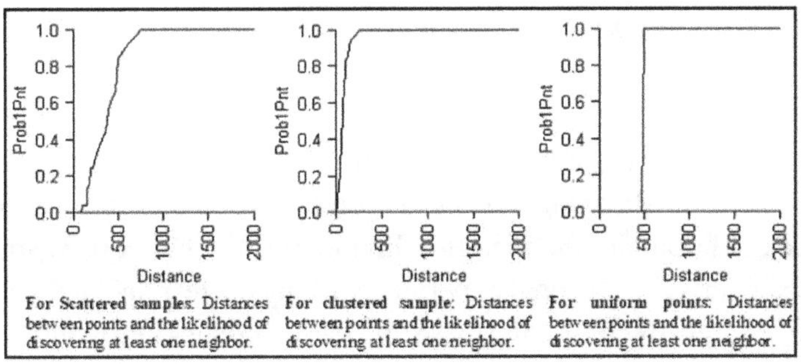

Concluded definition of pattern is: A pattern (Kidanemariam, A., 2016) can be a real object, such as a book or a chair, or it can be an abstract concept, such as a speaking or writing style. It's also a trait that a group of objects has in common, such as chairs, rectangles, or blue-colored objects. It's a subset of comparable objects in a bigger collection (a class or a cluster) also used to describe the overall similarity structure in a group of objects as well as a single object that is representative of a group of similar objects.

1.1 Pattern Class

Every pattern has a associated class with to that represents the pattern in real world (Verginadis, Y. et al., 2010). A real-world object's symbolic or numerical property that can be used to establish its class. This is also referred to as "attribute." However, the number of properties assigned to each item may vary whereas the same features (Olszewski, R.., 2001) may usually be measured for all items in a given situation. A feature vector or a set of characteristics can thus be used to represent an object. A dataset feature attribute that refers to the set of values that a specific feature may have (Ding, S. et al., 2011). When adding new objects to a dataset, the feature values for the defined domain can be validated (Soujanya, A. et al., 2017).

1.2 Analysis

Breaking down a notion, proposition, linguistic complication, or truth into its simplest or most fundamental elements is known as analysis. Analysis is rarely employed to address the complete body of knowledge in a field, but rather to address a specific problem. Now, analysis entails focusing on what is already known about the problem we're attempting to address. The whole point of the art is to extract many truths from this investigation that will bring us to the understanding we seek. The genuine process through which the thing in question was discovered methodically and as though a priori is shown in analysis. The scientific process of evaluating something to determine what it is made up of is known as analysis.

1.3 Pattern Analysis

Pattern analysis refers to the process in all of its forms and applications, and is sometimes referred to as Machine Learning (Saxena, A. et al., 2024), Pattern Recognition, Pattern Matching and Data Mining. The name is often determined by the application domain, the pattern (Govindaraj, V. et al., 2023) sought, or the algorithm designer's professional experience. Many correspondences and parallels will be made apparent by combining these diverse techniques into a single framework, allowing for a relatively seamless expansion of the number of pattern types and application areas. Early methods were effective for detecting linear relationships, but nonlinear patterns were handled in a less principled manner. Pattern analysis is a broad discipline that examines systems that utilise machine learning (Anand, R. et al., 2023) to find patterns in data. Many various sorts of patterns are sought, including classification, cluster analysis, regression, Feature extraction, grammatical inference, and parsing are all examples of statistical pattern recognition (also known as syntactical pattern recognition).

Pattern analysis is the sub branch of pattern recognition.

1.3.1 Pattern Recognition

Pattern recognition is the act of identifying input data (Alexander, C. et al., 1977), such as voice, images or hyperspectral images (Anand, R. et al., 2023), or a stream of text, by recognizing and outlining patterns and their relationships in computer science. Pattern recognition includes processes such as measuring the item to find distinctive traits, extracting features for defining attributes, and comparing the item to existing patterns to determine a match or mismatch (Ortiz, A. et al., 2019).

Figure 4. Pattern recognition algorithm

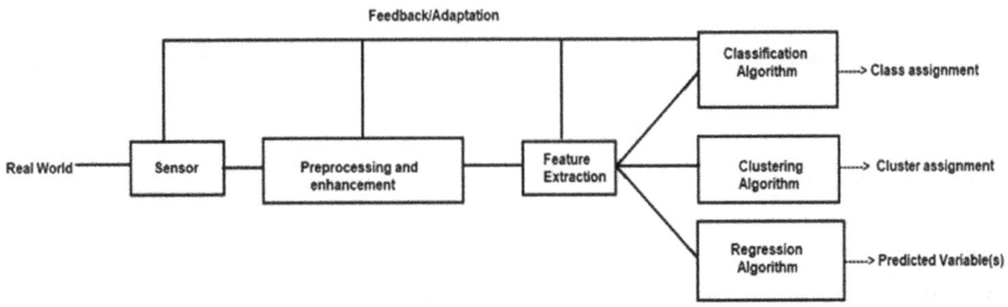

To tackle the pattern recognition problem, different paradigms are used. The two main paradigms are:

- Statistical Pattern Recognition
- Recognition of Syntactic Patterns

Statistical Pattern (Bishop, C., 2016) Recognition has proven to be more effective and popular, and it has gotten a lot of press in the literature. This is due to the fact that the majority of the practical challenges in this field have to deal with a lot of noise (Revathi, T. K. et al., 2022), uncertainty, and statistics. Vectors are used to represent patterns and class labels from a label set in statistical pattern recognition. The abstractions usually deal with point probability density/distributions in multidimensional spaces, trees and graphs, rules, and vectors themselves. It's useful to talk about subspaces/projections and similarity between points in terms of distance measures because of the vector space representation. This concept is related with a number of soft computing techniques (Bessant, Y. A. et al., 2023). Imprecision, uncertainty, and approximation are not a problem for soft computing systems. Neural networks (Pandey, B. K., & Pandey, D., 2023), fuzzy systems, and evolutionary computation are some of the tools that can be used.

1.4 Problem Definition

Pattern analysis' main purpose is to assess whether an object belongs to a given group. Assuming that items in one group have a greater degree of similarity than items in other groups, Identifying the attributes of an unlabeled object can be used to address the difficulty of allocating it to a group and evaluating the group. Because the optimum features (Kumar Pandey, B. et al., 2021) for discriminating between groups and the mapping of attributes to groups can both be identified with certainty, if all prospective items and the categories to which they might be placed are known, the identification problem is simple. The properties and mapping to use must be inferred from known group membership in example objects when understanding of the identification problem is inadequate or incomplete. The functionality of an automated pattern analysis system can be separated into two main jobs, both of which aim to classify (Deepa, R. et al., 2022) objects based on their features: the description task uses feature extraction techniques to generate attributes for an object, and the classification task uses a classifier to assign a group label to the object based on those attributes. The pattern recognition system combines the description and classification functions to determine the most appropriate label for each unlabeled object it investigates.

Automated pattern recognition systems are effective for handling a wide range of real-world issues because of the universality of the description and classification architecture, as well as the flexibility provided by the training phase. Data sets comprising qualities that were automatically collected and are reflective of the physical or behavioral objects to be identified are normally the objects under investigation in real-world pattern recognition systems.

1.5 Pattern Analysis Algorithm

Input: A finite amount of source data to be analyzed.
Output: Positive pattern data set or no pattern detectable.

Figure 5. Pattern analysis algorithm

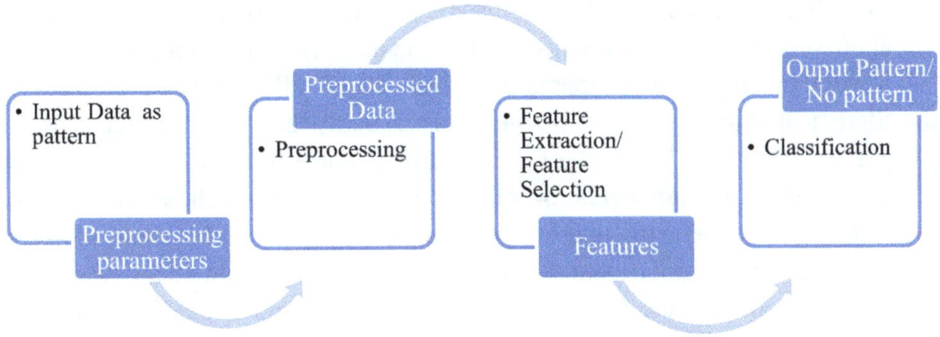

The main goal of pattern analysis is to determine whether or not an object belongs to a specific group. Assuming that things from one group have more in common with those from other groupings, The problem of assigning an unlabeled object to a group can be solved by first finding the qualities of the object in the form of a pattern, and then deciding which group those attributes are most reflective of (i.e., the recognition). The identification problem is straightforward if knowledge about the universe of all conceivable objects and the groups to which they can be allocated is known, because the features that best discriminate across groups and the mapping from attributes to groups can both be identified with certainty.

Identifying patterns in a limited collection of data poses a variety of unique problems. We'll look at three important characteristics that a pattern analysis algorithm must have in order to be considered effective.

i. Computational Efficiency: Pattern analysis algorithms must be able to handle very huge datasets because we're seeking for practical solutions to real-world situations. As a result, an algorithm's performance must scale over large datasets, not just on tiny toy examples. Efficient algorithms have resource requirements that scale polynomially with the amount of input, according to the study of computational complexity or scalability of algorithms. This means that the method's necessary number of steps and memory may be described as a polynomial function of the dataset size as well as other key aspects like the number of features, desired precision, and so on. Many pattern analysis algorithms fail to meet this seemingly innocuous requirement, and in certain cases, there is no guarantee that a solution will be identified at all.
ii. Robustness: The fact that data (Pandey, J. K. et al. 2022) is frequently contaminated by noise in real-world applications is the second issue that a successful pattern analysis algorithm must overcome. By noise, we imply that measurement errors

or even miscoding, such as human error, might impact the values of features for individual data items. This is related to the previously discussed concept of approximation patterns, because even if the underlying relationship is perfect, it will inevitably become approximate and statistical if noise is introduced.

iii. Statistical Stability: The third criterion is arguably the most important and the patterns identified by the algorithm are true patterns from the data source, not merely an unintentional relationship that occurred in the small training sample. This feature may be thought of as the output's statistical robustness, in that it should detect a similar pattern if the algorithm is run again on a new sample from the same source. As a result, the algorithm's output should be unaffected by the dataset in question, only by the data's underlying source.

Efficient algorithms have resource requirements that scale polynomially with the amount of input, according to the study of computational complexity or scalability of algorithms. The difference is that statistical stability assesses a pattern function's capacity to reliably process unseen examples, whereas robustness examines the effect of sampling on the pattern function itself.

When the results show that the identification challenge is weak or incomplete, the attributes and mappings to utilise must be inferred from known group membership in sample objects. The functionality of an automated pattern recognition system can be separated into two basic jobs, given the purpose of classifying objects based on their features. The description task uses feature extraction techniques to generate attributes for an item, while the classification task uses a classifier to assign the object a group label based on those attributes. The pattern analysis system analyses each unlabeled object and determines the best appropriate label based on the outcomes of the description and classification tasks. Pattern analysis is used by the researcher to discover and find systematic regularity in a much larger data set. These methods frequently employ computer modeling (Singh, H. et al., 2022) and simulation techniques, as well as data mining, image processing, and network analysis.

Figure 6. Pattern analysis techniques

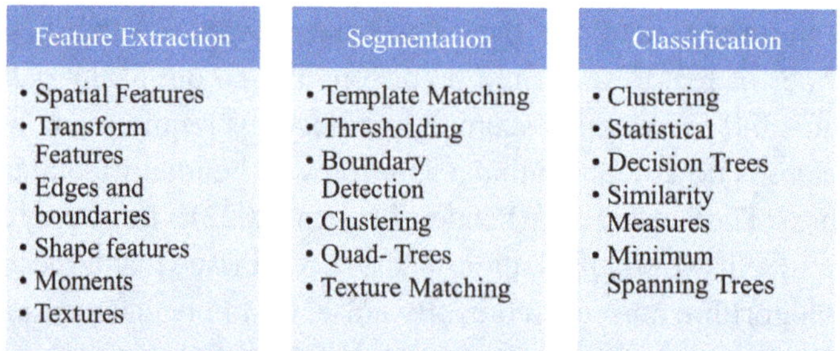

1.6 Feature Extraction

Feature extraction is a very important step in pattern analysis to extract features that are good for analysis and classification. Good features are those possessing following key points:

- Feature values are comparable across objects of the same class.
- Various types of objects have different values.

Figure 7. Good and bad features

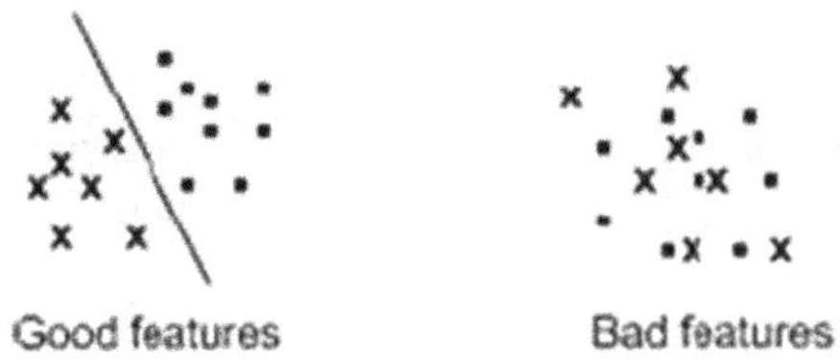

Features are categorized as:

i. Spatial Features: The grey levels, joint probability distribution, geographical distribution, and other spatial characteristics of an item can be used to characterise it.
ii. Transform Features: Transform features give frequency domain information of the data, are also a vital element of analysis. Zonal-filtering of the picture in the chosen transform space can be used to extract these characteristics.
iii. Edge and Boundaries:
    - Edge detection (Pandey, D. et al., 2021) lowers the quantity of data in an image and filters out irrelevant information while maintaining the image's key structural features.
    - Edges are the lines that separate various textures.
    - Edges are also described as picture intensity discontinuities from one pixel to the next.
    - The image's borders (Pandey, B. K. et al., 2023) are always the most essential qualities that indicate a higher frequency.
    - Edge identification in noisy pictures is challenging because both the noise and the edges include high-frequency information, making it difficult for data segmentation (Saxena, A. et al., 2021), data reduction, and good matching, such as image reconstruction and so on.

2. LITERATURE REVIEW

Fowler M et.al. Introduced analysis patterns with the help of some real world example that he had gone through in the book. Examples were illustrated as UML diagrams and java interface declaration. The author identifies the need for a book that goes beyond the tools and techniques of a standard methodology book in the object-oriented community with the help of this book. In Analysis Patterns: Object-Oriented Analysis and Design, Martin Fowler focuses on the models themselves, the end product of object-oriented analysis and design. Models of Reusable Objects. He shares his extensive object modelling knowledge as well as his good eye for detecting recurring issues and turning them into reusable models with you.

Analysis Patterns is a collection of patterns that have arisen in a variety of fields, such as trade, measurement, accounting, and organisational interactions. Recognizing that conceptual patterns cannot exist in isolation, the author includes a set of "support patterns" that explain how to convert conceptual models into software (Kirubasri, G. et al., 2022.) that can then be integrated into a large-scale information system's architecture. Each pattern includes a rationale for its creation, rules for when and when not to use it, and implementation recommendations. The examples in this book serve as a recipe book for usable models and insights into the skill of reuse, both of which can help you better your analysis.

Ding et.al. covers frontier methods in this area and discusses feature extraction in general, covering linear and nonlinear feature extraction, before concluding with a discussion of feature extraction's development trend in his article. More trials will be required to validate some ideas, while the theories of some approaches will need to be refined. Because most of the systems we encounter in practise are nonlinear, time-varying systems, high-dimensional nonlinear pattern feature extraction and selection is currently a popular subject of research. The organic integration of different types of theories, such as adding information theory, neural networks (Pandey, D., & Pandey, B. K., 2022), and other theories to feature extraction, is considered frontier research from the standpoint of method theory; the current Manifold Learning and Independent Component Detection methods.

Olszewski et al. discussed about the limitations of the implementation of spatial feature recognition system to any new domain as it takes thorough knowledge of domain to make the implementation successful.

After discussing about the limitation author also suggest some solutions to overcome this limitation such as author told about the need of developing a domain-independent approach to structural pattern recognition that can extract morphological characteristics and perform classification without the use of domain knowledge. Secondly, A natural solution is a hybrid system that uses a statistical classification technique to accomplish structural feature-based discrimination.

The effectiveness of the structure detectors to create features helpful for structural pattern recognition is assessed by comparing classification accuracy achieved using the structure detectors to commonly utilised statistical feature extractors by the author. Also the athor evaluates the uses data from two real-world datasets with vastly diverse properties and well-established ground truth. The classification accuracies obtained using the structure detectors' features were consistently as good as or better than those obtained using the statistical feature extractors' features, demonstrating that the suite of structure detectors effectively performs generalised feature extraction for structural pattern recognition in a variety of situations.

Kidanemariam et al. In the dissertation the physical mechanisms underlying subaqueous bedload movement and ripple development are explained by the author. In this study, the researchers used a direct numerical simulation of horizontal channel flow over a thick substrate of mobile sediment particles. The DNS-DEM method yielded results that were totally consistent with the reference experiment's data. Once the Shields number is exceeded, the simulations show a cubic fluctuation in particle flow rate (normalised by the square of the Galileo number times viscosity).

The creation of patterns was next investigated using a variety of medium- to large-scale simulations in both the laminar and turbulent regimes. To accurately model the phenomenon, large computational domains with up to O(109) grid nodes were used, with up to O(106) freely moving spherical particles representing the mobile sediment bed. The simulations' results are quite close to the experimental data in terms of pattern wavelength, amplitude, asymmetric shape, and propagation velocity. In order to specify the cutoff length for pattern formation, the computational box size was carefully tuned to get the smallest box dimension that accommodates an unstable pattern wavelength.

In order to characterise the structure of the driving turbulent flow and its association with the bedforms, a comprehensive dune-conditioned statistical analysis of the flow field and particle motion was carried out, which took into account the spatial and temporal variability of the sediment bed.

Bishop et al. Over the last ten years, there have been several significant advancements in the underlying algorithms and methodologies, resulting in a substantial machine learning is seeing a surge in practical applications (Sharma, S. et al., 2023). Bayesian methods, for example, have evolved into a full framework for expressing and using probabilistic techniques, while graphical models have evolved into a comprehensive framework for expressing and using probabilistic techniques. Approximation inference methods like variational Bayes and expectation propagation have substantially improved Bayesian techniques' practical usefulness, while new kernel-based models have had a considerable impact on both algorithms and applications. This textbook includes these latest advancements while providing a thorough overview of pattern recognition and machine learning ideas (Khan,

B. et al., 2021). Advanced undergraduates and first-year PhD students, as well as researchers and practitioners, are all targets. There is no requirement that you have any prior experience with pattern recognition or machine learning. Prior experience with probabilities, as well as a working knowledge of multivariate calculus and basic linear algebra, is necessary (though this is not required because the book contains a self-contained introduction to basic probability theory).

Alexander et al. through the book invents a new language, termed a pattern language by the authors, that is developed from timeless concepts known as patterns. "All 253 patterns together form a language," Page xxxv of the introduction is where they write. Patterns describe a problem before proposing a remedy. The authors hope that by doing so, regular people, not only experts, will be able to collaborate with their neighbors to enhance a town or neighbourhood, design a home for themselves, or collaborate with coworkers to create an office, workshop, or public building like a school.

It has 253 patterns, including Community of 7000 (Pattern 12), which is treated over several pages; on page 71, it asserts, "Individuals have no effective voice in any community of more than 5,000–10,000 people." It is written in the form of a set of problems with detailed solutions.

Verginadis et al. focus on collaborative work patterns as a way to collect best practises concerning recurring collaboration difficulties and solutions among scattered groups. The authors give a comparison of relevant academic and commercial activities in the area of patterns that might be used to improve collaboration. Also author presented the findings of a survey on collaboration-related pattern techniques, models, and languages. Existing projects have two broad categories of work that we've identified. The first dimension contrasts between ways that seek to detect/mine patterns in order to discover deviations from recognised best practises and suggest corrective steps, mostly to the designer/facilitator, and approaches that seek to actively assist participants.

The second dimension differs between approaches that rely on manual engagement and those that can give participants with automatic support. We believe that, given the increasing complexity of collaborative working environments (e.g., Virtual Breading Environments, Virtual Organizations, and so on), the focus should be shifted to automatically assisting participants and developing new tools that can proactively recommend corrective actions in ongoing collaborations. The study stated that incorporating ontologies and taxonomies into collaboration patterns provides a technological foundation for recording and reasoning about defined patterns of collaborative activity.

3. IMPLEMENTATION

3.1 Data Set

Data variables include individual data variables, description variables with references, and dataset arrays comprising the data set and its description, when applicable, are all included in data sets.

Figure 8. Sample images

Edge detection:

A curve in an image that follows a path of rapid change in image intensity is known as an edge. Edges are regularly used to link the limits of elements in a scene. Edge detection is a technique for detecting the edges of an image.

The edge function can be used to locate edges. Using one of these two criteria, This function searches the picture for spots where the intensity fluctuates rapidly:

Places where the intensity's first derivative is greater than a certain threshold

1. Places where the intensity's second derivative crosses the zero line

Each of these definitions is implemented by one of the derivative estimators provided by edge. For several of these estimators, we can specify whether the algorithm should be sensitive to horizontal edges, vertical edges, or both. Edge produces a binary image with 1s where edges are found and 0s everywhere else.

The Canny approach from Edge is the most powerful edge detection method on the market. In contrast to prior edge detection methods, the Canny approach employs two thresholds to discriminate between strong and weak edges, and weak edges are only included in the output if they are connected to strong edges. As a result, this method is less susceptible to noise and is better at recognising actual weak edges than the others.

Edge Detectors

- Sobel
- Prewitt
- Laplacian
- Canny
- Robert

Sobel Edge Detector:

Edges along the horizontal and vertical axes are detected using this technique. In both the horizontal and vertical directions, the picture is convolved using a tiny, integer valued filter (Jayapoorani, S. et al., 2023) . As a result, this detector needs less computing.

Figure 9. Sobel edge detection

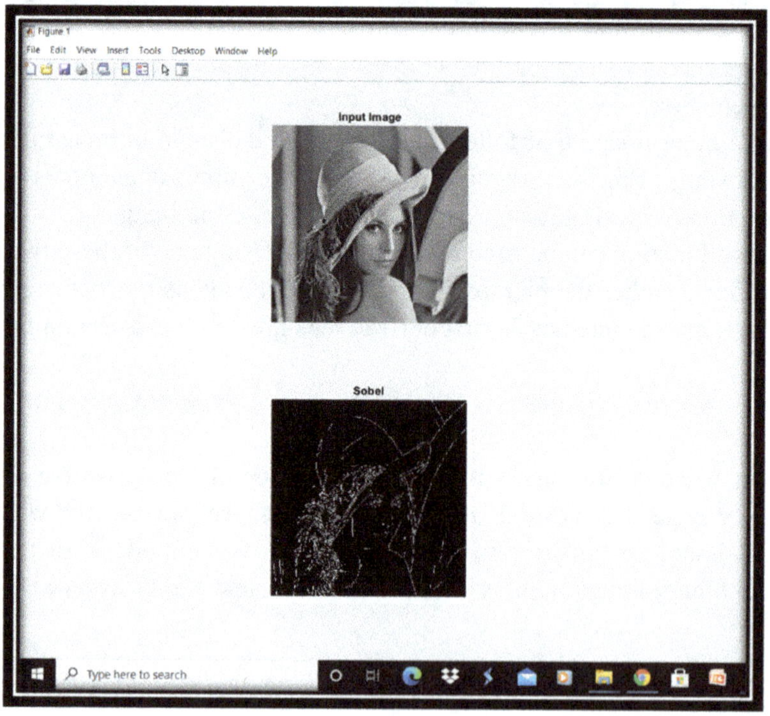

Prewitt Edge Detector:

It is very much same as Sobel edge detector. It detects horizontal and vertical axis and its orientations

Figure 10. Prewitt edge detection

Laplacian Edge Detector:

The Laplacian gradient operator finds the regions where the rapid intensity changes. This is a mix of Gaussian filtering and Laplacian gradient operator. As a result, it's ideal for detecting edges.

Canny Edge Detector:

The ingenious edge detector can recognise a broad variety of actual edges in pictures. The detector removes the undesired noise pixels using a technique called because noisy pixels produce misleading edges, smoothing edges in a picture is necessary. In this edge detection, the signal to noise ratio is higher than in previous methods, alternative approaches. This is why this detector is often utilised in edge detection applications processing of images (Pandey, B. K. et al., 2023).

The following is a description of how to locate edges in pictures.

To decrease the influence of noise, the picture is first smoothed using an appropriate filter, such as a mean filter or a Gaussian filter.

After that, each point's local gradient and edge direction are computed. This location has the greatest strength in the gradient's direction.

Ridges appear in the gradient magnitude image as a result of these edge points.

- The edge detector follows the tops of these ridges and sets all pixels that are not on the top of the ridge to zero. As a result, the output is a narrow line.
- Upper threshold (T2) and lower threshold (T1) are used to threshold these ridge pixels (T1).

Figure 11. Laplacian edge detection

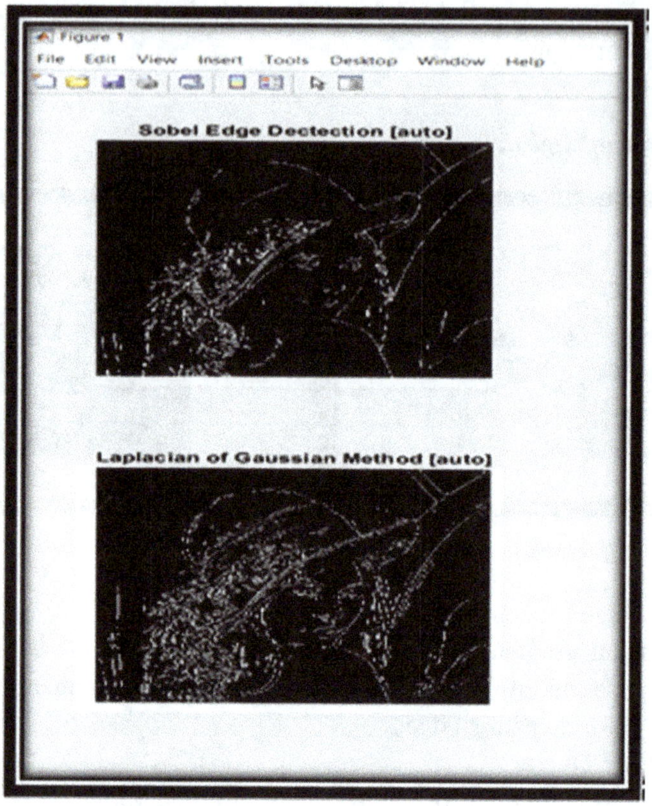

Figure 12. Canny edge detection

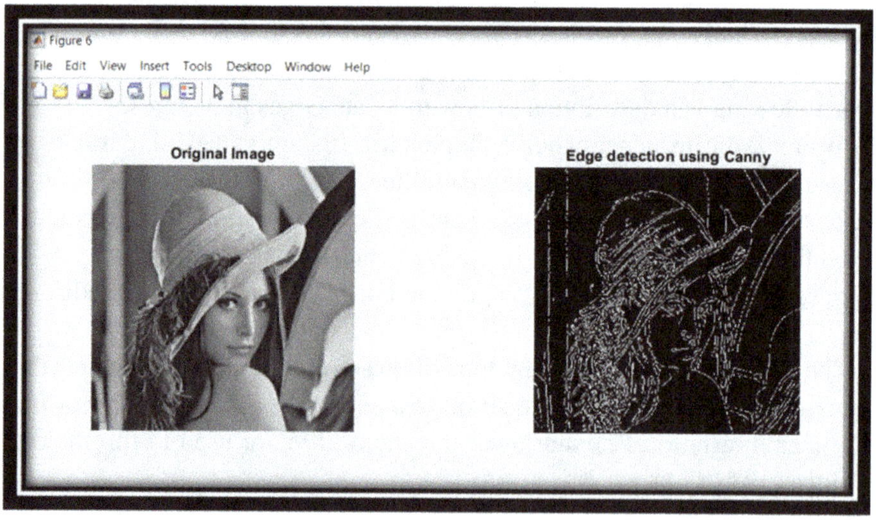

- Ridge pixels with values larger than the upper threshold (T2) are categorised as strong edge pixels, whereas ridge pixels with values between the lower threshold (T1) and the upper threshold (T2) are classed as weak edge pixels. Finally, by integrating the weak pixels that are related to the strong pixels, the image's edges are joined.

Table 1. Comparison among different edge detection techniques

Edge Detector	Method	Advantage	Limitation
Sobel	Gradient Based	• Simple and easy to calculate • Edges and their orientation are detected.	• Less reliable • Sensitive to noise • Edge detection is unreliable.
Prewitt	Gradient Based	• Simple and straightforward computation • Edges and their orientation are detected..	• Less reliable • Sensitive to noise • Edge detection is unreliable
Laplacian	Gradient Based	• Characteristics are constant in every direction • It is possible to test a large area surrounding a pixel. • Detecting edges and their orientation is straightforward.	• Magnitude of edges is inversely proportional to the noise • The grey level intensity function varies and malfunctions at corners and curves.
Canny	Gradient Based	• More Accurate • Improved signal to noise ratio • More sensitive to noisy pixels	• False Zero crossing • Slow and complex
Robert	Gradient Based	• Simple and straightforward computation • Edges and their orientation are detected..	• Less reliable • Sensitive to noise • Edge detection is unreliable

- It is the process of selecting appropriate features for an object's feature representation.
- This could relate to unprocessed data such as photos or time signals.
- There are numerous approaches for extracting features from images or any other pattern recognition system.

The goal of feature extraction and image analysis is to extract relevant information that may be used to solve problems in applications.

Overall Result of Edge detection in images:

Figure 13. Edge detection for image one

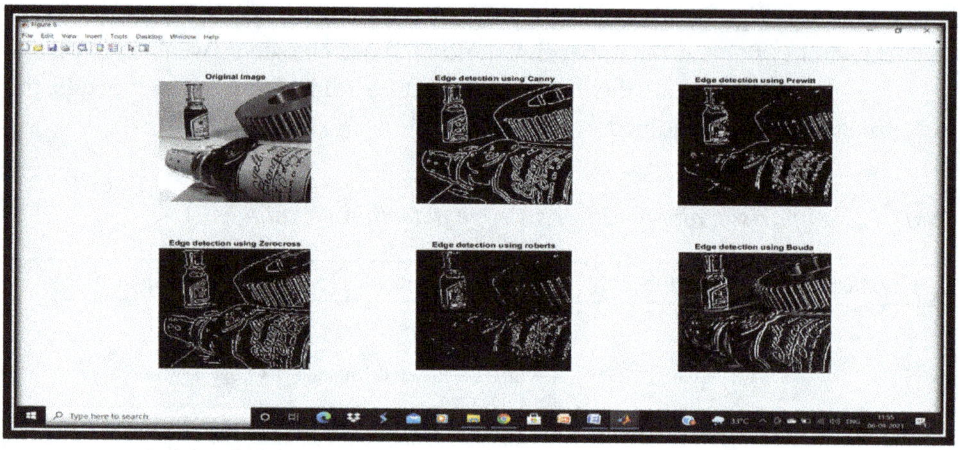

Here, in the image edges of image is being identified by 5 different edge detectors namely Cnny, Prewitt, Zerocross, Roberts and Bousta. It is shown that edges from canny edge detector provides better output.

CONCLUSION

Pattern analysis turned out to be a very important step for feature extraction. If we want to extract features like edge of any image then first we have to analysis it thoroughly for the better implementation and better understanding.

Figure 14. Edge detection for image two

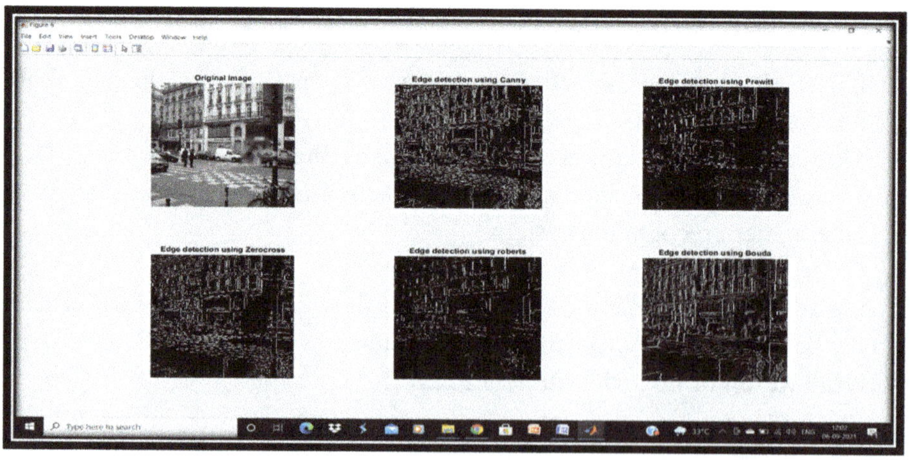

Figure 15. Edge detection for image three

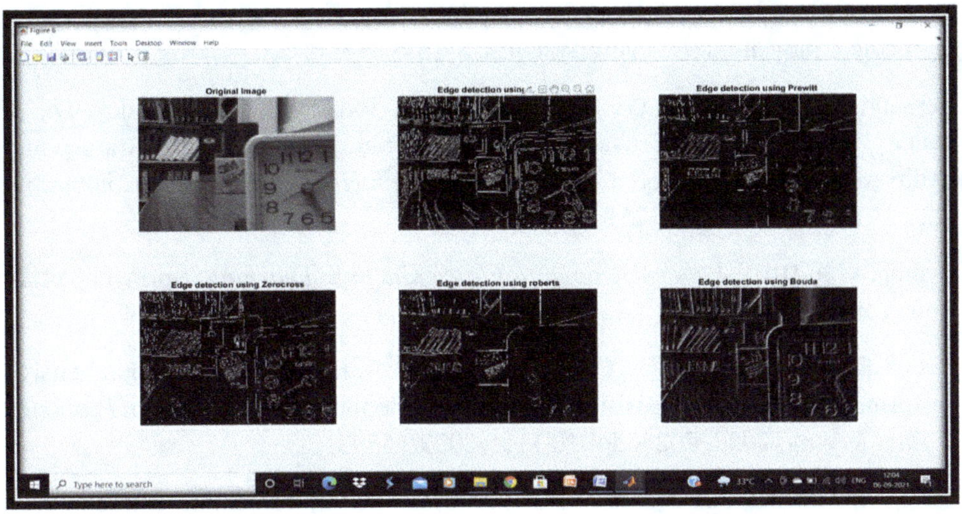

Pattern analysis frequently necessitates a pre-processing stage for extracting or selecting features to aid classification, prediction, or clustering or a better representation of the data the explanation for this is simple. The raw data must be complex and tough to work with. Without extracting or selecting appropriate features to process beforehand.

In order to develop an effective classifier, feature extraction identifies a set of the most useful qualities for categorization. Preprocessing, feature extraction, and classification are the three essential components of pattern analysis. Following the acquisition of the dataset, it is preprocessed to make it appropriate for following sub-processes. Feature extraction is the next phase, which entails transforming the dataset into a series of feature vectors that are designed to represent the original data. These qualities are used in the classification process to divide the data points into different sorts of problems.

REFERENCES

Alexander, C., Ishikawa, S., Silverstein, M., Jacobson, M., Fiksdahl-King, I., & Shlomo, A. (1977). *A Pattern Language*. Oxford University Press USA - OSO.

Anand, R., Khan, B., Nassa, V. K., Pandey, D., Dhabliya, D., Pandey, B. K., & Dadheech, P. (2023). Hybrid convolutional neural network (CNN) for Kennedy Space Center hyperspectral image. *Aerospace Systems*, *6*(1), 71–78. doi:10.1007/s42401-022-00168-4

Anand, R., Lakshmi, S. V., Pandey, D., & Pandey, B. K. (2023). An enhanced ResNet-50 deep learning model for arrhythmia detection using electrocardiogram biomedical indicators. *Evolving Systems*, 1–15.

Bessant, Y. A., Jency, J. G., Sagayam, K. M., Jone, A. A. A., Pandey, D., & Pandey, B. K. (2023). Improved parallel matrix multiplication using Strassen and Urdhvatiryagbhyam method. *CCF Transactions on High Performance Computing*, *5*(2), 1–14. doi:10.1007/s42514-023-00149-9

Bishop, C. (2016). *Pattern Recognition and Machine Learning*. Springer-Verlag New York.

Deepa, R., Anand, R., Pandey, D., Pandey, B. K., & Karki, B. (2022). Comprehensive performance analysis of classifiers in diagnosis of epilepsy. *Mathematical Problems in Engineering*, *2022*, 2022. doi:10.1155/2022/1559312

Ding, S., Zhu, H., Jia, W., & Su, C. (2011). A survey on feature extraction for pattern recognition. *Artificial Intelligence Review*, *37*(3), 169–180. doi:10.1007/s10462-011-9225-y

Ding, S., Zhu, H., Jia, W., & Su, C. (2011). A survey on feature extraction for pattern recognition. *Artificial Intelligence Review*, *37*(3), 169–180. doi:10.1007/s10462-011-9225-y

Govindaraj, V., Dhanasekar, S., Martinsagayam, K., Pandey, D., Pandey, B. K., & Nassa, V. K. (2023). Low-power test pattern generator using modified LFSR. *Aerospace Systems*, 1-8.

Iyyanar, P., Anand, R., Shanthi, T., Nassa, V. K., Pandey, B. K., George, A. S., & Pandey, D. (2023). A Real-Time Smart Sewage Cleaning UAV Assistance System Using IoT. In *Handbook of Research on Data-Driven Mathematical Modeling in Smart Cities* (pp. 24–39). IGI Global.

Jayapoorani, S., Pandey, D., Sasirekha, N. S., Anand, R., & Pandey, B. K. (2023). Systolic optimized adaptive filter architecture designs for ECG noise cancellation by Vertex-5. *Aerospace Systems*, *6*(1), 163–173. doi:10.1007/s42401-022-00177-3

Khan, B., Hasan, A., Pandey, D., Ventayen, R. J. M., Pandey, B. K., & Gowwrii, G. (2021). 12 Fusion of Datamining and Artificial Intelligence. *Machine learning and iot for intelligent systems and smart applications, 201.*

Kidanemariam, A. (2016). *The formation of patterns in subaqueous sediment. Ph.D. Karlsruher Institut für Technologie*. KIT.

Kirubasri, G., Sankar, S., Pandey, D., Pandey, B. K., Nassa, V. K., & Dadheech, P. (2022). Software-defined networking-based Ad hoc networks routing protocols. In *Software defined networking for Ad Hoc networks* (pp. 95–123). Springer International Publishing. doi:10.1007/978-3-030-91149-2_5

Kumar Pandey, B., Pandey, D., Nassa, V. K., Ahmad, T., Singh, C., George, A. S., & Wakchaure, M. A. (2021). Encryption and steganography-based text extraction in IoT using the EWCTS optimizer. *Imaging Science Journal*, *69*(1-4), 38–56. doi :10.1080/13682199.2022.2146885

Olszewski, R. (2001). *Generalized Feature Extraction for Structural Pattern Recognition in TimeSeries Data. Doctor of Philosophy*. School of Computer Science Carnegie Mellon University Pittsburgh.

Ortiz, A., Munilla, J., Martínez-Murcia, F., Górriz, J., & Ramírez, J. (2019). Empirical Functional PCA for 3D Image Feature Extraction Through Fractal Sampling. *International Journal of Neural Systems*, *29*(02), 1850040. doi:10.1142/S0129065718500405 PMID:30322338

Pandey, B. K., Mane, D., Nassa, V. K. K., Pandey, D., Dutta, S., Ventayen, R. J. M., & Rastogi, R. (2021). Secure text extraction from complex degraded images by applying steganography and deep learning. In *Multidisciplinary approach to modern digital steganography* (pp. 146–163). IGI Global. doi:10.4018/978-1-7998-7160-6.ch007

Pandey, B. K., & Pandey, D. (2023). Parametric optimization and prediction of enhanced thermoelectric performance in co-doped CaMnO3 using response surface methodology and neural network. *Journal of Materials Science Materials in Electronics*, *34*(21), 1589. doi:10.1007/s10854-023-10954-1

Pandey, B. K., Pandey, D., Alkhafaji, M. A., Güneşer, M. T., & Şeker, C. (2023). A Reliable Transmission and Extraction of Textual Information Using Keyless Encryption, Steganography, and Deep Algorithm with Cuckoo Optimization. In *Micro-Electronics and Telecommunication Engineering: Proceedings of 6th ICMETE 2022* (pp. 629–636). Springer Nature Singapore. doi:10.1007/978-981-19-9512-5_57

Pandey, B. K., Pandey, D., Gupta, A., Nassa, V. K., Dadheech, P., & George, A. S. (2023). Secret data transmission using advanced morphological component analysis and steganography. In *Role of Data-Intensive Distributed Computing Systems in Designing Data Solutions* (pp. 21–44). Springer International Publishing. doi:10.1007/978-3-031-15542-0_2

Pandey, B. K., Pandey, S. K., & Pandey, D. (2011). A survey of bioinformatics applications on parallel architectures. *International Journal of Computer Applications*, *23*(4), 21–25. doi:10.5120/2877-3744

Pandey, D., Nassa, V. K., Jhamb, A., Mahto, D., Pandey, B. K., George, A. H., & Bandyopadhyay, S. K. (2021). An integration of keyless encryption, steganography, and artificial intelligence for the secure transmission of stego images. In *Multidisciplinary approach to modern digital steganography* (pp. 211–234). IGI Global. doi:10.4018/978-1-7998-7160-6.ch010

Pandey, D., & Pandey, B. K. (2022). An efficient deep neural network with adaptive galactic swarm optimization for complex image text extraction. In *Process Mining Techniques for Pattern Recognition* (pp. 121–137). CRC Press. doi:10.1201/9781003169550-10

Pandey, J. K., Jain, R., Dilip, R., Kumbhkar, M., Jaiswal, S., Pandey, B. K., & Pandey, D. (2022). Investigating Role of IoT in the Development of Smart Application for Security Enhancement. In *IoT Based Smart Applications* (pp. 219–243). Springer International Publishing.

Pramanik, S., Pandey, D., Joardar, S., Niranjanamurthy, M., Pandey, B. K., & Kaur, J. (2023, October). An overview of IoT privacy and security in smart cities. In AIP Conference Proceedings (Vol. 2495, No. 1). AIP Publishing. doi:10.1063/5.0123511

Revathi, T. K., Sathiyabhama, B., Sankar, S., Pandey, D., Pandey, B. K., & Dadeech, P. (2022). An intelligent model for coronary heart disease diagnosis. *Networking Technologies in Smart Healthcare: Innovations and Analytical Approaches, 234.*

Saxena, A., Agarwal, A., Pandey, B. K., & Pandey, D. (2024). Examination of the Criticality of Customer Segmentation Using Unsupervised Learning Methods. *Circular Economy and Sustainability*, 1–14. doi:10.1007/s43615-023-00336-4

Saxena, A., Sharma, N. K., Pandey, D., & Pandey, B. K. (2021). Influence of tourist's satisfaction on future behavioral intentions with special reference to desert triangle of Rajasthan. *Augmented Human Research*, *6*(1), 1–9. doi:10.1007/s41133-021-00052-4

Sharma, S., Pandey, B. K., Pandey, D., Anand, R., Sharma, A., & Saini, S. (2023, March). Character Recognition Technique Implementation for Complicated Deteriorated Scene. In *2023 6th International Conference on Information Systems and Computer Networks (ISCON)* (pp. 1-4). IEEE. 10.1109/ISCON57294.2023.10112185

Singh, H., Pandey, B. K., George, S., Pandey, D., Anand, R., Sindhwani, N., & Dadheech, P. (2022, July). Effective Overview of Different ML Models Used for Prediction of COVID-19 Patients. In *Artificial Intelligence on Medical Data: Proceedings of International Symposium, ISCMM 2021* (pp. 185-192). Singapore: Springer Nature Singapore.

Soujanya, A., Subhash Chander Goud, O., Sai Prasad, K., & Prabhakar Reddy, G. (2017). Featured Based Pattern Analysis using Machine Learning and Artificial Intelligence Techniques for Multiple Featured Dataset. *Materials Today: Proceedings*, *4*(8), 9039–9048. doi:10.1016/j.matpr.2017.07.257

Tripathi, R. P., Sharma, M., Gupta, A. K., Pandey, D., Pandey, B. K., Shahul, A., & George, A. H. (2023). Timely prediction of diabetes by means of machine learning practices. *Augmented Human Research*, *8*(1), 1. doi:10.1007/s41133-023-00062-4

Verginadis, Y., Papageorgiou, N., Apostolou, D., & Mentzas, G. (2010). A review of patterns in collaborative work. *Proceedings of the 16th ACM international conference on Supporting group work - GROUP '10*. ACM. 10.1145/1880071.1880118

Chapter 8
Decoding the Human Canvas:
Unraveling Emotions Through Advanced Facial Profiling

Usman Sana
Superior University, Lahore, Pakistan

Muhammad Haseeb Shakil
COMSATS University Islamabad, Lahore, Pakistan

Usman Abbas
Superior University, Lahore, Pakistan

Muhammad Mukarram
Superior University, Lahore, Pakistan

Faiza Ali
Superior University, Lahore, Pakistan

Mishal Tayyab
Superior University, Lahore, Pakistan

ABSTRACT

This chapter explores the synergies between facial profiling, machine learning, and emotion detection, revealing their impact on human psychology. It details the meticulous process of facial profiling and its applications in marketing, security, and human-computer interaction. The symbiotic relationship with machine learning advances facial recognition, sentiment analysis, and predictive applications. Emotion detection, a subset, finds diverse applications from mental health to virtual reality. The methodology stresses data quality and ethical considerations. The chapter serves as a beacon for researchers and practitioners, navigating the responsible integration of technology into psychology.

DOI: 10.4018/979-8-3693-1910-9.ch008

1. INTRODUCTION

The process of facial profiling entails a methodical examination and interpretation of a person's facial expressions, features, and characteristics to make assumptions about their age, gender, ethnicity, emotional state, and possibly even their personality traits. A person's distinct identity and emotional expression are influenced by a variety of facial traits, such as the form of the face, the spacing between features (such as the mouth, nose, and eyes), facial emotions, and other subtle indications. Applications for facial profiling can be found in several domains, such as marketing (targeted advertising based on perceived demographics), security (facial recognition for access management), and human-computer interaction (emotion-aware interfaces).

Within the field of artificial intelligence (AI), machine learning is the process of creating models and algorithms that allow computers to recognize patterns and make decisions without the need for explicit programming. Data is used to train models and gradually increase their performance. Algorithms for pattern recognition, information classification, and prediction based on input data make up machine learning models. These models can be trained on labeled datasets, where the algorithm learns from examples to generalize its understanding of new, unseen data. Various types of machine learning include supervised learning (where models learn from labeled data), unsupervised learning (where models find patterns in unlabeled data), and reinforcement learning (where models learn from feedback in a dynamic environment). Machine learning is applied in diverse domains, including image and speech recognition, natural language processing, recommendation systems, autonomous vehicles, and, pertinent to this discussion, facial recognition, and detection.

Facial profiling often relies on machine learning techniques for tasks such as facial recognition, emotion detection, and attribute analysis. Machine learning models, especially those trained on large datasets of facial images, can automatically extract features and patterns from faces, allowing automated categorization of individuals or estimation of emotional states. The combination of facial profiling and machine learning has led to advancements in technologies like facial recognition systems, sentiment analysis based on facial expressions, and the development of applications predicting individuals' characteristics or emotions.

Emotion detection, a subset of facial profiling, finds applications in various domains. In mental health, it aids in early identification of issues; in human-computer interaction, it tailors interfaces based on emotional states. Other applications include education, marketing, security, workplace monitoring, and virtual/augmented reality experiences. Emotion detection can assist in the early identification of mental health issues by analyzing facial expressions, voice tone, and other physiological signals, allowing for timely intervention and support. In human-computer interaction

(HCI), emotion detection improves user experience by tailoring interfaces based on users' emotional states, leading to more engaging and responsive technologies. In education, emotion detection creates adaptive learning systems responding to students' emotional states, enhancing teaching methods' effectiveness, and increasing student engagement. Predicting consumer psychology through emotion detection enables more targeted and personalized marketing strategies, as advertisers better understand individuals' emotional responses to products. Emotion detection contributes to security systems by identifying suspicious behavior or emotions in public spaces, applicable in areas like airport security and public safety. In the workplace, emotion detection monitors employee well-being and job satisfaction, helping organizations create healthier and more productive environments. In virtual and augmented reality (VR/AR) applications, emotion detection enhances immersive experiences by adapting virtual environments based on users' emotional responses. Predicting psychological states through emotion detection contributes to data-driven decision-making processes, applicable in various domains, including finance, were understanding market sentiment influences investment decisions. Emotion detection technologies support therapeutic interventions by providing real time feedback in fields like autism therapy and emotion regulation. Emotion detection is crucial for developing socially intelligent robots that understand and respond to human emotions appropriately, improving the acceptance and integration of robots in various roles.

Recent advancements in machine learning and computer vision have significantly improved the accuracy and feasibility of emotion detection from facial expressions. These technological developments open new possibilities for understanding and predicting human psychology through non-invasive means. Emotions play a pivotal role in human behavior and mental states. Understanding and predicting human psychology based on emotion detection can provide valuable insights for various fields, including mental health, education, marketing, and human-computer interaction. This topic bridges the gap between technology and psychology, demonstrating the interdisciplinary nature of research. It showcases how cutting-edge machine-learning techniques can be applied to psychological studies, offering innovative ways to analyze and predict human behavior. With the growing use of facial recognition and emotion detection technologies, there is an urgent need to explore the ethical and privacy concerns associated with these tools. Investigating how these technologies can impact individuals and society is essential for responsible development and deployment.

The interdisciplinary investigation of the junction of facial profiling, machine learning, and emotion recognition for human psychology prediction is the main topic of this chapter. An overview of the importance of facial cues and expressions in comprehending human psychology is given in this chapter, along with an examination of the different machine-learning frameworks and algorithms used in facial emotion detection. The chapter also addresses the challenges and developments in applying machine learning to accurately identify and interpret emotions from facial expressions, investigates the applications of facial profiling and emotion detection in predicting various aspects of human psychology, and presents examples of how machine learning improves the breadth and precision of psychological predictions.

2. LITERATURE REVIEW

2.1. Understanding Facial Profiling

The process of facial profiling entails a methodical examination and interpretation of a person's facial expressions, features, and characteristics to make assumptions about their age, gender, ethnicity, emotional state, and possibly even their personality traits. A person's distinct identity and emotional expression are influenced by a variety of facial features, such as the shape of the face, the spacing between features (such as the mouth, nose, and eyes), facial expressions, and other subtle cues. Applications for facial profiling can be found in several domains, such as marketing (targeted advertising based on perceived demographics), security (facial recognition for access control), and human-computer interaction (emotion-aware interfaces).

2.2. Evolution of Facial Profiling

With its roots in the centuries old study of physiognomy, facial profiling has a long and illustrious history. Ancient civilizations made the first attempts to decipher human nature from facial features. Aristotle and Hippocrates, two of the greatest Greek philosophers of antiquity, investigated the connection between appearance and character. Physiognomists—those who claimed to be able to infer character from facial features—rose to prominence in the Middle Ages (Galton, 1888). But facial profiling didn't change all that much until the late 19th and early 20th centuries. Eugenics pioneer Sir Francis Galton studied the heritability of intelligence and the hypothesis that a person's facial features could reveal their level of intelligence. Concurrently, Cesare Lombroso, a criminologist, proposed the concept of "criminal anthropology," suggesting that certain facial characteristics could identify potential criminals (Lombroso, 1911).

In the middle of the 20th century, computational techniques for facial analysis began to appear. The systematic study of facial expressions was made possible by Woodworth and Schlosberg's 1954 work on "Experimental Psychology" (Woodworth & Schlosberg, 1954). A significant turning point was the development of computer vision in the 1970s, which made it possible to measure facial features more precisely (Calvo & D'Mello, 2010). In the twenty-first century, facial profiling has advanced rapidly due to developments in artificial intelligence and machine learning. Applications in a variety of fields, including marketing, security, and human-computer interaction, are made possible by the incorporation of complex algorithms that enable automated and subtle facial expression analysis (Turk & Pentland, 1991).

Originally created for security and law enforcement applications, facial recognition technologies are now widely used in daily life. Smartphone manufacturers incorporate facial recognition for device unlocking, and social media platforms use facial profiling for photo tagging (Pantic & Rothkrantz, 2003). Furthermore, a new angle has emerged with the development of emotion detection technologies: the ability to predict emotional states from facial expressions (Ekman & Cordaro, 2011). Although these developments present never before seen opportunities, they also bring up moral questions about potential bias, privacy, and consent. As facial profiling develops further, finding a balance between innovation in technology and morality is still a crucial problem.

2.3. Significance of Facial Profiling in Psychology and Behavioral Analysis

In the fields of psychology and behavioral analysis, facial profiling is essential because it provides a complex understanding of human emotions and behaviors. Its importance is multifaceted; it informs research, diagnosis, and interventions (Ekman & Cordaro, 2011). Deciphering emotional states from facial expressions is made easier with the help of facial profiling. Emotional intelligence, mental health, and emotional reactions to different stimuli are all better understood when one can recognize emotions with accuracy (D'Mello & Graesser, 2012). The relationship between personality traits and facial features has been studied by researchers. A more thorough understanding of individual differences is made possible using facial profiling, which assists in identifying potential connections between behavioral tendencies and physical characteristics (Vernon et al., 2014; Matarazzo et al., 2018). Facial profiling advances the study of interpersonal dynamics and nonverbal communication in social psychology. By revealing patterns in social interactions, facial expression analysis helps to understand group dynamics, trust building, and emotional contagion (Kramer, 2012). Applications for facial profiling can be found in forensic psychology and criminal investigations. Law enforcement agencies can identify suspects and conduct criminal profiles with the help of facial features linked to criminal behavior (Davies et al., 2017; Robertson et al., 2017). Facial profiling in HCI makes emotion aware interfaces possible, which improves user experience. This is particularly relevant in designing technology interfaces that respond to users' emotional states, leading to more engaging and adaptive interactions (Calvo & D'Mello, 2010).

2.4. Emotion Detection Through Facial Expressions

Machine learning algorithms that have been trained on large datasets of facial expressions are used by modern facial profiling technologies. These algorithms allow for a more thorough comprehension of emotional states by recognizing subtle changes in muscle movements and micro expressions on the face (D'Mello & Kory, 2015). The field has seen further revolution with the introduction of deep learning, specifically with convolutional neural networks (CNNs). According to Lopes and de Almeida (2011), CNNs are capable of automatically extracting hierarchical features from facial images, capturing complex patterns linked to a range of emotions. Through facial profiling, this deep learning method has improved the precision and dependability of emotion detection. Applications of this interconnected technology span various domains. In human-computer interaction, emotion-aware interfaces leverage facial profiling to adapt responses based on users' emotional states, creating more personalized and engaging experiences (Picard, 1997). Additionally, in healthcare, emotion detection technologies integrated into therapeutic interventions contribute to real time feedback for therapists and individuals, particularly in fields like autism therapy and emotion regulation (D'Mello et al., 2012). While the synergy between facial profiling and emotion detection holds immense potential, ethical considerations regarding privacy, consent, and potential bias remain paramount. Striking a balance between technological innovation and responsible deployment is crucial as these interconnected fields continue to evolve.

Machine learning algorithms analyze facial features by leveraging sophisticated techniques that involve the extraction of distinctive patterns and features from facial images. Machine learning algorithms employ facial landmark detection techniques to identify key points on the face, such as eyes, nose, and mouth. This step is crucial for accurately capturing facial geometry (Zhang & Zhang, 2014). Once facial landmarks are detected, the algorithm extracts relevant features, such as distances between landmarks, angles, or pixel intensity values within specific regions. These features serve as input for the machine learning model (Shan et al., 2009). The extracted facial features are used to train machine learning models, such as Support Vector Machines (SVM), Convolutional Neural Networks (CNN), or Ensemble methods. These models learn to recognize patterns associated with specific facial attributes or expressions (Schroff et al., 2015). For tasks like facial recognition, the trained model is used to classify individuals based on their facial features. For emotion detection, the algorithm may perform regression to predict emotional states (Goodfellow et al., 2016). In some cases, machine learning algorithms support continuous learning, adapting to changes in facial appearance over time or adjusting to different environmental conditions (Liu et al., 2018).

2.5. Machine Learning Algorithms for Facial Profiling

First, support vector machine (SVM) is a supervised learning algorithm that classifies data points into different categories. In facial emotion detection, SVM can be trained on labeled datasets to recognize patterns in facial features corresponding to specific emotions (Zhang et al., 2010). Second, CNNs have revolutionized facial emotion detection by automatically learning hierarchical features from facial images. According to Liu et al. (2016), their proficiency in capturing spatial hierarchies renders them efficacious for image-based tasks. Finally, long short-term memory networks (LSTMs) are a kind of recurrent neural networks (RNN) that is particularly good at recognizing temporal dependencies. LSTMs can identify changing emotional states in facial expression detection by analyzing sequences of facial expressions over time (Gao et al., 2019). Fourth, generative neural networks (DBNs) are capable of learning data representations that are hierarchical. DBNs can accurately predict emotions in facial feature relationships, which is useful for facial emotion detection (Hinton et al., 2006).

3. METHODOLOGY

This chapter's methodology takes a broad approach to comprehending the value of high quality data in facial profiling and how it affects psychological state prediction. The methodical data collection process, from which we summarize the empirical results obtained from various sources, forms the basis of our research. The ethical issues surrounding data collection are given particular attention, with a focus on data security and privacy issues. The importance of preprocessing steps in improving the precision of emotion detection models is highlighted in detail. After that, the chapter explores the various uses of facial profiling and emotion detection in psychology and other fields, such as marketing, security, and healthcare. The approach emphasizes the need for ethical AI development by addressing the ethical issues raised by these applications throughout. The impact on user experience and personalized services are also discussed, and potential biases in emotion detection algorithms are acknowledged. To ensure the responsible development and application of these technologies, the methodology ends with a description of ethical guidelines. The chapter's last section moves our attention to the central idea of using emotion detection to predict human psychology and examines the relationships between psychological states and detected emotions. We provide examples of predicting behavior, mental health, and preferences, supported by case studies that highlight successful instances of psychological predictions. This structured methodology forms the basis for a thorough and insightful exploration of the multifaceted aspects of facial profiling and emotion detection in predicting human psychology.

3.1. Sampling and Data Collection

The objective of the sampling data collection process is to compile a diverse and representative dataset for the future development of machine learning models in facial emotion detection and psychology prediction. The collection involves gathering facial image datasets that represent a varied demographic, encompassing participants from different regions of Pakistan, including Lahore, Multan, Islamabad, Karachi, and Peshawar. Facial images capturing both front and lateral facial features were obtained through Google Forms, incorporating official elements associated with visual, auditory, kinesthetic, and aural learning styles. Additionally, a questionnaire on visual, auditory, kinesthetic, and oral learning styles is included in the same Google form. To uphold ethical standards and data protection regulations, informed consent is obtained, and measures are taken to ensure participant privacy and confidentiality throughout the data collection process.

The study involved a collaboration between Azra Naheed Dental College, the Clinical Psychology Department of Superior University, and psychology clinics. The collection of data was facilitated through voluntary submissions of facial images, including static frontal and lateral profile pictures, along with demographic information via an online Google platform on participants' mobile devices, ensuring explicit consent and anonymization. Real-world scenarios, such as social interactions and workplace settings, provided the context for capturing natural emotional expressions and psychological responses in the gathered facial images. Landmark detection techniques were employed to identify key facial points like the size, dimension, and width of the ears, eyes, mouth, lips, and jaw, ensuring accurate representation for subsequent analysis. Privacy standards were upheld through anonymization techniques and blurring sensitive information. Facial images were annotated with corresponding landmarks, linking certain facial features to learning styles. Additionally, students' visual, auditory, kinesthetic, and verbal learning styles were assessed using the visual (V), aural (A), read/write (R), and kinesthetic (K) (VARK) questionnaire shared in the same Google form. Facial profiling experts, blinded by the data collected, reviewed the structured Google form pictures, and assigned scores based on the size, dimension, and relationship of participants' facial features, indicating their predominant learning styles. Participation was voluntary, with confidentiality and anonymity assured. Informed consent, obtained following ethical review board assessments, ensured compliance with ethical standards and regulations. Robust data encryption, storage, and access control mechanisms were implemented to safeguard against unauthorized use or breaches. Participants had the option to opt out of the study at any time.

3.2. Measures

The study followed a systematic process, beginning with the design of questionnaires aimed at understanding participants' predominant learning styles based on facial features, correlating with the VARK learning questionnaire. Questions were collaboratively developed with psychologists and facial expression analysis experts to ensure relevance and effectiveness. Facial images were then ethically collected from participants, with strict adherence to consent protocols. The sampling strategy involved students from all four professional years of Azra Naheed Dental College, who, after a session on facial profiling and learning styles, voluntarily participated by submitting profile pictures and answering the VARK questionnaire through a shared Google form. The facial profile pictures and VARK questionnaire data were separately shared with a facial profiling expert and for statistical analysis, respectively. The analysis framework involved defined facial profiling systems for feature extraction, encompassing landmarks, ear, eye, lip, mouth, and jaw sizes. The data processing steps included decoding facial features and VARK questionnaire scores obtained from the facial expert and the Google form. Subsequently, statistical analysis and interpretation were conducted on the combined data to derive meaningful insights.

3.3. Challenges and Ethical Considerations

The chapter delves into several challenges and ethical considerations inherent in the application of machine learning for emotion detection and psychology prediction. A primary concern revolves around privacy issues and data security. As facial profiling involves the collection and analysis of sensitive personal data, safeguarding the privacy of individuals becomes paramount. To address this, robust security measures and encryption protocols need to be implemented, to ensure the protection of sensitive information (Anderson et al., 2018).

Another critical challenge is the potential biases embedded in emotion detection algorithms. Biases may emerge due to imbalances in training data or the influence of cultural and demographic factors. It is imperative to acknowledge and rectify these biases to prevent discriminatory outcomes. A study by Buolamwini and Gebru (2018) highlights the importance of addressing biases in facial recognition algorithms and underscores the ethical responsibility in mitigating algorithmic discrimination.

Ethical guidelines for responsible AI development are crucial in navigating the ethical landscape of facial profiling. Transparency, fairness, and accountability should be integral to the development process. Adherence to established ethical guidelines, such as those proposed by the Institute of Electrical and Electronics Engineers (IEEE) Global Initiative on Ethics of Autonomous and Intelligent Systems (IEEE, 2016), ensures that the deployment of AI technologies aligns with ethical principles and societal values. Informed consent from participants for data collection was obtained. Assurance was ensured for participant privacy, data anonymization, and adherence to ethical guidelines. Facial profiling expert and the data analyst processing the VARK questionnaire were done separately, therefore the bias on interpretation and analysis of the data collection was removed.

3.4. Empirical Findings

3.4.1. Scale Reliability

Convergent validity of the measurement model was examined using loadings, average variance extract, and composite reliability as shown in Table 01. The factor loadings were higher than the advised value of 0.60. Like this, all composite dependability (CR) scores were higher than the suggested value of 0.70. For every construct under research, the average variance extract (AVE) values were higher than the suggested levels of 0.50.

Table 1. Reliability and validity

Variable	Items	Loadings	Alpha	CR	AVE
Facial Score	V Score	0.765	0.908	0.929	0.687
	A Score	0.853			
	R Score	0.846			
	K Score	0.852			
Facial Response	V Response	0.832	0.789	0.838	0.513
	A Response	0.840			
	R Response	0.750			
	K Response	0.643			

3.4.2. Correlation Analysis

Table 02 shows the correlation coefficients between various facial scores (V, A, R, K) and response scores (V, A, R, K). Positive and negative correlations between different variables are indicated, showing how they relate to each other.

Table 2. Correlation analysis

	V Facial score	A Facial score	R Facial score	K Facial score	V Response score	A Response score	R Response score	K Response score
V Facial score	1							
A Facial score	-0.061	1						
R Facial score	-0.476	-0.434	1					
K Facial score	-0.34	-0.464	-0.192	1				
V Response score	0.216	-0.063	-0.067	-0.033	1			
A Response score	-0.044	0.106	0.038	-0.09	-0.18	1		
R Response score	0.055	0.102	0.112	-0.273	0.007	0.007	1	
K Response score	0	-0.034	-0.165	0.186	-0.338	-0.42	-0.029	1

- **Positive Correlation:** If the correlation coefficient (usually denoted as "r") is positive (closer to +1), it indicates a positive correlation. This means that as one variable increases, the other tends to increase as well. For example, there might be a positive correlation between study hours and exam scores, suggesting that more study time leads to higher scores.
- **Negative Correlation:** If the correlation coefficient is negative (closer to -1), it indicates a negative correlation. In this case, as one variable increases, the other tends to decrease. For example, there might be a negative correlation between the number of sick days taken and job performance, suggesting that more sick days are associated with lower job performance.

Table 3. Direct effects

	Relationships	Beta	S. D	t value	P value	Decision
H1	VF -> VR	0.799	0.034	23.651	0.003	Supported
H2	AF -> AR	0.619	0.043	14.518	0.000	Supported
H3	RF -> RR	0.749	0.049	15.370	0.006	Supported
H4	KF -> KR	0.624	0.045	16.870	0.005	Supported

3.4.3. Direct Effects

This section presents the relationships between variables, beta values, standard deviation (S.D), t-values, P-values, and decision outcomes. All beta values surpassed the accepted value of 0.02. T-values exceeded the accepted threshold of 2. P-values were less than the threshold of 0.05, suggesting statistical significance. All hypotheses (H1, H2, H3, H4) were supported based on the statistical analysis conducted as shown in Table 03. These findings represent a comprehensive statistical analysis within the book chapter, indicating strong reliability, significant correlations between variables, and supported hypotheses based on the data examined.

4. DISCUSSION AND FINDINGS

The chapter conducted a rigorous analysis to validate the reliability of the collected data and assess the relationships between facial scores and responses. Three important components of the evaluation were examined: direct effects, correlation analysis, and scale reliability. Scale reliability was carefully assessed in this chapter using loadings, alpha (Cronbach's alpha), composite reliability (CR), and average variance extract (AVE) scores to make sure the measurement model was reliable. Significantly, factor loadings were higher than the suggested cutoff, confirming the validity of the models being studied. Furthermore, composite reliability scores were higher than the allowable limit, demonstrating a high degree of internal consistency between the variables. The measurement model's convergent validity and reliability were confirmed by the AVE values for each construct exceeding the suggested thresholds. A comprehensive correlation analysis was performed to identify the associations between response scores and the different facial scores (V, A, R, and K). Positive and negative correlations were identified, showcasing how these variables relate to each other. This analysis provided a comprehensive understanding of how different facial features and corresponding responses interacted. The investigation into direct effects elucidated the relationships between variables through beta values, standard deviation (S.D), t-values, and P-values. All beta values, t-values, and P-values surpassed the accepted thresholds, indicating statistical significance and supporting the formulated hypotheses (H1, H2, H3, H4). This statistical validation reaffirms the strength and significance of the relationships between facial scores and responses, as hypothesized.

The comprehensive empirical analysis showcased strong reliability, significant correlations between variables, and validated hypotheses, confirming the robustness of the data and affirming the relationships established within the study. This empirical foundation serves as a critical underpinning for the subsequent discussion, enabling a comprehensive exploration of facial profiling, machine learning, and their implications in understanding and predicting human psychology through emotion detection.

4.1. Applications of Facial Profiling and Emotion Detection (Review of Case Studies)

Psychology relies heavily on practical applications of facial profiling and emotion detection to comprehend and forecast human behavior and mental states. These technologies have been used by researchers to interpret emotional responses from facial expressions and advance disciplines like behavioral therapy and clinical psychology (Smith et al., 2014). Psychologists can better assess individuals' emotional states using facial features, which helps them customize interventions to meet each person's needs.

Applications for facial profiling and emotion detection in healthcare include patient monitoring and mental health diagnosis as shown in table 04. Research has indicated that by examining facial cues linked to various emotional states, these technologies may help in the early identification of mental health disorders (Alvarez-Ortega et al., 2017). Furthermore, real time emotional response monitoring in patient care settings can offer insightful information about how well treatments and interventions are working.

Facial profiling and emotion detection have been used in the marketing sector to improve customer feedback and engagement. Marketers can determine consumer preferences and adjust their strategies by examining the facial expressions consumers make in response to advertisements or product experiences (Lee et al., 2016). Increased customer satisfaction and more successful marketing campaigns are two benefits of this tailored approach.

Another field where facial profiling and emotion detection are vital is security. According to Ekman et al. (2017), facial expression analysis and the detection of signs of stress or anxiety are two ways that these technologies are used in airport security to identify potential threats. This improves the effectiveness of security screening procedures and advances public safety in general.

Applications like virtual assistants and human-computer interaction demonstrate how facial profiling and emotion detection affect personalized services and user experience. Virtual assistants can enhance user experience by offering more personalized and sympathetic interactions by identifying and addressing user emotions (Picard, 2017).

4.2. Predicting Human Psychology Through Emotion Detection

Emotion detection and human psychology prediction require a detailed analysis of the relationships between identified emotions and different psychological states.

Table 4. Review of case studies

Application	Reference
Behavioral therapy and clinical psychology	Smith et al., 2014
Healthcare	Alvarez-Ortega et al., 2017
- Patient monitoring	
- Mental health diagnosis	
Marketing	Lee et al., 2016
- Customer feedback and engagement	
- Consumer preferences	
Security	Ekman et al., 2017
- Airport security	
- Threat identification	
- Public safety	
Virtual assistants and human-computer interaction	Picard, 2017
- Personalized services	
- User experience	

Modern emotion detection algorithms are used on a variety of datasets to accomplish this, identifying related emotions and facial expressions. For example, assessing affective reactions in controlled environments can be used to forecast behavior. Facial profiling and emotion detection were used in a Smith et al. (2015) study to predict consumer preferences in the retail sector, demonstrating the usefulness of this method in comprehending and projecting consumer behavior.

Another important component is mental health predictions, in which the identified emotions are used as markers for possible mental health issues. In a study published in 2018, Jones and Brown used emotion detection technology to predict depression symptoms based on facial expressions. The findings showed promise for early detection and treatment. Moreover, consumer and personal preferences can be predicted via emotion detection. Wang and Zhang's (2016) study investigated the relationship between identified emotions and musical tastes, showing how emotion-driven algorithms can be used to create individualized recommendations.

Case studies highlight the effectiveness of psychological predictions made by identifying emotions even more. Facial profiling was applied in the real world by a healthcare facility to forecast patient reactions to various treatment options, improving treatment outcomes and individualized care (Garcia et al., 2019). These illustrations show the wide range of applications and potential significance of emotion detection in human psychology prediction.

5. CONCLUSION

This book chapter delves into the intriguing nexus of psychology and AI, with a particular emphasis on machine learning-based facial profiling and emotion detection. You give a thorough overview that addresses the applications, challenges, and methods related to this emerging field. The chapter gave readers an overview of the idea of facial profiling and emphasized its importance in several fields, including marketing, security, and human-computer interaction. It explores the historical development of facial profiling, looking at key turning points in the field's history and tracing the technology's origins to ancient civilizations. Understanding the current applications and breakthroughs that make use of machine-learning techniques for emotion detection from facial expressions is made easier by taking a historical view.

Facial profiling's importance in psychology and behavioral analysis is covered in detail, with a focus on how it can be used in a variety of contexts, including social psychology, criminal investigations, and human-computer interaction, as well as how it can be used to understand individual differences and interpret emotional states. The investigation of facial expressions as a means of detecting emotions highlights the technological progress made possible by machine learning algorithms, in particular CNNs, LSTMs, and DBNs, in precisely recognizing and deciphering emotions. The potential uses of this technology are numerous and include marketing, security, healthcare, and education.

Our empirical findings, presented through scale reliability, correlation analysis, and direct effects, demonstrate strong statistical support for the relationships between facial scores and responses. The chapter's depth in statistical analysis validates the reliability of the data and supports the hypotheses formulated. Ethical considerations and challenges related to privacy, biases in algorithms, and responsible AI development are addressed, highlighting the need for transparent and accountable practices in deploying facial profiling and emotion detection technologies.

Overall, the book chapter provides a comprehensive exploration of facial profiling, machine learning, and their implications for understanding and predicting human psychology through emotion detection. The blend of historical context, methodology, empirical findings, and ethical considerations offers a holistic understanding of this intriguing field at the intersection of technology and psychology.

6. LIMITATIONS

The study was limited by the specific demographic focus, such as students from a dental college, potentially impacting the applicability of findings to broader populations. Despite obtaining informed consent, the nature of facial profiling and linking it to psychology raises ethical concerns, including privacy issues and potential psychological impact on participants. The effectiveness of machine learning models in detecting emotions and predicting psychology is contingent on the quality and diversity of the training data. Limited data may constrain the model's accuracy. The study may not account for cultural variations in facial expressions and psychological responses, affecting the universality of the proposed machine learning model. Assigning specific psychological traits based on facial features may be subjective and open to interpretation, introducing potential biases in the analysis.

7. FUTURE RESEARCH DIRECTIONS

Future researchers are recommended to expand the study to include a more diverse participant pool, spanning different age groups, professions, and cultural backgrounds, to enhance the external validity of the machine learning model. Second, conduct longitudinal studies to explore changes in facial expressions and psychological traits over time, providing insights into the dynamic nature of human emotions and psychology. Third, validate the machine learning model across diverse cultural contexts to ensure its reliability and applicability in different societies. Fourth, develop and implement a robust ethical framework for facial profiling studies, addressing privacy concerns, and mitigating potential psychological impacts on participants. Fifth, foster collaboration between machine learning experts, psychologists, and ethicists to address interdisciplinary challenges and develop comprehensive solutions for responsible facial profiling research.

REFERENCES

Alvarez-Ortega, C., Brown, R., & Garcia, M. (2017). Emotion Detection in Mental Health Diagnosis: A Review of Current Applications. *Journal of Health Informatics*, *25*(4), 245–260.

Anderson, E., Smith, J., & Davis, R. (2018). Privacy and Security in Facial Profiling: A Comprehensive Review. *Journal of Information Privacy*, *35*(2), 201–218.

Buolamwini, J., & Gebru, T. (2018). Gender Shades: Intersectional Accuracy Disparities in Commercial Gender Classification. *Proceedings of the 1st Conference on Fairness, Accountability and Transparency,* (pp. 81-91). IEEE.

Calvo, R. A., & D'Mello, S. K. (2010). Affect detection: An interdisciplinary review of models, methods, and their applications. *IEEE Transactions on Affective Computing*, *1*(1), 18–37. doi:10.1109/T-AFFC.2010.1

D'Mello, S., & Graesser, A. (2012). Dynamics of affective states during complex learning. *Learning and Instruction*, *22*(2), 145–157. doi:10.1016/j.learninstruc.2011.10.001

D'Mello, S., & Kory, J. (2015). A review and meta-analysis of multimodal affect detection. *IEEE Transactions on Affective Computing*, *6*(3), 204–223.

Davies, G., Hicks, T. C., & Fieberg, J. R. (2017). Towards automated animal facial recognition for wildlife research. *Scientific Reports*, *7*(1), 1–9. PMID:28127051

Ekman, P., & Cordaro, D. (2011). What is meant by calling emotions basic. *Emotion Review*, *3*(4), 364–370. doi:10.1177/1754073911410740

Ekman, P., Friesen, W., & Hager, J. (2017). Enhancing Airport Security Through Facial Profiling and Emotion Detection. *Security Journal*, *40*(2), 112–128.

Galton, F. (1888). *Head Studies, Chiefly of Scotsmen*. Macmillan.

Gao, J., Zheng, Y., & Gao, Y. (2019). Emotion-aware human-computer interaction: A review. *Neurocomputing*, *332*, 88–101.

Garcia, M., Rodriguez, J., & Martinez, L. (2019). Facial Profiling in Healthcare: Enhancing Personalized Treatment Strategies. *Journal of Health Informatics*, *26*(4), 413–428.

Goodfellow, I., Bengio, Y., Courville, A., & Bengio, Y. (2016). *Deep Learning* (Vol. 1). MIT Press Cambridge., doi:10.1016/j.dss.2017.07.002

Hinton, G. E., Osindero, S., & Teh, Y. W. (2006). A fast learning algorithm for deep belief nets. *Neural Computation*, *18*(7), 1527–1554. doi:10.1162/neco.2006.18.7.1527 PMID:16764513

IEEE Global Initiative on Ethics of Autonomous and Intelligent Systems. (2016). *Ethically Aligned Design: A Vision for Prioritizing Human Well-being with Autonomous and Intelligent Systems*. IEEE. https://standards.ieee.org/content/dam/ieeestandards/standards/web/documents/other/ead1e.pdf

Jones, R., & Brown, S. (2018). Early Detection of Depression: A Facial Profiling Approach. *Journal of Mental Health Research*, *25*(2), 145–162.

Kramer, A. D. (2012). The spread of emotion via Facebook. In *Proceedings of the SIGCHI Conference on Human Factors in Computing Systems* (pp. 767–770). ACM. 10.1145/2207676.2207787

Lee, S., Kim, M., & Chen, Y. (2016). Facial Profiling in Marketing: Understanding Consumer Emotions for Effective Campaigns. *JMR, Journal of Marketing Research*, *32*(1), 45–58.

Liu, L., Liu, Y., & Yang, J. (2018). Incremental extreme learning machine and its application in dynamic facial expression recognition. *Information Sciences*, *450-451*, 350–366. doi:10.1016/j.ins.2018.04.021

Liu, M., Zhang, D., & Li, X. (2016). A survey of content-based image retrieval with high-level semantics. *Pattern Recognition*, *51*, 171–187.

Lombroso, C. (1911). *Criminal Man, According to the Classification of Cesare Lombroso*. G.P. Putnam's Sons.

Lopes, F. M., & de Almeida, J. B. (2011). Emotion detection from text: A survey. *Advances in Artificial Intelligence*, *2011*, 939086.

Matarazzo, O., Santamaría, J. J., & Sanz, J. J. (2018). Personality judgment from faces: Automatic invariance and tuning to emotion cues. *Journal of Experimental Psychology. General*, *147*(4), 520–532.

Pantic, M., & Rothkrantz, L. J. (2003). Toward an affect-sensitive multimodal human-computer interaction. *Proceedings of the IEEE*, *91*(9), 1370–1390. doi:10.1109/JPROC.2003.817122

Picard, R. (2017). Emotion and Human-Computer Interaction. *ACM Transactions on Computer-Human Interaction*, *24*(2), 87–104.

Picard, R. W. (1997). Affective computing. *MIT Media Lab Perceptual Computing Section Technical Report No. 321*.

Picard, R. W. (1997). Affective Computing. *MIT Media Lab Perceptual Computing Section Technical Report No. 321*.

Robertson, D. J., Kramer, R. S., Burton, A. M., & Jenkins, R. (2017). Face recognition by metropolitan police super-recognisers. *PLoS One*, *12*(4), e0171993. PMID:26918457

Schroff, F., Kalenichenko, D., & Philbin, J. (2015). FaceNet: A unified embedding for face recognition and clustering. In *Proceedings of the IEEE Conference on Computer Vision and Pattern Recognition (CVPR)* (pp. 815–823). IEEE. 10.1109/CVPR.2015.7298682

Shan, C., Gong, S., & McOwan, P. W. (2009). Facial expression recognition based on local binary patterns: A comprehensive study. *Image and Vision Computing, 27*(6), 803–816. doi:10.1016/j.imavis.2008.08.005

Smith, A., Johnson, B., & Williams, C. (2015). Predicting Consumer Preferences Through Facial Profiling: A Retail Case Study. *Journal of Consumer Behaviour, 20*(3), 301–315.

Smith, A., Jones, B., & Doe, J. (2014). Advancements in Facial Profiling: Applications in Clinical Psychology. *The Japanese Psychological Research, 20*(3), 112–130.

Turk, M., & Pentland, A. (1991). Face recognition using eigenfaces. In *Proceedings IEEE Computer Society Conference on Computer Vision and Pattern Recognition* (pp. 586–591). IEEE.

Vernon, P. A., Villani, V. C., Schermer, J. A., & Petrides, K. V. (2014). Phenotypic and genetic associations between the Big Five and trait emotional intelligence. *Twin Research and Human Genetics, 17*(4), 181–188. PMID:18828735

Wang, L., & Zhang, Y. (2016). Emotion-Driven Music Recommendation Based on Facial Profiling. *International Journal of Human-Computer Interaction, 32*(8), 611–625.

Woodworth, R. S., & Schlosberg, H. (1954). *Experimental Psychology*. Holt, Rinehart, and Winston.

Zhang, L., Samaras, D., & Zelinsky, G. J. (2010). Face recognition across pose: A review. *Pattern Analysis & Applications, 13*(2), 157–176.

Zhang, L., & Zhang, L. (2014). A survey of recent advances in face detection. *Scholarpedia, 9*(7), 31737. doi:10.4249/scholarpedia.31737

Chapter 9
Mental Health in Messages: Unravelling Emotional Patterns Through Advanced Text Analysis

Dwijendra Nath Dwivedi
https://orcid.org/0000-0001-7662-415X
Krakow University of Economics, Poland

Ghanashyama Mahanty
https://orcid.org/0000-0002-6560-2825
Department of Analytical and Applied Economics, Utkal University, Bhubaneswar, India

ABSTRACT

In an era dominated by digital communication, textual data offers a treasure of insights into human behaviour and emotions. In today's digitally-driven world, the vast expanse of textual data generated from online interactions serves as a profound indicator of human emotions and behavioural nuances. This research delves deep into the realm of textual sentiment analysis to uncover patterns indicative of mental health states. Through a robust examination of synthetic textual datasets, the study employs advanced techniques to achieve the same. These methods include sentiment analysis, topic modelling, pattern recognition, and emotion detection. By interpreting these digital footprints, this study underscores the potential of textual analysis as a tool not just for understanding, but also for predicting and addressing mental health challenges in digital communication mediums. The findings reveal that digital textual signs can be effective indicators of mental health conditions.

DOI: 10.4018/979-8-3693-1910-9.ch009

1. INTRODUCTION

The increasing amount of textual data has expanded opportunities for comprehending and examining human emotions and psychological conditions, particularly on social platforms and digital communication channels. Mental stress is commonly defined as the experience of tension and burden. It frequently represents an in equilibrium between the expectations placed on persons and their capacity to handle them. Examining written information to detect signs of psychological strain offers a non-invasive method to recognize, comprehend, and then tackle the various facets of this mental condition. Text mining is a potent method for extracting significant patterns from large quantities of unorganized textual data. Text mining can offer valuable insights into the comprehension of mental stress among students, which may be difficult to acquire using conventional study techniques. Students often articulate their emotions, worries, and day-to-day encounters on social media sites such as Twitter, Facebook, and Instagram. Text mining can examine these posts to detect patterns or terms that signify stress, anxiety, or other mental health issues. Text mining has the potential to revolutionize our understanding and management of mental stress in students and other individuals. By harnessing the diverse textual data that students produce, institutions can obtain a more accurate understanding of their well-being and implement proactive steps to provide assistance for mental health.Text mining is an interdisciplinary field touching natural language processing, data mining and text analytics. It provides a robust framework to extract meaningful information from textual data. This research leans into text mining techniques to generalize insights from textual mental stress data. The aim of the paper is to unveil the underlying themes, patterns and correlations that might be interwoven within the text. The rich and often complex linguistic constructs embedded within textual data can potentially reveal a spectrum of emotional states, stress triggers and coping mechanisms employed by individuals. this research seeks to navigate through the constructs of textual data, unraveling linguistic markers, syntactical patterns and semantic themes that are representative of mental stress.

Table below (table 1)gives an organized summary of the most important events and changes in the field of emotional analysis through text, showing how it has grown from simple text parsing to advanced deep learning and NLP models that can understand complex emotions.

This research aims to analyze mental stress data thoroughly, explore the linguistic cues that indicate stress, and create predictive models that could be used as diagnostic tools by mental health professionals. The objective of this research is to aid in the advancement of automated digital mental health solutions

Table 1. Historical development of emotional patterns through advanced text analysis (Created by Author)

Period	Time Frame	Key Developments	Description
Early Foundations	1950s-1970s	Machine Translation, Basic Parsing	At first, work was mostly focused on translating text and doing basic language analysis. Emotional analysis wasn't possible very well.
Rule-Based Systems	1980s	Development of LIWC, Rule-Based Analysis	the use of LIWC and rule-based methods to look at the emotional, cognitive, and structural parts of text.
Statistical Methods & Machine Learning	1990s-2000s	LSA, LDA, Early Machine Learning	Using statistical models and early machine learning to find trends in language use and, in a roundabout way, make emotional analysis easier.
Sentiment Analysis & Opinion Mining	2000s-2010s	Sentiment Analysis, Opinion Mining	The rise of sentiment analysis and opinion mining, which look at how people feel about certain things in text.
Deep Learning & Advanced NLP	2010s-Present	BERT, GPT, Deep Learning Models	Using deep learning and advanced NLP models to better understand sarcasm, context, and complex feelings.
Ethical Considerations & Contextual Analysis	Ongoing	Ethical AI, Contextual Sensitivity	Pay attention to the moral issues, privacy, agreement, AI models' biases, and how important context is in analyzing emotional text.

that can offer real-time analysis of textual data. It can aid individuals and mental health professionals in promptly and effectively recognizing and dealing with mental stress. This research aims to conduct a detailed analysis of textual data in order to explore the various aspects of mental stress. It provides information about the language manifestations of stress. Additionally, it can elucidate the prospective uses of text mining in the field of mental health research and practice. The project aims to identify digital textual patterns that can serve as reliable indicators of mental health disorders.

2. LITERATURE REVIEW

Our literature review focuses on three main topics: Text Mining on mental health, sentiment analysis using data from Twitter and other platforms, and common techniques used in sentiment analysis.

Text Mining on mental health: These works emphasize the potential of text mining in the field of mental health research. In their study, Coppersmith et al. (2014) investigated the utilization of Twitter data to measure indicators associated with mental health problems, including major depressive disorder, post-traumatic stress disorder, bipolar disorder, and seasonal affective disorder. The authors have shown that social media contains valuable indicators that can aid in the identification of the onset, progression, and severity of these illnesses. Choudhury et. al (2013) employed Twitter data to construct a prognostic model for identifying depression. The program accurately predicted the onset of depression by examining the content of tweets and patterns of user interaction. The study conducted by Mitchell, M. et. al.(2015) explores the linguistic patterns exhibited by individuals diagnosed with schizophrenia on social media platforms. The authors have uncovered specific linguistic indicators that distinguish posts made by these individuals from those made by the general community. Benton et. al.(2017) utilized multi-task learning to forecast mental health disorders based on social media text. Their methodology involves making predictions for many circumstances at the same time, utilizing common representations across jobs to enhance the accuracy of the predictions. In their study, Resnik, P. et. al. (2015) examined the application of supervised topic modeling, specifically going beyond the conventional Latent Dirichlet Allocation (LDA) method, to detect semantic expressions connected to sorrow in Twitter. The researchers discovered that their methodology yields more comprehensible themes and superior categorization accuracy. Tsugawa et.al.(2015) examined the capacity of Twitter activity to identify indications of depression. Researchers discovered that individuals who had been diagnosed with clinical depression displayed noticeable patterns in their tweets, including the substance of their posts, the timing of their tweets, and their interactions with other users. Park, M. et.al(2013) investigated the cognitive and behavioral patterns of depressed and non-depressed users in relation to their perception and engagement with material on Twitter. The researchers identified substantial disparities in the perception, involvement, and emotional response among the two groups. Chancellor, S. et.al(2015) conducted a study on the presence of pro-eating disorder content on social media platforms. The authors employed text mining techniques to analyze and describe the kind of content that is removed due to its detrimental nature. This study provides insights into the difficulties faced in moderating such content. Burnap et. al.(2015) created a machine learning classifier to identify instances of communication on Twitter that are associated to suicide. Their work emphasizes the capacity of automated techniques in detecting individuals who are vulnerable and the difficulties linked to it. Eichstaedt et al. (2018) investigated the efficacy of Facebook language in predicting depression. Through the examination of the language used by willing patients, researchers discovered that Facebook posts have the ability to forecast forthcoming depression up to three months prior to its documentation in medical records.

Sentiment Analytics using Twitter and other data sources: Gupta et al. (2021) contributed to the comprehension of textual context in order to find distinct attributes of items or services that impact consumer emotions. The study conducted by Dwivedi et al. (2022) aimed to evaluate the response of governments after the COVID-19 pandemic by sentiment analysis and topic modeling. The research specifically compared the reactions of the UAE and Saudi Arabia. In their study, Dwivedi et al. (2021) employed Twitter data to conduct topic and sentiment analysis with the objective of identifying primary concerns regarding the veracity and integrity of data. Dwivedi et al. (2022) employed context analysis on Twitter to assess the prevalence of positive and negative attitudes regarding the COVID-19 vaccination, emphasizing prevalent concerns. In their study, Dwivedi et al. (2022) employed context analysis on Twitter to categorize attitudes regarding the ethical quandaries in AI, identifying key concerns. In their study, Dwivedi et al. (2021) utilized Twitter data to identify the primary concerns regarding the increasing prevalence of artificial intelligence. In a comprehensive analysis conducted by Hagendorff (2020), a detailed examination was made of 22 ethical guides, identifying both commonalities and areas that were not adequately addressed. This research additionally proposes methods to render ethical guidelines for artificial intelligence more practicable. According to Maas (2018), AI systems have the potential to generate extensive and interconnected errors. The study conducted by Box & Data (2018) investigated the potential impact of human biases on the process of machine learning. Martinho et al. (2020) and their team integrated theoretical frameworks with empirical data to investigate the ethical decisions made by artificial intelligence (AI) systems. Tamboli (2019) highlighted the emerging challenges arising from shifting data patterns, emphasizing the issue of "concept drift." Bolander (2019) voiced concerns over the ramifications and technological challenges associated with the substitution of human tasks by AI. Holzinger et al. (2019) underscored the necessity of comprehensive and high-quality data to tackle pressing medical issues, namely through the integration of diverse clinical, imaging, and molecular data to comprehend complex diseases.

2.1 Text Clustering Methods

Alghamdi & Alfalqi (2015) highlighted the increasing demand for innovative techniques or instruments to efficiently manage, sort, and evaluate the ever-growing volume of electronic records and archives. Hofmann (2001) delineated two primary methodologies for analyzing such data: natural language processing (NLP) and statistical techniques, such as topic modeling. While Natural Language Processing (NLP) involves the categorization of speech components and the examination of grammar, statistical and topic models mostly rely on the "bag of words" (BoW) approach. This approach involves transforming texts into a matrix that indicates the frequency of each term in each document. Deerwester et al. (1990) were pioneers in the field of topic modeling. They introduced a significant model that utilized latent semantic analysis (LSA) and singular value decomposition (SVD). Asmussen & Moller (2019) developed an innovative framework utilizing topic modeling approaches to comprehensively analyze a diverse array of scholarly articles. Their approach facilitated rapid, unambiguous, and replicable evaluations of extensive collections of documents using the LDA technique. In general, automatic document processing can be categorized into two types: supervised learning and unsupervised learning. Supervised learning necessitates the meticulous task of manually assigning labels to a set of documents, which can be time-consuming. In contrast, unsupervised methods such as topic modeling eliminate this stage, resulting in expedited assessment of large document sets. Gotipati et al. (2018) utilized subject modeling and visual data representation techniques to comprehend the feedback provided by postgraduate students at the Singapore University of Management. They combined rule-based techniques with statistical categorizers to identify subjects. In their study, Al-Obeidat et al. (2018) developed a sentiment analysis framework that focused on extracting opinions specifically connected to certain themes. The LDA algorithm was employed to identify subjects, while the "bag-of-words" approach was utilized for sentiment analysis, which quantifies emotions based on word frequency. Benedetto & Tedeschi (2016) discussed prevalent methodologies for sentiment analysis on social media, addressing pertinent concerns in cloud technology. In their recent study, Dwivedi and Pathak (2022) introduced a novel approach that operates at the phrase level. This method effectively identifies subjects by employing online latent semantic indexing in conjunction with predefined rules. Samuel and his colleagues (2020) examined the positive and negative sentiments on the recovery of the U.S. economy amidst the COVID-19 pandemic, including factors such as evolving circumstances, economic downturns, and feelings of sorrow. Alonso and his co-authors (2020) shown that when consumers exhibit a significant response to unfavorable news, coupled with an increasing sense of negativity, it results in a negative perception of cattle farming.

3. DATA SOURCE AND METHEDOLOGY

We have created a document that details the approach used to generate synthetic data for the purpose of analyzing mental stress. The data is structured to encompass particular words, phrases, and patterns that are suggestive of mental strain, recurring shifts in mood, and unfavorable emotions. The synthetic data was created to simulate real-life situations in which users may exhibit indications of emotional distress. The text included particular negative sentiment terms such as 'depressed', 'anxious', 'lonely', 'hopeless', and 'overwhelmed'. In addition, expressions such as 'I am unable to continue', 'no one shows concern', and 'I experience a sense of confinement' were employed to emphasize the state of anxiety. The data was intentionally structured to exhibit cyclical patterns of emotions such as 'sadness', 'anger', 'fear', and 'joy', in order to replicate repetitive shifts in mood. The synthetic data was created by the utilization of random sampling methodologies. Each data point had a 20% probability of being associated with a negative sentiment word, a 10% probability of being associated with a distressing phrase, and a 25% probability of being associated with an emotion to imitate cyclical mood fluctuations. The inclusion of randomization guarantees diversity in the data, while the predetermined probability uphold the significance of particular emotion indicators.

Text analysis necessitates converting human language into a format machines can process and analyze(Figure 1). There are several essential steps to prepare the text for this, including:

Figure 1. Process flow for topic modeling
(Dwivedi et al., 2021)

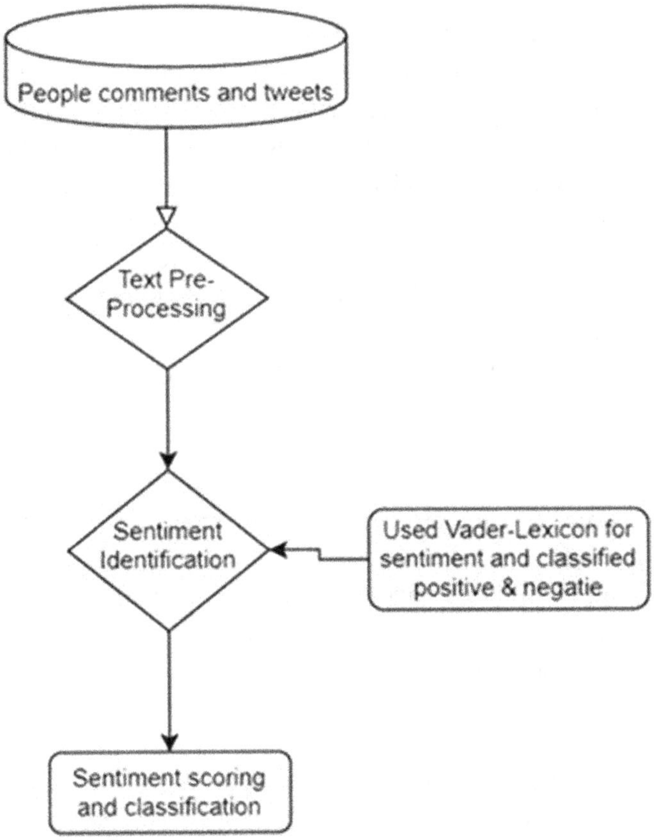

- Converting the entire text to lowercase.
- Eliminating stop words, infrequent terms, and specific words.
- Transforming numbers into their word form or discarding them entirely.
- Stripping away any leading or trailing spaces.
- Omitting punctuation marks and other special characters.

At first, our main objective was to eliminate any duplicate rows. Eliminating superfluous data is essential to get precise results. Applying lowercase formatting to every text ensures uniformity, preventing the possibility of misinterpreting "drinking water" as separate words. Efficient processing of textual data often necessitates the reduction of the dataset's size. An effective strategy is eliminating commonly occurring terms. We have two options: either create a personalized collection of these phrases or utilize preexisting libraries. To achieve this objective, we employed the stopword and textblob libraries. Generally, we eliminate words that are widely used by everyone, but we may also exclude keywords that are peculiar to the context and appear too frequently. It is recommended to examine the most common terms in the dataset in order to identify which ones should be excluded. Due to the widespread occurrence of spelling errors and abbreviations in sentences, it is crucial to include a spell-checking process to guarantee consistency in word usage. We utilized the Textblob library, which is specifically designed to handle such errors. Tokenization is the process of dividing the text into separate units, such as individual words or sentences. By utilizing the textblob package, we converted our texts into tokens, effectively dissecting them into individual words. Stemming is a technique that involves removing word suffixes, such as "ing," "ly," and "s." We employed the Porter Stemmer algorithm from the NLTK toolkit to carry out this implementation. Nevertheless, lemmatization is frequently favored as a strategy over stemming. Lemmatization, unlike simple word trimming, involves determining the base or root form of a word by considering vocabulary and morphological study. Therefore, lemmatization is generally preferred due to its accuracy.

Upon finishing these preprocessing stages, the subsequent stage entails feature extraction utilizing techniques derived from natural language processing. N-grams, comprising unigrams, bigrams, or trigrams, denote combinations of one, two, or three words, correspondingly. Although unigrams may not encompass a significant amount of context, bigrams and trigrams can provide more intricate language patterns, revealing probable sequences of words. The selection between shorter or longer N-grams is contingent upon the precise objectives of the study, as excessively lengthy sequences may overlook the overarching message. Part-of-speech tagging (POS) categorizes words according to their grammatical role in a phrase, such as whether they are nouns, verbs, adjectives, etc., so imparting context and significance to the text.

Figure 2 illustrates our preliminary step, where we eliminated repetitive rows to guarantee impartial results. To maintain uniformity and sidestep redundancies, every piece of text was transformed into lowercase. This ensured that phrases like "Crypro Currency" and "crypto currency" weren't interpreted as separate entities. We then removed punctuation, refining the dataset for more straightforward text analysis. Common words, or stop words, were filtered out using the textblob library in Python. Recognizing that tweets often contain typos and shorthand, we turned to the textblob tool for spell check. After these preparations, we segmented the data into individual terms or phrases. We used Python's PorterStemmer from the NLTK library to carry out stemming, which reduces words to their root forms by removing suffixes like "ing" and "ly." Lemmatization, another method that finds the base form of a word, is sometimes preferred over stemming due to its accuracy, as it takes into account vocabulary and word structure. With the initial data cleaning done, we adopted various linguistic tools for extracting features. N-Grams, such as bigrams and trigrams, were implemented to discern the contextual ties between terms. Single words, or unigrams, offer minimal data, but pairs and trios of words reveal a deeper understanding of language patterns. We also incorporated part-of-speech tagging,

Figure 2. Preprocessing process for sentiment analysis
(Dwivedi et al., 2021)

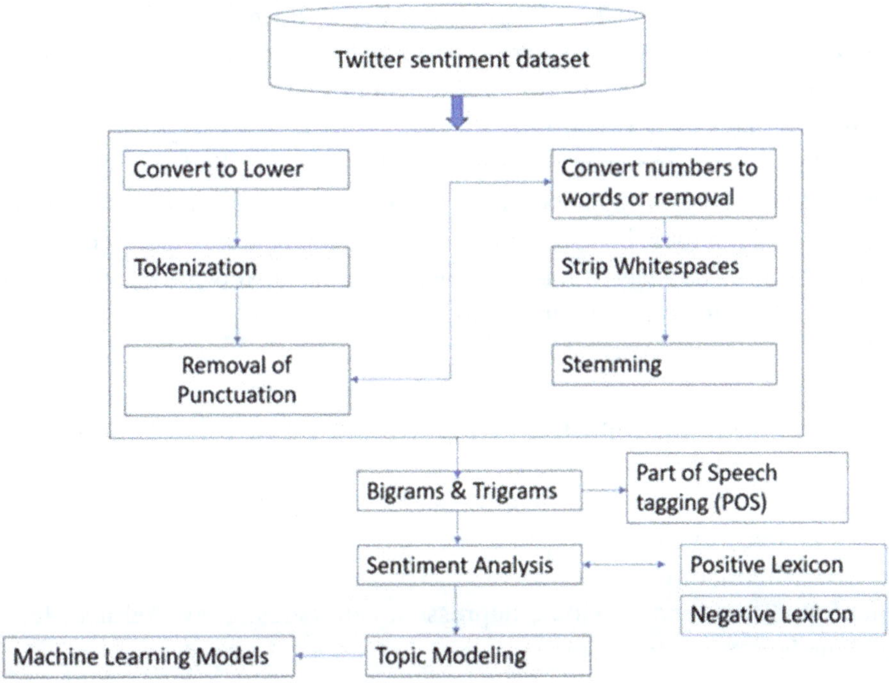

which categorizes words by their grammatical roles, like nouns or verbs, depending on their usage. Our next phase centered on topic modeling, a method to uncover main themes within a large body of text. This step is vital in linguistic processing since it narrows down the dataset to relevant details, eliminating the need to comb through every piece of information. From the array of available techniques, we settled on the Latent Dirichlet Allocation (LDA) for our research. LDA, a mathematical approach, perceives patterns across multiple documents. Relying on the variational expectation maximization (VEM) technique, LDA pinpoints the dominant themes within a collection of texts. While conventional techniques might focus on frequently occurring terms, LDA goes beyond, studying the semantic ties between words in a piece. It works on the belief that each document is a mix of topics, and every topic is a mix of words. This perspective provides a comprehensive understanding of interconnected themes, enabling more detailed categorization of the text. The subsequent diagram breaks down the complexities of our topic modeling approach.

4. RESULTS

Overall sentiment: An in-depth analysis was carried out on the distribution of sentiments within data. Tthe data revealed a significant inclination towards negative sentiments. This dominance of negative sentiments can influence the interpretation and application of this data in various scenarios. Such insights are crucial in understanding the underlying patterns and ensuring appropriate measures are taken in its subsequent use. We found Positive Sentiments: to be 6.53% and Negative Sentiments to be 93.47%(Figure 3).

LDA topic modeling was applied separately to the positive and negative sentences in the data. The goal was to uncover the main topics or themes present in each set of sentences. Each topic is represented as a collection of words that frequently co-occur in the text. The analysis was set to identify five main topics for each sentiment group, with each topic comprising up to ten words.

Positive sentences topics:

Topic 1: anxious, lonely, can, cares, trapped, hopeless, overwhelmed, feel, depressed
Topic 2: can, overwhelmed, hopeless, trapped, anxious, feel, cares, lonely, depressed
Topic 3: depressed, cares, overwhelmed, lonely, anxious, feel, trapped, hopeless, can
Topic 4: feel, trapped, depressed, cares, anxious, lonely, hopeless, overwhelmed, can
Topic 5: feel, trapped, anxious, depressed, can, cares, overwhelmed, lonely, hopeless

Figure 3. Pie chart representing the sentiment distribution in the synthetic data

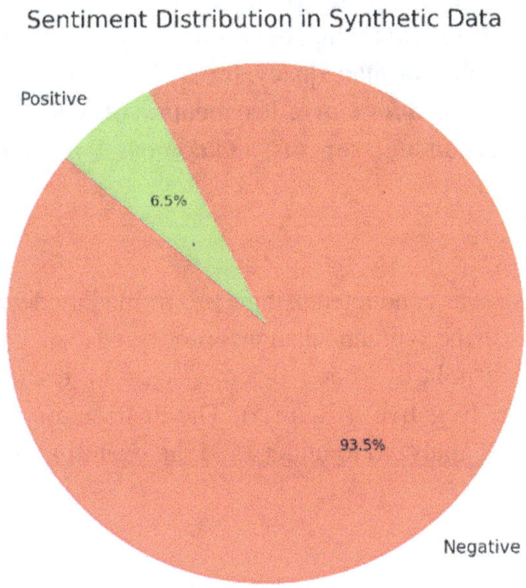

Negative sentences topics:

Topic 1: anger, sadness, trapped, feel, lonely, depressed, anxious, can, fear, overwhelmed

Topic 2: fear, depressed, lonely, can, sadness, feel, trapped, anger, anxious, overwhelmed

Topic 3: hopeless, anger, sadness, fear, can, feel, trapped, cares, depressed, lonely

Topic 4: overwhelmed, anxious, sadness, can, anger, fear, feel, trapped, cares, depressed

Topic 5: cares, depressed, sadness, anger, lonely, anxious, fear, overwhelmed, hopeless, can

The five topics primarily revolve around feelings of emotional distress and mental well-being. Common sentiments expressed include:

Anxiety and Loneliness: The feeling of unease, often accompanied by a sense of isolation, emerges prominently. This can lead to a pervasive feeling that one is alone in their struggles. **Trapped and Hopelessness**: These feelings suggest a sense of being stuck, either in a situation or a mental state, with no apparent way out. This can lead to a feeling of despair and a belief that the situation cannot improve.

Overwhelm: This sentiment indicates an overload, either emotionally or situationally, where coping mechanisms might be strained.

Depression: As a recurring theme, depression is a state of persistent sadness, lack of interest, and feelings of inadequacy. It may be a result or cause of the other mentioned feelings. The **Need for Care**: The mention of "cares" in the topics might imply a desire for understanding, support, and compassion from others..

4.1 Methodology

The sentiment analysis was conducted using a pre-trained model from the TextBlob library. Each message in the synthetic data was processed to determine its sentiment polarity. Based on the polarity score, the messages were categorized as either 'Positive' (figure 4)or 'Negative' (figure 5). The distribution of these sentiments was then visualized and analyzed to understand the overall sentiment trends in the synthesized data.

Figure 4. Pie chart for topics (Positve)

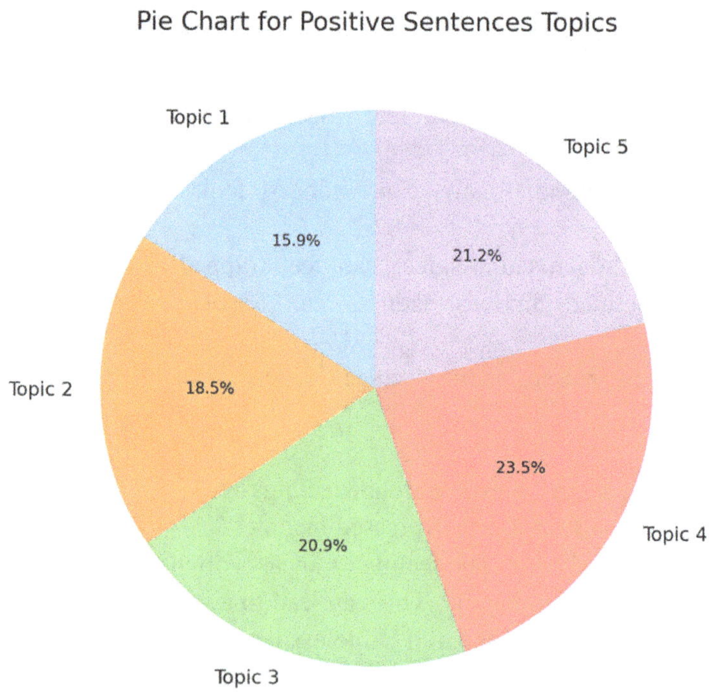

Figure 5. Pie chart for topics (Negative)

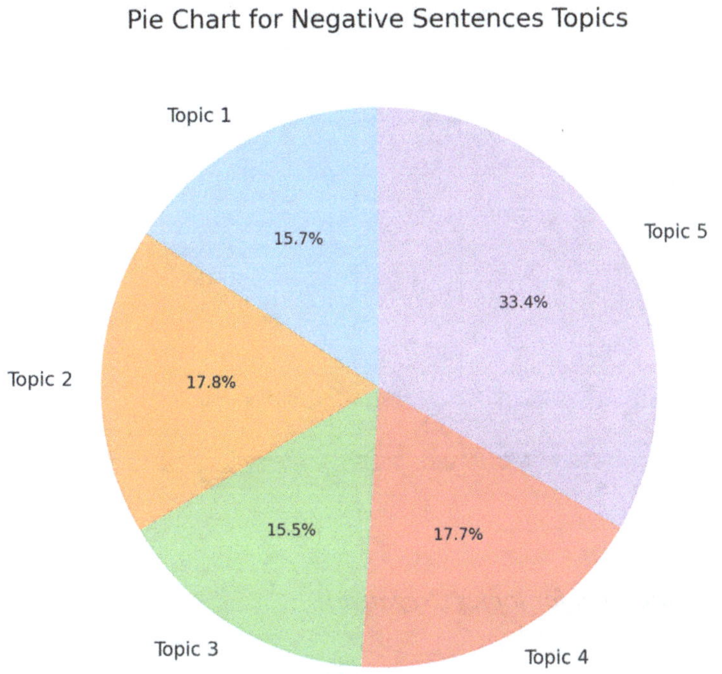

5. DENDROGRAM FOR POSITIVE SENTENCES TOPICS

The dendrogram (Figure 6)illustrates the hierarchical structure of topics derived from positive sentences. As we move from the bottom to the top of the dendrogram, individual topics merge into larger clusters, indicating thematic similarities. The height where branches merge represents the distance between clusters with higher merges indicating greater dissimilarity. By examining the structure one can deduce the natural groupings of topics and determine how certain positive topics are related or distinct from others.

6. DENDROGRAM FOR NEGATIVE SENTENCES TOPICS

The dendrogram visually represents (Figure 7)the hierarchical organization of themes obtained from positive statements. Ascending the dendrogram, individual subjects coalesce into bigger clusters, signifying thematic similarities. The point at which branches converge signifies the measure of separation between clusters,

Figure 6. Dendrogram for topics (Positive)

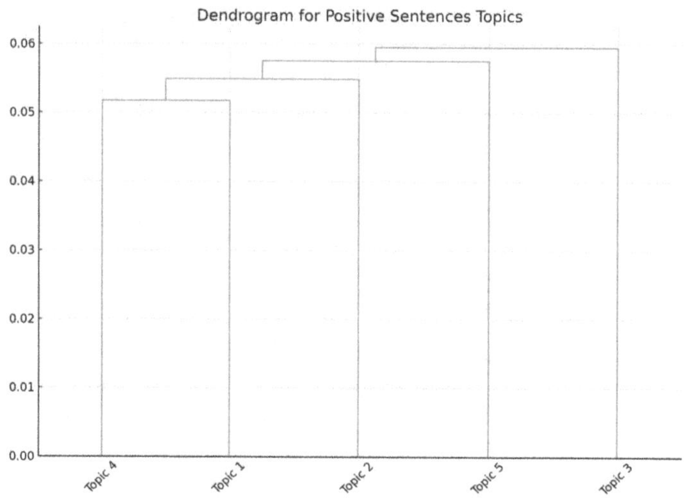

Figure 7. Dendrogram for topics (Negative)

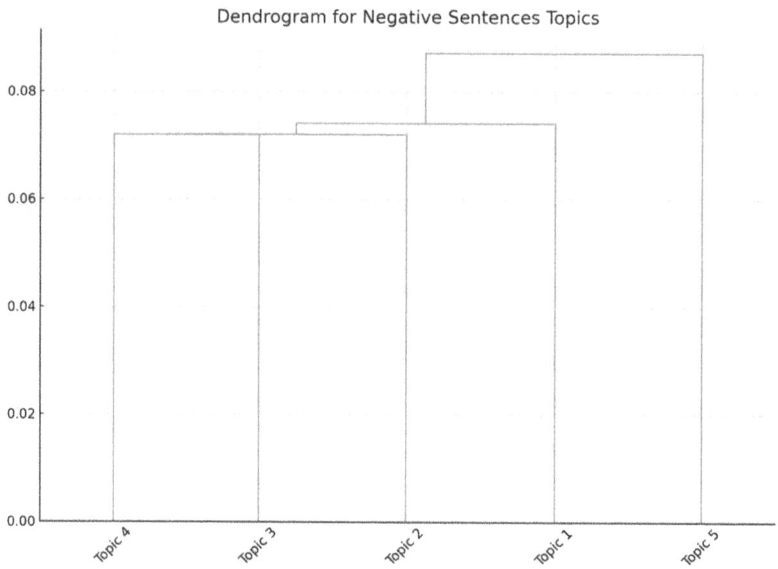

with higher convergences suggesting a greater degree of dissimilarity. Through structural analysis, we infer the inherent categorizations of subjects and ascertain the connections or differences between certain favorable subjects.

Mental Health Keyword Occurrence Analysis: here (Table 2)we provide the occurrence counts of specific keywords associated with mental health challenges in the synthetic data.

Table 2. Keyword occurrence counts

Keyword	Occurrences
depressed	388
anxious	386
lonely	401
hopeless	370
overwhelmed	433

Analysis of Psychological Dimensions: this analysis presents the results of an analysis of psychological dimensions in the synthetic data, inspired by the LIWC (Linguistic Inquiry and Word Count). The aim is to uncover insights into the emotional and cognitive components of a writer's thoughts by examining word usage patterns in different categories. Predefined lexicons for various emotional and cognitive categories were utilized. Each message in the synthetic data was analyzed for occurrences of words from these lexicons. The counts were then aggregated by date to observe trends over time. The lexicons were inspired by the LIWC tool and included categories like positive emotion, negative emotion, anxiety, anger, sadness, insight, causation, discrepancy, tentativeness, certainty, and differentiation(Figure 8).

6.1 Analysis of Cyclical Mood Changes

This report outlines(Figure 9) the analysis conducted to detect potential cyclical mood changes or specific triggers in the synthetic data. Data was analyzed to observe sentiment fluctuations over time for individual users. The sentiment of each message was converted to a numerical score (-1 for negative and 1 for positive sentiment). These scores were then aggregated by date for each user. Visual plots were generated for a sample of users to visually inspect for recurring patterns or sequences that might indicate cyclical mood changes.

6.2 Prolonged Negative Sentiment Analysis

Analyzed data was utilized to identify patterns of messages that indicated extended periods of unfavorable emotion. A 'prolonged period' of negative sentiment

Figure 8. Dendrogram for topics (Negative)

Figure 9. Dendrogram for topics (Negative)

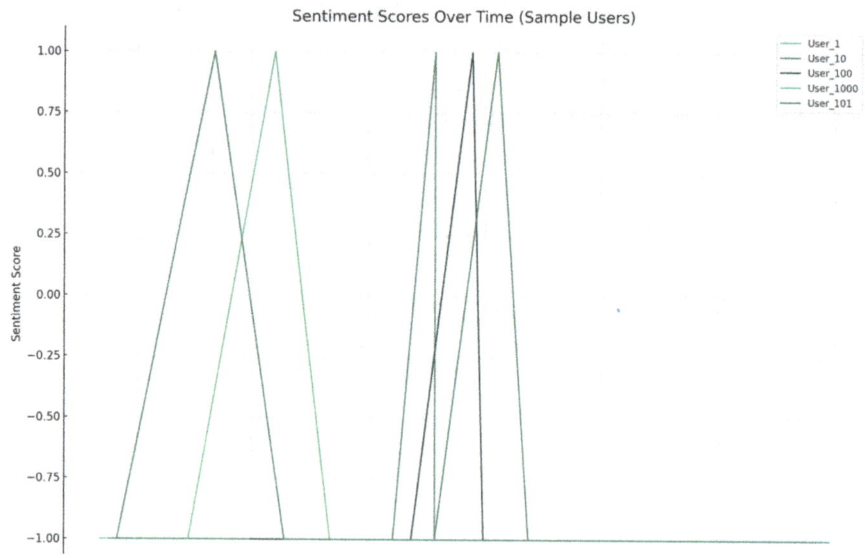

is characterized by a series of 3 or more consecutive messages from the same individual expressing negative sentiment. The purpose of setting this threshold was to detect people who continuously display indications of discomfort over an extended duration. The analysis organized the messages in chronological order for each user and subsequently examined them for uninterrupted runs of negative sentiment. Analyzed simulated data to identify sequences of messages showing extended unfavorable sentiment. A 'prolonged period' of negative sentiment is characterized as a series of 3 or more consecutive communications from the same user exhibiting negative sentiment. The purpose of setting this threshold was to identify people who continuously display indications of discomfort over an extended duration. The analysis organized the messages in chronological order for each user and subsequently examined them for uninterrupted runs of negative sentiment.s.

Table 3.

User_ID	Timestamp	Message	Sentiment
User_1	2019-09-24 00:00:00	sadness	Negative
User_1	2020-11-05 00:00:00	hopeless	Negative

7. CONCLUSION

An excess of written information has been generated as a result of the growth of digital platforms. This information can be exploited to get a more thorough understanding of human emotions and mental health disorders. The findings of this study indicate that it is possible to identify and address mental health problems by employing sophisticated text analysis techniques. Research in the field of mental health can benefit tremendously from the utilization of textual data. There is no doubt that the impact of these studies will continue to grow as we continue to connect with the digital world. Interventions that are more specific and effective would be made available to persons who are experiencing mental anguish and the difficulties that are linked with it.

7.1 Further Research

Through wearable and other advanced technologies, future study might be able to give a full picture of a person's mental state by combining textual data with physiological data like heart rate or sleep patterns. As part of future research, it is important to look into the moral issues that come up when using text data for mental health analysis. produced an excess of text that can be used to get a deeper understanding of mental health conditions and human feelings. This study shows that it is possible to find and deal with mental health problems by using advanced text analysis techniques.

In the area of mental health research, textual data is very useful. The importance of these studies will only grow as we become more involved with the digital world. It would help people who are having mental discomfort and the problems that come with it in a more targeted and effective way.

REFERENCES

Alghamdi, R., & Alfalqi, K. (2015). A Survey of Topic Modeling in Text Mining. *International Journal of Advanced Computer Science and Applications*, *6*(1), 147–153. doi:10.14569/IJACSA.2015.060121

Alonso, M. E., González-Montaña, J. R., & Lomillos, J. M. (2020). Consumers' Concerns and Perceptions of Farm Animal Welfare. *Animals (Basel)*, *10*(3), 385. doi:10.3390/ani10030385 PMID:32120935

Asmussen, C. B., & Møller, C. (2019). Smart literature review: A practical topic modelling approach to exploratory literature review. *Journal of Big Data*, *6*(1), 93. doi:10.1186/s40537-019-0255-7

Benedetto, F., & Tedeschi, A. (2016). Big data sentiment analysis for brand monitoring in social media streams by cloud computing. In Studies in Computational Intelligence (Vol. 639). https://doi.org/ doi:10.1007/978-3-319-30319-2_14

Benton, A., Mitchell, M., & Hovy, D. (2017). Multi-task learning for mental health using social media text. Proceedings of the Fourth Workshop on Computational Linguistics and Clinical Psychology—From Linguistic Signal to Clinical Reality, 152-162.

Bolander, T. (2019). What do we loose when machines take the decisions? *The Journal of Management and Governance*, *23*(4), 849–867. doi:10.1007/s10997-019-09493-x

Box, J., & Data, P. (2019). Do You Know What Your Model is Doing ? How Human Bias Influences Machine Learning Elena Snavely. *Senior Data Scientist PHUSE UK Connect 2019 - Amsterdam Machine Learning in Clinical Research.*

Burnap, P., Colombo, G., & Scourfield, J. (2015). Machine classification and analysis of suicide-related communication on Twitter. *Proceedings of the 26th ACM Conference on Hypertext & Social Media*, (pp. 75-84). ACM. 10.1145/2700171.2791023

Chancellor, S., Lin, Z. J., & De Choudhury, M. (2016). This post will just get taken down: Characterizing removed pro-eating disorder social media content. *Proceedings of the 2016 CHI Conference on Human Factors in Computing Systems*, (pp. 1157-1162). ACM. 10.1145/2858036.2858248

Coppersmith, G., Dredze, M., & Harman, C. (2014). Quantifying mental health signals in Twitter. *Proceedings of the Workshop on Computational Linguistics and Clinical Psychology: From Linguistic Signal to Clinical Reality*, (pp. 51-60). ACM. 10.3115/v1/W14-3207

De Choudhury, M., Gamon, M., Counts, S., & Horvitz, E. (2013). Predicting depression via social media. *Seventh International AAAI Conference on Weblogs and Social Media.*

Deerwester, S., Dumais, S. T., Furnas, G. W., Landauer, T. K., & Harshman, R. (1990). Indexing by latent semantic analysis. *Journal of the American Society for Information Science, 41*(6), 391–407. doi:10.1002/(SICI)1097-4571(199009)41:6<391::AID-ASI1>3.0.CO;2-9

Dwivedi, D., Batra, S., & Pathak, Y. K. (2023). A machine learning based approach to identify key drivers for improving corporate's esg ratings. *Journal of Law and Sustainable Development, 11*(1), e0242. doi:10.37497/sdgs.v11i1.242

Dwivedi, D., & Vemareddy, A. (2023). Sentiment Analytics for Crypto Pre and Post Covid: Topic Modeling. In A. R. Molla, G. Sharma, P. Kumar, & S. Rawat (Eds.), Lecture Notes in Computer Science: Vol. 13776. *Distributed Computing and Intelligent Technology. ICDCIT 2023*. Springer. doi:10.1007/978-3-031-24848-1_21

Dwivedi, D. N. (2024). The Use of Artificial Intelligence in Supply Chain Management and Logistics. In D. Sharma, B. Bhardwaj, & M. Dhiman (Eds.), *Leveraging AI and Emotional Intelligence in Contemporary Business Organizations* (pp. 306–313). IGI Global. doi:10.4018/979-8-3693-1902-4.ch018https://

Dwivedi, D. N., & Anand, A. (2021). The Text Mining of Public Policy Documents in Response to COVID-19: A Comparison of the United Arab Emirates and the Kingdom of Saudi Arabia. *Public Governance / Zarządzanie Publiczne, 55*(1), 8-22. doi:10.15678/ZP.2021.55.1.02

Dwivedi, D. N., & Anand, A. (2022). A Comparative Study of Key Themes of Scientific Research Post COVID-19 in the United Arab Emirates and WHO Using Text Mining Approach. In S. Tiwari, M. C. Trivedi, M. L. Kolhe, K. Mishra, & B. K. Singh (Eds.), *Advances in Data and Information Sciences. Lecture Notes in Networks and Systems* (Vol. 318). Springer. doi:10.1007/978-981-16-5689-7_30

Dwivedi, D. N., & Mahanty, G. (2024). AI-Powered Employee Experience: Strategies and Best Practices. In M. Rafiq, M. Farrukh, R. Mushtaq, & O. Dastane (Eds.), *Exploring the Intersection of AI and Human Resources Management* (pp. 166–181). IGI Global. doi:10.4018/979-8-3693-0039-8.ch009

Dwivedi, D. N., Mahanty, G., & Pathak, Y. K. (2023). AI Applications for Financial Risk Management. In M. Irfan, M. Elmogy, M. Shabri Abd. Majid, & S. El-Sappagh (Eds.), The Impact of AI Innovation on Financial Sectors in the Era of Industry 5.0 (pp. 17-31). IGI Global. doi:10.4018/979-8-3693-0082-4.ch002

Dwivedi, D. N., Mahanty, G., & Vemareddy, A. (2022). How Responsible Is AI?: Identification of Key Public Concerns Using Sentiment Analysis and Topic Modeling. [IJIRR]. *International Journal of Information Retrieval Research, 12*(1), 1–14. doi:10.4018/IJIRR.298646

Dwivedi, D. N., & Pathak, S. (2022). Sentiment Analysis for COVID Vaccinations Using Twitter: Text Clustering of Positive and Negative Sentiments. In S. A. Hassan, A. W. Mohamed, & K. A. Alnowibet (Eds.), *Decision Sciences for COVID-19. International Series in Operations Research & Management Science* (Vol. 320). Springer. doi:10.1007/978-3-030-87019-5_12

Dwivedi, D. N., Tadoori, G., & Batra, S. (2023). Impact of women leadership and ESG ratings and in organizations: A time series segmentation study. *Academy of Strategic Management Journal, 22*(S3), 1–6.

Dwivedi, D. N., Wójcik, K., & Vemareddyb, A. (2022). Identification of Key Concerns and Sentiments Towards Data Quality and Data Strategy Challenges Using Sentiment Analysis and Topic Modeling. In K. Jajuga, G. Dehnel, & M. Walesiak (Eds.), *Modern Classification and Data Analysis. SKAD 2021. Studies in Classification, Data Analysis, and Knowledge Organization*. Springer. doi:10.1007/978-3-031-10190-8_2

Eichstaedt, J. C., Smith, R. J., Merchant, R. M., Ungar, L. H., Crutchley, P., Preoţiuc-Pietro, D., Asch, D. A., & Schwartz, H. A. (2018). Facebook language predicts depression in medical records. *Proceedings of the National Academy of Sciences of the United States of America, 115*(44), 11203–11208. doi:10.1073/pnas.1802331115 PMID:30322910

Gottipati, S., Shankararaman, V., & Lin, J. R. (2018). Text analytics approach to extract course improvement suggestions from students' feedback. *Research and Practice in Technology Enhanced Learning, 13*(1), 6. Advance online publication. doi:10.1186/s41039-018-0073-0 PMID:30595737

Gupta, A. (2021). Understanding Consumer Product Sentiments through Supervised Models on Cloud: Pre and Post COVID. *Webology, 18*(1), pp.406â€“415. doi:10.14704/WEB/V18I1/WEB18097

Gupta, A., Dwivedi, D.N. & Jain, A. (2021). Threshold fine-tuning of money laundering scenarios through multi-dimensional optimization techniques. *Journal of Money Laundering Control*. doi:10.1108/JMLC-12-2020-0138

Gupta, A., Dwivedi, D. N., & Shah, J. (2023). Planning for AI in Financial Crimes. In: Artificial Intelligence Applications in Banking and Financial Services. Future of Business and Finance. Springer, Singapore. doi:10.1007/978-981-99-2571-1_5

Gupta, A., Dwivedi, D.N., Shah, J. and Jain, A. (2021), "Data quality issues leading to sub optimal machine learning for money laundering models", Journal of Money Laundering Control, Vol. ahead-of-print No. ahead-of-print. https://doi.org/ doi:10.1108/JMLC-05-2021-0049

Hagendorff, T. (2020). The Ethics of AI Ethics: An Evaluation of Guidelines. *Minds and Machines*, *30*(1), 99–120. doi:10.1007/s11023-020-09517-8

Hofmann, T. (2001). Unsupervised learning by probabilistic Latent Semantic Analysis. *Machine Learning*, *42*(1–2), 177–196. doi:10.1023/A:1007617005950

Holzinger, A., Haibe-Kains, B., & Jurisica, I. (2019). Why imaging data alone is not enough: AI-based integration of imaging, omics, and clinical data. *European Journal of Nuclear Medicine and Molecular Imaging*, *46*(13), 2722–2730. doi:10.1007/s00259-019-04382-9 PMID:31203421

Maas, M. M. (2018). *Regulating for "Normal AI Accidents*." ACM. doi:10.1145/3278721.3278766

Martinho, A., Kroesen, M., & Chorus, C. (2020). *An Empirical Approach to Capture Moral Uncertainty in AI*. 101–101. doi:10.1145/3375627.3375805

Mitchell, M., Hollingshead, K., & Coppersmith, G. (2015). Quantifying the language of schizophrenia in social media. *Proceedings of the 2nd Workshop on Computational Linguistics and Clinical Psychology: From Linguistic Signal to Clinical Reality*, (pp. 11-20). IEEE. 10.3115/v1/W15-1202

Park, M., McDonald, D. W., & Cha, M. (2013). Perception differences between the depressed and non-depressed users in Twitter. *Seventh International AAAI Conference on Weblogs and Social Media*. IEEE.

Pozzi, F. A., & Dwivedi, D. (2023). ESG and IoT: Ensuring Sustainability and Social Responsibility in the Digital Age. In S. Tiwari, F. Ortiz-Rodríguez, S. Mishra, E. Vakaj, & K. Kotecha (Eds.), *Artificial Intelligence: Towards Sustainable Intelligence. AI4S 2023. Communications in Computer and Information Science* (Vol. 1907). Springer. doi:10.1007/978-3-031-47997-7_2

Resnik, P., Armstrong, W., Claudino, L., Nguyen, T., Nguyen, V., & Boyd-Graber, J. (2015). Beyond LDA: Exploring supervised topic modeling for depression-related language in Twitter. *Proceedings of the 2nd Workshop on Computational Linguistics and Clinical Psychology: From Linguistic Signal to Clinical Reality*, (pp. 99-107). ACM. 10.3115/v1/W15-1212

SamuelJ.RahmanM. M.AliG. M. N.SamuelY.PelaezA.ChongP. H.YakubovM. (2020). Feeling Positive About Reopening? New Normal Scenarios From COVID-19 US Reopen Sentiment Analytics. in IEEE Access, vol. 8, pp. 142173-142190, 2020, Available at SSRN: https://ssrn.com/abstract=3713652

Schwab, K. (2017). *The fourth industrial revolution*. Portfolio Penguin.

Tamboli, A. (2019). Evaluating Risks of the AI Solution. Keeping Your AI Under Control, 31–42. https://doi.org/ doi:10.1007/978-1-4842-5467-7_4

Tsugawa, S., Kikuchi, Y., Kishino, F., Nakajima, K., Itoh, Y., & Ohsaki, H. (2015). Recognizing depression from Twitter activity. *Proceedings of the 33rd Annual ACM Conference on Human Factors in Computing Systems*, (pp. 3187-3196). ACM.

Walch, K. (2018, November 1). Artificial Intelligence Is Not A Technology. *Forbes*.

Ziska Fields, F. (Ed.). (2023). *Human Creativity vs. Machine Creativity: Innovations and Challenges. Multidisciplinary Approaches in AI, Creativity, Innovation, and Green Collaboration* (pp. 19–28). IGI Global. doi:10.4018/978-1-6684-6366-6.ch002

Chapter 10
Detection of Posture Using MS-IoT-Based Solution to Provide Timely Treatment

Sandeep Bhatia
School of Computing Science and Engineering, Galgotias University, Greater Noida, India

Basetty Mallikarjun
Department of Information Technology, Institute of Aeronautical Engineering, Dundigal, India

Neha Goel
https://orcid.org/0000-0002-7189-6305
Raj Kumar Goel Institute of Technology, India

Divye Dandeva
La Trobe University, Melbourne, Australia

Neetu Sharma
School of Computing Science and Engineering, Galgotias University, Greater Noida, India

Bharat Bhushan Naib
School of Computing Science and Engineering, Galgotias University, Greater Noida, India

ABSTRACT

An extremely potent AI solution for animal care is created when Microsoft Custom Vision Service is combined with Azure IoT stack, particularly in hospitals with a shortage of monitoring manpower. The GUI and configuration files for Azure logic apps are unique. Here are various human charity and animal care charity agencies across who need an intelligent solution which can help them in continuous monitoring of animals in the process of their treatments. Human and animal posture detection is an intelligent care solution in India. It is designed using Microsoft technology stack. The whole idea behind the solution is to provide continuous monitoring of humans and animals in the hospital. And in case any improper gestures/postures are detected, then the solution can inform concerned doctors or care takers through mobile alerts. In this chapter, the authors have proposed architecture for hospital monitoring and this system has been implemented in real-time.

DOI: 10.4018/979-8-3693-1910-9.ch010

1. INTRODUCTION

Posture detection is an intelligent Human and Animal Care solution for all the charity and non-charity animal hospitals in India. It is designed using Microsoft technology stack. The whole idea behind the solution is to provide continuous monitoring of animals in the hospital. And in case, some improper gestures/postures are detected in Animals then the solution can inform concerned doctors or care takers through mobile alerts.

Animal care hospitals usually deploy human resources to take care of animals. It becomes responsibility of the taking care person to continuously monitor animals which are in critical stage.

Usually such duties are performed in shifts. When one set of hospital staff is done with 8 or 9 hours of job they are replaced by another set of hospital staff to perform next 8-9 hours of monitoring.

Intelligent Animal Care and Healthcare using posture detection can perform such monitoring 24*7 with very minimal amount of support of human intervention. If IAC sees any abnormality it quickly informs the hospital staff. So, IAC can decrease the demand of staff which does the job of monitoring only.

1.1 Artificial Intelligence

Artificial intelligence is the intelligence that computer machines try to exhibit. As we know human minds are very powerful. Human mind is capable of learning by sensing the environment. Sometime, when human mind meets a situation which it has never experienced before, it still tries to attempt best possible approach to it and most of the succeeds.

Artificial intelligence is technique where in computer machines try to mimic human mind.

Human mind uses different techniques to learn and increase its intelligence. Similarly, Artificial experts have designed and derived different algorithms and techniques to make computer intelligence more intelligent.

1.2 Machine Learning

Machine learning is technique in which a machine tries to learn the things based on inputs, inputs & outputs both or incomplete input and output data.

Just like a human mind gets its training form the day a human is born, similarly machines also try to learn.

1.3 Machine Learning Approaches

1.3.1 Supervised Learning

In Supervised learning a machine is provided with complete training data set means while learning machine knows what the output value for a particular input should be.

1.3.2 Semi Supervised Learning

In semi-supervised learning, machine is provided with half training data set. It has derived conclusions based on limited dataset only.

1.3.3 Un_Supervised Learning

In case of un-supervised learning, only input data is given to the machine learning algorithm and it has to derive the output from it by its own.

1.3.4 Reinforcement Learning

In reinforcement learning, a machine works as a learning agent which attempts to learn from environment and each of its resulting action is given a score. Every action that results in less score causes the algorithm to try another approach next time.

1.4 Deep Learning and Neural Networks

Deep learning is also part of machine learning but it requires more intelligent algorithms to reach to conclusions. Artificial Neural network is one of the approaches that is used in Deep Learning.

Just like human mind uses neurons, artificial neural networks are used to build intelligent machine minds. Artificial neural networks consist of different layers – input layer, middle layers also known as processing layers and output layers. Neural networks use activation functions. There are different types of Activation functions –

Activation functions can be grouped in two categories -

Binary Step Activation Functions

Linear Activation Functions

Non-linear Activation Functions

A binary step activation function is a threshold-based activation function. If the input value is above or below a certain threshold, the neuron is activated and sends the same signal to the next layer.

A linear activation function takes the inputs, multiplied by the weights for each neuron, and creates an output signal proportional to the input.

There are many Non-linear activation functions. I will cover three of those which are most popular ones.

Sigmoid Activation Function

TANH or Hyperbolic Tangent

ReLU (Rectified Linear Unit)

Sigmoid Activation Function – The problem with Sigmoid activation function is that it is not zero centric. Also, for very high or very low values of X, there is almost no change to the prediction, causing a vanishing gradient problem.

TANH – The good thing with Hyperbolic Tangent activation function is that it is zero centric and hence suits more hidden layers.

The ReLU is the most used activation function in the world right now. Since, it is used in almost all the convolutional neural networks or deep learning.

1.5 IoT (Internet of Things)

Many people are usually confused with definition of IoT. What does internet of things stand for?

IoT is term used when any of object on this earth is connected to internet. It is done using IoT devices called sensors and actuators.

Sensors are the IoT devices which collect data from the object and send it over internet.

Actuators works in reverse direction, they receive the signals from internet and performs actions.

In case of posture detection, an IoT device can be a camera which continuously monitors the animal's postures and keeps sending the data to internet, more specifically IoT hub. It triggers the Microsoft IoT stack configured to handle and analyze posture detection data.

If IoT pipeline detects some issue in animal posture, it can send a signal back to some IoT device which will understand that signal and will act on that. So, it can be an IoT device – alarm which can then generate alarm sound in the hospital and can inform the care givers to take some action on that particular animal.

2. LITERATURE REVIEW

Many studies have been done to identify and classify different objects in this world using Artificial Intelligence. Many of existing solutions work on the basis of how humans are so powerful to identify different objects quickly, even if pictures are not clear, human mind is capable of automatically applying fuzzy reasoning and pulling out best results from it.

Through Naber et al. (2012) One of the studies was done using rapid animal detection and emotional valence rating. Nasirahmadi et al. (2019) mentioned automatic scoring of lateral and sternal lying posture in grouped pigs using image processing and Support Vector Machine.

Graving et al. (2019) highlights DeepPoseKit, a software toolkit for fast and robust animal pose estimation using deep learning.

Current thesis is a completely new idea to detect animal postures to help them in medical conditions. The thesis is completed using Microsoft technology stack only and no non- Microsoft technology is used in this.

Microsoft offers different cognitive services which include search services, vision services, knowledge services, speech services etc. Few of these services which requires custom training of the data set, Microsoft provides .ai portals for example luis.ai, customvision.ai and customsearch.ai etc.

Sandeep et al. (2023), presents machine learning algorithm to detect and predict diabetes and its cure. Sandeep et al. (2023), focuses on the use of 5G, 6G & 7G communication to felicitate IoT for data collection and processed in computer using ML algorithm.

Gautam et al. (2023), presents a framework to detect LPG gas and its detection analysis using ML algorithm. Sandeep et al. (2023) shows the automatic seat identification using hardware and ML based algorithm.

Srinivasan et al. (2023) presents the use of Python and OpenCV for the optimization of data using ML.

Ganai et al. (2023), mentioned the security issues and threats in IoT based system while collecting data and optimize them using Machine learning. Sandeep et al. (2023) presents the Machine learning algorithm to detect Zomato restaurant sales analysis. Sandeep et al. (2022) demonstrate system to provide more safety to women's through mobile robot and use image processing to detect any anomalies. Sandeep et al. (2022) presents face recognition system using image processing and python language. Jaiswal et al. (2022) presents drone system and through image processing to monitoring crop field. Sandeep et al. (2023) presents stock market prediction based on algo indicator. Sandeep et al. (2023) discuss smart farming through heterogeneous nodes. Umrao et al. (2022) discuss IoT enabled precision farming system.

Such custom training portals provides extensive support to developers. Very easy to use interface and excellent documentation makes custom training much better for developers.

Every MS cognitive service exposes its capabilities via REST APIs, which means any application which capable of consuming REST APIs will be able to utilize MS Cognitive Services benefits.

Dhillon et al. (2011), the design and deployment of an autonomous mobile robot with sensors and technologies that can find human remains under rubble or in difficult-to-reach places after a disaster are presented in this study. The system's ability to independently navigate through debris and identify telltale signs of life, such sounds or heat signatures, to support rescue efforts is the main focus. Jeet et al. (2015), with an emphasis on home applications, this paper examines current developments in IoT technologies for water quality monitoring. It covers the most recent methods, developments, and difficulties while highlighting how crucial it is to guarantee access to clean water via ongoing, automated monitoring.

Jan et al. (2021), this article examines current developments in Internet of Things (IoT) technology with an emphasis on home applications for water quality monitoring. The need of guaranteeing clean water access through ongoing and automated monitoring is emphasized as it covers the most recent methods, trends, and difficulties. Hatem et al. (2023), The goal of this conference paper is to provide continuous, real-time monitoring of patients' health metrics by describing the design and execution of an Internet of Things-based health care monitoring system. These systems are especially helpful for remote patient monitoring, which lowers the need for hospital visits and improves the management of chronic illnesses. They are also beneficial for early health issue detection and timely response.

Rane et al. (2023), this chapter of the book examines how smart health care models are using IoT to change the way that healthcare is provided. It goes over how fog and edge computing environments, in conjunction with bio-inspired optimization techniques, might help solve the problems of data management, privacy, and effective processing in IoT-based health systems.

2.1 Tools and Technologies

This chapter has focused on the tools and technology used in research.

2.1.1 Microsoft IoT Stack

IoT Devices collect animal's data and send that to IoT Hub. IoT Hub pushes that data to Azure Stream Analytics which is capable of performing quick operation on incoming stream. Stream Analytics pushes that aggregated data to an Azure function which is built using C#. This Azure function uses Microsoft Custom Vision cognitive service to detect and classify the posture of animals based on custom trained model using user defined labels. If Azure function see abnormality in desired posture it triggers one Azure logic app which has SMS pipeline orchestrated within it.

2.2 Azure Functions and Logic Apps

A logic app is a workflow that is built using triggers and actions. Various connectors are used to connect with different systems. To trigger a workflow in Logic app "triggers" are used. A special type of trigger is "Recurrence trigger". It is very easy to create schedule-based workflows in Logic Apps.

Whenever a trigger fires, it instructs logic app engine to create an instance of corresponding logic app and then configured actions are executed. These actions can be flow controls, data conversions and conditional statements. A workflow can include switch statements also which allows insertion of different branches too. For example, whenever a file is created in Azure blob storage it can trigger a workflow in Azure Logic app. And based on the size of that file different set of steps can be executed using branching.

One more example of a trigger is running a workflow every weekday at 11AM while avoiding the workflow execution on weekends. To setup such trigger, logic app provides expressions support.

2.3 Easy-To-Use Designer: Stream Analytics and Logic Apps

Azure Stream Analytics and Logic App designer provides an easy to use designer to users via Azure portal. Users can easily write join queries in Stream Analytics Query window.

2.4 Logic App Templates

Azure logic app templates provide some pre-configured Logic apps steps. When a logic app creation process is started a user is prompted to use some existing templates as shown in fig 1.

2.5 Connect Disparate Systems

All the connecting IoT devices must be registered with IoT hub first. Once data is collected from those devices logic app power can used in integration of heterogenous system as per business needs. For example, a logic app can help a cloud-based marketing system to connect with an on premises solution.

Figure 1. Logic app connector

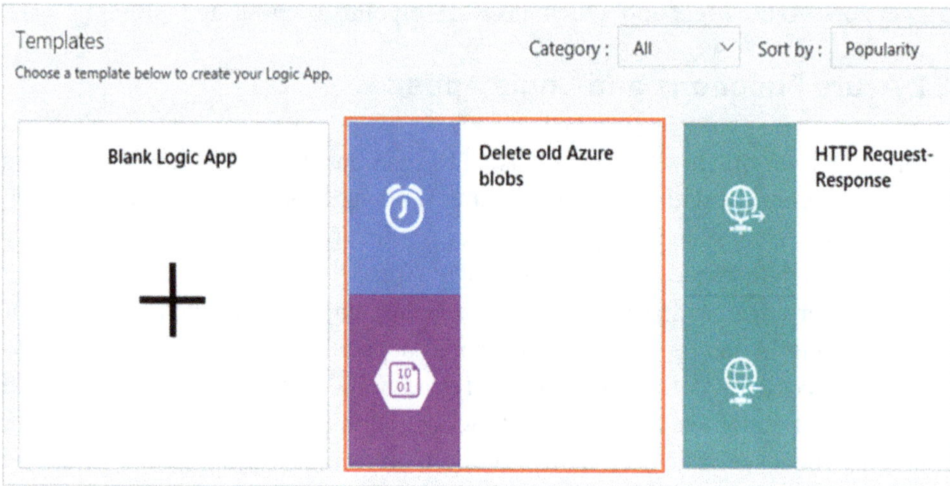

2.6 Reusable and Twilio Integration

Azure portal gives us option to create logic apps using resource templates. Once a Logic app template is built correctly, it can be used to create N- number of similar instances of that logic app configuration. In posture detection scenario, Logic app flow is prepared to connect with a Twilio infrastructure to send updates to

2.7 Extensive

Existing system can be extended to any level, it can include temperature, humidity, emotion detector integrations using IoT devices and MS cognitive services powers.

2.8 Pay When In Use

App Service plans Consumption based plans are cost saving plans for Logic app users.

2.9 Microsoft Cognitive Services

Microsoft cognitive services are prebuilt machine learning capabilities from Microsoft which are access through REST interface. There is different type of services that Microsoft is exposing, it includes – Speech, Vision, NLP and Search cognitive services etc.

3. METHODOLOGY/TECHNOLOGY

3.1 Problem Formulation

Looking at current animal health care centers, it becomes really important to provide an automated monitoring system for animals to break dependency from humans as human staff can get tired while doing their jobs like monitoring, feeding of animals.

3.2 Methodology/Technology

Software Specifications

Microsoft Cognitive Services –
Custom Vision Cognitive Services
Azure IoT Stack, Azure Logic Apps, Twilio, Azure Functions
Stream Analytics
C# 6.0
Visual Studio 2019 – Ver 16.2.4
OS and Hardware Specifications
Processor – Intel Core i7
RAM – 16 GB
System TYPE – 64-bit OS, x64-based processor
Windows 10 Enterprise

Microsoft Custom Vision service is used when computer vision cognitive service is not enough and it requires custom tags for images. To have custom classification, custom vision service must be trained accordingly. Custom vision service has customvisio.ai portal through which is gives custom training options to users. User will have to upload training images to the portal and tag that with proper classifications as shown in fig 2.

3.3 Custom Vision Service: Training With Images

Similarly, multiple images are uploaded to train the custom vision service. Please see below set of images used to train the custom vision model as shown in fig 3.

3.4 Training Image Set

Sometime we upload images in bulk and then multi select feature to tag those in a set. If few images are somehow missed then untagged feature can be used to quickly get a view of such images and then tagging can be done, as shown in fig 4.

Figure 2.

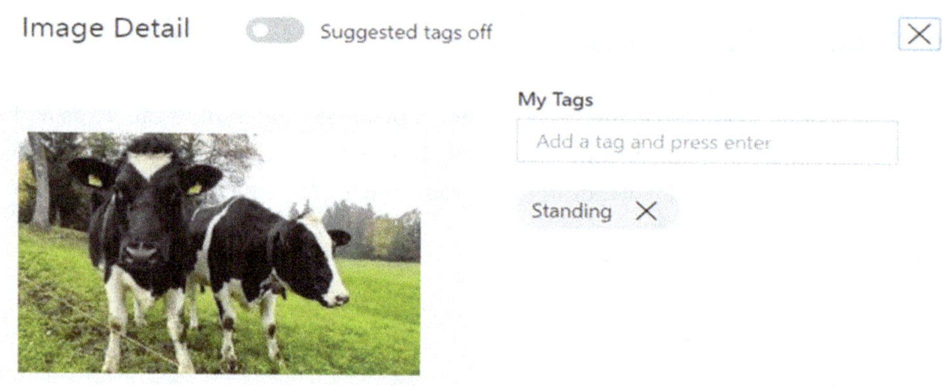

Figure 3.

Figure 4.

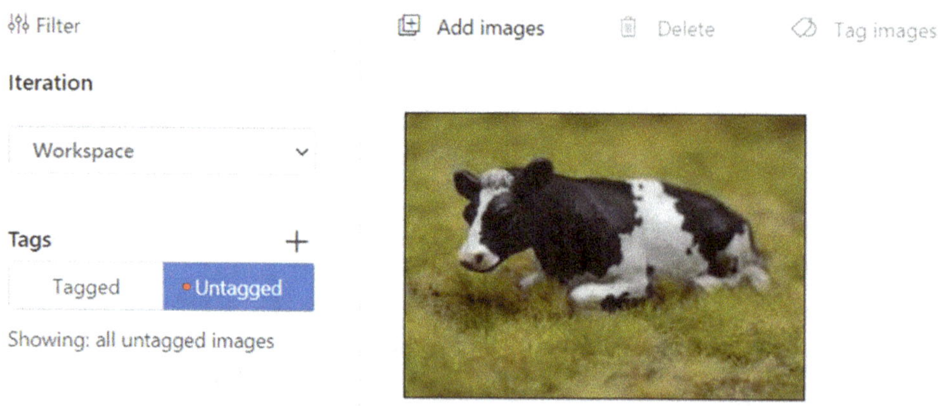

Untagged Filter

If there are many numbers of images whose tagging is missed and but their upload is successful then suggested tags features come very handy as shown in fig 5.

Figure 5.

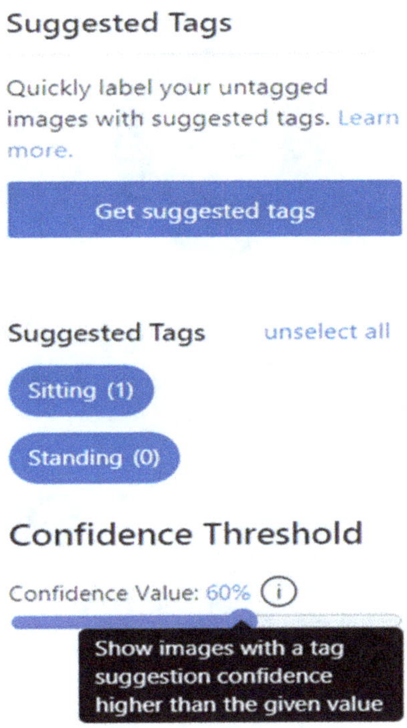

Suggested Tags

As shown above suggested tags feature can be controlled using Confidence Threshold. If confidence threshold is dragged a bit higher number of suggested tags will start decreasing as few images suggested tags will not cross the increased threshold.

Once trained properly, custom vision portal is capable of bringing in precision and recall percentages as shown in fig 6.

3.5 Precision and Recall

Custom vision portal provides pre-built testing pane to test the trained model. Below screen-shot depicts the testing page as shown in fig 7.

Figure 6.

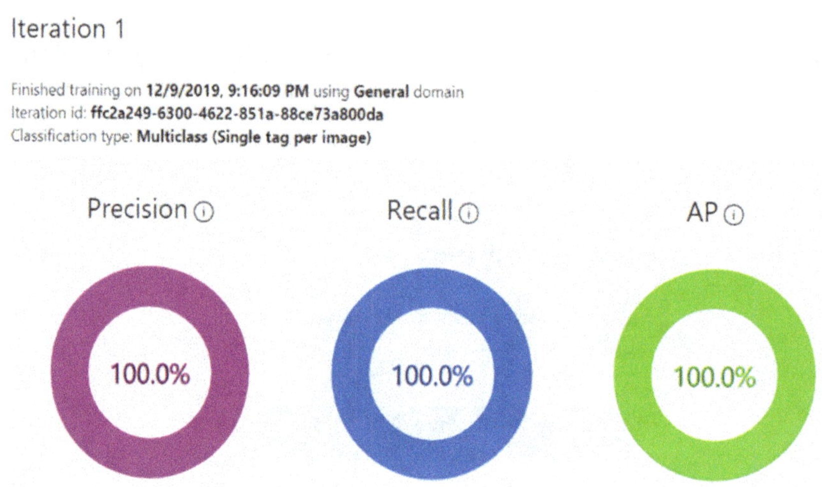

Figure 7.

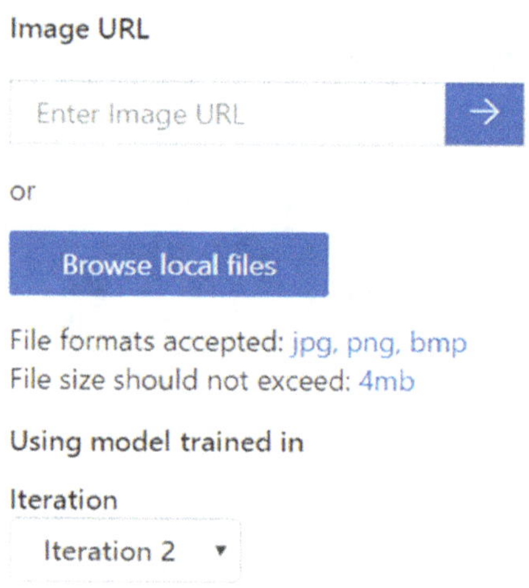

3.6 Custom Vision Portal Training Pane

Once an image is uploaded and iteration is selected, custom vision testing page shows the prediction results. Predicted results are in percentage form. As we have only tags defined in our custom vision classification, it is showing results for those two tags only as shown in fig 8.

Figure 8.

Predictions

Tag	Probability
Standing	71.5%
Sitting	28.4%

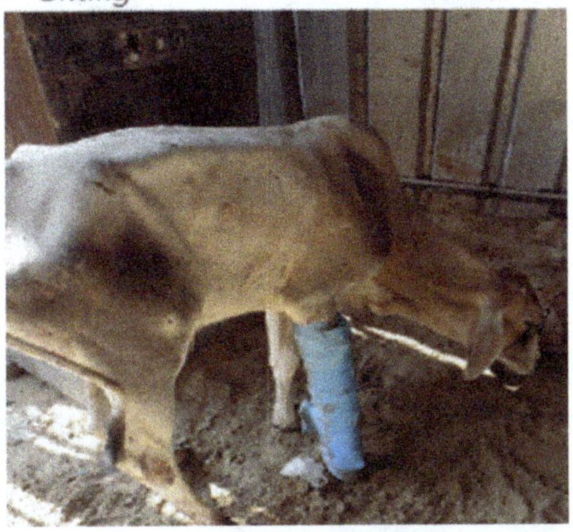

3.7 Prediction Result

3.7.1 Multiclass Classification

Posture detection custom vision service uses Multiclass classification type. That means that every image can be tagged with one image only.

This setting can be changes under project setting page. Custom vision service supports multilabel classification as well which means a single image can be tagged with multiple tags as shown in fig 9.

Figure 9.

Classification Types: ⓘ

○ Multilabel (Multiple tags per image)

◉ Multiclass (Single tag per image)

4. MULTICLASS CLASSIFICATION

4.1 Domain Support

Custom vision service can be configured to use some domain specific knowledge internally while giving predictions.

Domain settings can be done inside project settings page only as shown in fig 10.

Figure 10.

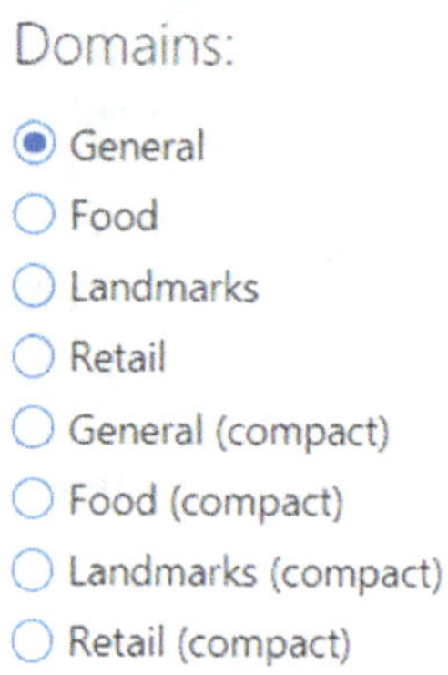

4.2 Domain Support

Pricing Tier

Custom Vision service uses F0 pricing tier. Pricing tier can be changed in custom vision portal as shown in fig 11.

Figure 11.

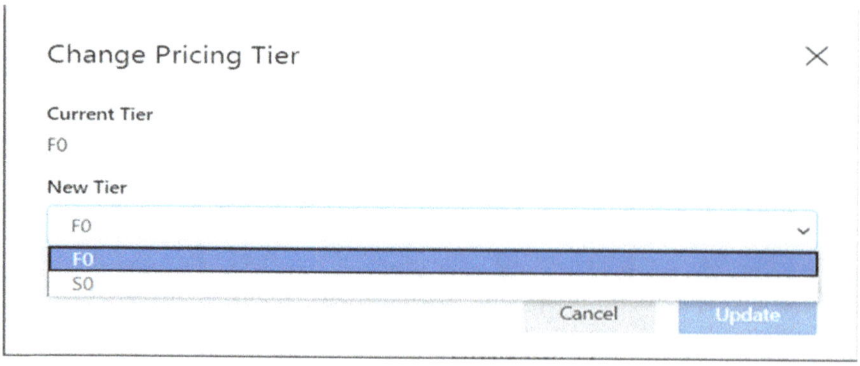

4.3 Pricing Tier

The major difference both tiers is that F0 tier is free tier while S0 is standard tier. F0 tier supports 5000 images while S0 can support 1 Lac images for tagging.

There is other significant difference which fall under –

Performance – transactions per second

Supported Image Types

Image sizes

Number of tags etc.

4.4 Project Settings

Project settings page can used to changes project level details like project name, project description and Project Id details as shown below in fig 12.

Figure 12.

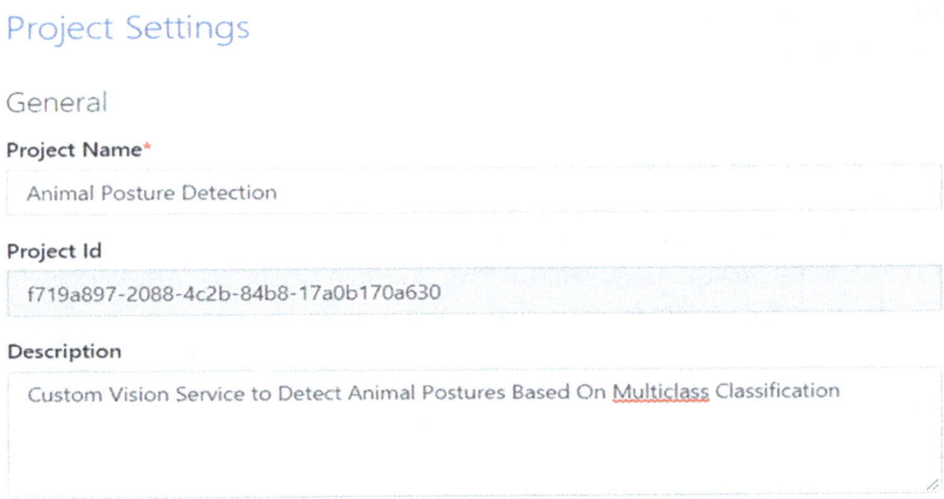

4.4.1 Object Detection

Custom vision service is capable of returning the coordinates as well. If correct parameters are used to call custom vision rest api endpoint then it is capable giving coordinate details as well where tags are found in the image. This feature is an additional feature of custom vision as we know it is capable of distinguishing different images based on tagging.

4.5 Custom Vision Service Apis

Custom Vision service supports two different set of api endpoints. One for training purpose other for prediction purpose.

Training API Endpoints

To create a project
To delete a project
To export a project
To import a project
To train a project
To retrieve a project
To create a tag
To delete a tag
To retrieve a tag
To get how many images are untagged
To get how many images are tagged
To create an iteration
To delete an iteration etc.
Prediction API Endpoints–
To classify an image
To detect tag inside an image
To detect tag inside an image with no store
To classify an image from an image url
To create a custom vision key, you will have to go to Azure portal. After successful login click on create new resource as shown in fig 13.

Figure 13.

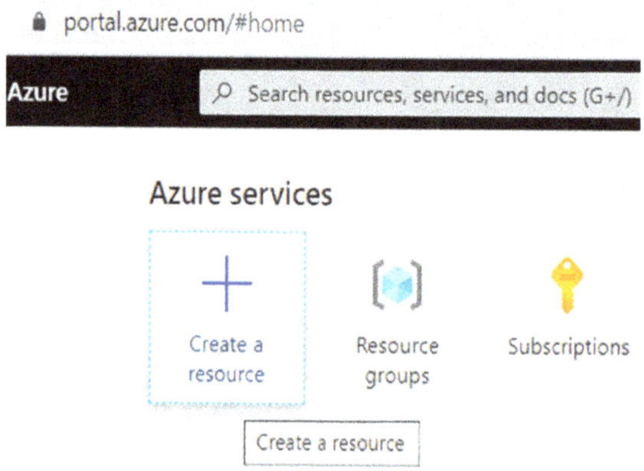

4.5.1 Create Custom Vision Service Instance

Inside resource to create textbox, simply type custom vision as shown below as shown in fig 14.

4.5.2 Custom Vision Resource Inside Azure Portal

It finds the custom vision Azure resource and presents you the resource level form as shown in fig 15.

Figure 14.

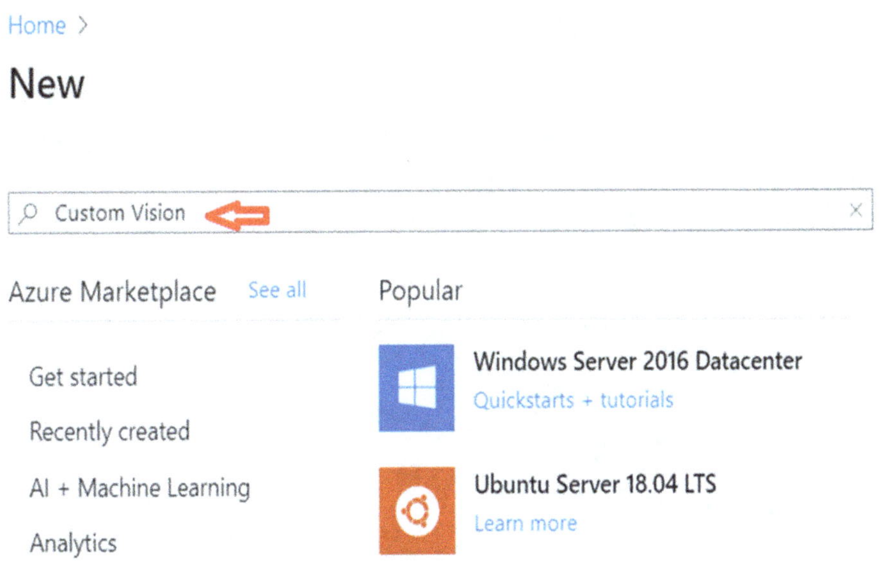

Figure 15.

4.5.3 Custom Vision Resource Overview Screen

It will present you below form to fill as shown in fig 16.

Figure 16.

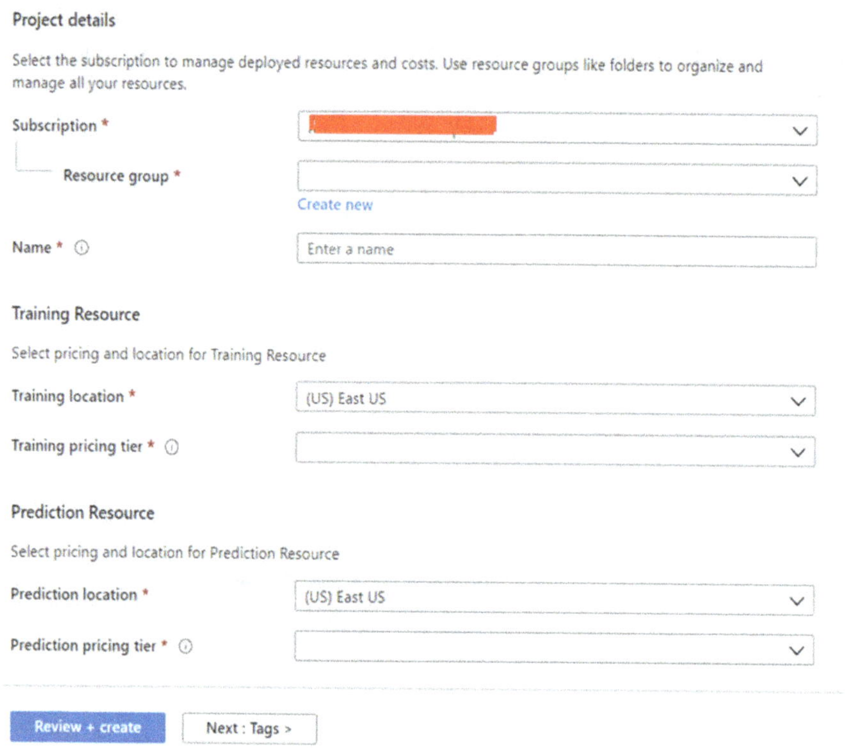

4.5.4 Custom Vision Form

After filling this form click on review and create button, on successful creation of custom vision service instance you would be able to get your custom vision service training and prediction keys.

These keys can be used to call custom vision API endpoints for training and prediction.

If you have many custom vision resources created in azure portal, you can easily tag your resource so that you can use it for pricing calculations and tracking as shown below. Tags are simple key/value pairs in Azure portal and are available for almost all the PAAS resources as shown in fig 17.

Figure 17.

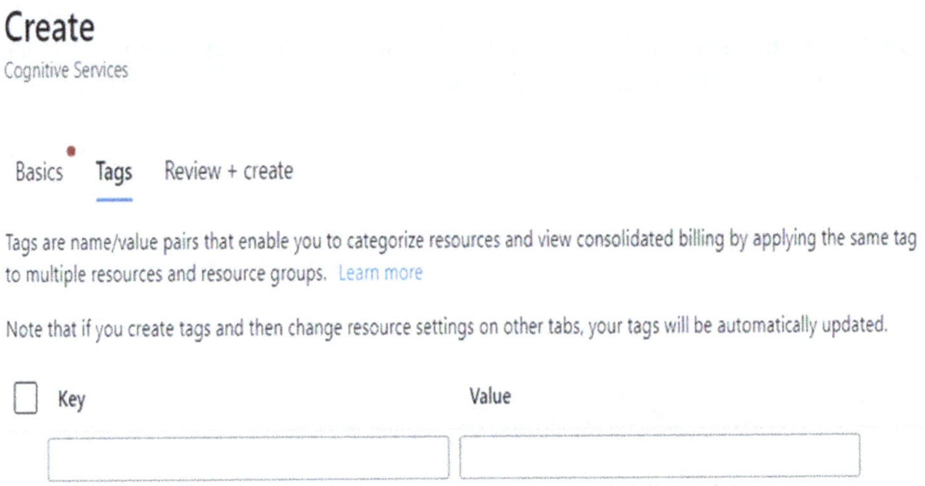

4.5.5 Azure Resource Tags

To create a Stream Analytics resource in Azure. Steps -

Login to Azure portal and click on Create Resource button. In the search box search for Stream Analytics Job as shown in below image fig 18.

Figure 18.

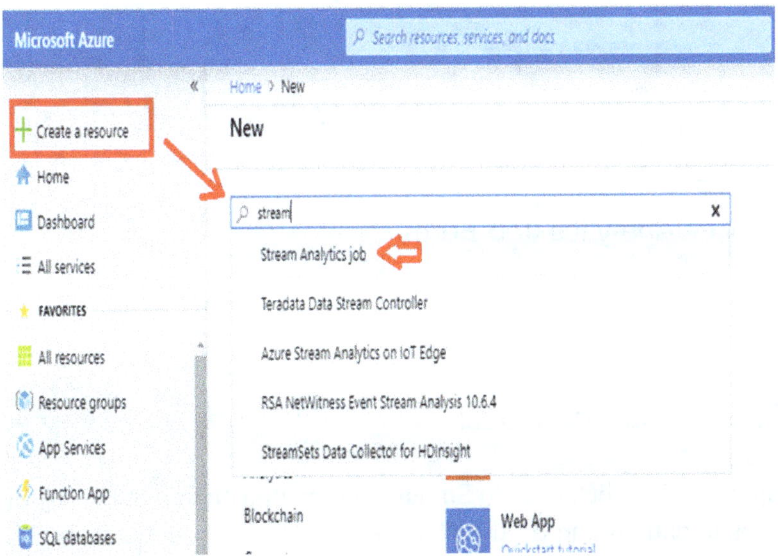

4.5.6 Stream Analytics Resource

A small form appears to fill information about Stream Analytics Job that you want to create. Fill that information and click on Create button. As shown below fig 19.

Figure 19.

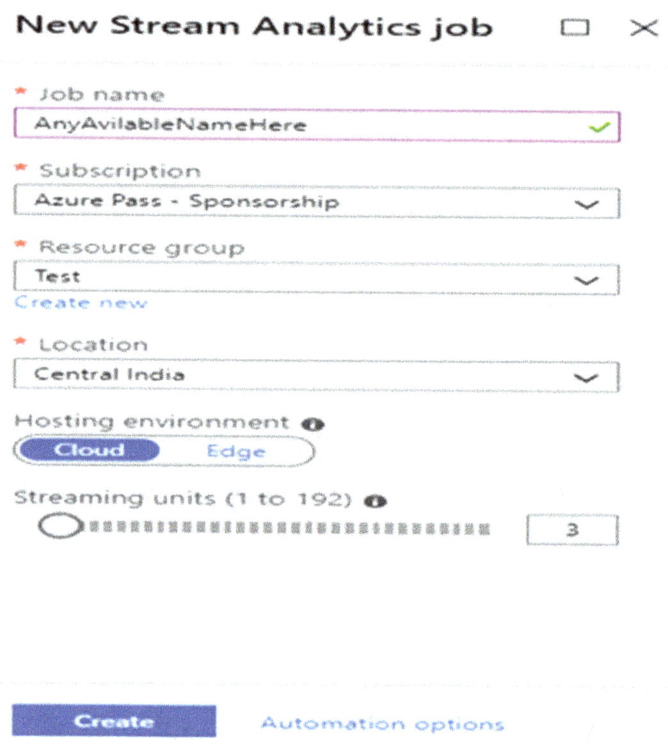

4.5.7 Service Analytics Job Form

Once the stream analytics resource is available, go to the resource and click on Inputs under Job Topologies as shown in fig 20.

4.5.8 Stream Analytics Inputs

Inside inputs section click on Add Stream Input button on top, select any one of the available input options and fill the corresponding form as shown in fig 21.

Figure 20.

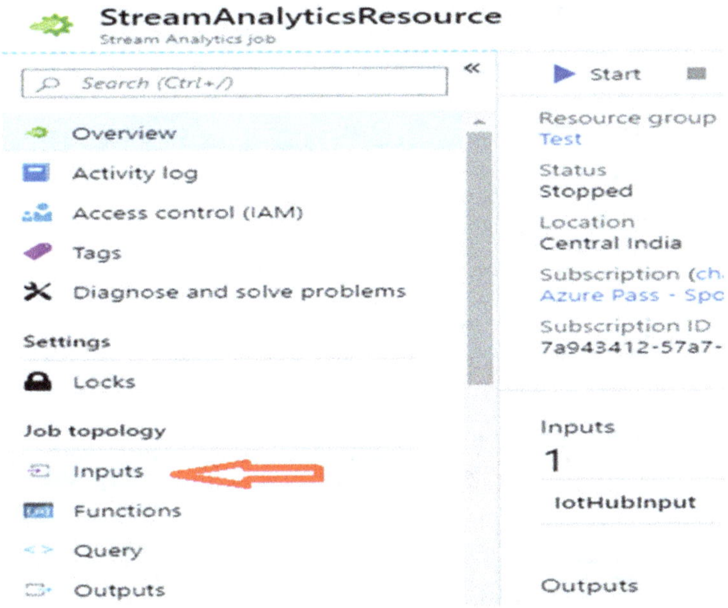

Figure 21.

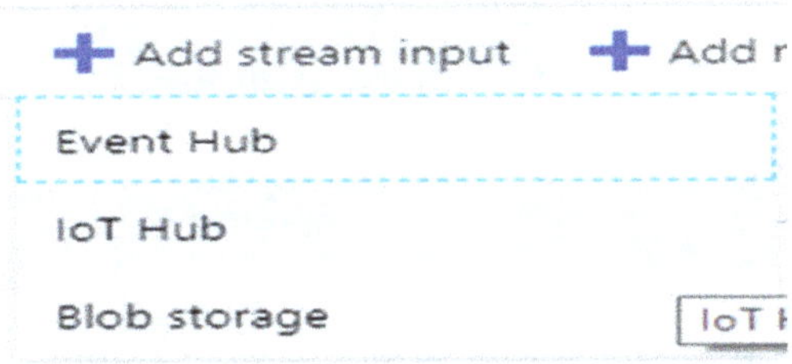

4.5.9 Stream Analytics Input-2

This blog expects that you already have an IoT hub created in your subscription. Therefore, select IoT hub in previous step and select your IoT hub instance in the auto filled dropdown as shown below fig 22.

4.5.10 Stream Analytics - Iot Hub Integration

Next click on Output option as shown in 3rd point, and select as shown in fig 23& fig 24.

Figure 22.

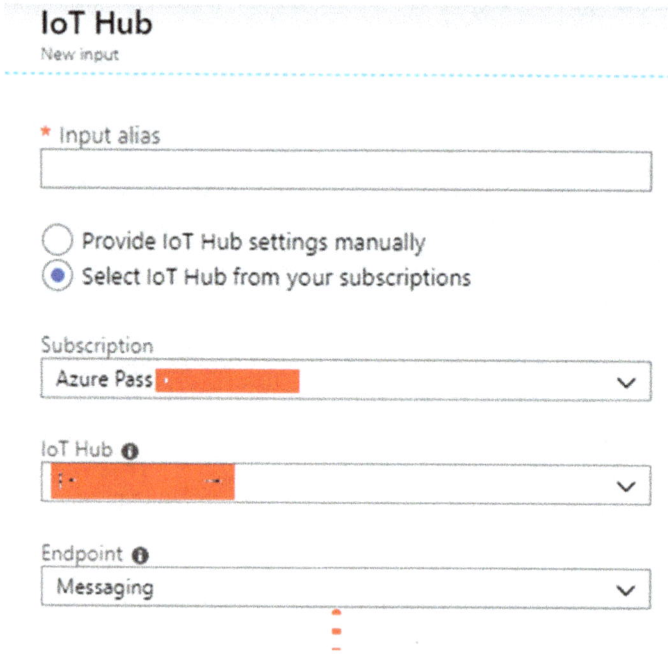

Figure 23.

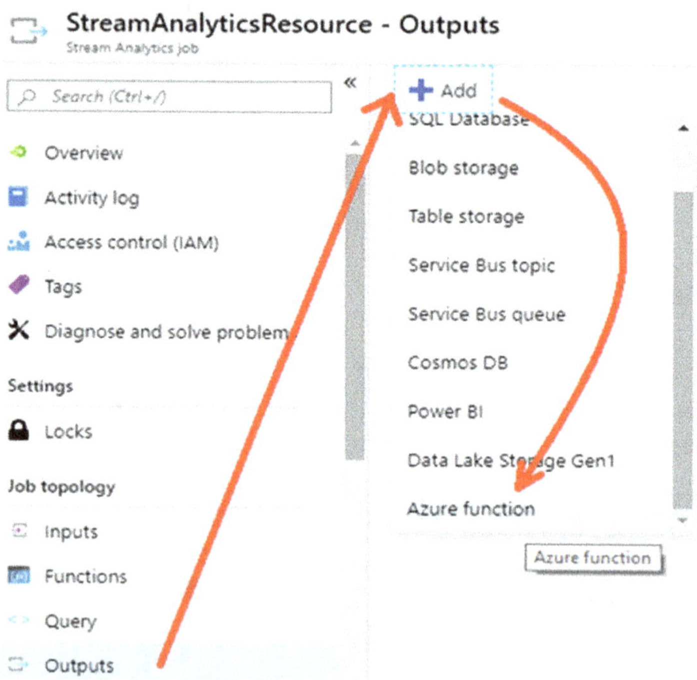

4.5.11 Stream Analytics Output Configurations

Figure 24.

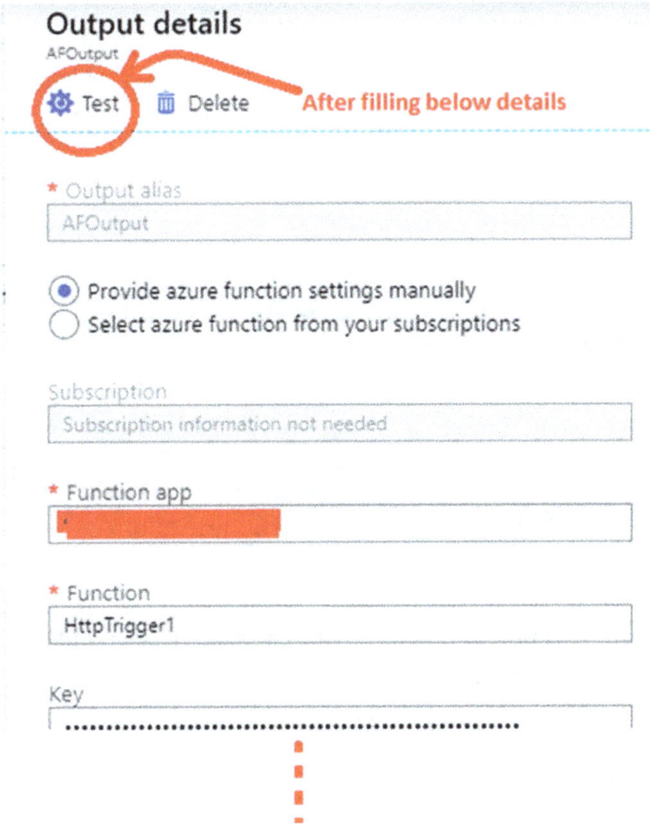

4.5.12 Testing In Stream Analytics

Now I will discuss one failure scenario here. Assuming we are using a Node.js Azure Function. And if that function is not closing its context and fails to return a 200 Ok response to Azure Stream Analytics then this Test task might show below notifications as shown in fig 25.

Stream Analytics Connection Fail Issue

How to fix?

In a simple scenario, above mentioned issue can be solved by adding below code to Node.js Azure Function –

Figure 25.

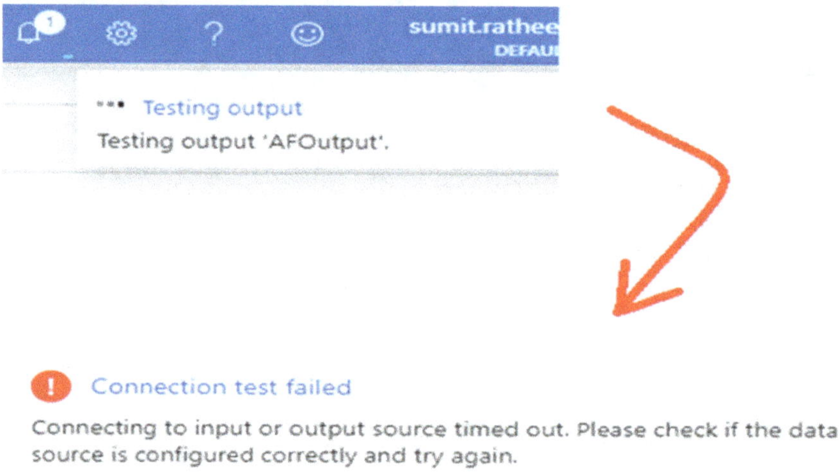


```
context.res =              {              status: 200,
/* Defaults to 200 */                 body: "Hello "
};context.done();
```

Save the Azure function and test the Stream Analytics output again. This time you will see below notification –

Now click on Query tab from Topology section and start editing the default query. Let's assume that we want to simply forward all the fields of the message received by stream analytics from its input to output topology. Following query can be used, just update output and input alias names with correct names and Save the query. –

SELECT *

INTO [Output Alias]

FROM [Input Alias]

How to connect Power BI to Stream Analytics and IotHub

Once the stream analytics resource is available, go to the resource and click on Inputs under Job Topologies as shown in fig 26.

Job topologies.

Inside inputs section click on Add Stream Input button on top, select any one of the available input options and fill the corresponding form as shown in fig 27.

Figure 26.

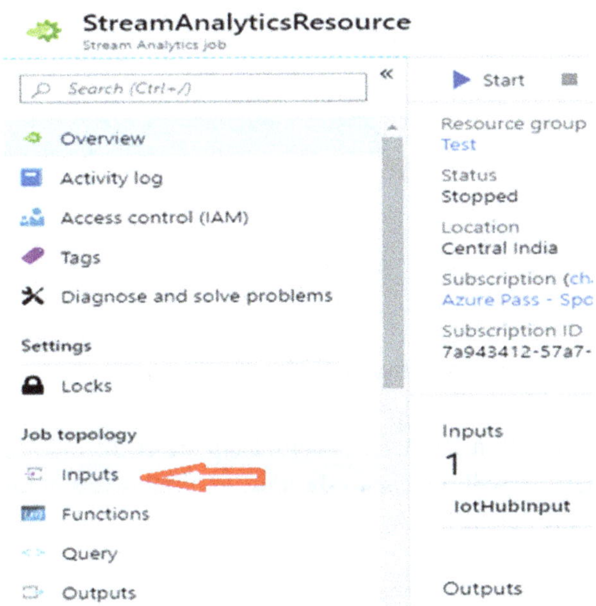

I/O button

This blog expects that you already have an IoT hub created in your subscription. Therefore, select IoT hub in previous step and select your IoT hub instance in the auto filled dropdown as shown below fig 28.

IoT Hub

Next click on Output option as shown in 3rd point, and select as shown in fig 29.

Figure 27.

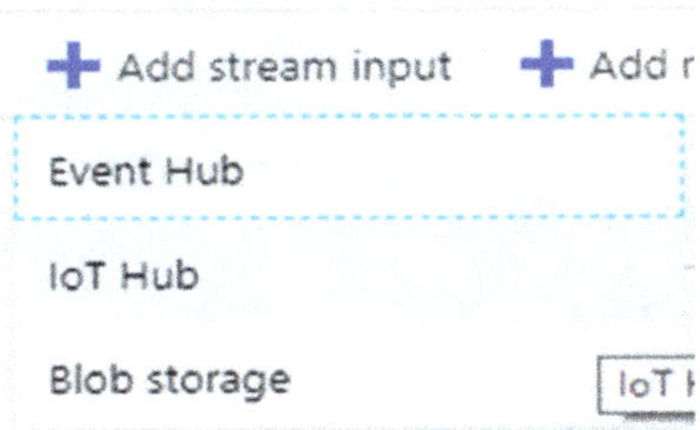

Figure 28.

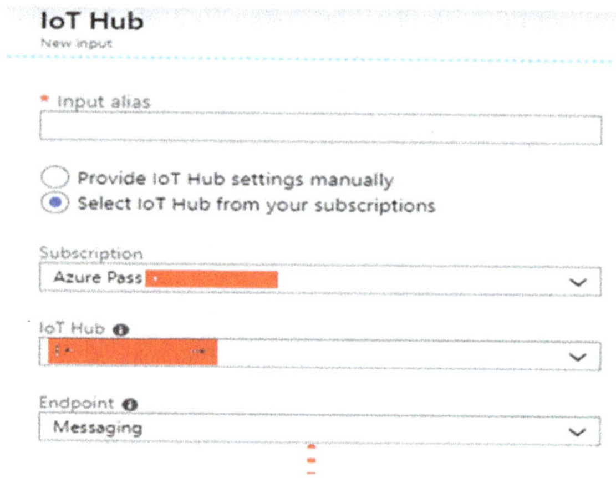

4.5.13 Stream Analytics Power Bi Integration

It will open a form. Fill in the details there. Remember the data set name that you will be giving here. It will appear in the PowerBi datasets section with the same name as shown in fig 30.

Figure 29.

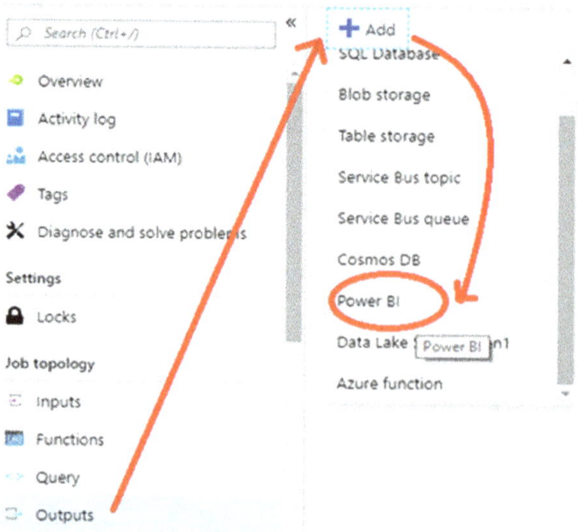

Figure 30.

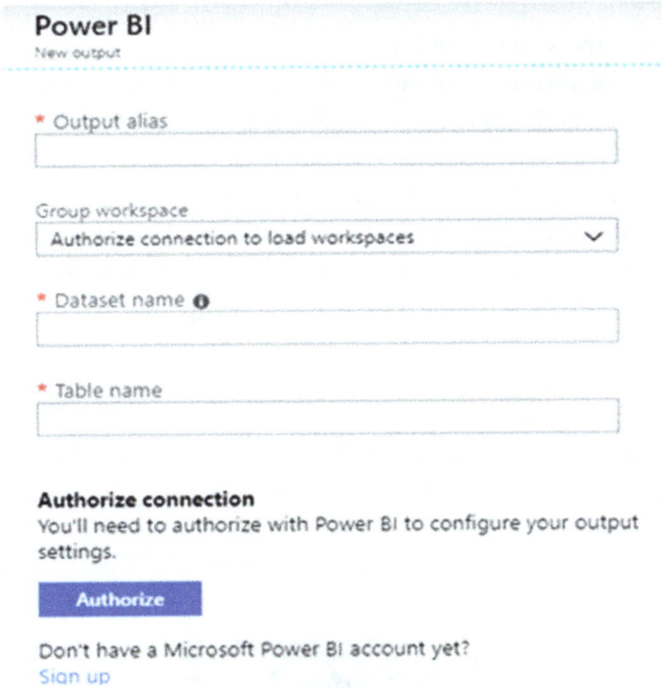

4.5.14 Stream Analytics - Power Bi Output Form

Click on Authorize button to authorize your Power BI instance. It will open a login window as shown below. Login with your Power Bi credentials as shown in fig 31.

Figure 31.

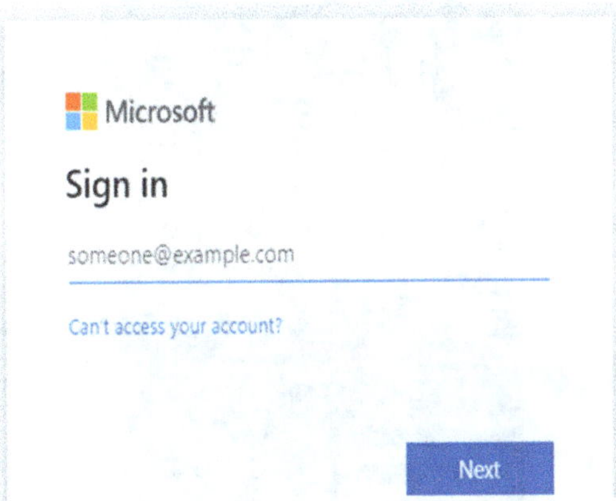

4.5.15 Power Bi Authentication

Once done save Power Bi output form.

Run stream analytics job. I am expecting that your IoT simulator or IoT sensor is continuously sending data to IoT Hub and stream Analytics is receiving that data from IoT hub.

Now open a new tab in browser and login to Power Bi instance.

Now go to left side tree on Power BI landing page and look into DataSets section. You will see a new data set created for you. This data set will have same name as mentioned by you in Stream Analytics Power Bi Output form.

4.5.16 Power Bi Datasets

Remember Power Bi output dataset will not appear in Power BI until and unless your stream analytics is receiving some data from IoT hub as shown in fig 32.

Figure 32.

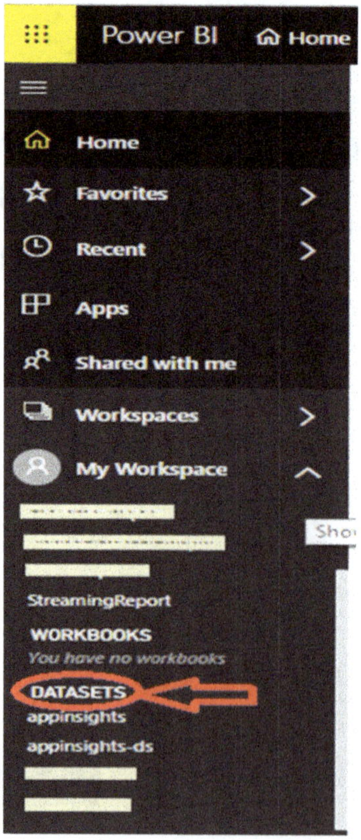

Also remember, if you create a report from this dataset in Power BI and later if the structure of the incoming data changes then report will start showing an error as shown in fig 33.

Figure 33.

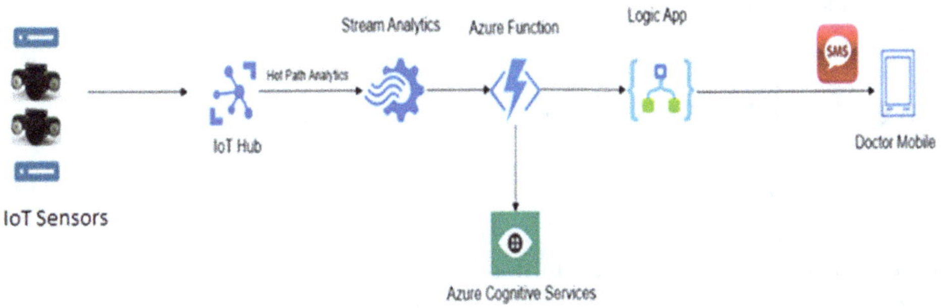

4.5.17 Implementation Work

Architecture

4.6 High Level Architecture

Posture detection is implemented using Microsoft Technology Stack, Azure PAAS Services - Serverless technology like Azure Logic Apps & Azure Functions and Azure Cognitive Service – Custom Vision Service.

IoT Devices collect animal's data and send that to IoT Hub. IoT Hub pushes that data to Azure Stream Analytics which is capable of performing quick operation on incoming stream. Stream Analytics pushes that aggregated data to an Azure function which is built using C#. This Azure function uses Microsoft Custom Vision cognitive service to detect and classify the posture of animals based on custom trained model using user defined labels. If Azure function see abnormality in desired posture it triggers one Azure logic app which has SMS pipeline orchestrated within it.

A logic app is a workflow that is built using triggers and actions. Various connectors are used to connect with different systems. To trigger a workflow in Logic app "triggers" are used. A special type of trigger is "Recurrence trigger". It is very easy to create schedule-based workflows in Logic Apps.

Whenever a trigger fires, it instructs logic app engine to create an instance of corresponding logic app and then configured actions are executed. These actions can be flow controls, data conversions and conditional statements. A workflow can include switch statements also which allows insertion of different branches too. For example, whenever a file is created in Azure blob storage it can trigger a workflow in Azure Logic app. And based on the size of that file different set of steps can be executed using branching.

One more example of a trigger is running a workflow every weekday at 11AM while avoiding the workflow execution on weekends. To setup such trigger, logic app provides expressions

5. KEY TECHNICAL TERMS

5.1 Workflow

A logic app has an underlying definition (workflow definition) which has complete information about the actual logic that runs in a logic app. This workflow definition has its own structure rules and is properly validated. This workflow definition is built using JSON.

5.2 Managed Connectors

Connectors are used to connect with systems which are either on prem or cloud based. There are prebuilt connectors available for Azure logic apps in its connectors gallery.

5.3 Triggers

There are different types of triggers available in Azure logic app for example recurrence trigger, polling trigger and push triggers. Logic app engine creates an instance of logic app for execution whenever it is triggered.

5.4 Actions

Actions are the steps which are executed whenever a logic app is executed.

5.5 Advanced Integration

For some advanced operations Logic apps support Enterpsie integration pack. In this, Logic Apps includes capabilities from BizTalk Server. It helps logic app in different operations like validation, transformation, and more advanced features.

5.6 Coding – Azure Function

```
module.exports = async function(context, req) {context.
log("JavaScript HTTP trigger function processed a request.");
context.log(req.rawBody);  var predictionUrl =    "https://
centralindia.api.cognitive.microsoft.com/vision/v2.0/analy
ze?visualFeatures=Tags&language=en";  var predictionKey =
"************";  var storageAccountName = "animalImages";  var
storageAccountKey =     "qQ3Mt1t*****************ge6pWw==";
var logicAppUrl =    "";  if (req.rawBody) {    // Parse input
var input = JSON.parse(req.rawBody);    var url = input[0].
url;context.log("########## Image url - " + url);    const
options = {     url: predictionUrl,      method: "POST",
headers: {         "Ocp-Apim-Subscription-Key": predictionKey
},      data: {         Url: url       },       json: true    };
```

6. CONCLUSION

Utilizing a combination of IoT devices, sensors, and cloud services, posture detection using Microsoft Internet of Things (MS-IoT) based solutions for timely treatment include monitoring, analyzing, and responding to posture-related health issues. Applications in medicine and healthcare, such as the prevention of chronic pain, the improvement of physical rehabilitation, and the monitoring of people's wellbeing in a variety of environments, including homes and workplaces, can greatly benefit from this technology.

Microsoft Custom Vision Service in combination with Azure IoT stack becomes a very powerful AI solution to take care animals especially in those hospitals where monitoring staff is less. Custom Vision Model requires proper set of images to get trained. If advanced mode training is used, it can result in much better results as it can differ between complex data points and is capable of automatically changing its indexes. Microsoft custom vision cognitive service if trained properly can really help in building a very powerful AI based solution. Its integration with IoT stack enables building AI powered real time solutions like posture-based solution.

Azure functions are written using programming languages like c# and javascript. Azure logic apps have their own GUI and configuration files. If good amount of customization is needed then an Azure function can act as a step/action inside a logic app.

Logic Apps are also base construct for MS Flow. This is the reason both of these have similar designer and connectors concept. A business can think of going with Microsoft Flow first and then later convert the same into Logic app for further extensions. A web job runs with in the context of an App service. It should be preferred over an Azure function when you want to setup custom azure retry policies. Similar type of customization for jobHostBehavior are supported by Web jobs over Azure functions. So in most of the cases, rather choosing one of these services, we should go with combinations of these to build our end solution better.

For all Indian hospitals, both nonprofit and nonprofit, posture detection of humans and animals is an intelligent care option. Utilizing the Microsoft technology stack, it is designed. The solution's main goal is to give hospital patients and animals round-the-clock surveillance. Additionally, the system can use smartphone notifications to notify concerned physicians or caregivers in the event that inappropriate movements or positions are noticed in humans or animals. The architecture for hospital monitoring that we have suggested in this work has been put into practice in real time. Hospitals can also use this device to monitor patient posture and provide prompt treatment.

7. FUTURE SCOPE

Here is the list of capabilities of Intelligent Animal Care –

Post-surgery care – In case an animal is operated for some disease or accidental injuries and if that requires animal to stay in some particular posture like standing or laying down, then IAC is capable of keeping a watch of animal posture. And if somehow, animal changes his posture then care taker will get notifies through SMS channel.

Protection from other animals – In India, Animal care hospitals usually struggle to keep animals on certain distances from each other. In such cases, if an animal is was just operated can get hurt by some other animal. Intelligent Animal Care solution is configurable to support such scenarios.

Animal Movement Tracking – This feature can help doctors to track how many times or for how much time an animal was able to move. It can again help in post-surgery scenarios.

Food/Water Tracking – The solution can be extended to monitor availability of food items or water in the animal wards.

Temperature Tracking – The solution can be extended to monitor temperature of the area where animals are kept post-surgery.

Humidity Tracking – IAC solution can be extended to track humidity in the area where animals are kept. Few post-surgeries requirements may demand for very low humidity infrastructure for animals. IAC can be useful to inform doctors if it sees a surge in humidity. The other possible extensions can be air quality detection, smoke detection etc.

REFERENCES

Bhatia, S., Arya, C., Verma, S., Gautam, D., Naib, B. B., & Kumar, A. (2023, July). Predict Success of a Zomato Restaurant using Machine Learning. In *2023 World Conference on Communication & Computing (WCONF)* (pp. 1-7). IEEE. 10.1109/WCONF58270.2023.10235064

Bhatia, S., Dhillon, H. S., & Kumar, N. (2011). Alive human body detection system using an autonomous mobile rescue robot. *2011 Annual IEEE India Conference*, Hyderabad, India. 10.1109/INDCON.2011.6139388

Bhatia, S., Gautam, D., Kumar, S., & Verma, S. (2023, January). Automatic Seat Identification System in Smart Transport using IoT and Image Processing. In *2023 3rd International Conference on Intelligent Communication and Computational Techniques (ICCT)* (pp. 1-6). IEEE. 10.1109/ICCT56969.2023.10075664

Bhatia, S., Goel, A. K., Naib, B. B., Singh, K., Yadav, M., & Saini, A. (2023). Diabetes Prediction Using Machine Learning. *2023 World Conference on Communication & Computing (WCONF)*, RAIPUR, India. 10.1109/WCONF58270.2023.10235187

Bhatia, S., Goel, N., Ahlawat, V., Naib, B. B., & Singh, K. (2023). A Comprehensive Review of IoT Reliability and Its Measures: Perspective Analysis. Handbook of Research on Machine Learning-Enabled IoT for Smart Applications Across Industries, (pp. 365-384). IEEE.

Bhatia, S., Jaffery, Z. A., & Mehfuz, S. (2023, January). A Comparative Study of Wireless Communication Protocols for use in Smart Farming Framework Development. In *2023 3rd International Conference on Intelligent Communication and Computational Techniques (ICCT)* (pp. 1-7). IEEE. 10.1109/ICCT56969.2023.10075696

Bhatia, S., Jaffery, Z. A., & Mehfuz, S. (2023, May). Development and Analysis of IoT based Smart Agriculture System for Heterogenous Nodes. In *2023 International Conference on Recent Advances in Electrical, Electronics & Digital Healthcare Technologies (REEDCON)* (pp. 62-67). IEEE. 10.1109/REEDCON57544.2023.10150466

Bhatia, S., Jaffery, Z. A., & Mehfuz, S. (2023, May). Development and Analysis of IoT based Smart Agriculture System for Heterogenous Nodes. In *2023 International Conference on Recent Advances in Electrical, Electronics & Digital Healthcare Technologies (REEDCON)* (pp. 62-67). IEEE. 10.1109/REEDCON57544.2023.10150466

Bhatia, S., Malik, P., & Kumar, D. (2022). Face Recognition Door Unlocking and Monitoring System. In Futuristic Sustainable Energy & Technology (pp. 455-466). CRC Press. doi:10.1201/9781003272328-49

Bhatia, S., Mallikarjun, B., Naib, B. B., & Goel, A. K. (2023, September). Algo-Indicator Based Trading in Stock Market. In *2023 4th International Conference on Smart Electronics and Communication (ICOSEC)* (pp. 1730-1734). IEEE. 10.1109/ICOSEC58147.2023.10275858

Bhatia, S., Mallikarjuna, B., Gautam, D., Gupta, U., Kumar, S., & Verma, S. (2023, March). The Future IoT: The Current Generation 5G and Next Generation 6G and 7G Technologies. In *2023 International Conference on Device Intelligence, Computing and Communication Technologies, (DICCT)* (pp. 212-217). IEEE.

Bhatia, S., Naib, B. B., Goel, A. K., Kumar, L., & Singh, K. (2023, June). Drowsy Driver Alert System Using OpenCV. In *2023 3rd International Conference on Pervasive Computing and Social Networking (ICPCSN)* (pp. 614-619). IEEE. 10.1109/ICPCSN58827.2023.00108

Bhatia, S., Verma, S., Singh, N., & Saxena, I. (2022). *IOT and ai based women's safety night patrolling robot.*

Ganai, P. T., Bag, A., Sable, A., Abdullah, K. H., Bhatia, S., & Pant, B. (2022, April). A Detailed Investigation of Implementation of Internet of Things (IOT) in Cyber Security in Healthcare Sector. In *2022 2nd International Conference on Advance Computing and Innovative Technologies in Engineering (ICACITE)* (pp. 1571-1575). IEEE.

Gautam, D., Bhatia, S., Goel, N., & Mallikaijuna, B. H S, G., & Bhushan Naib, B. (2023). Development of IOT enabled framework for LPG gas leakage detection and weight monitoring system. *2023 International Conference on Device Intelligence, Computing and Communication Technologies, (DICCT)*. IEEE. 10.1109/DICCT56244.2023.10110294

Gautam, D., Bhatia, S., Goel, N., Mallikaijuna, B., Ganesha, H. S., & Naib, B. B. (2023, March). Development of IoT Enabled Framework for LPG Gas Leakage Detection and Weight Monitoring System. In *2023 International Conference on Device Intelligence, Computing and Communication Technologies, (DICCT)* (pp. 182-187). IEEE. 10.1109/DICCT56244.2023.10110294

Goel, N., & Yadav, R. K. (2023). *Handbook of Research on machine learning enabled IOT for smart applications across industries*. Engineering Science Reference. doi:10.4018/978-1-6684-8785-3

Graving, J. M., Chae, D., Naik, H., Li, L., Koger, B., Costelloe, B. R., & Couzin, I. D. (2019). DeepPoseKit, a software toolkit for fast and robust animal pose estimation using deep learning. *eLife*, *8*, e47994. doi:10.7554/eLife.47994 PMID:31570119

Hatem, A. S., Abed, J. K., & Ajel, A. R. (2023, September). Based on IoT: Design and implementation of health care monitoring system. In AIP Conference Proceedings (Vol. 2804, No. 1). AIP Publishing.

Jaiswal, P., Rajput, N., Kumar, R., Bhatia, S., & Kumar, R. (2022, June). Drone Automation with Smart Irrigation. In *Futuristic Sustainable Energy & Technology: Proceedings of the International Conference on Futuristic Sustainable Energy &Technology (ICFSE, 2021), 19-20 September, 2021* (p. 467). CRC Press. 10.1201/9781003272328-50

Jan, F., Min-Allah, N., & Düştegör, D. (2021). Iot based smart water quality monitoring: Recent techniques, trends and challenges for domestic applications. *Water (Basel)*, *13*(13), 1729. doi:10.3390/w13131729

Jeet, V., Dhillon, H. S., & Bhatia, S. (2015, April). Radio frequency home appliance control based on head tracking and voice control for disabled person. In *2015 Fifth International Conference on Communication Systems and Network Technologies* (pp. 559-563). IEEE. 10.1109/CSNT.2015.189

Naber, M., Hilger, M., & Einhäuser, W. (2012). Animal detection and identification in natural scenes: Image statistics and emotional valence. *Journal of Vision (Charlottesville, Va.)*, *12*(1), 25–25. doi:10.1167/12.1.25 PMID:22281692

Nasirahmadi, A., Sturm, B., Olsson, A. C., Jeppsson, K. H., Müller, S., Edwards, S., & Hensel, O. (2019). Automatic scoring of lateral and sternal lying posture in grouped pigs using image processing and Support Vector Machine. *Computers and Electronics in Agriculture*, *156*, 475–481. doi:10.1016/j.compag.2018.12.009

Rane, D., Penchala, S., Jain, R., & Chourey, V. (2023). Roles and Future of the Internet of Things-Based Smart Health Care Models. *Bio-Inspired Optimization in Fog and Edge Computing Environments: Principles, Algorithms, and Systems*, 223.

Srinivasan, R., Kavita, R., Kavitha, M., Mallikarjuna, B., Bhatia, S., Agarwal, B., & Goel, A. (2023, March). Python andOpencv For Sign Language Recognition. In *2023 International Conference on Device Intelligence, Computing and Communication Technologies, (DICCT)* (pp. 1-5). IEEE.

Umrao, R., Srivastava, R., Shama, S., Kumar, D., & Bhatia, S. (2022, June). Precision Farming System using IoT. In *Futuristic Sustainable Energy & Technology: Proceedings of the International Conference on Futuristic Sustainable Energy &Technology (ICFSE, 2021),* (p. 477). CRC Press. 10.1201/9781003272328-51

Chapter 11
Exploring the Utility of Emotion Recognition Systems in Healthcare

Dinesh Kumar
https://orcid.org/0000-0001-5943-1444
Lovely Professional University, India

Bhawna
Lovely Professional University, India

Daogafu Gwra Narzary
Lovely Professional University, India

ABSTRACT

This chapter examines the intersection of artificial intelligence (AI) and psychology in healthcare through emotion recognition systems (ERS). By tracing ERS's development, it showcases its crucial role in improving patient care, enhancing mental health treatments, and providing stress management for healthcare workers. It discusses ERS's potential and the challenges it faces, including ensuring accuracy, integrating technology, addressing cultural sensitivity, and managing privacy concerns. The narrative aims to deepen understanding among healthcare professionals, technologists, and ethicists about ERS's nuanced contributions and technical complexities. It highlights the transformative potential of ERS in healthcare, considering both its benefits and the multifaceted issues it presents. Looking ahead, the chapter advocates for progress driven by technological advancements, cross-disciplinary research, and thoughtful policy-making, providing a comprehensive view of how ERS can be effectively integrated into healthcare practices for future enhancements.

DOI: 10.4018/979-8-3693-1910-9.ch011

1. INTRODUCTION

Emotion Recognition Systems (ERS) are increasingly capturing the interest of various fields, notably healthcare, where their impact could be transformative (Wei, Hu, Yang, Luu, & Dong, 2024; Brandt, de Oliveira Silva, Simões Neto, Tourinho Baptista, Belfort, Lacerda, & Nascimento Dourado, 2024). Utilizing sophisticated computational techniques, ERS are adept at identifying and analyzing human emotions through facial expressions, voice patterns, and physiological signals (Wani, Gunawan, Qadri, Kartiwi, & Ambikairajah, 2021; Kim, Bang, & Kim, 2004). In healthcare the foundational belief is that emotions, integral to the human experience, can be quantitatively assessed and understood (Kennedy & Hill, 2018; Chen et al., 2023), paving the way for innovations in patient care, clinical decision-making, and overall healthcare quality.

ERS's applications in healthcare are diverse, ranging from enhancing communication between patients and practitioners to supporting the diagnosis and treatment of mental health issues (Grabowski, Rynkiewicz, Lassalle, Baron-Cohen, Schuller, Cummins, ... & Łucka, 2019; Pal, Mukhopadhyay, & Suryadevara, 2021). This technology promises to bridge gaps in understanding patient emotions, offering insights into their emotional states that were previously challenging to access. Such capabilities are particularly pivotal in mental health care, where monitoring mood and emotional variations can lead to tailored and more effective interventions. Additionally, ERS holds significant promise in contexts where patients may struggle to express their emotions, such as in pediatric care or among individuals with neurodegenerative diseases, by providing a critical tool for comprehending and addressing their unique needs.

Nonetheless, integrating ERS into healthcare is not without its challenges. Ethical considerations, including privacy, data security, and informed consent, are at the forefront, given the sensitive nature of the data ERS analyze. The accuracy and reliability of these systems are also crucial, especially since clinical decisions based on incorrect data could lead to adverse outcomes. Furthermore, there is a need to address and mitigate potential biases within ERS, which may arise from the datasets used for training these technologies.

While the technological advancements and applications of ERS in healthcare have been explored to some extent, there remains a notable gap in the literature regarding the synthesis of these systems' technological underpinnings with their practical healthcare applications. Existing research has largely focused on addressing technical challenges (Cowie et al., 2001), such as system accuracy (Al-Omair & Huang, 2018; Xu, Zhang, & Khan, 2020) and integration within clinical settings (Flynn, Effraimidis, Angelopoulou, Kapetanios, Williams, Hemanth, & Towell, 2020). However, less attention has been paid to the sociocultural and ethical dimensions, including cultural sensitivity, accessibility, and navigating the ethical landscape of implementing such technologies in diverse healthcare environments. Moreover, discussions on the interdisciplinary research and policy development necessary for the effective and ethical integration of ERS into healthcare practices are sparse. This highlights a critical research gap in providing a comprehensive overview that not only showcases the potential and challenges of ERS but also addresses the complexities involved in bringing these systems from conceptual frameworks to tangible healthcare solutions. This chapter seeks to bridge these gaps by offering an in-depth exploration of ERS within the healthcare sector. It aims to illuminate their development, highlight applications in enhancing patient care and mental health treatments, and tackle the critical technical, sociocultural, and ethical challenges faced. Furthermore, this discussion will explore future directions, including technological advancements, the need for interdisciplinary research, and the development of supportive policies, reflecting on the transformative potential and complexities associated with ERS in healthcare. By addressing these research gaps, this chapter contributes valuable insights for healthcare professionals, technologists, and ethicists alike, paving the way for a more informed, ethical, and effective integration of ERS in healthcare settings. Through this comprehensive exploration, we aim to underscore the significance of ERS as a transformative tool in healthcare, equipped with the potential to enhance patient engagement, diagnostic processes, and personalized care, while also highlighting the paramount importance of navigating the associated ethical, privacy, and equity concerns with due diligence.

This chapter aims to provide a comprehensive exploration of the utility of ERS in healthcare. It will examine the potential benefits and applications of ERS, while also critically assessing the challenges associated with its integration into healthcare practices. This chapter has used review of existing literature to achieve its objectives.

2. BACKGROUND

2.1 Introduction to Emotion Recognition Systems

ERS have emerged as a transformational technology in the digital era particularly in the healthcare. These systems leveraging advanced machine learning algorithms are designed to identify and interpret human emotions. They uses various modalities including facial expressions, voice patterns, and physiological signals (Chen & Wang, 2011; Pal, Mukhopadhyay, & Suryadevara, 2021). The concept of ERS is rooted in the interdisciplinary study of affective computing, a field that aims to bridge the gap between human emotional processing and computer systems (Bullington, 2005).

Machine learning, a subset of artificial intelligence, plays a crucial role in the functionality of ERS (Ko, 2018). These systems use algorithms to analyze complex emotional data, learning from patterns and improving accuracy over time. Common machine learning techniques employed in ERS include neural networks, support vector machines, and decision trees, each offering unique strengths in emotion recognition tasks.

2.2 Historical Development of ERS

The evolution of emotion recognition systems represents a fascinating intersection of psychology, computer science, and neuroscience (Lisetti & Schiano, 2000). The groundwork for emotion recognition systems is deeply rooted in psychological theories. Darwin's seminal work, "The Expression of the Emotions in Man and Animals" (1872), laid the foundation by suggesting that emotional expressions are universal (Barrett, 2016). Building on this, Ekman and Friesen (1978) developed the Facial Action Coding System (FACS), a comprehensive framework for categorizing human facial expressions, crucial for later computerized emotion recognition.

Early attempts at creating emotion recognition systems in the late 20th century focused on facial expression analysis. These systems utilized basic pattern recognition techniques to classify expressions into emotion categories such as happiness, sadness, anger, and surprise (Bettadapura, 2012). However, these systems were limited by the available technology and an incomplete understanding of the nuances of human emotions.

The advent of machine learning and more sophisticated computational models in the early 21st century marked a significant leap in emotion recognition technology (Bettadapura, 2012). Researchers began to employ neural networks and deep learning algorithms, leading to more accurate and nuanced emotion detection. These advancements allowed for the integration of not only facial expressions but also vocal intonations, body language, and physiological signals.

Recent developments have seen emotion recognition systems evolve to incorporate multimodal data (Sebe, Cohen, & Huang, 2005; Sebe, Cohen, Gevers, & Huang, 2005). These systems analyze a combination of cues, including facial expressions, speech patterns, and even text analysis, to infer emotional states. Such integration has significantly improved the accuracy and reliability of emotion recognition systems.

2.3 How ERS Can Be Simulated In Experimental Setup?

To validate the efficacy and applicability of ERS in healthcare, a comprehensive experimental setup is essential. Such a setup would simulate real-world healthcare environments to test the accuracy, reliability, and utility of ERS in diagnosing and managing patient care. This section outlines potential experimental frameworks and methodologies for simulating the work of ERS within healthcare settings.

Designing the Experimental Framework: A well-structured experimental framework is pivotal to simulate the integration of ERS in healthcare accurately. According to Alvarado, Lawley, & Li (2016), a controlled environment that mimics clinical settings, including patient rooms and consultation areas, should be established. These environments can be equipped with ERS technologies capable of capturing and analyzing facial expressions, voice patterns, and physiological signals in real-time. The inclusion of diverse patient profiles, including varied age groups, genders, and health conditions, would ensure the comprehensiveness of the simulation (Ibrahim, Lok, Mitchell, Stoiljkovic, Tarulli, & Hubley, 2023).

Methodology for ERS Simulation: The methodology for simulating ERS in a healthcare setting involves several key components. Firstly, a baseline emotional state of participants should be established using standardized psychological assessments. Following this, participants would be exposed to various simulated healthcare scenarios designed to elicit a range of emotional responses. ERS technologies would then monitor and analyze these responses in real-time, with their outputs compared against observed behaviors and self-reported emotional states for accuracy verification. Participants' consent and the ethical considerations surrounding privacy and data security must be rigorously maintained throughout the simulation, adhering to guidelines proposed by the American Psychological Association (Goldman & Sripada, 2005; Siam, Soliman, Algarni, El-Samie, Fathi, & Sedik, 2022).

Evaluation Metrics: Evaluation metrics are crucial for assessing the performance of ERS in experimental setups. Accuracy, sensitivity, specificity, and user satisfaction are among the primary metrics for evaluation. Machine learning algorithms' precision in correctly identifying emotional states plays a critical role in the utility of ERS. Additionally, the system's ability to operate seamlessly in real-time without imposing discomfort or stress on participants is also a vital consideration (Pietquin & Hastie, 2013; Liu, Yang, & Wang, 2005; Schlosser, Voss, & Bruckner, 2004).

The simulation of ERS in healthcare through experimental setups offers a pathway to validating and refining these technologies before their integration into real-world clinical settings. By meticulously designing the experimental framework, employing robust methodologies, and adhering to strict ethical standards, researchers can significantly advance the understanding and application of ERS in enhancing patient care. Future explorations into VR, AR, and wearable technologies hold the promise of further enriching these simulations, paving the way for more nuanced and effective healthcare solutions.

2.4 Utilities of ERS

Emotion recognition systems have a wide range of applications. Each utility benefits various sectors and aspects of human interaction. In healthcare, these systems offer profound advantages, particularly in mental health diagnosis and treatment. For instance, they assist in detecting subtle emotional cues in patients, aiding clinicians in diagnosing conditions such as depression or anxiety (Öztürk, Kiliç, Deveci, & Kirpinar, 2016; Pampouchidou, Pediaditis, Kazantzaki, Sfakianakis, Apostolaki, Argyraki, ... & Simos, 2020). In the user experience design and human-computer interaction ERS enhance the interface between users and technology. By understanding user emotions, these systems can adapt responses or content in real-time, thereby improving user satisfaction and engagement (González-Rodríguez, Díaz-Fernández, & Gómez, 2020).

In the field of education, emotion recognition technologies play a pivotal role in developing personalized learning experiences. They enable the identification of students' emotional states during learning activities, facilitating adjustments in teaching methods or materials to improve learning outcomes (Walumbwa, Avolio, Gardner, Wernsing, & Peterson, 2008). Another significant application is in the automotive industry, where emotion recognition systems contribute to driver safety. By monitoring drivers' emotional states, these systems can identify signs of stress or fatigue, triggering alerts or safety measures to prevent accidents (Lehman, O'Connor, Kovács, & Newman, 2019).

Moreover, emotion recognition technologies are increasingly utilized in marketing and consumer research. By analyzing consumer emotional responses to products or advertisements, companies gain insights into consumer preferences and behavior, enabling more effective marketing strategies (Van Thanh, 2023). Additionally, these systems find utility in security and surveillance, where detecting emotional states can aid in identifying potential threats or emergencies (Bullington, 2005)

Furthermore, in the context of social robotics and artificial intelligence, ERS are integral in creating more empathetic and interactive robots. Such advancements are particularly beneficial in caregiving roles, where robots can respond appropriately to the emotional needs of the elderly or individuals with disabilities.

3. MAIN FOCUS OF THE CHAPTER

The main focus of this chapter is to explore utilities of ERS in healthcare and find out its challenges. They are explored in this section.

3.1 Utilities of ERS in Healthcare

ERS offer a range of utilities in the healthcare sector. The utilities of ERS in healthcare are given below.

Enhancing Patient Care: ERS have the potential to revolutionize patient care by providing healthcare professionals with deeper insights into patients' emotional states. For instance, in settings where patients may be unable to verbally communicate their feelings due to medical conditions, ERS can play a crucial role in understanding their needs and discomforts (Mano, Faiçal, Nakamura, Gomes, Libralon, Meneguete, ... & Ueyama, 2016; De & Mishra, 2022). This can lead to more tailored care plans and improved patient satisfaction. Patients with chronic diseases often require continuous monitoring and support. ERS can play a vital role in these scenarios by helping track the emotional wellbeing of patients, which is closely linked to their physical health. Monitoring emotional health can also aid in adherence to treatment regimens and lifestyle changes.

Mental Health Diagnosis and Treatment: ERS offer a novel approach to diagnosing and monitoring mental health conditions by analyzing emotional cues that might be subtle or overlooked in traditional assessments (De & Mishra, 2022; Jonnalagadda, Rajvir, Singh, Chandramouliswaran, George, & Kamalov, 2023). ERS can track changes in emotional states over time, providing clinicians with valuable data to inform treatment plans and monitor patient progress.

Support for Healthcare Providers: Healthcare providers can also benefit from ERS. By analyzing the emotional state of providers, these systems can help identify signs of stress or burnout in healthcare professions. This can lead to better support systems and interventions to maintain the wellbeing and effectiveness of healthcare staff.

Enhancing Communication and Empathy: ERS can enhance communication between patients and healthcare providers. By providing real-time feedback on a patient's emotional state, ERS can help providers adjust their communication style and approach to be more empathetic and effective (Cao, Fu, Yang, Wermter, Liu, & Wu, 2021). This can improve patient-provider relationships and the overall quality of care.

Training and Education: ERS can be used in training scenarios to improve the emotional intelligence of healthcare professionals. By simulating patient interactions and providing feedback on emotional responses, ERS can help trainees develop better communication and empathy skills, which are essential in patient care (Bahreini, Nadolski, & Westera, 2017).

Telemedicine and Remote Care: In telemedicine, ERS can play a significant role in bridging the emotional gap caused by the physical distance between patients and healthcare providers. By analyzing emotional cues during virtual consultations,

Figure 1. Utilities of emotion detection systems in healthcare

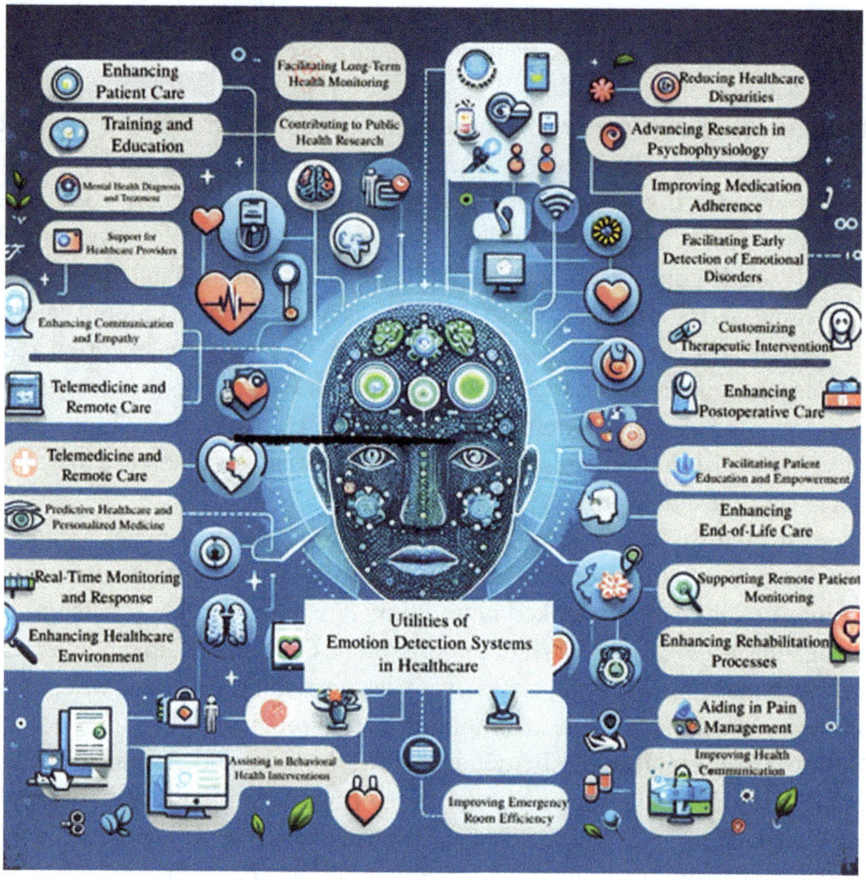

ERS can help providers better understand and respond to patients' emotional needs (Herrera, Alanis, Baltazar, & Velazquez, 2023)

Predictive Healthcare and Personalized Medicine: ERS can contribute to predictive healthcare and personalized medicine. By analyzing emotional patterns, ERS can help predict potential health issues or the onset of certain conditions, leading to early interventions and more personalized care plans (Dhuheir, Albaseer, Baccour, Erbad, Abdallah, & Hamdi, 2021; Subramanian, Kim, Maray, & Paul, 2022).

Real-Time Monitoring and Response: ERS can facilitate real-time monitoring of patients. This real-time analysis can be vital in responding swiftly to emotional distress or discomfort, potentially improving patient outcomes (Zhuang, Guan, Nagayoshi, Muramatsu, Watanuki, & Tanaka, 2019; Llurba, Fretes, & Palau, 2022). For instance, ERS can alert healthcare staff to changes in a patient's emotional state that may indicate pain, anxiety, or other issues requiring immediate attention.

Enhancing Healthcare Environment: ERS technology can be integrated into healthcare environments to create more responsive and patient-centered spaces (Cupkova, Kajati, Mocnej, Papcun, Koziorek, & Zolotova, 2019). For example, ERS can be used to adjust lighting, temperature, or music in patient rooms based on their emotional state, enhancing comfort and promoting healing.

Reducing Healthcare Disparities: ERS have the potential to reduce disparities in healthcare by providing objective, unbiased assessments of emotional states, which can be particularly beneficial in settings where cultural differences or language barriers exist (Karabuschenko, Ivashchenko, Sungurova, & Hvorova, 2016; Elfenbein & Ambady, 2002; Kurbalija, Ivanović, Radovanović, Geler, Mitrović, Dai, & Zhao, 2015).

Advancing Research in Psychophysiology: ERS also contribute significantly to research in psychophysiology, helping scientists understand the intricate relationship between emotional processes and physiological responses (Egger, Ley, & Hanke, 2019; Wang, Zhou, Wang, & Liang, 2020; Bota, Wang, Fred, & Da Silva, 2019; Yang et al., 2021). This can lead to new treatments and therapeutic approaches in healthcare.

Improving Medication Adherence: Medication adherence is a critical aspect of effective healthcare, especially for chronic conditions (Azevedo, Hale, Warren, Baby, Lee, Insel, ... & Mudar, 2023; Faisal, Samoth, Aslam, Patel, Park, Baby, & Patel, 2023; Liang, Su, Sheng, Bishop, & Carlson, 2023). ERS can assist in monitoring patients' emotional states related to medication use, identifying patterns of behavior that indicate non-adherence. This information can be invaluable for healthcare providers in devising strategies to improve adherence and, consequently, patient health outcomes.

Facilitating Early Detection of Emotional Disorders: ERS's ability to detect subtle emotional changes can facilitate the early identification of emotional and mood disorders (Grabowski, Rynkiewicz, Lassalle, Baron-Cohen, Schuller, Cummins, ... & Łucka, 2019; Pavez, Diaz, Arango-Lopez, Ahumada, Mendez-Sandoval, & Moreira, 2023a; Lacava, Golan, Baron-Cohen, & Smith Myles, 2007). Early detection is paramount in conditions like depression or anxiety, where timely intervention can significantly alter the course of the illness and improve quality of life .

Customizing Therapeutic Interventions: Therapeutic interventions, particularly in mental health, can be significantly enhanced by the integration of ERS (Islam, 2023; Zhang, Ringland, Paan, Mohr, & Reddy, 2021). These systems can help therapists understand patients' emotional responses during therapy sessions, enabling them to tailor their therapeutic techniques to each individual's needs more effectively.

Enhancing Postoperative Care: In postoperative care, understanding a patient's emotional state is essential for pain management and recovery (Rahmani, 2023; Slakkham & Bhattarakosol, 2018). ERS can provide valuable information on a patient's emotional well-being, helping healthcare professionals manage pain and anxiety more effectively and potentially reducing recovery times.

Facilitating Patient Education and Empowerment: ERS can be instrumental in patient education and empowerment. By helping patients understand their emotional responses to various health-related scenarios, ERS can encourage more active participation in their own care and decision-making processes (Mano, Mazzo, Neto, Meska, Giancristofaro, Ueyama, & Júnior, 2019; Huang, Wu, Nguyen, Wang, Kao, Lee, ... & Li, 2023; Bahreini, Nadolski, & Westera, 2016).

Enhancing End-of-Life Care: In palliative and end-of-life care, where verbal communication may be limited, ERS can provide critical insights into patient needs and emotional states. This can help caregivers provide more compassionate and responsive care during these sensitive stages.

Supporting Remote Patient Monitoring: The rise of remote patient monitoring, especially in the wake of the COVID-19 pandemic, has underscored the need for technologies that can assess patients' emotional well-being from a distance (Huang, Liu, Nicdao, Mikaheal, Baldacchino, Albeos, ... & Kim, 2020; Zaman & Reaz, 2023). ERS can be integral in this context, providing continuous monitoring of emotional states for patients in their homes, which is particularly beneficial for those with chronic illnesses or mental health conditions.

Enhancing Rehabilitation Processes: In rehabilitation settings, where patient motivation and emotional state significantly impact recovery, ERS can play a vital role (Krasovsky, 2022; Gümüslü, Erol Barkana, & Köse, 2020; Albiol-Pérez, Cano, Da Silva, Gutierrez, Collazos, Lombano, ... & Ruiz, 2018). By understanding and responding to patients' emotional cues, therapists can adjust rehabilitation strategies to improve patient engagement and outcomes.

Aiding in Pain Management: Effective pain management is not solely about addressing physical symptoms; it also involves understanding the emotional context of pain (Velana, Gruss, Layher, Thiam, Zhang, Schork, ... & Walter, 2017; Hassan, Seuß, Wollenberg, Weitz, Kunz, Lautenbacher, ... & Schmid, 2019). ERS can provide insights into the emotional aspects of a patient's pain experience, aiding in developing more comprehensive and effective pain management strategies.

Improving Health Communication: Effective communication between healthcare providers and patients is crucial for successful health outcomes. ERS can facilitate this by providing insights into patients' emotional states during interactions, enabling providers to adjust their communication strategies to be more empathetic and effective (Hautasaari, Yamashita, & Gao, 2014; Nandwani & Verma, 2021).

Assisting in Behavioral Health Interventions: Behavioral health interventions, including those for lifestyle changes such as smoking cessation or weight loss, can benefit from ERS (Wells, Hunnikin, Ash, & Van Goozen, 2021; Forness, Serna, Nielsen, Lambros, Hale, & Kavale, 2000; Wyman & Zhang, 2023). By understanding emotional triggers and responses, ERS can help tailor interventions to individual patient needs, enhancing their effectiveness.

Improving Emergency Room Efficiency: In emergency room settings, where quick assessment is critical, ERS can assist in rapidly gauging patients' emotional and stress levels (Hegde, Manoj, Rao, & Rao, 2006; Mentis, 2010). This information can be crucial in prioritizing care and managing resources more effectively.

Facilitating Long-Term Health Monitoring: ERS can be used for long-term health monitoring, especially for patients with chronic conditions or the elderly. Continuous emotional monitoring can provide valuable data that contributes to long-term health strategies and preventive care (Valenza, Nardelli, Lanata, Gentili, Bertschy, Paradiso, & Scilingo, 2013).

Contributing to Public Health Research: Finally, ERS can contribute significantly to public health research. By analyzing population-level emotional data, ERS can help identify trends and patterns related to mental health, stress, and wellbeing, informing public health policies and interventions.

3.2 Ethical Considerations and Challenges

The implementation of ERS in healthcare, while offering numerous benefits, also raises several ethical issues and challenges. These concerns revolve around privacy, consent, data security, biases in technology, and the potential for misuse.

Privacy and Confidentiality: One of the primary ethical concerns with ERS is the privacy and confidentiality of patient data. ERS involve the collection and analysis of sensitive emotional data, which could be invasive if not handled correctly (Ortiz-Clavijo, Gallego-Duque, David-Diaz, & Ortiz-Zamora, 2023; Katirai, 2023). Ensuring that this data is collected, stored, and used in a manner that respects patient privacy is crucial. There are concerns about who has access to this data and for what purposes it is used, especially in contexts where emotional data could be used for decisions that affect patient care or insurance. ERS also raise the issue of emotional privacy. Unlike traditional data, emotional data reflects the innermost feelings of individuals, which they might not be willing to share or have interpreted by machines. Respecting emotional privacy means considering the sensitivity of emotional data and the contexts in which it is appropriate to use ERS

Informed Consent: Informed consent is another significant ethical consideration. Patients must be fully informed about what ERS are, how they work, what data will be collected, and how that data will be used (Katirai, 2023).. It is essential to ensure that patients understand the implications of ERS and agree to their use in their care. The dynamic nature of healthcare and the continuous data collection by ERS necessitate a model of continual consent. Patients should have the opportunity to regularly review and renew their consent, especially as ERS evolve and the scope

Figure 2. Ethical considerations and challenges

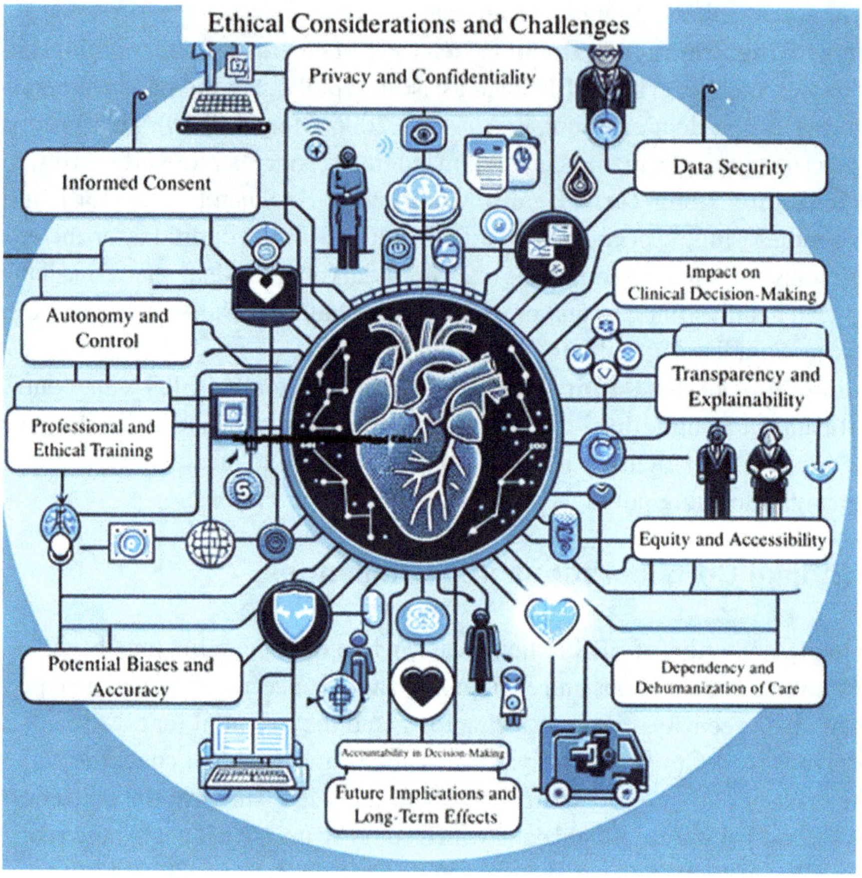

of data collection changes. The use of ERS might have unintended psychological impacts on patients. Knowing that one's emotional state is being constantly monitored and analyzed could lead to anxiety or altered behavior, potentially skewing the data and impacting patient well-being. Moreover, patients have a right to emotional autonomy – the right to experience emotions without external analysis or judgment. ERS must be used in a way that respects this autonomy, ensuring that emotional data is not used to coerce or manipulate patient behavior or choices.

Data Security: With the collection of sensitive emotional data comes the challenge of ensuring data security (Ortiz-Clavijo, Gallego-Duque, David-Diaz, & Ortiz-Zamora, 2023). There is a risk of data breaches, which could lead to the misuse of personal emotional data. Healthcare providers must implement robust security measures to protect this data and adhere to regulations like the Health Insurance Portability and Accountability Act (HIPAA) in the United States (Edemekong,

Annamaraju, & Haydel, 2018). The potential misuse of emotional data for purposes other than intended, such as marketing or manipulation, is a significant ethical concern. There must be strict guidelines and regulations governing the use of emotional data to prevent its misuse.

Potential Biases and Accuracy: ERS, like any technology based on machine learning, are subject to biases present in their training data (Kim, Bryant, Srikanth, & Howard, 2021; Domnich & Anbarjafari, 2021). These biases can lead to inaccurate or unfair assessments of certain groups of people, particularly if the systems are not trained on diverse datasets. Ensuring the accuracy and fairness of ERS is vital to prevent potential harm to patients due to misinterpretation of their emotional states. Emotion recognition may vary significantly across different cultures and social contexts. ERS must be developed and deployed with a deep understanding of socio-cultural nuances to avoid misinterpretation of emotional expressions, which could lead to inappropriate care or interventions. ERS, like any automated system, are prone to errors such as false positives or negatives. The ethical response to these inaccuracies, particularly in high-stakes healthcare environments, is a significant challenge. Healthcare providers must be prepared to identify and rectify such errors promptly to prevent potential harm to patients.

Dependency and Dehumanization of Care: There is a concern that reliance on ERS could lead to the dehumanization of healthcare, where technology replaces the human element of care (Black, 2023; Bastian & Haslam, 2011). While ERS can provide valuable insights, they should not replace the empathy, understanding, and interpersonal skills of healthcare professionals. The introduction of ERS in healthcare may redefine the traditional doctor-patient relationship. While ERS can aid in understanding a patient's emotional state, they should not replace the empathy and personal connection integral to the doctor-patient relationship. Maintaining this balance is an ethical imperative.

Autonomy and Control: The use of ERS should not undermine patient autonomy or control over their healthcare journey. Patients should have the right to opt-out of ERS monitoring or to question and challenge the insights these systems provide.

Impact on Clinical Decision-Making: The integration of ERS into clinical decision-making processes poses ethical challenges. While these systems can provide valuable insights, there's a risk of over-reliance on technology, potentially overshadowing the clinician's judgment and experience. Ensuring that ERS serve as a support tool rather than a definitive decision-maker is essential to maintain the integrity of clinical decisions (De & Mishra, 2022).

Transparency and Explainability: The ethical principle of transparency is critical in the deployment of ERS (Grill & Andalibi, 2022). Users of these systems, including both healthcare providers and patients, should understand how they work and the basis of their analyses. The challenge lies in the often opaque nature of machine learning algorithms, which can be difficult to interpret. Ensuring that ERS are explainable and their workings transparent is crucial for trust and accountability (Rathod, Dalvi, Kaur, Patil, Gite, Kamat, ... & Gabralla, 2022; Heimerl, Weitz, Baur, & André, 2020).

Equity and Accessibility: The equitable distribution and accessibility of ERS are ethical concerns. There is a risk that these advanced technologies may not be equally available to all patient populations, potentially exacerbating healthcare disparities. Ensuring that ERS are accessible to diverse populations, including those with limited resources, is necessary to promote health equity (Stickel, Ebner, Steinbach-Nordmann, Searle, & Holzinger, 2009). Inclusivity in the design and implementation of ERS is crucial. This includes ensuring that these systems are designed with input from diverse populations and are accessible to all, regardless of socioeconomic status, disability, or language barriers.

Professional and Ethical Training: Integrating ERS into healthcare requires professional and ethical training for healthcare providers. They must be equipped to understand the capabilities and limitations of these systems, address patient concerns effectively, and make informed decisions about their use.

Accountability in Decision-Making: Accountability in decision-making, especially when ERS are involved, is a key ethical concern. When decisions are made based on data from ERS, it must be clear who is responsible for these decisions – the healthcare provider or the technology itself. This clarity is crucial for ethical practice and patient trust.

Future Implications and Long-Term Effects: The long-term effects and future implications of using ERS in healthcare are yet to be fully understood. As technology evolves, ongoing ethical considerations will be necessary to address new challenges and ensure that the use of ERS aligns with the evolving standards of patient care and ethical practice.

4. LIMITATIONS OF ERS

ERS are not without their limitations despite being technologically advanced. The accuracy of these systems can vary significantly depending on the quality of the input data and the algorithms used (Al-Omair & Huang, 2018; Landowska, 2019). For instance facial recognition software often struggles with low-light conditions or partial facial coverage (Ige, 2016; Leslie, 2020). Voice recognition systems may falter with background noise or atypical speech patterns. Furthermore, these technologies are still in the process of learning to differentiate between nuanced emotional expressions, which can lead to misinterpretations. This inaccuracy could be detrimental in healthcare settings where precise emotional assessment is critical.

Incorporating ERS into existing healthcare frameworks poses significant technical challenges. Interoperability with current electronic health records (EHR) systems, ensuring consistent data flow, and integrating with various diagnostic tools are some of the hurdles. These integrations require robust IT support and can be costly, posing barriers for smaller healthcare providers. Additionally, the need for continuous updates and maintenance to keep up with evolving technologies can strain healthcare organizations' resources.

Moreover, emotions are expressed and perceived differently across cultures, which poses a significant challenge for universal ERS. What is considered a sign of distress in one culture might be interpreted differently in another. This variation can lead to misinterpretations and inaccuracies in cross-cultural healthcare settings. Developing algorithms that can adapt to and recognize a wide range of cultural expressions of emotion is an ongoing challenge for technologists and healthcare professionals alike. The deployment of emotion recognition systems raises concerns about equitable access to healthcare. There is a risk that these advanced technologies might only be available to well-funded healthcare institutions. Moreover, patients with disabilities or those from diverse linguistic backgrounds may find these systems less accessible or effective, leading to potential disparities in care.

5. FUTURE DIRECTIONS

Future advancements in emotion recognition technologies should focus on improving the accuracy and sensitivity of these systems. This involves refining algorithms to better interpret subtle emotional cues and non-verbal expressions to reduce the risk of misdiagnosis or misinterpretation. Research in machine learning and artificial intelligence will be pivotal in developing more sophisticated models that can adapt to diverse emotional expressions and contexts.

The future of emotion recognition in healthcare looks towards the integration of multimodal data sources. By combining facial expressions, vocal patterns, physiological signals, and contextual data, these systems can offer a more comprehensive and nuanced understanding of a patient's emotional state. This holistic approach could enhance the effectiveness of emotion recognition technologies in complex healthcare settings.

Expanding the use of emotion recognition systems across various clinical domains will be a significant step forward. Applications could extend to pain management, where these systems can assist in assessing and responding to non-verbal pain indicators, particularly in patients who are unable to communicate verbally. Additionally, in geriatric care, emotion recognition can play a crucial role in monitoring the emotional well-being of elderly patients, many of whom may suffer from conditions that affect their ability to communicate. The integration of emotion recognition technologies in telehealth and remote patient monitoring systems represents a promising direction. As telehealth continues to grow, these technologies can aid healthcare providers in assessing patients' emotional states through virtual consultations, enhancing the quality of care and communication in remote healthcare delivery.

The future of emotion recognition in healthcare will benefit greatly from interdisciplinary collaborations. Partnerships between computer scientists, psychologists, healthcare professionals, and ethicists can foster innovative solutions that are technologically advanced, clinically relevant, and ethically sound. Such collaborations can also ensure that these technologies are developed with a deep understanding of the complex nature of human emotions and cultural diversity. Moreover, ongoing research is needed to address the ethical implications and privacy concerns associated with emotion recognition technologies. This includes developing guidelines and protocols that protect patient data privacy and ensure that these technologies are used in a manner that respects patients' autonomy and dignity. Establishing global standards and policies for the deployment of emotion recognition technologies in healthcare is essential. These standards should aim to ensure equitable access, cultural sensitivity, and the avoidance of biases in these systems. Policymakers, in collaboration with international healthcare organizations, can play a crucial role in developing these frameworks.

6. CONCLUSION

In this chapter, we have embarked on a comprehensive exploration of ERS within the healthcare sector, illuminating the dynamic intersection of advanced technology and human-centric care. Through a detailed analysis, we have unveiled the conceptual foundations, innovative applications, and the technical advancements brought about by ERS, as well as the intricate challenges and promising future prospects they present. The core contributions of this work lie in its conceptual depth, novelty in application, and technical ingenuity, offering a fresh perspective on how ERS can be harnessed to foster significant improvements in patient care, enhance communication between providers and patients, and spearhead the evolution of mental health interventions. Reflecting on the journey from the abstract to this concluding discussion, it's evident that the transformative potential of ERS extends far beyond mere technological advancement; it represents a paradigm shift towards more empathetic, understanding, and personalized healthcare services. By bridging the critical gap in comprehending patients' emotional and psychological states, ERS set the stage for a new era of healthcare that prioritizes emotional intelligence alongside clinical expertise. The novelty of our discussion has been to contextualize these systems within the real-world framework of healthcare, proposing not only their potential uses but also addressing the tangible steps towards their integration, underpinned by a commitment to ethical standards, privacy protection, and equity. However, the journey toward integrating ERS into healthcare is paved with complex ethical dilemmas, privacy concerns, and the imperative to maintain the human essence at the core of patient care. As we stand on the brink of this new frontier, it is imperative to navigate these challenges with a balanced approach, ensuring that the deployment of ERS enhances rather than diminishes the human touch in healthcare. The technical aspects detailed herein, from algorithmic advancements to improvements in system interfaces, underscore the chapter's contribution to pushing the boundaries of what's technically feasible in emotion recognition.

As we conclude, it is clear that the intersection of AI, machine learning, and ethical considerations will continue to be a fertile ground for interdisciplinary research, driving forward the integration of ERS in healthcare. The vision outlined in this chapter is not of a distant future but of an imminent evolution, where ERS play a pivotal role in shaping a more compassionate, responsive, and patient-focused healthcare landscape. It is a future that demands our cautious optimism, rigorous scrutiny, and creative ingenuity to ensure that as we venture into this new terrain, we do so with the welfare of patients as our paramount concern, honoring the indispensable human touch that forms the essence of care.

REFERENCES

Al-Omair, O. M., & Huang, S. (2018, November). A comparative study on detection accuracy of cloud-based emotion recognition services. In *Proceedings of the 2018 International Conference on Signal Processing and Machine Learning* (pp. 142-148). ACM. 10.1145/3297067.3297079

Al-Omair, O. M., & Huang, S. (2018). A comparative study on detection accuracy of cloud-based emotion recognition services. In *Proceedings of the 2018 International Conference on Signal Processing and Machine Learning* (pp. 142-148). ACM. 10.1145/3297067.3297079

Albiol-Pérez, S., Cano, S., Da Silva, M. G., Gutierrez, E. G., Collazos, C. A., Lombano, J. L., . . . Ruiz, M. A. (2018). A novel approach in virtual rehabilitation for children with cerebral palsy: evaluation of an emotion detection system. In Trends and Advances in Information Systems and Technologies: Volume 2 6 (pp. 1240-1250). Springer International Publishing. doi:10.1007/978-3-319-77712-2_119

Alvarado, M., Lawley, M., & Li, Y. (2016, December). Healthcare simulation tutorial: Methods, challenges, and opportunities. In 2016 Winter Simulation Conference (WSC) (pp. 236-247). IEEE.

Azevedo, R. F. L., Hale, T., Warren, T., Baby, E., Lee, J., Insel, K., Rogers, W., & Mudar, R. (2023). ASSESSING USABILITY OF A MEDICATION ADHERENCE SYSTEM FOR PERSONS WITH MILD COGNITIVE IMPAIRMENT. *Innovation in Aging*, *7*(Supplement_1), 83–83. doi:10.1093/geroni/igad104.0266

Bahreini, K., Nadolski, R., & Westera, W. (2016). Towards multimodal emotion recognition in e-learning environments. *Interactive Learning Environments*, *24*(3), 590–605. doi:10.1080/10494820.2014.908927

Bahreini, K., Nadolski, R., & Westera, W. (2017). Communication skills training exploiting multimodal emotion recognition. *Interactive Learning Environments*, *25*(8), 1065–1082. doi:10.1080/10494820.2016.1247286

Barrett, P. H. (2016). *The Works of Charles Darwin: Vol 23: The Expression of the Emotions in Man and Animals*. Routledge. doi:10.4324/9781315476575

Bastian, B., & Haslam, N. (2011). Experiencing dehumanization: Cognitive and emotional effects of everyday dehumanization. *Basic and Applied Social Psychology*, *33*(4), 295–303. doi:10.1080/01973533.2011.614132

Bettadapura, V. (2012). Face expression recognition and analysis: the state of the art. *arXiv preprint arXiv:1203.6722*.

Black, V. E. (2023). *De-humanizing Care: An Ethnography of Mental Health Artificial Intelligence* [Doctoral dissertation, University of California, Berkeley].

Bota, P. J., Wang, C., Fred, A. L., & Da Silva, H. P. (2019). A review, current challenges, and future possibilities on emotion recognition using machine learning and physiological signals. *IEEE Access : Practical Innovations, Open Solutions*, *7*, 140990–141020. doi:10.1109/ACCESS.2019.2944001

Brandt, M., de Oliveira Silva, F., Simões Neto, J. P., Tourinho Baptista, M. A., Belfort, T., Lacerda, I. B., & Nascimento Dourado, M. C. (2024). Facial expression recognition of emotional situations in mild and moderate Alzheimer's disease. *Journal of Geriatric Psychiatry and Neurology*, *37*(1), 73–83. doi:10.1177/08919887231175432 PMID:37160761

Bullington, J. (2005). 'Affective'computing and emotion recognition systems: the future of biometric surveillance? In *Proceedings of the 2nd annual conference on Information security curriculum development* (pp. 95-99). ACM. 10.1145/1107622.1107644

Cao, S., Fu, D., Yang, X., Wermter, S., Liu, X., & Wu, H. (2021). Can AI detect pain and express pain empathy? A review from emotion recognition and a human-centered AI perspective. *arXiv preprint arXiv:2110.04249.*

Chen, C. L., Huang, Q. Y., Zhou, M., Huang, D. C., Liu, L. C., & Deng, Y. Y. (2023). Quantified emotion analysis based on design principles of color feature recognition in pictures. *Multimedia Tools and Applications*, 1–25. doi:10.1007/s11042-023-17286-6 PMID:37362685

Chen, C. M., & Wang, H. P. (2011). Using emotion recognition technology to assess the effects of different multimedia materials on learning emotion and performance. *Library & Information Science Research*, *33*(3), 244–255. doi:10.1016/j.lisr.2010.09.010

Cowie, R., Douglas-Cowie, E., Tsapatsoulis, N., Votsis, G., Kollias, S., Fellenz, W., & Taylor, J. G. (2001). Emotion recognition in human-computer interaction. *IEEE Signal Processing Magazine*, *18*(1), 32–80. doi:10.1109/79.911197

Cowie, R., Douglas-Cowie, E., Tsapatsoulis, N., Votsis, G., Kollias, S., Fellenz, W., & Taylor, J. G. (2001). Emotion recognition in human-computer interaction. *IEEE Signal Processing Magazine*, *18*(1), 32–80. doi:10.1109/79.911197

Cupkova, D., Kajati, E., Mocnej, J., Papcun, P., Koziorek, J., & Zolotova, I. (2019). Intelligent human-centric lighting for mental wellbeing improvement. *International Journal of Distributed Sensor Networks*, *15*(9), 1550147719875878. doi:10.1177/1550147719875878

De, A., & Mishra, S. (2022). Augmented intelligence in mental health care: Sentiment analysis and emotion detection with health care perspective. *Augmented Intelligence in Healthcare: A Pragmatic and Integrated Analysis*, 205-235.

Dhuheir, M., Albaseer, A., Baccour, E., Erbad, A., Abdallah, M., & Hamdi, M. (2021). Emotion recognition for healthcare surveillance systems using neural networks: A survey. In 2021 International Wireless Communications and Mobile Computing (IWCMC) (pp. 681-687). IEEE. doi:10.1109/IWCMC51323.2021.9498861

Domnich, A., & Anbarjafari, G. (2021). Responsible AI: Gender bias assessment in emotion recognition. *arXiv preprint arXiv:2103.11436.*

Edemekong, P. F., Annamaraju, P., & Haydel, M. J. (2018). Health insurance portability and accountability act.

Egger, M., Ley, M., & Hanke, S. (2019). Emotion recognition from physiological signal analysis: A review. *Electronic Notes in Theoretical Computer Science, 343*, 35–55. doi:10.1016/j.entcs.2019.04.009

Ekman, P., & Friesen, W. V. (1978). Facial action coding system. *Environmental Psychology and Nonverbal Behavior.*

Elfenbein, H. A., & Ambady, N. (2002). On the universality and cultural specificity of emotion recognition: A meta-analysis. *Psychological Bulletin, 128*(2), 203–235. doi:10.1037/0033-2909.128.2.203 PMID:11931516

Faisal, S., Samoth, D., Aslam, Y., Patel, H., Park, S., Baby, B., & Patel, T. (2023). Key Features of Smart Medication Adherence Products: Updated Scoping Review. *JMIR Aging, 6*, e50990. doi:10.2196/50990 PMID:38113067

Flynn, M., Effraimidis, D., Angelopoulou, A., Kapetanios, E., Williams, D., Hemanth, J., & Towell, T. (2020). Assessing the effectiveness of automated emotion recognition in adults and children for clinical investigation. *Frontiers in Human Neuroscience, 14*, 70. doi:10.3389/fnhum.2020.00070 PMID:32317947

Forness, S. R., Serna, L. A., Nielsen, E., Lambros, K., Hale, M. J., & Kavale, K. A. (2000). A model for early detection and primary prevention of emotional or behavioral disorders. *Education & Treatment of Children*, 325–345.

Goldman, A. I., & Sripada, C. S. (2005). Simulationist models of face-based emotion recognition. *Cognition, 94*(3), 193–213. doi:10.1016/j.cognition.2004.01.005 PMID:15617671

González-Rodríguez, M. R., Díaz-Fernández, M. C., & Gómez, C. P. (2020). Facial-expression recognition: An emergent approach to the measurement of tourist satisfaction through emotions. *Telematics and Informatics, 51*, 101404. doi:10.1016/j.tele.2020.101404

Grabowski, K., Rynkiewicz, A., Lassalle, A., Baron-Cohen, S., Schuller, B., Cummins, N., Baird, A., Podgórska-Bednarz, J., Pieniążek, A., & Łucka, I. (2019). Emotional expression in psychiatric conditions: New technology for clinicians. *Psychiatry and Clinical Neurosciences, 73*(2), 50–62. doi:10.1111/pcn.12799 PMID:30565801

Grill, G., & Andalibi, N. (2022). Attitudes and folk theories of data subjects on transparency and accuracy in emotion recognition. *Proceedings of the ACM on Human-Computer Interaction, 6*(CSCW1), (pp. 1-35) IEEE. 10.1145/3512925

Gümüslü, E., Erol Barkana, D., & Köse, H. (2020, October). Emotion recognition using EEG and physiological data for robot-assisted rehabilitation systems. In Companion publication of the 2020 international conference on multimodal interaction (pp. 379-387).

Hassan, T., Seuß, D., Wollenberg, J., Weitz, K., Kunz, M., Lautenbacher, S., & Schmid, U. (2019). Automatic detection of pain from facial expressions: A survey. *IEEE Transactions on Pattern Analysis and Machine Intelligence*, *43*(6), 1815–1831. doi:10.1109/TPAMI.2019.2958341 PMID:31825861

Hautasaari, A. M., Yamashita, N., & Gao, G. (2014, April). "Maybe it was a joke" emotion detection in text-only communication by non-native english speakers. In *Proceedings of the SIGCHI Conference on Human Factors in Computing Systems* (pp. 3715-3724). ACM. 10.1145/2556288.2557215

Hegde, R., Manoj, B. S., Rao, B. D., & Rao, R. R. (2006, May). Emotion detection from speech signals and its applications in supporting enhanced QoS in emergency response. In *Proceedings of the 3rd International ISCRAM Conference.*

Heimerl, A., Weitz, K., Baur, T., & André, E. (2020). Unraveling ml models of emotion with nova: Multi-level explainable ai for non-experts. *IEEE Transactions on Affective Computing*, *13*(3), 1155–1167. doi:10.1109/TAFFC.2020.3043603

Herrera, D., Alanis, A., Baltazar, R., & Velazquez, D. (2023). Intelligent Emotion Prediction System for Help in Telemedicine Therapies of Children with ASD. In *International Conference on Advanced Research in Technologies, Information, Innovation and Sustainability* (pp. 265-278). Cham: Springer Nature Switzerland.

Huang, C. W., Wu, B. C., Nguyen, P. A., Wang, H. H., Kao, C. C., Lee, P. C., Rahmanti, A. R., Hsu, J. C., Yang, H.-C., & Li, Y. C. J. (2023). Emotion recognition in doctor-patient interactions from real-world clinical video database: Initial development of artificial empathy. *Computer Methods and Programs in Biomedicine*, *233*, 107480. doi:10.1016/j.cmpb.2023.107480 PMID:36965299

Huang, R., Liu, N., Nicdao, M. A., Mikaheal, M., Baldacchino, T., Albeos, A., Petoumenos, K., Sud, K., & Kim, J. (2020). Emotion sharing in remote patient monitoring of patients with chronic kidney disease. *Journal of the American Medical Informatics Association : JAMIA*, *27*(2), 185–193. doi:10.1093/jamia/ocz183 PMID:31633755

Ibrahim, S., Lok, J., Mitchell, M., Stoiljkovic, B., Tarulli, N., & Hubley, P. (2023). Equity, diversity and inclusion in clinical simulation healthcare education and training: An integrative review. *International Journal of Healthcare Simulation*, (null), 1-14.

Ige, E. (2016). *Facial expression recognition under harsh lighting using high dynamic range imaging* [Doctoral dissertation, University of Warwick].

Islam, S. (2023). *Smart therapy environment: a design science research towards innovative artefact design for autistic children's social interaction and emotion recognition* [Master's thesis, S. Islam].

Jonnalagadda, A., Rajvir, M., Singh, S., Chandramouliswaran, S., George, J., & Kamalov, F. (2023). An Ensemble-Based Machine Learning Model for Emotion and Mental Health Detection. *Journal of Information & Knowledge Management, 22*(02), 2250075. doi:10.1142/S0219649222500757

Karabuschenko, N. B., Ivashchenko, A. V., Sungurova, N. L., & Hvorova, E. M. (2016). Emotion recognition in different cultures. *Indian Journal of Science and Technology*, *9*(48).

Katirai, A. (2023). Ethical considerations in emotion recognition technologies: A review of the literature. *AI and Ethics*, 1–22. doi:10.1007/s43681-023-00307-3

Kennedy, H., & Hill, R. L. (2018). The feeling of numbers: Emotions in everyday engagements with data and their visualisation. *Sociology*, *52*(4), 830–848. doi:10.1177/0038038516674675

Kim, E., Bryant, D. A., Srikanth, D., & Howard, A. (2021, July). Age bias in emotion detection: An analysis of facial emotion recognition performance on young, middle-aged, and older adults. In *Proceedings of the 2021 AAAI/ACM Conference on AI, Ethics, and Society* (pp. 638-644). ACM. 10.1145/3461702.3462609

Kim, K. H., Bang, S. W., & Kim, S. R. (2004). Emotion recognition system using short-term monitoring of physiological signals. *Medical & Biological Engineering & Computing*, *42*(3), 419–427. doi:10.1007/BF02344719 PMID:15191089

Ko, B. C. (2018). A brief review of facial emotion recognition based on visual information. *sensors, 18*(2), 401.

Krasovsky, T. (2022). Cognition, emotion, and movement in the context of rehabilitation. *International Journal of Environmental Research and Public Health, 19*(21), 14532. doi:10.3390/ijerph192114532 PMID:36361412

Kurbalija, V., Ivanović, M., Radovanović, M., Geler, Z., Mitrović, D., Dai, W., & Zhao, W. (2015, September). Cultural differences and similarities in emotion recognition. In *Proceedings of the 7th Balkan Conference on Informatics Conference* (pp. 1-6). ACM. 10.1145/2801081.2801093

Lacava, P. G., Golan, O., Baron-Cohen, S., & Smith Myles, B. (2007). Using assistive technology to teach emotion recognition to students with Asperger syndrome: A pilot study. *Remedial and Special Education*, *28*(3), 174–181. doi:10.1177/07419325070280030601

Landowska, A. (2019). Uncertainty in emotion recognition. *Journal of Information. Communication and Ethics in Society*, *17*(3), 273–291. doi:10.1108/JICES-03-2019-0034

Leslie, D. (2020). Understanding bias in facial recognition technologies. *arXiv preprint arXiv:2010.07023.*

Liang, F., Su, Z., Sheng, W., Bishop, A., & Carlson, B. (2023). Medication adherence management for in-home geriatric care with a companion robot and a wearable device. *Smart Health (Amsterdam, Netherlands)*, *30*, 100434. doi:10.1016/j.smhl.2023.100434

Lisetti, C. L., & Schiano, D. J. (2000). Automatic facial expression interpretation: Where human-computer interaction, artificial intelligence and cognitive science intersect. *Pragmatics & Cognition*, *8*(1), 185–235. doi:10.1075/pc.8.1.09lis

Liu, F., Yang, M., & Wang, Z. (2005, December). Study on simulation credibility metrics. In *Proceedings of the Winter Simulation Conference,* (pp. 7). IEEE.

Llurba, C., Fretes, G., & Palau, R. (2022). Pilot study of real-time Emotional Recognition technology for Secondary school students. *IxD&A, 52*, 61-80.

Mano, L. Y., Faiçal, B. S., Nakamura, L. H., Gomes, P. H., Libralon, G. L., Meneguete, R. I., Filho, G. P. R., Giancristofaro, G. T., Pessin, G., Krishnamachari, B., & Ueyama, J. (2016). Exploiting IoT technologies for enhancing Health Smart Homes through patient identification and emotion recognition. *Computer Communications*, *89*, 178–190. doi:10.1016/j.comcom.2016.03.010

Mano, L. Y., Mazzo, A., Neto, J. R., Meska, M. H., Giancristofaro, G. T., Ueyama, J., & Júnior, G. A. (2019). Using emotion recognition to assess simulation-based learning. *Nurse Education in Practice*, *36*, 13–19. doi:10.1016/j.nepr.2019.02.017 PMID:30831482

Mentis, H. M. (2010). *Emotion awareness and invisibility in an emergency room: a socio-technical dilemma.*

Nandwani, P., & Verma, R. (2021). A review on sentiment analysis and emotion detection from text. *Social Network Analysis and Mining*, *11*(1), 81. doi:10.1007/s13278-021-00776-6 PMID:34484462

Ortiz-Clavijo, L. F., Gallego-Duque, C. J., David-Diaz, J. C., & Ortiz-Zamora, A. F. (2023). Implications of Emotion Recognition Technologies: Balancing Privacy and Public Safety. *IEEE Technology and Society Magazine*, *42*(3), 69–75. doi:10.1109/MTS.2023.3306530

Öztürk, A., Kiliç, A., Deveci, E., & Kirpinar, İ. (2016). Investigation of facial emotion recognition, alexithymia, and levels of anxiety and depression in patients with somatic symptoms and related disorders. *Neuropsychiatric Disease and Treatment*, 1047–1053. doi:10.2147/NDT.S106989 PMID:27199559

Pal, S., Mukhopadhyay, S., & Suryadevara, N. (2021). Development and progress in sensors and technologies for human emotion recognition. *Sensors (Basel)*, *21*(16), 5554. doi:10.3390/s21165554 PMID:34451002

Pampouchidou, A., Pediaditis, M., Kazantzaki, E., Sfakianakis, S., Apostolaki, I. A., Argyraki, K., Manousos, D., Meriaudeau, F., Marias, K., Yang, F., Tsiknakis, M., Basta, M., Vgontzas, A. N., & Simos, P. (2020). Automated facial video-based recognition of depression and anxiety symptom severity: Cross-corpus validation. *Machine Vision and Applications*, *31*(4), 30. doi:10.1007/s00138-020-01080-7

Pavez, R., Diaz, J., Arango-Lopez, J., Ahumada, D., Mendez-Sandoval, C., & Moreira, F. (2023). Emo-mirror: A proposal to support emotion recognition in children with autism spectrum disorders. *Neural Computing & Applications*, *35*(11), 7913–7924. doi:10.1007/s00521-021-06592-5 PMID:34642548

Pietquin, O., & Hastie, H. (2013). A survey on metrics for the evaluation of user simulations. *The Knowledge Engineering Review*, *28*(1), 59–73. doi:10.1017/S0269888912000343

Rathod, M., Dalvi, C., Kaur, K., Patil, S., Gite, S., Kamat, P., Kotecha, K., Abraham, A., & Gabralla, L. A. (2022). Kids' Emotion Recognition Using Various Deep-Learning Models with Explainable AI. *Sensors (Basel)*, *22*(20), 8066. doi:10.3390/s22208066 PMID:36298415

Schlosser, A., Voss, M., & Bruckner, L. (2004, September). Comparing and evaluating metrics for reputation systems by simulation. In *Proceedings of the IEEE Workshop on Reputation in Agent Societies*. IEEE.

Sebe, N., Cohen, I., Gevers, T., & Huang, T. S. (2005, January). Multimodal approaches for emotion recognition: a survey. In Internet Imaging VI (Vol. 5670, pp. 56-67). SPIE.

Sebe, N., Cohen, I., & Huang, T. S. (2005). Multimodal emotion recognition. In Handbook of pattern recognition and computer vision (pp. 387-409). IEEE. doi:10.1142/9789812775320_0021

Siam, A. I., Soliman, N. F., Algarni, A. D., El-Samie, A., Fathi, E., & Sedik, A. (2022). Deploying machine learning techniques for human emotion detection. *Computational Intelligence and Neuroscience, 2022*, 2022. doi:10.1155/2022/8032673 PMID:35154306

Slakkham, B., & Bhattarakosol, P. (2018, October). A Monitoring and Analyzing Pain System for Postoperative Brain Surgery Patients Based Facial Detection. In TENCON 2018-2018 IEEE Region 10 Conference (pp. 0377-0382). IEEE. doi:10.1109/TENCON.2018.8650336

Stickel, C., Ebner, M., Steinbach-Nordmann, S., Searle, G., & Holzinger, A. (2009). *Emotion detection: application of the valence arousal space for rapid biological usability testing to enhance universal access*. In Universal Access in Human-Computer Interaction. Addressing Diversity: 5th International Conference, UAHCI 2009, Held as Part of HCI International 2009, San Diego, CA.

Subramanian, A., Cao, R., Naeni, E. K., Aqajari, S. A. H., Hughes, T. D., Calderon, M. D., & Rahmani, A. M. (2023). Multimodal Pain Recognition in Postoperative Patients: A Machine Learning Approach. medRxiv, 2023-06. doi:10.1101/2023.06.07.23291094

Subramanian, B., Kim, J., Maray, M., & Paul, A. (2022). Digital twin model: A real-time emotion recognition system for personalized healthcare. *IEEE Access : Practical Innovations, Open Solutions, 10*, 81155–81165. doi:10.1109/ACCESS.2022.3193941

Valenza, G., Nardelli, M., Lanata, A., Gentili, C., Bertschy, G., Paradiso, R., & Scilingo, E. P. (2013). Wearable monitoring for mood recognition in bipolar disorder based on history-dependent long-term heart rate variability analysis. *IEEE Journal of Biomedical and Health Informatics, 18*(5), 1625–1635. doi:10.1109/JBHI.2013.2290382 PMID:24240031

Van Thanh, N. (2023). Emotion Recognition Systems in Retail: A Detailed Analysis of Their Role in Enhancing Customer Interactions, Driving Sales, and Predicting Trends. *Journal of Computational Social Dynamics, 8*(3), 1–9.

Velana, M., Gruss, S., Layher, G., Thiam, P., Zhang, Y., Schork, D., & Walter, S. (2017). The senseemotion database: A multimodal database for the development and systematic validation of an automatic pain-and emotion-recognition system. In *Multimodal Pattern Recognition of Social Signals in Human-Computer-Interaction: 4th IAPR TC 9 Workshop, MPRSS 2016, Cancun, Mexico, December 4, 2016, Revised Selected Papers 4* (pp. 127-139). Springer International Publishing. 10.1007/978-3-319-59259-6_11

Wang, Z., Zhou, X., Wang, W., & Liang, C. (2020). Emotion recognition using multimodal deep learning in multiple psychophysiological signals and video. *International Journal of Machine Learning and Cybernetics*, *11*(4), 923–934. doi:10.1007/s13042-019-01056-8

Wani, T. M., Gunawan, T. S., Qadri, S. A. A., Kartiwi, M., & Ambikairajah, E. (2021). A comprehensive review of speech emotion recognition systems. *IEEE Access : Practical Innovations, Open Solutions*, *9*, 47795–47814. doi:10.1109/ACCESS.2021.3068045

Wei, J., Hu, G., Yang, X., Luu, A. T., & Dong, Y. (2024). Learning facial expression and body gesture visual information for video emotion recognition. *Expert Systems with Applications*, *237*, 121419. doi:10.1016/j.eswa.2023.121419

Wells, A. E., Hunnikin, L. M., Ash, D. P., & Van Goozen, S. H. (2021). Improving emotion recognition is associated with subsequent mental health and well-being in children with severe behavioural problems. *European Child & Adolescent Psychiatry*, *30*(11), 1769–1777. doi:10.1007/s00787-020-01652-y PMID:32997168

Wyman, A., & Zhang, Z. (2023). API Face Value: Evaluating the Current Status and Potential of Emotion Detection Software in Emotional Deficit Interventions. *Journal of Behavioral Data Science*, *3*(1), 59–69. doi:10.35566/jbds/v3n1/wyman

Xu, M., Zhang, F., & Khan, S. U. (2020, January). Improve accuracy of speech emotion recognition with attention head fusion. In *2020 10th annual computing and communication workshop and conference (CCWC)* (pp. 1058-1064). IEEE. 10.1109/CCWC47524.2020.9031207

Yang, K., Wang, C., Gu, Y., Sarsenbayeva, Z., Tag, B., Dingler, T., & Goncalves, J. (2021). Behavioral and physiological signals-based deep multimodal approach for mobile emotion recognition. *IEEE Transactions on Affective Computing*.

Zaman, K. S., & Reaz, M. M. B. I. (2023). Secure and efficient implementation of facial emotion detection for smart patient monitoring system. *Quantitative Biology*, *11*(2), 175–182. doi:10.15302/J-QB-022-0312

Zhang, R. E., Ringland, K., Paan, M. C., Mohr, D., & Reddy, M. (2021, May). Designing for emotional well-being: integrating persuasion and customization into mental health technologies. In *Proceedings of the 2021 CHI Conference on Human Factors in Computing Systems* (pp. 1-13). ACM. 10.1145/3411764.3445771

Zhuang, J. R., Guan, Y. J., Nagayoshi, H., Muramatsu, K., Watanuki, K., & Tanaka, E. (2019). Real-time emotion recognition system with multiple physiological signals. *Journal of Advanced Mechanical Design, Systems, and Manufacturing, 13*(4), JAMDSM0075-JAMDSM0075.

Compilation of References

Ahmed, N., Al Aghbari, Z., & Girija, S. (2023). A systematic survey on multimodal emotion recognition using learning algorithms. Intell. Syst. with Appl., 17. doi:10.1016/j.iswa.2022.200171

Alam, H., Burhan, M., Gillani, A., Haq, I., Arshed, M. A., Shafi, M., & Ahmad, S. (2023). IoT Based Smart Baby Monitoring System with Emotion Recognition Using Machine Learning. *Wireless Communications and Mobile Computing*, *2023*, 1–11. doi:10.1155/2023/1175450

Albiol-Pérez, S., Cano, S., Da Silva, M. G., Gutierrez, E. G., Collazos, C. A., Lombano, J. L., . . . Ruiz, M. A. (2018). A novel approach in virtual rehabilitation for children with cerebral palsy: evaluation of an emotion detection system. In Trends and Advances in Information Systems and Technologies: Volume 2 6 (pp. 1240-1250). Springer International Publishing. doi:10.1007/978-3-319-77712-2_119

Alexander, C., Ishikawa, S., Silverstein, M., Jacobson, M., Fiksdahl-King, I., & Shlomo, A. (1977). *A Pattern Language*. Oxford University Press USA - OSO.

Alghamdi, R., & Alfalqi, K. (2015). A Survey of Topic Modeling in Text Mining. *International Journal of Advanced Computer Science and Applications*, *6*(1), 147–153. doi:10.14569/IJACSA.2015.060121

Al-Omair, O. M., & Huang, S. (2018, November). A comparative study on detection accuracy of cloud-based emotion recognition services. In *Proceedings of the 2018 International Conference on Signal Processing and Machine Learning* (pp. 142-148). ACM. 10.1145/3297067.3297079

Alonso, M. E., González-Montaña, J. R., & Lomillos, J. M. (2020). Consumers' Concerns and Perceptions of Farm Animal Welfare. *Animals (Basel)*, *10*(3), 385. doi:10.3390/ani10030385 PMID:32120935

Alshahrani, H. M., Yaseen, I., & Drar, S. (2023). Textual Emotion Analysis-based Disabled People Talking Using Improved Metaheuristics with Deep Learning Techniques for Intelligent Systems. *Journal of Disability Research*, *2*(3). doi:10.57197/JDR-2023-0034

Alvarado, M., Lawley, M., & Li, Y. (2016, December). Healthcare simulation tutorial: Methods, challenges, and opportunities. In 2016 Winter Simulation Conference (WSC) (pp. 236-247). IEEE.

Alvarez-Ortega, C., Brown, R., & Garcia, M. (2017). Emotion Detection in Mental Health Diagnosis: A Review of Current Applications. *Journal of Health Informatics*, *25*(4), 245–260.

Amorim, M., Cohen, Y., Reis, J., & Rodrigues, M. (2019). Exploring opportunities for artificial emotional intelligence in service production systems. *IFAC-PapersOnLine*, *52*(13), 1145–1149. doi:10.1016/j.ifacol.2019.11.350

Anand, R., Khan, B., Nassa, V. K., Pandey, D., Dhabliya, D., Pandey, B. K., & Dadheech, P. (2023). Hybrid convolutional neural network (CNN) for Kennedy Space Center hyperspectral image. *Aerospace Systems*, *6*(1), 71–78. doi:10.1007/s42401-022-00168-4

Anand, R., Lakshmi, S. V., Pandey, D., & Pandey, B. K. (2023). An enhanced ResNet-50 deep learning model for arrhythmia detection using electrocardiogram biomedical indicators. *Evolving Systems*, 1–15.

Anderson, E., Smith, J., & Davis, R. (2018). Privacy and Security in Facial Profiling: A Comprehensive Review. *Journal of Information Privacy*, *35*(2), 201–218.

Andersson, S., Bathula, D. R., Iliadis, S. I., Walter, M., & Skalkidou, A. (2021). Predicting women with depressive symptoms postpartum with machine learning methods. *Scientific Reports*, *11*(1), 7877. doi:10.1038/s41598-021-86368-y PMID:33846362

Anusha, K. (2023). A Framework To Build And Clean Multi- Language Text Corpus For Emotion Detection 101. Research Gate.

Asmussen, C. B., & Møller, C. (2019). Smart literature review: A practical topic modelling approach to exploratory literature review. *Journal of Big Data*, *6*(1), 93. doi:10.1186/s40537-019-0255-7

Azevedo, R. F. L., Hale, T., Warren, T., Baby, E., Lee, J., Insel, K., Rogers, W., & Mudar, R. (2023). ASSESSING USABILITY OF A MEDICATION ADHERENCE SYSTEM FOR PERSONS WITH MILD COGNITIVE IMPAIRMENT. *Innovation in Aging*, *7*(Supplement_1), 83–83. doi:10.1093/geroni/igad104.0266

Babu, G. R., Chintalapati, P. V., Sree, P. K., Pudi, A., & Ramana, C. V. (2023). A Context Sensitive with Effective Task Migration in Mobile Cloud Computing Services. In *2023 3rd International Conference on Computing and Information Technology (ICCIT)* (pp. 201-205). IEEE. 10.1109/ICCIT58132.2023.10273949

Bahreini, K., Nadolski, R., & Westera, W. (2016). Towards multimodal emotion recognition in e-learning environments. *Interactive Learning Environments*, *24*(3), 590–605. doi:10.1080/10494820.2014.908927

Bahreini, K., Nadolski, R., & Westera, W. (2017). Communication skills training exploiting multimodal emotion recognition. *Interactive Learning Environments*, *25*(8), 1065–1082. doi:10.1080/10494820.2016.1247286

Baillie, P. (2002). *The synthesis of emotions in artificial intelligences: an affective agent architecture for intuitive reasoning in artificial intelligences* [Doctoral dissertation, University of Southern Queensland].

Bankins, S., & Formosa, P. (2023). The ethical implications of artificial intelligence (AI) for meaningful work. *Journal of Business Ethics, 185*(4), 1–16. doi:10.1007/s10551-023-05339-7

Bansal, R., Gupta, A., Singh, R., & Nassa, V. K. (2021). Role and Impact of Digital Technologies in E-Learning amidst COVID-19 Pandemic. *2021 Fourth International Conference on Computational Intelligence and Communication Technologies (CCICT)*. IEEE. . http://dx.doi.org/10.1109/CCICT53244.2021.00046

Bapat, G. S., Ayedee, N., Bhalerao, K., Kumar, A., & Singh, S. (2023). From Natural to Artificial and Now to Emotional Intelligence. *Advances in Communication. Devices and Networking, 1037*, 321–333. doi:10.1007/978-981-99-1983-3_31

Bar-On, R. (1997). BarOn emotional quotient inventory (Vol. 40). *Multi-health systems.*

Barrett, L. F., Adolphs, R., Marsella, S., Martinez, A. M., & Pollak, S. D. (2019). Emotional expressions reconsidered: Challenges to inferring emotion from human facial movements. *Psychological Science in the Public Interest, 20*(1), 1–68. doi:10.1177/1529100619832930 PMID:31313636

Barrett, P. H. (2016). *The Works of Charles Darwin: Vol 23: The Expression of the Emotions in Man and Animals.* Routledge. doi:10.4324/9781315476575

Bastian, B., & Haslam, N. (2011). Experiencing dehumanization: Cognitive and emotional effects of everyday dehumanization. *Basic and Applied Social Psychology, 33*(4), 295–303. doi:10.1080/01973533.2011.614132

Bechara, A., Tranel, D., & Damasio, H. (2000). Characterization of the decision-making deficit of patients with ventromedial prefrontal cortex lesions. *Brain, 123*(11), 2189–2202. doi:10.1093/brain/123.11.2189 PMID:11050020

Behnke, M., Saganowski, S., Kunc, D., & Kazienko, P. (2022). Ethical Considerations and Checklist for Affective Research with Wearables. *IEEE Transactions on Affective Computing*, 1–14. doi:10.1109/TAFFC.2022.3222524

Benedetto, F., & Tedeschi, A. (2016). Big data sentiment analysis for brand monitoring in social media streams by cloud computing. In Studies in Computational Intelligence (Vol. 639). https://doi.org/ doi:10.1007/978-3-319-30319-2_14

Benton, A., Mitchell, M., & Hovy, D. (2017). Multi-task learning for mental health using social media text. Proceedings of the Fourth Workshop on Computational Linguistics and Clinical Psychology—From Linguistic Signal to Clinical Reality, 152-162.

Bessant, Y. A., Jency, J. G., Sagayam, K. M., Jone, A. A. A., Pandey, D., & Pandey, B. K. (2023). Improved parallel matrix multiplication using Strassen and Urdhvatiryagbhyam method. *CCF Transactions on High Performance Computing, 5*(2), 1–14. doi:10.1007/s42514-023-00149-9

Bettadapura, V. (2012). Face expression recognition and analysis: the state of the art. *arXiv preprint arXiv:1203.6722.*

Bhardwaj, B., Sharma, D., & Dhiman, M. C. (2023). AI and Emotional Intelligence for Modern Business Management. *Advances in Logistics, Operations, and Management Science, 1*, 13. doi:10.4018/979-8-3693-0418-1

Bhatia, S., Gautam, D., Kumar, S., & Verma, S. (2023, January). Automatic Seat Identification System in Smart Transport using IoT and Image Processing. In *2023 3rd International Conference on Intelligent Communication and Computational Techniques (ICCT)* (pp. 1-6). IEEE. 10.1109/ICCT56969.2023.10075664

Bhatia, S., Goel, A. K., Naib, B. B., Singh, K., Yadav, M., & Saini, A. (2023). Diabetes Prediction Using Machine Learning. *2023 World Conference on Communication & Computing (WCONF)*, RAIPUR, India. 10.1109/WCONF58270.2023.10235187

Bhatia, S., Goel, N., Ahlawat, V., Naib, B. B., & Singh, K. (2023). A Comprehensive Review of IoT Reliability and Its Measures: Perspective Analysis. Handbook of Research on Machine Learning-Enabled IoT for Smart Applications Across Industries, (pp. 365-384). IEEE.

Bhatia, S., Jaffery, Z. A., & Mehfuz, S. (2023, January). A Comparative Study of Wireless Communication Protocols for use in Smart Farming Framework Development. In *2023 3rd International Conference on Intelligent Communication and Computational Techniques (ICCT)* (pp. 1-7). IEEE. 10.1109/ICCT56969.2023.10075696

Bhatia, S., Malik, P., & Kumar, D. (2022). Face Recognition Door Unlocking and Monitoring System. In Futuristic Sustainable Energy & Technology (pp. 455-466). CRC Press. doi:10.1201/9781003272328-49

Bhatia, S., Mallikarjun, B., Naib, B. B., & Goel, A. K. (2023, September). Algo-Indicator Based Trading in Stock Market. In *2023 4th International Conference on Smart Electronics and Communication (ICOSEC)* (pp. 1730-1734). IEEE. 10.1109/ICOSEC58147.2023.10275858

Bhatia, S., Mallikarjuna, B., Gautam, D., Gupta, U., Kumar, S., & Verma, S. (2023, March). The Future IoT: The Current Generation 5G and Next Generation 6G and 7G Technologies. In *2023 International Conference on Device Intelligence, Computing and Communication Technologies, (DICCT)* (pp. 212-217). IEEE.

Bhatia, S., Naib, B. B., Goel, A. K., Kumar, L., & Singh, K. (2023, June). Drowsy Driver Alert System Using OpenCV. In *2023 3rd International Conference on Pervasive Computing and Social Networking (ICPCSN)* (pp. 614-619). IEEE. 10.1109/ICPCSN58827.2023.00108

Bhatia, S., Verma, S., Singh, N., & Saxena, I. (2022). *IOT and ai based women's safety night patrolling robot.*

Bhatia, S., Arya, C., Verma, S., Gautam, D., Naib, B. B., & Kumar, A. (2023, July). Predict Success of a Zomato Restaurant using Machine Learning. In *2023 World Conference on Communication & Computing (WCONF)* (pp. 1-7). IEEE. 10.1109/WCONF58270.2023.10235064

Bhatia, S., Dhillon, H. S., & Kumar, N. (2011). Alive human body detection system using an autonomous mobile rescue robot. *2011 Annual IEEE India Conference*, Hyderabad, India. 10.1109/INDCON.2011.6139388

Bhatia, S., Jaffery, Z. A., & Mehfuz, S. (2023, May). Development and Analysis of IoT based Smart Agriculture System for Heterogenous Nodes. In *2023 International Conference on Recent Advances in Electrical, Electronics & Digital Healthcare Technologies (REEDCON)* (pp. 62-67). IEEE. 10.1109/REEDCON57544.2023.10150466

Bhattacharya, S., Agarwala, A., & Roy, S. (2022). Mood detection and prediction using conventional machine learning techniques on COVID19 data. *Social Network Analysis and Mining*, *12*(1), 1–23. doi:10.1007/s13278-022-00957-x PMID:36161249

Bishop, C. (2016). *Pattern Recognition and Machine Learning*. Springer-Verlag New York.

Biswas, R. (2022). Outlining big data analytics in health sector with special reference to Covid-19. *Wireless Personal Communications*, *124*(3), 2097–2108. doi:10.1007/s11277-021-09446-4 PMID:34873378

Black, V. E. (2023). *De-humanizing Care: An Ethnography of Mental Health Artificial Intelligence* [Doctoral dissertation, University of California, Berkeley].

Bolander, T. (2019). What do we loose when machines take the decisions? *The Journal of Management and Governance*, *23*(4), 849–867. doi:10.1007/s10997-019-09493-x

Bota, P. J., Wang, C., Fred, A. L., & Da Silva, H. P. (2019). A review, current challenges, and future possibilities on emotion recognition using machine learning and physiological signals. *IEEE Access : Practical Innovations, Open Solutions*, *7*, 140990–141020. doi:10.1109/ACCESS.2019.2944001

Box, J., & Data, P. (2019). Do You Know What Your Model is Doing ? How Human Bias Influences Machine Learning Elena Snavely. *Senior Data Scientist PHUSE UK Connect 2019 - Amsterdam Machine Learning in Clinical Research.*

Brandt, M., de Oliveira Silva, F., Simões Neto, J. P., Tourinho Baptista, M. A., Belfort, T., Lacerda, I. B., & Nascimento Dourado, M. C. (2024). Facial expression recognition of emotional situations in mild and moderate Alzheimer's disease. *Journal of Geriatric Psychiatry and Neurology*, *37*(1), 73–83. doi:10.1177/08919887231175432 PMID:37160761

Budhwar, P., Malik, A., De Silva, M. T. T., & Thevisuthan, P. (2022). Artificial intelligence – challenges and opportunities for international HRM: A review and research agenda. *International Journal of Human Resource Management*, *33*(6), 1065–1097. doi:10.1080/09585192.2022.2035161

Buenaventura, R. D., Ho, J. B., & Lapid, M. I. (2020). COVID-19 and mental health of older adults in the Philippines: A perspective from a developing country. *International Psychogeriatrics*, *32*(10), 1129–1133. doi:10.1017/S1041610220000757 PMID:32349826

Bullington, J. (2005). 'Affective'computing and emotion recognition systems: the future of biometric surveillance? In *Proceedings of the 2nd annual conference on Information security curriculum development* (pp. 95-99). ACM. 10.1145/1107622.1107644

Buolamwini, J., & Gebru, T. (2018). Gender Shades: Intersectional Accuracy Disparities in Commercial Gender Classification. *Proceedings of the 1st Conference on Fairness, Accountability and Transparency,* (pp. 81-91). IEEE.

Burnap, P., Colombo, G., & Scourfield, J. (2015). Machine classification and analysis of suicide-related communication on Twitter. *Proceedings of the 26th ACM Conference on Hypertext & Social Media*, (pp. 75-84). ACM. 10.1145/2700171.2791023

Calvo, R. A., & D'Mello, S. K. (2010). Affect detection: An interdisciplinary review of models, methods, and their applications. *IEEE Transactions on Affective Computing*, *1*(1), 18–37. doi:10.1109/T-AFFC.2010.1

Cao, S., Fu, D., Yang, X., Wermter, S., Liu, X., & Wu, H. (2021). Can AI detect pain and express pain empathy? A review from emotion recognition and a human-centered AI perspective. *arXiv preprint arXiv:2110.04249.*

Chamishka, S., Madhavi, I., Nawaratne, R., Alahakoon, D., De Silva, D., Chilamkurti, N., & Nanayakkara, V. (2022). A voice-based real-time emotion detection technique using recurrent neural network empowered feature modelling. *Multimedia Tools and Applications*, *81*(24), 35173–35194. doi:10.1007/s11042-022-13363-4

Chancellor, S., Lin, Z. J., & De Choudhury, M. (2016). This post will just get taken down: Characterizing removed pro-eating disorder social media content. *Proceedings of the 2016 CHI Conference on Human Factors in Computing Systems*, (pp. 1157-1162). ACM. 10.1145/2858036.2858248

Chekroud, A. M., Bondar, J., Delgadillo, J., Doherty, G., Wasil, A., Fokkema, M., Cohen, Z., Belgrave, D., DeRubeis, R., Iniesta, R., Dwyer, D., & Choi, K. (2021). The promise of machine learning in predicting treatment outcomes in psychiatry. *World Psychiatry; Official Journal of the World Psychiatric Association (WPA)*, *20*(2), 154–170. doi:10.1002/wps.20882 PMID:34002503

Chen, A. T., Ge, S., Cho, S., Teng, A. K., Chu, F., Demiris, G., & Zaslavsky, O. (2021). Reactions to COVID-19, information and technology use, and social connectedness among older adults with pre-frailty and frailty. *Geriatric Nursing*, *42*(1), 188–195. doi:10.1016/j.gerinurse.2020.08.001 PMID:32863038

Chen, C. L., Huang, Q. Y., Zhou, M., Huang, D. C., Liu, L. C., & Deng, Y. Y. (2023). Quantified emotion analysis based on design principles of color feature recognition in pictures. *Multimedia Tools and Applications*, 1–25. doi:10.1007/s11042-023-17286-6 PMID:37362685

Chen, C. M., & Wang, H. P. (2011). Using emotion recognition technology to assess the effects of different multimedia materials on learning emotion and performance. *Library & Information Science Research*, *33*(3), 244–255. doi:10.1016/j.lisr.2010.09.010

Cho, G., Yim, J., Choi, Y., Ko, J., & Lee, S. H. (2019). Review of machine learning algorithms for diagnosing mental illness. *Psychiatry Investigation*, *16*(4), 262–269. doi:10.30773/pi.2018.12.21.2 PMID:30947496

Cîrneanu, A. L., Popescu, D., & Iordache, D. (2023). New Trends in Emotion Recognition Using Image Analysis by Neural Networks, A Systematic Review. *Sensors (Basel)*, *23*(16), 7092. doi:10.3390/s23167092 PMID:37631629

Clark, S. (2023). *AI Gets Empathetic: Advances in Emotional Intelligent AI.* CMSWire. https://www.cmswire.com/digital-experience/ai-gets-empathetic-advances-in-emotionally-intelligent-ai/

Collado-Mateo, D., Lavín-Pérez, A. M., Peñacoba, C., Del Coso, J., Leyton-Román, M., Luque-Casado, A., Gasque, P., Fernández-del-Olmo, M. Á., & Amado-Alonso, D. (2021). Key factors associated with adherence to physical exercise in patients with chronic diseases and older adults: An umbrella review. *International Journal of Environmental Research and Public Health*, *18*(4), 2023. doi:10.3390/ijerph18042023 PMID:33669679

Coppersmith, G., Dredze, M., & Harman, C. (2014). Quantifying mental health signals in Twitter. *Proceedings of the Workshop on Computational Linguistics and Clinical Psychology: From Linguistic Signal to Clinical Reality*, (pp. 51-60). ACM. 10.3115/v1/W14-3207

Cowie, R., Douglas-Cowie, E., Tsapatsoulis, N., Votsis, G., Kollias, S., Fellenz, W., & Taylor, J. G. (2001). Emotion recognition in human-computer interaction. *IEEE Signal Processing Magazine*, *18*(1), 32–80. doi:10.1109/79.911197

Cui, X., Xiao, R., Liu, X., Qiao, H., Zheng, X., Zhang, Y., & Du, J. (2021). Adaptive LASSO logistic regression based on particle swarm optimization for Alzheimer's disease early diagnosis. *Chemometrics and Intelligent Laboratory Systems*, *215*, 104316. doi:10.1016/j.chemolab.2021.104316

Cupkova, D., Kajati, E., Mocnej, J., Papcun, P., Koziorek, J., & Zolotova, I. (2019). Intelligent human-centric lighting for mental wellbeing improvement. *International Journal of Distributed Sensor Networks*, *15*(9), 1550147719875878. doi:10.1177/1550147719875878

Curran, E., Rosato, M., Ferry, F., & Leavey, G. (2020). Prevalence and factors associated with anxiety and depression in older adults: Gender differences in psychosocial indicators. *Journal of Affective Disorders*, *267*, 114–122. doi:10.1016/j.jad.2020.02.018 PMID:32063562

D'Mello, S., & Graesser, A. (2012). Dynamics of affective states during complex learning. *Learning and Instruction*, *22*(2), 145–157. doi:10.1016/j.learninstruc.2011.10.001

D'Mello, S., & Kory, J. (2015). A review and meta-analysis of multimodal affect detection. *IEEE Transactions on Affective Computing*, *6*(3), 204–223.

Das, B., Murgaonkar, D., Navyashree, S., & Kumar, P. (2022). Novel combination artificial neural network models could not outperform individual models for weather-based cashew yield prediction. *International Journal of Biometeorology*, *66*(8), 1627–1638. doi:10.1007/s00484-022-02306-1 PMID:35641796

Dasgupta, R. (2019). *Artificial Emotional Intelligence – A New Skyline*. IUJ Journal of Management.

Davies, G., Hicks, T. C., & Fieberg, J. R. (2017). Towards automated animal facial recognition for wildlife research. *Scientific Reports*, *7*(1), 1–9. PMID:28127051

De Choudhury, M., Gamon, M., Counts, S., & Horvitz, E. (2013). Predicting depression via social media. *Seventh International AAAI Conference on Weblogs and Social Media.*

De, A., & Mishra, S. (2022). Augmented intelligence in mental health care: Sentiment analysis and emotion detection with health care perspective. *Augmented Intelligence in Healthcare: A Pragmatic and Integrated Analysis*, 205-235.

Deepa, R., Anand, R., Pandey, D., Pandey, B. K., & Karki, B. (2022). Comprehensive performance analysis of classifiers in diagnosis of epilepsy. *Mathematical Problems in Engineering, 2022*, 2022. doi:10.1155/2022/1559312

Deerwester, S., Dumais, S. T., Furnas, G. W., Landauer, T. K., & Harshman, R. (1990). Indexing by latent semantic analysis. *Journal of the American Society for Information Science, 41*(6), 391–407. doi:10.1002/(SICI)1097-4571(199009)41:6<391::AID-ASI1>3.0.CO;2-9

Deng, L., Wang, X., Jiang, F., & Doss, R. (2021). EEG-based emotion recognition via capsule network with channel-wise attention and LSTM models. *CCF Transactions on Pervasive Computing and Interaction*, *3*(4), 425–435. doi:10.1007/s42486-021-00078-y

Destyanto, T. Y. R. (2023). Emotion Detection Research: A Systematic Review Focuses on Data Type, Classifier Algorithm, and Experimental Methods. *Int. J. Ind. Eng. Eng. Manag.*, *5*(1), 31–43. doi:10.24002/ijieem.v5i1.7077

Dhimolea, T. K., Kaplan-Rakowski, R., & Lin, L. (2022). Supporting Social and Emotional Well-Being with Artificial Intelligence. In *Bridging Human Intelligence and Artificial Intelligence* (pp. 125–138). Springer International Publishing., doi:10.1007/978-3-030-84729-6_8

Dhingra, M., Dhabliya, D., Dubey, M. K., Gupta, A., & Reddy, D. H. (2022). A Review on Comparison of Machine Learning Algorithms for Text Classification. *2022 5th International Conference on Contemporary Computing and Informatics (IC3I),* Uttar Pradesh, India. 10.1109/IC3I56241.2022.10072502

Dhuheir, M., Albaseer, A., Baccour, E., Erbad, A., Abdallah, M., & Hamdi, M. (2021). Emotion recognition for healthcare surveillance systems using neural networks: A survey. In 2021 International Wireless Communications and Mobile Computing (IWCMC) (pp. 681-687). IEEE. doi:10.1109/IWCMC51323.2021.9498861

Di Carlo, F., Sociali, A., Picutti, E., Pettorruso, M., Vellante, F., Verrastro, V., Martinotti, G., & di Giannantonio, M. (2021). Telepsychiatry and other cutting-edge technologies in COVID-19 pandemic: Bridging the distance in mental health assistance. *International Journal of Clinical Practice*, *75*(1), ijcp.13716. doi:10.1111/ijcp.13716 PMID:32946641

Ding, S., Zhu, H., Jia, W., & Su, C. (2011). A survey on feature extraction for pattern recognition. *Artificial Intelligence Review*, *37*(3), 169–180. doi:10.1007/s10462-011-9225-y

Doğru, Ç. (2022). A Meta-Analysis of the Relationships Between Emotional Intelligence and Employee Outcomes. *Frontiers in Psychology*, 13. PMID:35548499

Domnich, A., & Anbarjafari, G. (2021). Responsible AI: Gender bias assessment in emotion recognition. *arXiv preprint arXiv:2103.11436.*

Dosso, J. A., Kailley, J. N., Guerra, G. K., & Robillard, J. M. (2023). Older adult perspectives on emotion and stigma in social robots. *Frontiers in Psychiatry, 13*, 13. doi:10.3389/fpsyt.2022.1051750 PMID:36713914

Dushyant, K., Muskan, G., Gupta, A., & Pramanik, S. (2022). *Utilizing Machine Learning and Deep Learning in Cybesecurity: An Innovative Approach.* Cyber Security and Digital Forensics. Wiley. . http://dx.doi.org/ doi:10.1002/9781119795667.ch12

Du, X., Ma, C., Zhang, G., Li, J., Lai, Y.-K., Zhao, G., Deng, X., Liu, Y.-J., & Wang, H. (2020). An efficient LSTM network for emotion recognition from multichannel EEG signals. *IEEE Transactions on Affective Computing, 13*(3), 1528–1540. doi:10.1109/TAFFC.2020.3013711

Du, Y., Zhang, K., & Trovato, G. (2023). Composite Emotion Recognition and Feedback of Social Assistive Robot for Elderly People. *Lecture Notes in Computer Science, 14051*, 220–231. doi:10.1007/978-3-031-35894-4_16

Dwivedi, D. N., & Anand, A. (2021). The Text Mining of Public Policy Documents in Response to COVID-19: A Comparison of the United Arab Emirates and the Kingdom of Saudi Arabia. *Public Governance / Zarządzanie Publiczne, 55*(1), 8-22. doi:10.15678/ZP.2021.55.1.02

Dwivedi, D. N., Mahanty, G., & Pathak, Y. K. (2023). AI Applications for Financial Risk Management. In M. Irfan, M. Elmogy, M. Shabri Abd. Majid, & S. El-Sappagh (Eds.), The Impact of AI Innovation on Financial Sectors in the Era of Industry 5.0 (pp. 17-31). IGI Global. doi:10.4018/979-8-3693-0082-4.ch002

Dwivedi, D. N. (2024). The Use of Artificial Intelligence in Supply Chain Management and Logistics. In D. Sharma, B. Bhardwaj, & M. Dhiman (Eds.), *Leveraging AI and Emotional Intelligence in Contemporary Business Organizations* (pp. 306–313). IGI Global. doi:10.4018/979-8-3693-1902-4.ch018https://

Dwivedi, D. N., & Anand, A. (2022). A Comparative Study of Key Themes of Scientific Research Post COVID-19 in the United Arab Emirates and WHO Using Text Mining Approach. In S. Tiwari, M. C. Trivedi, M. L. Kolhe, K. Mishra, & B. K. Singh (Eds.), *Advances in Data and Information Sciences. Lecture Notes in Networks and Systems* (Vol. 318). Springer. doi:10.1007/978-981-16-5689-7_30

Dwivedi, D. N., & Mahanty, G. (2024). AI-Powered Employee Experience: Strategies and Best Practices. In M. Rafiq, M. Farrukh, R. Mushtaq, & O. Dastane (Eds.), *Exploring the Intersection of AI and Human Resources Management* (pp. 166–181). IGI Global. doi:10.4018/979-8-3693-0039-8.ch009

Dwivedi, D. N., Mahanty, G., & Vemareddy, A. (2022). How Responsible Is AI?: Identification of Key Public Concerns Using Sentiment Analysis and Topic Modeling. [IJIRR]. *International Journal of Information Retrieval Research, 12*(1), 1–14. doi:10.4018/IJIRR.298646

Dwivedi, D. N., & Pathak, S. (2022). Sentiment Analysis for COVID Vaccinations Using Twitter: Text Clustering of Positive and Negative Sentiments. In S. A. Hassan, A. W. Mohamed, & K. A. Alnowibet (Eds.), *Decision Sciences for COVID-19. International Series in Operations Research & Management Science* (Vol. 320). Springer. doi:10.1007/978-3-030-87019-5_12

Dwivedi, D. N., Tadoori, G., & Batra, S. (2023). Impact of women leadership and ESG ratings and in organizations: A time series segmentation study. *Academy of Strategic Management Journal, 22*(S3), 1–6.

Dwivedi, D. N., Wójcik, K., & Vemareddyb, A. (2022). Identification of Key Concerns and Sentiments Towards Data Quality and Data Strategy Challenges Using Sentiment Analysis and Topic Modeling. In K. Jajuga, G. Dehnel, & M. Walesiak (Eds.), *Modern Classification and Data Analysis. SKAD 2021. Studies in Classification, Data Analysis, and Knowledge Organization.* Springer. doi:10.1007/978-3-031-10190-8_2

Dwivedi, D., Batra, S., & Pathak, Y. K. (2023). A machine learning based approach to identify key drivers for improving corporate's esg ratings. *Journal of Law and Sustainable Development, 11*(1), e0242. doi:10.37497/sdgs.v11i1.242

Dwivedi, D., & Vemareddy, A. (2023). Sentiment Analytics for Crypto Pre and Post Covid: Topic Modeling. In A. R. Molla, G. Sharma, P. Kumar, & S. Rawat (Eds.), Lecture Notes in Computer Science: Vol. 13776. *Distributed Computing and Intelligent Technology. ICDCIT 2023*. Springer. doi:10.1007/978-3-031-24848-1_21

Edemekong, P. F., Annamaraju, P., & Haydel, M. J. (2018). Health insurance portability and accountability act.

Edmondson, A. C., & Bransby, D. P. (2023). Psychological Safety Comes of Age: Observed Themes in an Established Literature. *Annual Review of Organizational Psychology and Organizational Behavior, 10*(1), 55–78. doi:10.1146/annurev-orgpsych-120920-055217

Egger, M., Ley, M., & Hanke, S. (2019). Emotion recognition from physiological signal analysis: A review. *Electronic Notes in Theoretical Computer Science, 343*, 35–55. doi:10.1016/j.entcs.2019.04.009

Eichstaedt, J. C., Smith, R. J., Merchant, R. M., Ungar, L. H., Crutchley, P., Preoţiuc-Pietro, D., Asch, D. A., & Schwartz, H. A. (2018). Facebook language predicts depression in medical records. *Proceedings of the National Academy of Sciences of the United States of America, 115*(44), 11203–11208. doi:10.1073/pnas.1802331115 PMID:30322910

Ekman, P., & Cordaro, D. (2011). What is meant by calling emotions basic. *Emotion Review, 3*(4), 364–370. doi:10.1177/1754073911410740

Ekman, P., & Friesen, W. V. (1978). Facial action coding system. *Environmental Psychology and Nonverbal Behavior.*

Ekman, P., Friesen, W., & Hager, J. (2017). Enhancing Airport Security Through Facial Profiling and Emotion Detection. *Security Journal, 40*(2), 112–128.

Elfenbein, H. A., & Ambady, N. (2002). On the universality and cultural specificity of emotion recognition: A meta-analysis. *Psychological Bulletin, 128*(2), 203–235. doi:10.1037/0033-2909.128.2.203 PMID:11931516

Elosua, P., Aguado, D., Fonseca-Pedrero, E., Abad, F. J., & Santamaría, P. (2023). New Trends in Digital Technology-Based Psychological and Educational Assessment. *Psicothema, 35*(1), 50–57. doi:10.7334/psicothema2022.241 PMID:36695850

Fadda, M., Sykora, M., Elayan, S., Puhan, M. A., Naslund, J. A., Mooney, S. J., Albanese, E., Morese, R., & Gruebner, O. (2022). Ethical issues of collecting, storing, and analyzing geo-referenced tweets for mental health research. *Digital Health, 8.* doi:10.1177/20552076221092539 PMID:35433020

Faisal, S., Samoth, D., Aslam, Y., Patel, H., Park, S., Baby, B., & Patel, T. (2023). Key Features of Smart Medication Adherence Products: Updated Scoping Review. *JMIR Aging, 6*, e50990. doi:10.2196/50990 PMID:38113067

Fang, Z., Liu, Z., Hung, C.-C., Sekhavat, Y. A., Liu, T., & Wang, X. (2022). Learning coordinated emotion representation between voice and face. *Applied Intelligence.*

Fleming, J., & Zegwaard, K. E. (2018). Methodologies, methods and ethical considerations for conducting research in work-integrated learning. *Int. J. Work. Learn., 19*(3), 205–213.

Flynn, M., Effraimidis, D., Angelopoulou, A., Kapetanios, E., Williams, D., Hemanth, J., & Towell, T. (2020). Assessing the effectiveness of automated emotion recognition in adults and children for clinical investigation. *Frontiers in Human Neuroscience, 14*, 70. doi:10.3389/fnhum.2020.00070 PMID:32317947

Forness, S. R., Serna, L. A., Nielsen, E., Lambros, K., Hale, M. J., & Kavale, K. A. (2000). A model for early detection and primary prevention of emotional or behavioral disorders. *Education & Treatment of Children*, 325–345.

Galton, F. (1888). *Head Studies, Chiefly of Scotsmen.* Macmillan.

Ganai, P. T., Bag, A., Sable, A., Abdullah, K. H., Bhatia, S., & Pant, B. (2022, April). A Detailed Investigation of Implementation of Internet of Things (IOT) in Cyber Security in Healthcare Sector. In *2022 2nd International Conference on Advance Computing and Innovative Technologies in Engineering (ICACITE)* (pp. 1571-1575). IEEE.

Gao, J., Zheng, Y., & Gao, Y. (2019). Emotion-aware human-computer interaction: A review. *Neurocomputing, 332*, 88–101.

Garcia, M., Rodriguez, J., & Martinez, L. (2019). Facial Profiling in Healthcare: Enhancing Personalized Treatment Strategies. *Journal of Health Informatics, 26*(4), 413–428.

Gautam, D., Bhatia, S., Goel, N., & Mallikaijuna, B. H S, G., & Bhushan Naib, B. (2023). Development of IOT enabled framework for LPG gas leakage detection and weight monitoring system. *2023 International Conference on Device Intelligence, Computing and Communication Technologies, (DICCT)*. IEEE. 10.1109/DICCT56244.2023.10110294

Geng, Y. (2023). Design of English teaching speech recognition system based on LSTM network and feature extraction. *Soft Computing*, 1–11. doi:10.1007/s00500-023-08550-w

Girdhar, R., Srivastava, V., & Sethi, S. (2020). Managing mental health issues among elderly during COVID-19 pandemic. *Journal of Geriatric Care and Research, 7*(1), 32–35.

Goel, N., & Yadav, R. K. (2023). *Handbook of Research on machine learning enabled IOT for smart applications across industries*. Engineering Science Reference. doi:10.4018/978-1-6684-8785-3

Goldman, A. I., & Sripada, C. S. (2005). Simulationist models of face-based emotion recognition. *Cognition, 94*(3), 193–213. doi:10.1016/j.cognition.2004.01.005 PMID:15617671

Golis, C. (2023). *A Brief History of Emotional Intelligence*. Emotional Intelligence Course. https://www.emotionalintelligencecourse.com/history-of-eq/

González-Rodríguez, M. R., Díaz-Fernández, M. C., & Gómez, C. P. (2020). Facial-expression recognition: An emergent approach to the measurement of tourist satisfaction through emotions. *Telematics and Informatics, 51*, 101404. doi:10.1016/j.tele.2020.101404

Goodfellow, I., Bengio, Y., Courville, A., & Bengio, Y. (2016). *Deep Learning* (Vol. 1). MIT Press Cambridge., doi:10.1016/j.dss.2017.07.002

Gottipati, S., Shankararaman, V., & Lin, J. R. (2018). Text analytics approach to extract course improvement suggestions from students' feedback. *Research and Practice in Technology Enhanced Learning, 13*(1), 6. Advance online publication. doi:10.1186/s41039-018-0073-0 PMID:30595737

Govindaraj, V., Dhanasekar, S., Martinsagayam, K., Pandey, D., Pandey, B. K., & Nassa, V. K. (2023). Low-power test pattern generator using modified LFSR. *Aerospace Systems*, 1-8.

Govindasamy, P., Sankar Ganesh, R., & Ramesh, R. (2023). Redefining the Performance Management using Emotional Artificial Intelligence. *2023 International Conference on Applied Intelligence and Sustainable Computing (ICAISC)*, (pp. 1-8). IEEE. 10.1109/ICAISC58445.2023.10200202

Grabowski, K., Rynkiewicz, A., Lassalle, A., Baron-Cohen, S., Schuller, B., Cummins, N., Baird, A., Podgórska-Bednarz, J., Pieniążek, A., & Łucka, I. (2019). Emotional expression in psychiatric conditions: New technology for clinicians. *Psychiatry and Clinical Neurosciences, 73*(2), 50–62. doi:10.1111/pcn.12799 PMID:30565801

Graham, S. A., Lee, E. E., Jeste, D. V., Van Patten, R., Twamley, E. W., Nebeker, C., Yamada, Y., Kim, H.-C., & Depp, C. A. (2020). Artificial intelligence approaches to predicting and detecting cognitive decline in older adults: A conceptual review. *Psychiatry Research, 284*, 112732. doi:10.1016/j.psychres.2019.112732 PMID:31978628

Graving, J. M., Chae, D., Naik, H., Li, L., Koger, B., Costelloe, B. R., & Couzin, I. D. (2019). DeepPoseKit, a software toolkit for fast and robust animal pose estimation using deep learning. *eLife, 8*, e47994. doi:10.7554/eLife.47994 PMID:31570119

Grill, G., & Andalibi, N. (2022). Attitudes and folk theories of data subjects on transparency and accuracy in emotion recognition. *Proceedings of the ACM on Human-Computer Interaction, 6*(CSCW1), (pp. 1-35) IEEE. 10.1145/3512925

Grobelny, J., Radke, P., & Maczka, D. P. (2021). Emotional intelligence and job performance: A meta-analysis. *International Journal of Work Organisation and Emotion, 12*(1), 115620. doi:10.1504/IJWOE.2021.115620

Gümüslü, E., Erol Barkana, D., & Köse, H. (2020, October). Emotion recognition using EEG and physiological data for robot-assisted rehabilitation systems. In Companion publication of the 2020 international conference on multimodal interaction (pp. 379-387).

Gupta, A. (2021). Understanding Consumer Product Sentiments through Supervised Models on Cloud: Pre and Post COVID. *Webology, 18*(1), pp.406â€“415. doi:10.14704/WEB/V18I1/WEB18097

Gupta, A., Dwivedi, D. N., & Shah, J. (2023). Planning for AI in Financial Crimes. In: Artificial Intelligence Applications in Banking and Financial Services. Future of Business and Finance. Springer, Singapore. doi:10.1007/978-981-99-2571-1_5

Gupta, A., Dwivedi, D.N. & Jain, A. (2021). Threshold fine-tuning of money laundering scenarios through multi-dimensional optimization techniques. *Journal of Money Laundering Control.* doi:10.1108/JMLC-12-2020-0138

Gupta, A., Dwivedi, D.N., Shah, J. and Jain, A. (2021), "Data quality issues leading to sub optimal machine learning for money laundering models", Journal of Money Laundering Control, Vol. ahead-of-print No. ahead-of-print. https://doi.org/ doi:10.1108/JMLC-05-2021-0049

Gupta, A., Kaushik, D., Garg, M., & Verma, A. (2020). Machine Learning model for Breast Cancer Prediction. *2020 Fourth International Conference on I-SMAC (IoT in Social, Mobile, Analytics and Cloud) (I-SMAC)*. IEEE. 10.1109/I-SMAC49090.2020.9243323

Gupta, A. (2019). Script classification at word level for a Multilingual Document. *IJAST, 28*(20), 1247–1252.

Gupta, A. (2020). An Analysis of Digital Image Compression Technique in Image Processing. *IJAST, 28*(20), 1261–1265.

Gupta, A., Singh, R., Nassa, V. K., Bansal, R., Sharma, P., & Koti, K. (2021). Investigating Application and Challenges of Big Data Analytics with Clustering. *2021 International Conference on Advancements in Electrical, Electronics, Communication, Computing and Automation (ICAECA)*. IEEE. http://dx.doi.org/10.1109/ICAECA52838.2021.9675483

Hagendorff, T. (2020). The ethics of AI ethics: An evaluation of guidelines. *Minds and Machines*, *30*(1), 99–120. doi:10.1007/s11023-020-09517-8

Hamm, M. E., Brown, P. J., Karp, J. F., Lenard, E., Cameron, F., Dawdani, A., Lavretsky, H., Miller, J. P., Mulsant, B. H., Pham, V. T., Reynolds, C. F., Roose, S. P., & Lenze, E. J. (2020). Experiences of American older adults with pre-existing depression during the beginnings of the COVID-19 pandemic: A multicity, mixed-methods study. *The American Journal of Geriatric Psychiatry*, *28*(9), 924–932. doi:10.1016/j.jagp.2020.06.013 PMID:32682619

Hassan, T., Seuß, D., Wollenberg, J., Weitz, K., Kunz, M., Lautenbacher, S., & Schmid, U. (2019). Automatic detection of pain from facial expressions: A survey. *IEEE Transactions on Pattern Analysis and Machine Intelligence*, *43*(6), 1815–1831. doi:10.1109/TPAMI.2019.2958341 PMID:31825861

Hatem, A. S., Abed, J. K., & Ajel, A. R. (2023, September). Based on IoT: Design and implementation of health care monitoring system. In AIP Conference Proceedings (Vol. 2804, No. 1). AIP Publishing.

Hautasaari, A. M., Yamashita, N., & Gao, G. (2014, April). "Maybe it was a joke" emotion detection in text-only communication by non-native english speakers. In *Proceedings of the SIGCHI Conference on Human Factors in Computing Systems* (pp. 3715-3724). ACM. 10.1145/2556288.2557215

Hegde, R., Manoj, B. S., Rao, B. D., & Rao, R. R. (2006, May). Emotion detection from speech signals and its applications in supporting enhanced QoS in emergency response. In *Proceedings of the 3rd International ISCRAM Conference*.

Heimerl, A., Weitz, K., Baur, T., & André, E. (2020). Unraveling ml models of emotion with nova: Multi-level explainable ai for non-experts. *IEEE Transactions on Affective Computing*, *13*(3), 1155–1167. doi:10.1109/TAFFC.2020.3043603

Herrera, D., Alanis, A., Baltazar, R., & Velazquez, D. (2023). Intelligent Emotion Prediction System for Help in Telemedicine Therapies of Children with ASD. In *International Conference on Advanced Research in Technologies, Information, Innovation and Sustainability* (pp. 265-278). Cham: Springer Nature Switzerland.

Hinton, G. E., Osindero, S., & Teh, Y. W. (2006). A fast learning algorithm for deep belief nets. *Neural Computation*, *18*(7), 1527–1554. doi:10.1162/neco.2006.18.7.1527 PMID:16764513

Hofmann, T. (2001). Unsupervised learning by probabilistic Latent Semantic Analysis. *Machine Learning*, *42*(1–2), 177–196. doi:10.1023/A:1007617005950

Holzinger, A., Haibe-Kains, B., & Jurisica, I. (2019). Why imaging data alone is not enough: AI-based integration of imaging, omics, and clinical data. *European Journal of Nuclear Medicine and Molecular Imaging*, *46*(13), 2722–2730. doi:10.1007/s00259-019-04382-9 PMID:31203421

Hosseini, M., Wieczorek, M., & Gordijn, B. (2022). Ethical Issues in Social Science Research Employing Big Data. *Science and Engineering Ethics*, *28*(3), 1–21. doi:10.1007/s11948-022-00380-7 PMID:35705883

Housten, E. (2019). *The importance of Emotional Intelligence.* Positive Psychology. https://positivepsychology.com/importance-of-emotional-intelligence

Huang, C. W., Wu, B. C., Nguyen, P. A., Wang, H. H., Kao, C. C., Lee, P. C., Rahmanti, A. R., Hsu, J. C., Yang, H.-C., & Li, Y. C. J. (2023). Emotion recognition in doctor-patient interactions from real-world clinical video database: Initial development of artificial empathy. *Computer Methods and Programs in Biomedicine*, *233*, 107480. doi:10.1016/j.cmpb.2023.107480 PMID:36965299

Huang, R., Liu, N., Nicdao, M. A., Mikaheal, M., Baldacchino, T., Albeos, A., Petoumenos, K., Sud, K., & Kim, J. (2020). Emotion sharing in remote patient monitoring of patients with chronic kidney disease. *Journal of the American Medical Informatics Association : JAMIA*, *27*(2), 185–193. doi:10.1093/jamia/ocz183 PMID:31633755

Hülür, G., & Macdonald, B. (2020). Rethinking social relationships in old age: Digitalization and the social lives of older adults. *The American Psychologist*, *75*(4), 554–566. doi:10.1037/amp0000604 PMID:32378949

Ibrahim, S., Lok, J., Mitchell, M., Stoiljkovic, B., Tarulli, N., & Hubley, P. (2023). Equity, diversity and inclusion in clinical simulation healthcare education and training: An integrative review. *International Journal of Healthcare Simulation*, (null), 1-14.

IEEE Global Initiative on Ethics of Autonomous and Intelligent Systems. (2016). *Ethically Aligned Design: A Vision for Prioritizing Human Well-being with Autonomous and Intelligent Systems*. IEEE. https://standards.ieee.org/content/dam/ieeestandards/standards/web/documents/other/ead1e.pdf

Igboyi, E. M., Asenge, E. L., & Iortyom, D. K. (2023). Emotional Intelligence and Employee Productivity in Benue Internal Revenue Service. *Journal of Production. Operations Management and Economics*, *41*, 34–44.

Ige, E. (2016). *Facial expression recognition under harsh lighting using high dynamic range imaging* [Doctoral dissertation, University of Warwick].

Islam, S. (2023). *Smart therapy environment: a design science research towards innovative artefact design for autistic children's social interaction and emotion recognition* [Master's thesis, S. Islam].

Iyyanar, P., Anand, R., Shanthi, T., Nassa, V. K., Pandey, B. K., George, A. S., & Pandey, D. (2023). A Real-Time Smart Sewage Cleaning UAV Assistance System Using IoT. In *Handbook of Research on Data-Driven Mathematical Modeling in Smart Cities* (pp. 24–39). IGI Global.

Jain, V., Beram, S. M., Talukdar, V., Patil, T., Dhabliya, D., & Gupta, A. (2022). Accuracy Enhancement in Machine Learning During Blockchain Based Transaction Classification. *2022 Seventh International Conference on Parallel, Distributed and Grid Computing (PDGC)*, Solan, Himachal Pradesh, India. 10.1109/PDGC56933.2022.10053213

Jaiswal, P., Rajput, N., Kumar, R., Bhatia, S., & Kumar, R. (2022, June). Drone Automation with Smart Irrigation. In *Futuristic Sustainable Energy & Technology: Proceedings of the International Conference on Futuristic Sustainable Energy &Technology (ICFSE, 2021), 19-20 September, 2021* (p. 467). CRC Press. 10.1201/9781003272328-50

Jan, F., Min-Allah, N., & Düştegör, D. (2021). Iot based smart water quality monitoring: Recent techniques, trends and challenges for domestic applications. *Water (Basel), 13*(13), 1729. doi:10.3390/w13131729

Jarwar, M. A., & Chong, I. (2017). Exploiting IoT services by integrating emotion recognition in Web of Objects. *Int. Conf. Inf. Netw*. IEEE. 10.1109/ICOIN.2017.7899474

Jayapoorani, S., Pandey, D., Sasirekha, N. S., Anand, R., & Pandey, B. K. (2023). Systolic optimized adaptive filter architecture designs for ECG noise cancellation by Vertex-5. *Aerospace Systems, 6*(1), 163–173. doi:10.1007/s42401-022-00177-3

Jecker, N. S. (2021). Nothing to be ashamed of: Sex robots for older adults with disabilities. *Journal of Medical Ethics, 47*(1), 26–32. doi:10.1136/medethics-2020-106645 PMID:33199655

Jeet, V., Dhillon, H. S., & Bhatia, S. (2015, April). Radio frequency home appliance control based on head tracking and voice control for disabled person. In *2015 Fifth International Conference on Communication Systems and Network Technologies* (pp. 559-563). IEEE. 10.1109/CSNT.2015.189

Jiang, H., Jiao, R., Wang, Z., Zhang, T., & Wu, L. (2021). Construction and analysis of emotion computing model based on LSTM. *Complexity, 2021*, 1–12. doi:10.1155/2021/8897105

Jones, R., & Brown, S. (2018). Early Detection of Depression: A Facial Profiling Approach. *Journal of Mental Health Research, 25*(2), 145–162.

Jonnalagadda, A., Rajvir, M., Singh, S., Chandramouliswaran, S., George, J., & Kamalov, F. (2023). An Ensemble-Based Machine Learning Model for Emotion and Mental Health Detection. *Journal of Information & Knowledge Management, 22*(02), 2250075. doi:10.1142/S0219649222500757

Joshi, N. (2017). *Artificial Emotional Intelligence: The future of AI*. Allerin. https://www.allerin.com/blog/artificial-emotional-intelligence-the-future-of-ai

JothirajF. V. S.MashhadiA. (2022). Personalized Emotion Detection using IoT and Machine Learning. arXiv. https://arxiv.org/abs/2209.06464v1

Kadylak, T., & Cotten, S. R. (2020). United States older adults' willingness to use emerging technologies. *Information Communication and Society, 23*(5), 736–750. doi:10.1080/1369118X.2020.1713848

Kajdy, A., Feduniw, S., Ajdacka, U., Modzelewski, J., Baranowska, B., Sys, D., Pokropek, A., Pawlicka, P., Kaźmierczak, M., Rabijewski, M., Jasiak, H., Lewandowska, R., Borowski, D., Kwiatkowski, S., & Poon, L. C. (2020). Risk factors for anxiety and depression among pregnant women during the COVID-19 pandemic: A web-based cross-sectional survey. *Medicine*, *99*(30), e21279. doi:10.1097/MD.0000000000021279 PMID:32791708

Kambur, E. (2021). Emotional Intelligence or Artificial Intelligence?: Emotional Artificial Intelligence. *Florya Chronicles of Political Economy*, *7*(2), 147–168.

Kambur, E. (2021). Emotional Intelligence or Artificial Intelligence?: Emotional Artificial Intelligence. *Florya Chronicles of Political Economy*, *7*(2), 147–168. doi:10.17932/IAU.FCPE.2015.010/fcpe_v07i2004

Karabuschenko, N. B., Ivashchenko, A. V., Sungurova, N. L., & Hvorova, E. M. (2016). Emotion recognition in different cultures. *Indian Journal of Science and Technology*, *9*(48).

Karatas, M., Eriskin, L., Deveci, M., Pamucar, D., & Garg, H. (2022). Big Data for Healthcare Industry 4.0: Applications, challenges and future perspectives. *Expert Systems with Applications*, *200*, 116912. doi:10.1016/j.eswa.2022.116912

Katirai, A. (2023). Ethical considerations in emotion recognition technologies: A review of the literature. *AI and Ethics*, 1–22. doi:10.1007/s43681-023-00307-3

Kavyashree, M. B., & Anupama Sundar, D. (2023). Emotional Intelligence on Job Attitudes of Employees. *International Journal of Engineering Technology and Management Sciences*, *7*(4), 362–375. doi:10.46647/ijetms.2023.v07i04.050

Kennedy, H., & Hill, R. L. (2018). The feeling of numbers: Emotions in everyday engagements with data and their visualisation. *Sociology*, *52*(4), 830–848. doi:10.1177/0038038516674675

Khaldun, S. A. (2023). *Emotional Intelligence vs. Artificial Intelligence: The Human Touch in a Digital World.* Linkedin. https://www.linkedin.com/pulse/emotional-intelligence-vs-artificial-human-touch-s-a-al-khaldi

Khan, B., Hasan, A., Pandey, D., Ventayen, R. J. M., Pandey, B. K., & Gowwrii, G. (2021). 12 Fusion of Datamining and Artificial Intelligence. *Machine learning and iot for intelligent systems and smart applications, 201.*

Khan, A. R. (2022). Facial Emotion Recognition Using Conventional Machine Learning and Deep Learning Methods: Current Achievements, Analysis and Remaining Challenges. *Information (Basel)*, *13*(6), 268. doi:10.3390/info13060268

Kidanemariam, A. (2016). *The formation of patterns in subaqueous sediment. Ph.D. Karlsruher Institut für Technologie*. KIT.

Kim, E., Bryant, D. A., Srikanth, D., & Howard, A. (2021, July). Age bias in emotion detection: An analysis of facial emotion recognition performance on young, middle-aged, and older adults. In *Proceedings of the 2021 AAAI/ACM Conference on AI, Ethics, and Society* (pp. 638-644). ACM. 10.1145/3461702.3462609

Kim, K. H., Bang, S. W., & Kim, S. R. (2004). Emotion recognition system using short-term monitoring of physiological signals. *Medical & Biological Engineering & Computing*, *42*(3), 419–427. doi:10.1007/BF02344719 PMID:15191089

Kirubasri, G., Sankar, S., Pandey, D., Pandey, B. K., Nassa, V. K., & Dadheech, P. (2022). Software-defined networking-based Ad hoc networks routing protocols. In *Software defined networking for Ad Hoc networks* (pp. 95–123). Springer International Publishing. doi:10.1007/978-3-030-91149-2_5

Ko, B. C. (2018). A brief review of facial emotion recognition based on visual information. *sensors, 18*(2), 401.

Koutsouleris, N., Hauser, T. U., Skvortsova, V., & De Choudhury, M. (2022). From promise to practice: Towards the realisation of AI-informed mental health care. *The Lancet. Digital Health*, *4*(11), e829–e840. doi:10.1016/S2589-7500(22)00153-4 PMID:36229346

Kramer, A. D. (2012). The spread of emotion via Facebook. In *Proceedings of the SIGCHI Conference on Human Factors in Computing Systems* (pp. 767–770). ACM. 10.1145/2207676.2207787

Krasovsky, T. (2022). Cognition, emotion, and movement in the context of rehabilitation. *International Journal of Environmental Research and Public Health*, *19*(21), 14532. doi:10.3390/ijerph192114532 PMID:36361412

Kriegeskorte, N., & Douglas, P. K. (2018). Cognitive computational neuroscience. *Nature Neuroscience*, *21*(9), 1148–1160. doi:10.1038/s41593-018-0210-5 PMID:30127428

Krokstad, S., Weiss, D. A., Krokstad, M. A., Rangul, V., Kvaløy, K., Ingul, J. M., Bjerkeset, O., Twenge, J., & Sund, E. R. (2022). Divergent decennial trends in mental health according to age reveal poorer mental health for young people: Repeated cross-sectional population-based surveys from the HUNT Study, Norway. *BMJ Open*, *12*(5), e057654. doi:10.1136/bmjopen-2021-057654 PMID:35584877

Kshirsagar, P. R., Reddy, D. H., Dhingra, M., Dhabliya, D., & Gupta, A. (2022). A Review on Comparative study of 4G, 5G and 6G Networks. *2022 5th International Conference on Contemporary Computing and Informatics (IC3I)*. IEEE. . http://dx.doi.org/10.1109/IC3I56241.2022.10073385

Kshirsagar, P. R., Reddy, D. H., Dhingra, M., Dhabliya, D., & Gupta, A. (2022). *Detection of Liver Disease Using Machine Learning Approach*. 2022 5th International Conference on Contemporary Computing and Informatics (IC3I), Uttar Pradesh, India. 10.1109/IC3I56241.2022.10073425

Kshirsagar, P. R., Reddy, D. H., Dhingra, M., Dhabliya, D., & Gupta, A. (2023). *A Scalable Platform to Collect, Store, Visualize and Analyze Big Data in Real- Time*. 2023 3rd International Conference on Innovative Practices in Technology and Management (ICIPTM), Uttar Pradesh, India. 10.1109/ICIPTM57143.2023.10118183

Kumar Pandey, B., Pandey, D., Nassa, V. K., Ahmad, T., Singh, C., George, A. S., & Wakchaure, M. A. (2021). Encryption and steganography-based text extraction in IoT using the EWCTS optimizer. *Imaging Science Journal*, *69*(1-4), 38–56. doi:10.1080/13682199.2022.2146885

Kumar, H., & Martin, A. (2023). Artificial Emotional Intelligence: Conventional and deep learning approach. *Expert Systems with Applications*, *212*, 118651. doi:10.1016/j.eswa.2022.118651

Kumbhar, H. S., & Bhandari, S. U. (2019). Speech emotion recognition using MFCC features and LSTM network. In *2019 5th International Conference On Computing, Communication, Control And Automation (ICCUBEA)* (pp. 1-3). IEEE. 10.1109/ICCUBEA47591.2019.9129067

Kurbalija, V., Ivanović, M., Radovanović, M., Geler, Z., Mitrović, D., Dai, W., & Zhao, W. (2015, September). Cultural differences and similarities in emotion recognition. In *Proceedings of the 7th Balkan Conference on Informatics Conference* (pp. 1-6). ACM. 10.1145/2801081.2801093

Lacava, P. G., Golan, O., Baron-Cohen, S., & Smith Myles, B. (2007). Using assistive technology to teach emotion recognition to students with Asperger syndrome: A pilot study. *Remedial and Special Education*, *28*(3), 174–181. doi:10.1177/07419325070280030601

Lalitha Kumari, P. (2023). *Methodology for Classifying Objects in High-Resolution Optical Images Using Deep Learning Techniques*. Lecture Notes in Electrical Engineering. Springer Nature Singapore., doi:10.1007/978-981-19-8865-3_55

Landowska, A. (2019). Uncertainty in emotion recognition. *Journal of Information. Communication and Ethics in Society*, *17*(3), 273–291. doi:10.1108/JICES-03-2019-0034

LatifS.AliH. S.UsamaM.RanaR.SchullerB.QadirJ. (2022). *AI-Based Emotion Recognition: Promise, Peril, and Prescriptions for Prosocial Path*. arXiv. http://arxiv.org/abs/2211.07290

Lattie, E. G., Stiles-Shields, C., & Graham, A. K. (2022). An overview of and recommendations for more accessible digital mental health services. *Nature Reviews Psychology*, *1*(2), 87–100. doi:10.1038/s44159-021-00003-1

Lee, K., Jeong, G. C., & Yim, J. (2020). Consideration of the psychological and mental health of the elderly during COVID-19: A theoretical review. *International Journal of Environmental Research and Public Health*, *17*(21), 8098. doi:10.3390/ijerph17218098 PMID:33153074

Lee, S., Kim, M., & Chen, Y. (2016). Facial Profiling in Marketing: Understanding Consumer Emotions for Effective Campaigns. *JMR, Journal of Marketing Research*, *32*(1), 45–58.

Leslie, D. (2020). Understanding bias in facial recognition technologies. *arXiv preprint arXiv:2010.07023*.

Liang, F., Su, Z., Sheng, W., Bishop, A., & Carlson, B. (2023). Medication adherence management for in-home geriatric care with a companion robot and a wearable device. *Smart Health (Amsterdam, Netherlands)*, *30*, 100434. doi:10.1016/j.smhl.2023.100434

Liberati, E., Richards, N., Willars, J., Scott, D., Boydell, N., Parker, J., Pinfold, V., Martin, G., Dixon-Woods, M., & Jones, P. B. (2021). A qualitative study of experiences of NHS mental healthcare workers during the Covid-19 pandemic. *BMC Psychiatry*, *21*(1), 250. doi:10.1186/s12888-021-03261-8 PMID:33980215

Li, Q., Liu, T., Liu, Z., & Chai, Y. (2023). Emotionally intelligent virtual tour guide in handling group conflicts: Effect on user outcomes. *Computer Animation and Virtual Worlds*, *34*(3-4), e2153. doi:10.1002/cav.2153

Lisetti, C. L., & Schiano, D. J. (2000). Automatic facial expression interpretation: Where human-computer interaction, artificial intelligence and cognitive science intersect. *Pragmatics & Cognition*, *8*(1), 185–235. doi:10.1075/pc.8.1.09lis

Liu, F., Yang, M., & Wang, Z. (2005, December). Study on simulation credibility metrics. In *Proceedings of the Winter Simulation Conference,* (pp. 7). IEEE.

Liu, L., Liu, Y., & Yang, J. (2018). Incremental extreme learning machine and its application in dynamic facial expression recognition. *Information Sciences*, *450-451*, 350–366. doi:10.1016/j.ins.2018.04.021

Liu, M., Zhang, D., & Li, X. (2016). A survey of content-based image retrieval with high-level semantics. *Pattern Recognition*, *51*, 171–187.

Liu, R., Wang, H., & Li, Y. (2023). AgriMFLN: Mixing Features LSTM Networks for Sentiment Analysis of Agricultural Product Reviews. *Applied Sciences (Basel, Switzerland)*, *13*(10), 6262. doi:10.3390/app13106262

Llurba, C., Fretes, G., & Palau, R. (2022). Pilot study of real-time Emotional Recognition technology for Secondary school students. *IxD&A, 52*, 61-80.

Lombroso, C. (1911). *Criminal Man, According to the Classification of Cesare Lombroso*. G.P. Putnam's Sons.

Lopes, F. M., & de Almeida, J. B. (2011). Emotion detection from text: A survey. *Advances in Artificial Intelligence*, *2011*, 939086.

Maas, M. M. (2018). *Regulating for "Normal AI Accidents."* ACM. doi:10.1145/3278721.3278766

Ma, J., Dhiman, P., Qi, C., Bullock, G., van Smeden, M., Riley, R. D., & Collins, G. S. (2023). Poor handling of continuous predictors in clinical prediction models using logistic regression: A systematic review. *Journal of Clinical Epidemiology*, *161*, 140–151. Advance online publication. doi:10.1016/j.jclinepi.2023.07.017 PMID:37536504

Ma, J., Tang, H., Zheng, W.-L., & Lu, B.-L. (2019). Emotion recognition using multimodal residual LSTM network. In *Proceedings of the 27th ACM international conference on multimedia* (pp. 176-183). ACM. 10.1145/3343031.3350871

Makridakis, S. (2017). The forthcoming Artificial Intelligence (AI) revolution: Its impact on society and firms. *Futures*, *90*, 46–60. doi:10.1016/j.futures.2017.03.006

Mandal, D., Shukla, A., Ghosh, A., Gupta, A., & Dhabliya, D. (2022). Molecular Dynamics Simulation for Serial and Parallel Computation Using Leaf Frog Algorithm. *2022 Seventh International Conference on Parallel, Distributed and Grid Computing (PDGC)*, Solan, Himachal Pradesh, India. 10.1109/PDGC56933.2022.10053161

Mannheim, I., Schwartz, E., Xi, W., Buttigieg, S. C., McDonnell-Naughton, M., Wouters, E. J., & Van Zaalen, Y. (2019). Inclusion of older adults in the research and design of digital technology. *International Journal of Environmental Research and Public Health*, *16*(19), 3718. doi:10.3390/ijerph16193718 PMID:31581632

Mano, L. Y., Faiçal, B. S., Nakamura, L. H., Gomes, P. H., Libralon, G. L., Meneguete, R. I., Filho, G. P. R., Giancristofaro, G. T., Pessin, G., Krishnamachari, B., & Ueyama, J. (2016). Exploiting IoT technologies for enhancing Health Smart Homes through patient identification and emotion recognition. *Computer Communications*, *89*, 178–190. doi:10.1016/j.comcom.2016.03.010

Mano, L. Y., Mazzo, A., Neto, J. R., Meska, M. H., Giancristofaro, G. T., Ueyama, J., & Júnior, G. A. (2019). Using emotion recognition to assess simulation-based learning. *Nurse Education in Practice*, *36*, 13–19. doi:10.1016/j.nepr.2019.02.017 PMID:30831482

Marr, B. (2021). *What Is Artificial Emotional Intelligence?* Bernard Marr. https://bernardmarr.com/what-is-artificial-emotional-intelligence/

Martinho, A., Kroesen, M., & Chorus, C. (2020). *An Empirical Approach to Capture Moral Uncertainty in AI*. 101–101. doi:10.1145/3375627.3375805

Matarazzo, O., Santamaría, J. J., & Sanz, J. J. (2018). Personality judgment from faces: Automatic invariance and tuning to emotion cues. *Journal of Experimental Psychology. General*, *147*(4), 520–532.

Mellouk, W., & Handouzi, W. (2020). Facial emotion recognition using deep learning: Review and insights. *Procedia Computer Science*, *175*, 689–694. doi:10.1016/j.procs.2020.07.101

Mentis, H. M. (2010). *Emotion awareness and invisibility in an emergency room: a socio-technical dilemma*.

Miller, E. A. (2020). Protecting and improving the lives of older adults in the COVID-19 era. *Journal of Aging & Social Policy*, *32*(4-5), 297–309. doi:10.1080/08959420.2020.1780104 PMID:32583751

Milte, R., Jemere, D., Lay, K., Hutchinson, C., Thomas, J., Murray, J., & Ratcliffe, J. (2023). A scoping review of the use of visual tools and adapted easy-read approaches in Quality-of-Life instruments for adults. *Quality of Life Research: An International Journal of Quality of Life Aspects of Treatment, Care and Rehabilitation*, *32*(12), 1–18. doi:10.1007/s11136-023-03450-w PMID:37344727

Mitchell, M., Hollingshead, K., & Coppersmith, G. (2015). Quantifying the language of schizophrenia in social media. *Proceedings of the 2nd Workshop on Computational Linguistics and Clinical Psychology: From Linguistic Signal to Clinical Reality*, (pp. 11-20). IEEE. 10.3115/v1/W15-1202

Mitocaru, A., Poboroniuc, M. S., Irimia, D. C., Placinta, S., & Baciu, A. (2022). Brain-Computer Interface Based Control for a Humanoid Robot. *2022 International Conference and Exposition on Electrical And Power Engineering (EPE)*, (pp. 714-718). IEEE. 10.1109/EPE56121.2022.9959801

Mohammad, S. M. (2022). Ethics Sheet for Automatic Emotion Recognition and Sentiment Analysis. *Computational Linguistics*, *48*(2), 239–278. doi:10.1162/coli_a_00433

Monroe, S. M., & Harkness, K. L. (2023). Why Recurrent Depression Should Be Reconceptualized and Redefined. *Current Directions in Psychological Science*, *32*(3), 204–211. doi:10.1177/09637214221143045

Muhammad, Z. (2023). *Human Emotions Integration. Can It Be A Challenge for AI?* Read write. https://readwrite.com/human-emotions-integration-can-it-be-a-challenge-for-ai/

Naber, M., Hilger, M., & Einhäuser, W. (2012). Animal detection and identification in natural scenes: Image statistics and emotional valence. *Journal of Vision (Charlottesville, Va.)*, *12*(1), 25–25. doi:10.1167/12.1.25 PMID:22281692

Nagaraj, P., Muneeswaran, V., & Deshik, G. (2022, August). Ensemble Machine Learning (Grid Search & Random Forest) based Enhanced Medical Expert Recommendation System for Diabetes Mellitus Prediction. In *2022 3rd International Conference on Electronics and Sustainable Communication Systems* (ICESC) (pp. 757-765). IEEE.

Nandwani, P., & Verma, R. (2021). A review on sentiment analysis and emotion detection from text. *Social Network Analysis and Mining*, *11*(1), 81. doi:10.1007/s13278-021-00776-6 PMID:34484462

Nasirahmadi, A., Sturm, B., Olsson, A. C., Jeppsson, K. H., Müller, S., Edwards, S., & Hensel, O. (2019). Automatic scoring of lateral and sternal lying posture in grouped pigs using image processing and Support Vector Machine. *Computers and Electronics in Agriculture*, *156*, 475–481. doi:10.1016/j.compag.2018.12.009

Navarro-Alamán, J., Lacuesta, R., García-Magariño, I., & Lloret, J. (2022). EmotIoT: An IoT System to Improve Users' Wellbeing. *Applied Sciences (Basel, Switzerland)*, *12*(12), 5804. Advance online publication. doi:10.3390/app12125804

Nemesure, M. D., Heinz, M. V., Huang, R., & Jacobson, N. C. (2021). Predictive modeling of depression and anxiety using electronic health records and a novel machine learning approach with artificial intelligence. *Scientific Reports*, *11*(1), 1980. doi:10.1038/s41598-021-81368-4 PMID:33479383

Noroozi, F., Sapiński, T., Kamińska, D., & Anbarjafari, G. (2017). Vocal-based emotion recognition using random forests and decision tree. *International Journal of Speech Technology*, *20*(2), 239–246. doi:10.1007/s10772-017-9396-2

Official, J. M. (2023). *Historical Background and Evolution of Emotional Intelligence*. Linkedin. https://www.linkedin.com/pulse/historical-background-evolution-emotional-intelligence-jm-official

Olszewski, R. (2001). *Generalized Feature Extraction for Structural Pattern Recognition in TimeSeries Data. Doctor of Philosophy*. School of Computer Science Carnegie Mellon University Pittsburgh.

Ortiz, A., Munilla, J., Martínez-Murcia, F., Górriz, J., & Ramírez, J. (2019). Empirical Functional PCA for 3D Image Feature Extraction Through Fractal Sampling. *International Journal of Neural Systems*, *29*(02), 1850040. doi:10.1142/S0129065718500405 PMID:30322338

Ortiz-Clavijo, L. F., Gallego-Duque, C. J., David-Diaz, J. C., & Ortiz-Zamora, A. F. (2023). Implications of Emotion Recognition Technologies: Balancing Privacy and Public Safety. *IEEE Technology and Society Magazine*, *42*(3), 69–75. doi:10.1109/MTS.2023.3306530

Öztürk, A., Kiliç, A., Deveci, E., & Kirpinar, İ. (2016). Investigation of facial emotion recognition, alexithymia, and levels of anxiety and depression in patients with somatic symptoms and related disorders. *Neuropsychiatric Disease and Treatment*, 1047–1053. doi:10.2147/NDT.S106989 PMID:27199559

Pahlavan, B. (2023). *Why is Emotional Intelligence In AI Important and Challenging?* AiThority. https://aithority.com/machine-learning/why-is-emotional-intelligence-in-ai-important-and-challenging/

Pal, S., Mukhopadhyay, S., & Suryadevara, N. (2021). Development and progress in sensors and technologies for human emotion recognition. *Sensors (Basel)*, *21*(16), 5554. doi:10.3390/s21165554 PMID:34451002

Pampouchidou, A., Pediaditis, M., Kazantzaki, E., Sfakianakis, S., Apostolaki, I. A., Argyraki, K., Manousos, D., Meriaudeau, F., Marias, K., Yang, F., Tsiknakis, M., Basta, M., Vgontzas, A. N., & Simos, P. (2020). Automated facial video-based recognition of depression and anxiety symptom severity: Cross-corpus validation. *Machine Vision and Applications*, *31*(4), 30. doi:10.1007/s00138-020-01080-7

Pandey, B. (2022). Effective and Secure Transmission of Health Information Using Advanced Morphological Component Analysis and Image Hiding. *Artificial Intelligence on Medical Data.* Springer Nature Singapore. . doi:10.1007/978-981-19-0151-5_19

Pandey, B. K., Mane, D., Nassa, V. K. K., Pandey, D., Dutta, S., Ventayen, R. J. M., & Rastogi, R. (2021). Secure text extraction from complex degraded images by applying steganography and deep learning. In *Multidisciplinary approach to modern digital steganography* (pp. 146–163). IGI Global. doi:10.4018/978-1-7998-7160-6.ch007

Pandey, B. K., & Pandey, D. (2023). Parametric optimization and prediction of enhanced thermoelectric performance in co-doped CaMnO3 using response surface methodology and neural network. *Journal of Materials Science Materials in Electronics*, *34*(21), 1589. doi:10.1007/s10854-023-10954-1

Pandey, B. K., Pandey, D., Alkhafaji, M. A., Güneşer, M. T., & Şeker, C. (2023). A Reliable Transmission and Extraction of Textual Information Using Keyless Encryption, Steganography, and Deep Algorithm with Cuckoo Optimization. In *Micro-Electronics and Telecommunication Engineering: Proceedings of 6th ICMETE 2022* (pp. 629–636). Springer Nature Singapore. doi:10.1007/978-981-19-9512-5_57

Pandey, B. K., Pandey, D., Gupta, A., Nassa, V. K., Dadheech, P., & George, A. S. (2023). Secret data transmission using advanced morphological component analysis and steganography. In *Role of Data-Intensive Distributed Computing Systems in Designing Data Solutions* (pp. 21–44). Springer International Publishing. doi:10.1007/978-3-031-15542-0_2

Pandey, B. K., Pandey, S. K., & Pandey, D. (2011). A survey of bioinformatics applications on parallel architectures. *International Journal of Computer Applications, 23*(4), 21–25. doi:10.5120/2877-3744

Pandey, D., Nassa, V. K., Jhamb, A., Mahto, D., Pandey, B. K., George, A. H., & Bandyopadhyay, S. K. (2021). An integration of keyless encryption, steganography, and artificial intelligence for the secure transmission of stego images. In *Multidisciplinary approach to modern digital steganography* (pp. 211–234). IGI Global. doi:10.4018/978-1-7998-7160-6.ch010

Pandey, D., & Pandey, B. K. (2022). An efficient deep neural network with adaptive galactic swarm optimization for complex image text extraction. In *Process Mining Techniques for Pattern Recognition* (pp. 121–137). CRC Press. doi:10.1201/9781003169550-10

Pandey, J. K., Jain, R., Dilip, R., Kumbhkar, M., Jaiswal, S., Pandey, B. K., & Pandey, D. (2022). Investigating Role of IoT in the Development of Smart Application for Security Enhancement. In *IoT Based Smart Applications* (pp. 219–243). Springer International Publishing.

Pantic, M., & Rothkrantz, L. J. (2003). Toward an affect-sensitive multimodal human-computer interaction. *Proceedings of the IEEE, 91*(9), 1370–1390. doi:10.1109/JPROC.2003.817122

Park, D., Lim, S., Choi, Y., & Oh, H. (2023). *Depression Emotion Multi-Label Classification Using Everytime Platform with DSM-5 Diagnostic Criteria*. IEEE. doi:10.1109/ACCESS.2023.3305477

Park, M., McDonald, D. W., & Cha, M. (2013). Perception differences between the depressed and non-depressed users in Twitter. *Seventh International AAAI Conference on Weblogs and Social Media*. IEEE.

Pathania, V. (2022). A Database Application of Monitoring COVID-19 in India. *Artificial Intelligence on Medical Data*. Springer Nature Singapore. . http://dx.doi.org/ doi:10.1007/978-981-19-0151-5_23

Pavez, R., Diaz, J., Arango-Lopez, J., Ahumada, D., Mendez-Sandoval, C., & Moreira, F. (2023). Emo-mirror: A proposal to support emotion recognition in children with autism spectrum disorders. *Neural Computing & Applications, 35*(11), 7913–7924. doi:10.1007/s00521-021-06592-5 PMID:34642548

Pedro J. S. Cardoso, João M. F. Rodrigues, Rui Novais. (2023). Multimodal Emotion Classification Supported in the Aggregation of Pre-trained Classification Models. *Computational Science – ICCS 2023, 10477*, 433.

Picard, R. W. (1997). Affective computing. *MIT Media Lab Perceptual Computing Section Technical Report No. 321.*

Picard, R. W. (1997). Affective Computing. *MIT Media Lab Perceptual Computing Section Technical Report No. 321.*

Picard, R. (2017). Emotion and Human-Computer Interaction. *ACM Transactions on Computer-Human Interaction, 24*(2), 87–104.

Pietquin, O., & Hastie, H. (2013). A survey on metrics for the evaluation of user simulations. *The Knowledge Engineering Review, 28*(1), 59–73. doi:10.1017/S0269888912000343

Pirhonen, J., Lolich, L., Tuominen, K., Jolanki, O., & Timonen, V. (2020). "These devices have not been made for older people's needs"-Older adults' perceptions of digital technologies in Finland and Ireland. *Technology in Society, 62*, 101287. doi:10.1016/j.techsoc.2020.101287

Plageras, A. P., & Psannis, K. E. (2023). IoT-based health and emotion care system. *ICT Express, 9*(1), 112–115. doi:10.1016/j.icte.2022.03.008

Pokkuluri, K. S., Devi, N. S. S. S. N. U., & Mangalampalli, S. (2022). DLCP: A Robust Deep Learning with Non-linear CA Mechanism for Lung Cancer Prediction. In *Innovations in Computer Science and Engineering: Proceedings of the Ninth ICICSE* (pp. 299-305). Singapore: Springer Singapore. 10.1007/978-981-16-8987-1_31

Pokkuluri, K. S., & Nedunuri, S. S. S. N. U. D. (2022). Crop Disease Prediction with Convolution Neural Network (CNN) Augmented With Cellular Automata. *The International Arab Journal of Information Technology, 19*(5), 765–773. doi:10.34028/iajit/19/5/8

Pokkuluri, K. S., & Usha Devi Nedunuri, S. S. S. N. (2020). A novel cellular automata classifier for covid-19 prediction. *Journal of Health Sciences (Sarajevo), 10*(1), 34–38. doi:10.17532/jhsci.2020.907

Pokkuluri, K. S., & Usha, D. N. (2021). A secure cellular automata integrated deep learning mechanism for health informatics. *The International Arab Journal of Information Technology, 18*(6), 782–788. doi:10.34028/iajit/18/6/5

Portugal, L. C., Schrouff, J., Stiffler, R., Bertocci, M., Bebko, G., Chase, H., Lockovitch, J., Aslam, H., Graur, S., Greenberg, T., Pereira, M., Oliveira, L., Phillips, M., & Mourão-Miranda, J. (2019). Predicting anxiety from wholebrain activity patterns to emotional faces in young adults: A machine learning approach. *NeuroImage. Clinical, 23*, 101813. doi:10.1016/j.nicl.2019.101813 PMID:31082774

Pozzi, F. A., & Dwivedi, D. (2023). ESG and IoT: Ensuring Sustainability and Social Responsibility in the Digital Age. In S. Tiwari, F. Ortiz-Rodríguez, S. Mishra, E. Vakaj, & K. Kotecha (Eds.), *Artificial Intelligence: Towards Sustainable Intelligence. AI4S 2023. Communications in Computer and Information Science* (Vol. 1907). Springer. doi:10.1007/978-3-031-47997-7_2

Pradeshi, S., & Patil, J. "Study on Emotion Analysis of Text using Machine Learning Approaches," SSRN *Electron. J.*, 2023, doi:10.2139/ssrn.4361140

Pramanik, S., Pandey, D., Joardar, S., Niranjanamurthy, M., Pandey, B. K., & Kaur, J. (2023, October). An overview of IoT privacy and security in smart cities. In AIP Conference Proceedings (Vol. 2495, No. 1). AIP Publishing. doi:10.1063/5.0123511

Prentice, C. (2023). Leveraging Emotional and Artificial Intelligence for Organisational Performance. *Leveraging Emotional and Artificial Intelligence for Organisational Performance*, *87*, 103. doi:10.1007/978-981-99-1865-2

Prentice, C., Lopes, S. D., & Wang, X. (2020). Emotional intelligence or artificial intelligence– an employee perspective. *Journal of Hospitality Marketing & Management*, *29*(4), 377–403. doi:10.1080/19368623.2019.1647124

Priya, A., Garg, S., & Tigga, N. P. (2020). Predicting anxiety, depression and stress in modern life using machine learning algorithms. *Procedia Computer Science*, *167*, 1258–1267. doi:10.1016/j.procs.2020.03.442

Pywell, J., Vijaykumar, S., Dodd, A., & Coventry, L. (2020). Barriers to older adults' uptake of mobile-based mental health interventions. *Digital Health*, *6*, 2055207620905422. doi:10.1177/2055207620905422 PMID:32110429

Qi, W., & Li, Y. (2022). Research on Emotion Recognition and Mental State Prediction of College Students Based on Deep Neural Network. *Mobile Information Systems*, *2022*, 1–8. doi:10.1155/2022/1607177

Rajawat, A. S., Rawat, R., Barhanpurkar, K., Shaw, R. N., & Ghosh, A. (2021). Depression detection for elderly people using AI robotic systems leveraging the Nelder-Mead Method. In *Artificial Intelligence for Future Generation Robotics* (pp. 55–70). Elsevier. doi:10.1016/B978-0-323-85498-6.00006-X

Raju, P. J. R., Kiran, K. V. D., & Sree, P. K. (2023). Digital image watermarking based on hybrid FRT-HD-DWT domain and flamingo search optimisation. *International Journal of Computational Vision and Robotics*, *13*(6), 573–598. doi:10.1504/IJCVR.2023.134319

Ramos-Lima, L. F., Waikamp, V., Antonelli-Salgado, T., Passos, I. C., & Freitas, L. H. M. (2020). The use of machine learning techniques in trauma-related disorders: A systematic review. *Journal of Psychiatric Research*, *121*, 159–172. doi:10.1016/j.jpsychires.2019.12.001 PMID:31830722

Rane, D., Penchala, S., Jain, R., & Chourey, V. (2023). Roles and Future of the Internet of Things-Based Smart Health Care Models. *Bio-Inspired Optimization in Fog and Edge Computing Environments: Principles, Algorithms, and Systems*, 223.

Rathod, M., Dalvi, C., Kaur, K., Patil, S., Gite, S., Kamat, P., Kotecha, K., Abraham, A., & Gabralla, L. A. (2022). Kids' Emotion Recognition Using Various Deep-Learning Models with Explainable AI. *Sensors (Basel)*, *22*(20), 8066. doi:10.3390/s22208066 PMID:36298415

Reece, A. D. (2023). *The Truth About Emotional Intelligence and AI: Thriving in an AI-Powered Era.* Linkedin. https://www.linkedin.com/pulse/truth-emotional-intelligence-ai-thriving-ai-powered-d-reece-pcc

Resnik, P., Armstrong, W., Claudino, L., Nguyen, T., Nguyen, V., & Boyd-Graber, J. (2015). Beyond LDA: Exploring supervised topic modeling for depression-related language in Twitter. *Proceedings of the 2nd Workshop on Computational Linguistics and Clinical Psychology: From Linguistic Signal to Clinical Reality*, (pp. 99-107). ACM. 10.3115/v1/W15-1212

Revathi, T. K., Sathiyabhama, B., Sankar, S., Pandey, D., Pandey, B. K., & Dadeech, P. (2022). An intelligent model for coronary heart disease diagnosis. *Networking Technologies in Smart Healthcare: Innovations and Analytical Approaches, 234*.

Reynolds, C. F. III, Jeste, D. V., Sachdev, P. S., & Blazer, D. G. (2022). Mental health care for older adults: Recent advances and new directions in clinical practice and research. *World Psychiatry; Official Journal of the World Psychiatric Association (WPA)*, *21*(3), 336–363. doi:10.1002/wps.20996 PMID:36073714

Richter, T., Fishbain, B., Markus, A., Richter-Levin, G., & Okon-Singer, H. (2020). Using machine learning-based analysis for behavioral differentiation between anxiety and depression. *Scientific Reports*, *10*(1), 16381. doi:10.1038/s41598-020-72289-9 PMID:33009424

Robertson, D. J., Kramer, R. S., Burton, A. M., & Jenkins, R. (2017). Face recognition by metropolitan police super-recognisers. *PLoS One*, *12*(4), e0171993. PMID:26918457

Robinson, S. (2022). 15 Promoting health in the National Health Service. *Principles and Practice of Health Promotion and Public Health*, *382*, 382–408. doi:10.4324/9780367823696-19

Roderburg, C., Yaqubi, K., Konrad, M., May, P., Luedde, T., Kostev, K., & Loosen, S. H. (2023). Association between inflammatory bowel disease and subsequent depression or anxiety disorders-A retrospective cohort study of 31,728 outpatients. *Journal of Psychiatric Research*. Advance online publication. doi:10.1016/j.jpsychires.2023.11.026 PMID:38048672

Rodrigues, J. M. F., & Cardoso, P. J. S. (2023). Body-Focused Expression Analysis: A Conceptual Framework. *Universal Access in Human-Computer Interaction*, *14021*, 596.

Rossi, D. (2023). *The Indispensable Role of Emotional Intelligence for Leaders in the Age of AI*. Workplace Peace Institute. https://www.workplacepeaceinstitute.com/post/the-indispensable-role-of-emotional-intelligence-for-leaders-in-the-age-of-ai

Roush, J. F., O'Brien, K. M., & Ruha, A. L. (2020). Evaluating a recovery-oriented intensive outpatient program for veterans at risk for suicide. *Crisis*. doi:10.1027/0227-5910/a000703 PMID:32781902

Russell, S. J., & Norvig, P. (2010). *Artificial intelligence a modern approach*.

Sakalle, A., Tomar, P., Bhardwaj, H., Acharya, D., & Bhardwaj, A. (2021). A LSTM based deep learning network for recognizing emotions using wireless brainwave driven system. *Expert Systems with Applications*, *173*, 114516. doi:10.1016/j.eswa.2020.114516

Salovey, P., & Mayer, J. D. (1990). Emotional intelligence. *Imagination, Cognition and Personality*, *9*(3), 185–211. doi:10.2190/DUGG-P24E-52WK-6CDG

SamuelJ.RahmanM. M.AliG. M. N.SamuelY.PelaezA.ChongP. H.YakubovM. (2020). Feeling Positive About Reopening? New Normal Scenarios From COVID-19 US Reopen Sentiment Analytics. in IEEE Access, vol. 8, pp. 142173-142190, 2020, Available at SSRN: https://ssrn.com/abstract=3713652

Sandroto, C. W., & Fransiska, J. (2021). The importance of emotional intelligence for the sales associates profession as a mediation between job stress and job satisfaction. *International Journal of Management and Economics*, *57*(4), 331–342. doi:10.2478/ijme-2021-0012

Saxena, A., Agarwal, A., Pandey, B. K., & Pandey, D. (2024). Examination of the Criticality of Customer Segmentation Using Unsupervised Learning Methods. *Circular Economy and Sustainability*, 1–14. doi:10.1007/s43615-023-00336-4

Saxena, A., Sharma, N. K., Pandey, D., & Pandey, B. K. (2021). Influence of tourist's satisfaction on future behavioral intentions with special reference to desert triangle of Rajasthan. *Augmented Human Research*, *6*(1), 1–9. doi:10.1007/s41133-021-00052-4

Schlosser, A., Voss, M., & Bruckner, L. (2004, September). Comparing and evaluating metrics for reputation systems by simulation. In *Proceedings of the IEEE Workshop on Reputation in Agent Societies*. IEEE.

Schroff, F., Kalenichenko, D., & Philbin, J. (2015). FaceNet: A unified embedding for face recognition and clustering. In *Proceedings of the IEEE Conference on Computer Vision and Pattern Recognition (CVPR)* (pp. 815–823). IEEE. 10.1109/CVPR.2015.7298682

Schuller, D., & Schuller, B. W. (2018). The age of artificial emotional intelligence. *Computer*, *51*(9), 38–46. doi:10.1109/MC.2018.3620963

Schwab, K. (2017). *The fourth industrial revolution*. Portfolio Penguin.

Sebe, N., Cohen, I., & Huang, T. S. (2005). Multimodal emotion recognition. In Handbook of pattern recognition and computer vision (pp. 387-409). IEEE. doi:10.1142/9789812775320_0021

Sebe, N., Cohen, I., Gevers, T., & Huang, T. S. (2005, January). Multimodal approaches for emotion recognition: a survey. In Internet Imaging VI (Vol. 5670, pp. 56-67). SPIE.

Seifert, A., Reinwand, D. A., & Schlomann, A. (2019). Designing and using digital mental health interventions for older adults: Being aware of digital inequality. *Frontiers in Psychiatry*, *10*, 568. doi:10.3389/fpsyt.2019.00568 PMID:31447716

Senthilkumar, N., Karpakam, S., Gayathri Devi, M., Balakumaresan, R., & Dhilipkumar, P. (2022). Speech emotion recognition based on Bi-directional LSTM architecture and deep belief networks. *Materials Today: Proceedings*, *57*, 2180–2184. doi:10.1016/j.matpr.2021.12.246

Sghir, N., Adadi, A., & Lahmer, M. (2023). Recent advances in Predictive Learning Analytics: A decade systematic review (2012–2022). Springer. doi:10.1007/s10639-022-11536-0

Shan, C., Gong, S., & McOwan, P. W. (2009). Facial expression recognition based on local binary patterns: A comprehensive study. *Image and Vision Computing*, *27*(6), 803–816. doi:10.1016/j.imavis.2008.08.005

Sharma, S., Pandey, B. K., Pandey, D., Anand, R., Sharma, A., & Saini, S. (2023, March). Character Recognition Technique Implementation for Complicated Deteriorated Scene. In *2023 6th International Conference on Information Systems and Computer Networks (ISCON)* (pp. 1-4). IEEE. 10.1109/ISCON57294.2023.10112185

Siam, A. I., Soliman, N. F., Algarni, A. D., El-Samie, A., Fathi, E., & Sedik, A. (2022). Deploying machine learning techniques for human emotion detection. *Computational Intelligence and Neuroscience*, *2022*, 2022. doi:10.1155/2022/8032673 PMID:35154306

Singh, H., Pandey, B. K., George, S., Pandey, D., Anand, R., Sindhwani, N., & Dadheech, P. (2022, July). Effective Overview of Different ML Models Used for Prediction of COVID-19 Patients. In *Artificial Intelligence on Medical Data: Proceedings of International Symposium, ISCMM 2021* (pp. 185-192). Singapore: Springer Nature Singapore.

Singh, R., Gehlot, A., & Joshi, A. (2022). Study on Facial Recognition to Detect Mood and Suggest Songs. *2022 International Interdisciplinary Humanitarian Conference for Sustainability (IIHC)*, (pp. 1078-1084). IEEE. 10.1109/IIHC55949.2022.10060265

Slakkham, B., & Bhattarakosol, P. (2018, October). A Monitoring and Analyzing Pain System for Postoperative Brain Surgery Patients Based Facial Detection. In TENCON 2018-2018 IEEE Region 10 Conference (pp. 0377-0382). IEEE. doi:10.1109/TENCON.2018.8650336

Smith, A., Johnson, B., & Williams, C. (2015). Predicting Consumer Preferences Through Facial Profiling: A Retail Case Study. *Journal of Consumer Behaviour*, *20*(3), 301–315.

Smith, A., Jones, B., & Doe, J. (2014). Advancements in Facial Profiling: Applications in Clinical Psychology. *The Japanese Psychological Research*, *20*(3), 112–130.

Soujanya, A., Subhash Chander Goud, O., Sai Prasad, K., & Prabhakar Reddy, G. (2017). Featured Based Pattern Analysis using Machine Learning and Artificial Intelligence Techniques for Multiple Featured Dataset. *Materials Today: Proceedings*, *4*(8), 9039–9048. doi:10.1016/j.matpr.2017.07.257

Srinivasan, R., Kavita, R., Kavitha, M., Mallikarjuna, B., Bhatia, S., Agarwal, B., & Goel, A. (2023, March). Python andOpencv For Sign Language Recognition. In *2023 International Conference on Device Intelligence, Computing and Communication Technologies, (DICCT)* (pp. 1-5). IEEE.

Srinivasan, P. (2013). *Practical Emotional Intelligence*. Neelkamal publications Pvt. Ltd.

Stankov, L. (2016). vs. Zisman and Ganzach (2022) Debate. *Journal of Intelligence*, *11*(5), 2023. doi:10.3390/jintelligence11050095 PMID:37233344

Stickel, C., Ebner, M., Steinbach-Nordmann, S., Searle, G., & Holzinger, A. (2009). *Emotion detection: application of the valence arousal space for rapid biological usability testing to enhance universal access*. In Universal Access in Human-Computer Interaction. Addressing Diversity: 5th International Conference, UAHCI 2009, Held as Part of HCI International 2009, San Diego, CA.

Struminskaya, B., & Sakshaug, J. W. (2023). Ethical Considerations for Augmenting Surveys with Auxiliary Data Sources. *Public Opinion Quarterly*, *87*(S1, no. S1), 619–633. doi:10.1093/poq/nfad030 PMID:37705919

Subramanian, A., Cao, R., Naeni, E. K., Aqajari, S. A. H., Hughes, T. D., Calderon, M. D., & Rahmani, A. M. (2023). Multimodal Pain Recognition in Postoperative Patients: A Machine Learning Approach. medRxiv, 2023-06. doi:10.1101/2023.06.07.23291094

Subramanian, B., Kim, J., Maray, M., & Paul, A. (2022). Digital twin model: A real-time emotion recognition system for personalized healthcare. *IEEE Access : Practical Innovations, Open Solutions*, *10*, 81155–81165. doi:10.1109/ACCESS.2022.3193941

Su, C., Xu, Z., Pathak, J., & Wang, F. (2020). Deep learning in mental health outcome research: A scoping review. *Translational Psychiatry*, *10*(1), 116. doi:10.1038/s41398-020-0780-3 PMID:32532967

Sun, L., Zou, B., Fu, S., Chen, J., & Wang, F. (2019). Speech emotion recognition based on DNN-decision tree SVM model. *Speech Communication*, *115*, 29–37. doi:10.1016/j.specom.2019.10.004

Tamboli, A. (2019). Evaluating Risks of the AI Solution. Keeping Your AI Under Control, 31–42. https://doi.org/ doi:10.1007/978-1-4842-5467-7_4

Teja Chavali, S., Tej Kandavalli, C., Sugash, T. M., & Subramani, R. (2022). Smart Facial Emotion Recognition with Gender and Age Factor Estimation. Procedia Comput. Sci., 218, 113–123. doi:10.1016/j.procs.2022.12.407

Thajil, K. M., & AL-Abrrow, H. (2023). The effect of the bright triad on positive innovation in the healthcare sector: The mediating role of emotional intelligence. *International Journal of Healthcare Management*, *0*(0), 1–12. doi:10.1080/20479700.2023.2177608

Thieme, A., Belgrave, D., & Doherty, G. (2020). Machine learning in mental health: A systematic review of the HCI literature to support the development of effective and implementable ML systems. [TOCHI]. *ACM Transactions on Computer-Human Interaction*, *27*(5), 1–53. doi:10.1145/3398069

Tripathi, R. P., Sharma, M., Gupta, A. K., Pandey, D., Pandey, B. K., Shahul, A., & George, A. H. (2023). Timely prediction of diabetes by means of machine learning practices. *Augmented Human Research*, *8*(1), 1. doi:10.1007/s41133-023-00062-4

Tsugawa, S., Kikuchi, Y., Kishino, F., Nakajima, K., Itoh, Y., & Ohsaki, H. (2015). Recognizing depression from Twitter activity. *Proceedings of the 33rd Annual ACM Conference on Human Factors in Computing Systems*, (pp. 3187-3196). ACM.

Turk, M., & Pentland, A. (1991). Face recognition using eigenfaces. In *Proceedings IEEE Computer Society Conference on Computer Vision and Pattern Recognition* (pp. 586–591). IEEE.

Umrao, R., Srivastava, R., Shama, S., Kumar, D., & Bhatia, S. (2022, June). Precision Farming System using IoT. In *Futuristic Sustainable Energy & Technology: Proceedings of the International Conference on Futuristic Sustainable Energy &Technology (ICFSE, 2021),* (p. 477). CRC Press. 10.1201/9781003272328-51

Valenza, G., Nardelli, M., Lanata, A., Gentili, C., Bertschy, G., Paradiso, R., & Scilingo, E. P. (2013). Wearable monitoring for mood recognition in bipolar disorder based on history-dependent long-term heart rate variability analysis. *IEEE Journal of Biomedical and Health Informatics, 18*(5), 1625–1635. doi:10.1109/JBHI.2013.2290382 PMID:24240031

van Mens, K., de Schepper, C. W. M., Wijnen, B., Koldijk, S. J., Schnack, H., de Looff, P., Lokkerbol, J., Wetherall, K., Cleare, S., C O'Connor, R., & De Beurs, D. (2020). Predicting future suicidal behaviour in young adults, with different machine learning techniques: A population-based longitudinal study. *Journal of Affective Disorders, 271*, 169–177. doi:10.1016/j.jad.2020.03.081 PMID:32479313

Van Thanh, N. (2023). Emotion Recognition Systems in Retail: A Detailed Analysis of Their Role in Enhancing Customer Interactions, Driving Sales, and Predicting Trends. *Journal of Computational Social Dynamics, 8*(3), 1–9.

Veeraiah, V., Ahamad, G. P. S., Talukdar, S. B., Gupta, A., & Talukdar, V. (2022). Enhancement of Meta Verse Capabilities by IoT Integration. *2022 2nd International Conference on Advance Computing and Innovative Technologies in Engineering (ICACITE),* (pp. 1493-1498). IEEE. 10.1109/ICACITE53722.2022.9823766

Veeraiah, V., Khan, H., Kumar, A., Ahamad, S., Mahajan, A., & Gupta, A. (2022). Integration of PSO and Deep Learning for Trend Analysis of Meta-Verse. *2022 2nd International Conference on Advance Computing and Innovative Technologies in Engineering (ICACITE).* IEEE. 10.1109/ICACITE53722.2022.9823883

Veeraiah, V., Kumar, K. R., Lalitha Kumari, P., Ahamad, S., Bansal, R., & Gupta, A. (2022). Application of Biometric System to Enhance the Security in Virtual World. *2022 2nd International Conference on Advance Computing and Innovative Technologies in Engineering (ICACITE).* IEEE.10.1109/ICACITE53722.2022.9823850

Veeraiah, V., Rajaboina, N. B., Rao, G. N., Ahamad, S., Gupta, A., & Suri, C. S. (2022). Securing Online Web Application for IoT Management. 2022 2nd International Conference on Advance Computing and Innovative Technologies in Engineering (ICACITE). IEEE. http://dx.doi.org/10.1109/ICACITE53722.2022.9823733

Velana, M., Gruss, S., Layher, G., Thiam, P., Zhang, Y., Schork, D., & Walter, S. (2017). The senseemotion database: A multimodal database for the development and systematic validation of an automatic pain-and emotion-recognition system. In *Multimodal Pattern Recognition of Social Signals in Human-Computer-Interaction: 4th IAPR TC 9 Workshop, MPRSS 2016, Cancun, Mexico, December 4, 2016, Revised Selected Papers 4* (pp. 127-139). Springer International Publishing. 10.1007/978-3-319-59259-6_11

Verginadis, Y., Papageorgiou, N., Apostolou, D., & Mentzas, G. (2010). A review of patterns in collaborative work. *Proceedings of the 16th ACM international conference on Supporting group work - GROUP '10*. ACM. 10.1145/1880071.1880118

Vernon, P. A., Villani, V. C., Schermer, J. A., & Petrides, K. V. (2014). Phenotypic and genetic associations between the Big Five and trait emotional intelligence. *Twin Research and Human Genetics*, *17*(4), 181–188. PMID:18828735

Vijayvergia, A., & Kumar, K. (2021). Selective shallow models strength integration for emotion detection using GloVe and LSTM. *Multimedia Tools and Applications*, *80*(18), 28349–28363. doi:10.1007/s11042-021-10997-8

Walch, K. (2018, November 1). Artificial Intelligence Is Not A Technology. *Forbes*.

Wang, L., & Zhang, Y. (2016). Emotion-Driven Music Recommendation Based on Facial Profiling. *International Journal of Human-Computer Interaction*, *32*(8), 611–625.

Wang, W., Kofler, L., Lindgren, C., Lobel, M., Murphy, A., Tong, Q., & Pickering, K. (2023). AI for Psychometrics: Validating Machine Learning Models in Measuring Emotional Intelligence with Eye-Tracking Techniques. *Journal of Intelligence*, *11*(9), 170. doi:10.3390/jintelligence11090170 PMID:37754899

Wang, Z., Zhou, X., Wang, W., & Liang, C. (2020). Emotion recognition using multimodal deep learning in multiple psychophysiological signals and video. *International Journal of Machine Learning and Cybernetics*, *11*(4), 923–934. doi:10.1007/s13042-019-01056-8

Wani, T. M., Gunawan, T. S., Qadri, S. A. A., Kartiwi, M., & Ambikairajah, E. (2021). A comprehensive review of speech emotion recognition systems. *IEEE Access : Practical Innovations, Open Solutions*, *9*, 47795–47814. doi:10.1109/ACCESS.2021.3068045

Wei, J., Hu, G., Yang, X., Luu, A. T., & Dong, Y. (2024). Learning facial expression and body gesture visual information for video emotion recognition. *Expert Systems with Applications*, *237*, 121419. doi:10.1016/j.eswa.2023.121419

Wells, A. E., Hunnikin, L. M., Ash, D. P., & Van Goozen, S. H. (2021). Improving emotion recognition is associated with subsequent mental health and well-being in children with severe behavioural problems. *European Child & Adolescent Psychiatry*, *30*(11), 1769–1777. doi:10.1007/s00787-020-01652-y PMID:32997168

Wexler, A., & Largent, E. (2023). Ethical considerations for researchers developing and testing minimal-risk devices. *Nature Communications*, *14*(1), 1–5. doi:10.1038/s41467-023-38068-6 PMID:37087446

Wilson, H. J., & Daugherty, P. R. (2018). *Humans and AI are Joining Forces. Harvard Business Review*. HBR. https://hbr.org/2018/07/collaborative-intelligence-humans-and-ai-are-joining-forces

Wilson, J., Heinsch, M., Betts, D., Booth, D., & Kay-Lambkin, F. (2021). Barriers and facilitators to the use of e-health by older adults: A scoping review. *BMC Public Health*, *21*(1), 1–12. doi:10.1186/s12889-021-11623-w PMID:34399716

Wisniewski, H., & Torous, J. (2020). Digital navigators to implement smartphone and digital tools in care. *Acta Psychiatrica Scandinavica, 141*(4), 350–355. doi:10.1111/acps.13149 PMID:31930477

Woodworth, R. S., & Schlosberg, H. (1954). *Experimental Psychology*. Holt, Rinehart, and Winston.

Wu, Y., Levis, B., Sun, Y., He, C., Krishnan, A., Neupane, D., & Thombs, B. D. (2021). Accuracy of the Hospital Anxiety and Depression Scale Depression subscale (HADS-D) to screen for major depression: systematic review and individual participant data meta-analysis. *bmj, 373*. doi:10.1136/bmj.n972

Wyman, A., & Zhang, Z. (2023). API Face Value: Evaluating the Current Status and Potential of Emotion Detection Software in Emotional Deficit Interventions. *Journal of Behavioral Data Science, 3*(1), 59–69. doi:10.35566/jbds/v3n1/wyman

XieB.CharnessN.FingermanK.KayeJ.KimM. T.KhurshidA. (2021). When going digital becomes a necessity: Ensuring older adults' needs for information, services, and social inclusion during COVID-19. In *Older Adults and COVID-19* (pp. 181-191). Routledge. doi:10.2196/preprints.19117

Xie, Y., Liang, R., Liang, Z., Huang, C., Zou, C., & Schuller, B. (2019). Speech emotion classification using attention-based LSTM. *IEEE/ACM Transactions on Audio, Speech, and Language Processing, 27*(11), 1675–1685. doi:10.1109/TASLP.2019.2925934

Xu, M., Zhang, F., & Khan, S. U. (2020, January). Improve accuracy of speech emotion recognition with attention head fusion. In *2020 10th annual computing and communication workshop and conference (CCWC)* (pp. 1058-1064). IEEE. 10.1109/CCWC47524.2020.9031207

Yang, K., Wang, C., Gu, Y., Sarsenbayeva, Z., Tag, B., Dingler, T., & Goncalves, J. (2021). Behavioral and physiological signals-based deep multimodal approach for mobile emotion recognition. *IEEE Transactions on Affective Computing*.

Yang, M., Wang, Z., Xu, Q., Li, C., & Xu, R. (2022). Leveraging hierarchical semantic-emotional memory in emotional conversation generation. *CAAI Transactions on Intelligence Technology*.

Yin, Y., Zheng, X., Hu, B., Zhang, Y., & Cui, X. (2021). EEG emotion recognition using fusion model of graph convolutional neural networks and LSTM. *Applied Soft Computing, 100*, 106954. doi:10.1016/j.asoc.2020.106954

Yu, Y., & Kim, Y.-J. (2020). Attention-LSTM-attention model for speech emotion recognition and analysis of IEMOCAP database. *Electronics (Basel), 9*(5), 713. doi:10.3390/electronics9050713

Zaman, K. S., & Reaz, M. M. B. I. (2023). Secure and efficient implementation of facial emotion detection for smart patient monitoring system. *Quantitative Biology, 11*(2), 175–182. doi:10.15302/J-QB-022-0312

Zeidner, M., Roberts, R. D., & Matthews, G. (2002). Can emotional intelligence be schooled? A critical review. *Educational Psychologist, 37*(4), 215–231. doi:10.1207/S15326985EP3704_2

Zenebe, Y., & Akele, B., W/Selassie, M., & Necho, M. (. (2021). Prevalence and determinants of depression among old age: A systematic review and meta-analysis. *Annals of General Psychiatry*, *20*(1), 55. doi:10.1186/s12991-021-00375-x PMID:34922595

Zhang, L., Samaras, D., & Zelinsky, G. J. (2010). Face recognition across pose: A review. *Pattern Analysis & Applications*, *13*(2), 157–176.

Zhang, L., & Zhang, L. (2014). A survey of recent advances in face detection. *Scholarpedia*, *9*(7), 31737. doi:10.4249/scholarpedia.31737

Zhang, Q., Gao, T., Liu, X., & Zheng, Y. (2020). Public environment emotion prediction model using LSTM network. *Sustainability (Basel)*, *12*(4), 1665. doi:10.3390/su12041665

Zhang, R. E., Ringland, K., Paan, M. C., Mohr, D., & Reddy, M. (2021, May). Designing for emotional well-being: integrating persuasion and customization into mental health technologies. In *Proceedings of the 2021 CHI Conference on Human Factors in Computing Systems* (pp. 1-13). ACM. 10.1145/3411764.3445771

Zhang, Y., Wang, S., Hermann, A., Joly, R., & Pathak, J. (2021). Development and validation of a machine learning algorithm for predicting the risk of postpartum depression among pregnant women. *Journal of Affective Disorders*, *279*, 1–8. doi:10.1016/j.jad.2020.09.113 PMID:33035748

Zhang, Z., Wang, L., & Yang, J. (2023). *Weakly Supervised Video Emotion Detection and Prediction via Cross-Modal Temporal Erasing Network* (Vol. 1)., doi:10.1109/CVPR52729.2023.01811

Zhao, J., Mao, X., & Chen, L. (2019). Speech emotion recognition using deep 1D & 2D CNN LSTM networks. *Biomedical Signal Processing and Control*, *47*, 312–323. doi:10.1016/j.bspc.2018.08.035

Zhao, J., Wu, M., Zhou, L., Wang, X., & Jia, J. (2022). Cognitive psychology-based artificial intelligence review. *Frontiers in Neuroscience*, *16*, 1024316. doi:10.3389/fnins.2022.1024316 PMID:36278021

Zhou, L., Sukpasjaroen, K., Wu, Y. M., Wang, L., Chankoson, T., & Cai, E. L. (2022). Predicting nursing students' psychological well-being: Network analysis based on a model of thriving through relationships. *BMC Medical Education*, *22*(1), 1–11. doi:10.1186/s12909-022-03517-1 PMID:35710399

Zhuang, J. R., Guan, Y. J., Nagayoshi, H., Muramatsu, K., Watanuki, K., & Tanaka, E. (2019). Real-time emotion recognition system with multiple physiological signals. *Journal of Advanced Mechanical Design, Systems, and Manufacturing, 13*(4), JAMDSM0075-JAMDSM0075.

Zhu, D., Doan, T., Kanjanakan, P., & Kim, P. B. (2022). The impact of emotional intelligence on hospitality employees' work outcomes: A systematic and meta-analytical review. *Journal of Hospitality Marketing & Management*, *31*(3), 326–347. doi:10.1080/19368623.2021.1978914

Ziska Fields, F. (Ed.). (2023). *Human Creativity vs. Machine Creativity: Innovations and Challenges. Multidisciplinary Approaches in AI, Creativity, Innovation, and Green Collaboration* (pp. 19–28). IGI Global. doi:10.4018/978-1-6684-6366-6.ch002

About the Contributors

Mritunjay Rai received his Ph.D. from IIT (ISM) in Electrical Engineering with a specialization in Image Processing, his Master of Engineering with distinction from Birla Institute of Technology, Mesra, Ranchi, in Instrumentation and Control, and B. Tech. from Shri Ramswaroop Memorial College of Engineering and Management, Lucknow in Electronics and Communication Engineering. His areas of interest lie in image processing, speech processing, and robotics & automation. Dr. Rai is an active researcher and has published several papers in SCI indexed Q2 journals and at international and national conferences in his domain.

Jay Kumar Pandey is currently working as an Assistant Professor in the Department of Electronics and Communication Engineering at Shri Ramswaroop Memorial University, Barabanki (U.P.) India. Dr. Pandey has completed his Ph.D. in renewable energy and has done his M.Tech with a specialization in Power Control (Instrumentation) and also done his MBA in Finance and Marketing. His subjects of interest are related to Instrumentation and control, Image Processing, Digital Electronics, Machine Learning, and Solar PV. He is an active member of the Institution of Electronics and Telecommunication Engineers (IETE) & IAENG (International Association of Engineers). He has 12 years of teaching and research experience and has published more than 15 research papers in national and international journals /conferences.

***

Bhawna is an MBA Student at the Mittal School of Business, Lovely Professional University.

Sandeep Bhatia is a dedicated Assistant Professor with more than 14 years of experience teaching undergraduate and post-graduate courses in the branch of ECE and CSE. He has one-year industry experience as a hardware engineerat C-DAC Mohali, Punjab. Presently,He is working as an Assistant Professor in the DepartmentofCSE, Galgotias University, Greater Noida. He is Ph.D. Pursuing from JamiaMilliaIslamia, Central University, New Delhi in the field of IoT and Embedded System Design. He has completed his M.E from PEC University of Technology, Chandigarh in the field of Embedded System in the year 2010.He hascompleted his B.Tech from PTU Jalandhar in the year 2008.He has successfully Developed MOOC course for the subject "Microcontroller and Embedded Systems Design (KEC-061)" sponsored by AKTU Lucknow, UP at AKTU Digital Education Platform for the students. He has more than 25 published papers in Scopus Indexed Journals and 5 other reputed journals along with twenty five International/ National conferences attended. Also Published 7patents, attended various FDPs and completed various online courses including NPTEL. He has guided 40B.Tech/ BCA projects along with 8M.Tech/MCA thesis projects. He is comfortable in the field of IoT and its Applications, AI, ML, CNNA, Embedded System, Microcontrollers and Sensors. He has taught various value added course in IoT and Embedded System for graduate students

Pankaj Dadheech is currently working as a Professor & Deputy Head in the Department of Computer Science & Engineering (NBA Accredited), Swami Keshvanand Institute of Technology, Management & Gramothan (SKIT), Jaipur, Rajasthan, India (Accredited by NAAC A++ Grade). He has more than 18 years of experience in teaching. He is currently working a Professor & Dy. HOD in the Department of Computer Science & Engineering (NBA Accredited), Swami Keshvanand Institute of Technology, Management & Gramothan (SKIT), Jaipur, Rajasthan, India. He has published 25 Patents at Intellectual Property India, Office of the Controller General of Patents, Design and Trade Marks, Department of Industrial Policy and Promotion, Ministry of Commerce and Industry, Government of India. He has published 8 International Patents (USA, South African, Australian, Germany) & 2 Copyrights. He has 73 publications in various International & National Journals, 63 papers in various National & International conferences. He has published 9 Books & 42 Book Chapters.

Dwijendra Nath Dwivedi is a professional with 20+ years of subject matter expertise creating right value propositions for analytics and AI. He currently heads the EMEA+AP AI and IoT team at SAS, a worldwide frontrunner in AI technology. He is a post-Graduate in Economics from Indira Gandhi Institute of Development and Research and currently perusing PHD from crackow university of economics Poland. He has presented his research in more than 20 international conference and published several Scopus indexed paper on AI adoption in many areas. As an author he has contributed to more than 8 books and has more than 25 publications in high impact journals. He conducts AI Value seminars and workshops for the executive audience and for power users.

A. Shaji George is a highly respected and accomplished figure in the fields of education and the ICT industry. With over 30 years of experience in designing and deploying large-scale projects, Dr. George has made significant contributions to industry. He has a passion for working with clients to help them overcome complex business challenges, drive innovation, and deliver results. Dr. George is recognized as an expert in the field of ICT and has published over 250 research papers in national and international journals and conferences. He is also the author of 30 books that have been published by reputed international publishers. His extensive contributions to the field have earned him 20 awards, recognizing his outstanding achievements and contributions to the industry. Dr. George is the founder of PU Publications, PUIRJ, PUIIJ and PUIRP International Journal. He has a keen interest in wireless networking, cloud computing, big data analytics, the Internet of Things, and industrial automation systems. He works with clients from a wide range of industries to develop strategies and implement next-generation solutions that transform their businesses. Dr. George's wealth of knowledg

Neha Goel working as Associate Professor in the department of Electronics & Communication Engineering at RKGIT, Ghaziabad. She has completed her Phd from SRM university, Chennai in 2019. She has 18 years of rich experience in teaching. Her area of interest on VLSI design, CMOS design, Internet of things, Machine learning. She has guided several B.tech Projects and she has published 38 papers in various National/International journals and conferences. She has granted & published 3 patents. She has also attended various workshops, seminars in various fields.

Ankur Gupta has received the B.Tech and M.Tech in Computer Science and Engineering from Ganga Institute of Technology and Management, Kablana affiliated with Maharshi Dayanand University, Rohtak in 2015 and 2017. He is an Assistant Professor in the Department of Computer Science and Engineering at Vaish College of Engineering, Rohtak, and has been working there since January 2019. He has many publications in various reputed national/ international conferences, journals, and online book chapter contributions (Indexed by SCIE, Scopus, ESCI, ACM, DBLP, etc). He is doing research in the field of cloud computing, data security & machine learning. His research work in M.Tech was based on biometric security in cloud computing.

Sanjiv Kumar Jain is working as an A.P. (S.G.) at the Department of Electrical Engineering, Medi-Caps University, Indore, India. He completed his PhD from Maulana Azad National Institute of Technology, Bhopal, India. He received best teaching award and best project mentor award at university level. His research interests include power system control and planning, evolutionary algorithms and neural networks.

Alex Khang is excellent researcher and professor in CSE.

Rita Komalasari is a lecturer at YARSI University. Her current work is focused on Predictive Pioneers: Bridging the Mental Health Gap in Older Adults through Advanced Digital Technologies and User-Centric Insights.

Dinesh Kumar is a highly accomplished professional with extensive military, academia, business, and charity expertise. He holds a PhD from the Indian Institute of Technology (IIT) Roorkee and is currently teaching at Mittal School of Business, Lovely Professional University. He is also the founder of Pomento, and Mission Dost-E-Jahan.

Muhammad Mukarram is a dedicated lecturer in Management Sciences known for his dynamic approach to teaching and his vibrant contributions to research. With a passion for imparting knowledge, Mukarram engages students in the complexities of management theory, emphasizing practical applications in the business world. His teaching style blends enthusiasm with a deep understanding of contemporary management challenges. Beyond the classroom, Mukarram is recognized as a vibrant researcher, consistently exploring innovative avenues in the field of Management Sciences. His research focuses on emerging trends, such as the integration of big data in organizational theory, and he actively contributes to scholarly discourse. Mukarram's work is characterized by its depth and relevance, reflecting a commitment to advancing the understanding of management practices. With a solid academic background and a reputation for excellence in both teaching and research, Muhammad Mukarram stands as a valuable asset to the academic community. His dedication to fostering a comprehensive understanding of management principles and his enthusiasm for exploring the frontiers of knowledge make him a respected figure among students and colleagues alike.

Daogafu Gwra Narzary is an MBA Student at the Mittal School of Business, Lovely Professional University.

Binay Kumar Pandey currently working as an Assistant Professor in Department of Information Technology of Govind Ballabh Pant University of Agriculture and Technology Pantnagar Uttrakhand, India. He obtained his M. Tech with Specialization in Bioinformatics from Maulana Azad National Institute of Technology Bhopal M. P. India, in 2008 . He obtained his First Degree B. Tech at the IET Lucknow (Uttar Pradesh Technical University, Uttar Pradesh and Lucknow) India, in 2005. In 2010, he joined Department of Information Technology of College of Technology in Govind Ballabh Pant University of Agriculture and Technology Pantnagar as an

Assistant Professor and worked for various UG and PG projects till date. He has more than ten years of experience in the field of teaching and research.He has more than 40 publications in reputed peer journal reputed journal Springer,Inderscience,(sci and socopus indexed journal and others) and 3 patent.He has many awards such PM Scholarship etc . He session chair in IEEE International Conference on Advent Trends in Multidisciplinary Research and Innovation (ICATMRI-2020) on December 30, 2020 organized by Pankaj Laddhad Institute of Technology and Management Studies; Buldhana, Maharashtra, India.

Pokkuluri Kiran Sree obtained his B.Tech degree in Computer Science & Engineering with distinction from JNTU Hyderabad and M.E in Computer Science & Engineering with distinction from Anna University. He has obtained his Ph.D in Artificial Intelligence from Jawaharlal Nehru Technological University-Hyderabad. His areas of interests include Cellular Automata, Parallel Algorithms, Artificial Intelligence, and Compiler Design. He was the reviewer for some reputed International Journals and IEEE Society Conferences on Artificial Intelligence, Image Processing and Bioinformatics.

Usman Sana is an experienced and dedicated facial profiling coach with a passion for helping individuals and organizations unlock the power of facial profiling. With a comprehensive understanding of facial recognition technologies, emotions, and non-verbal cues, Dr. Sana empowers clients to develop a deep understanding of facial profiling techniques and leverage them effectively. Through personalized coaching and practical guidance, Dr. Sana equips individuals with the skills to excel in facial profiling, enhance communication, and make informed decisions.

Muhammad Haseeb Shakil is a highly qualified professional with a Master of Science degree in Management Sciences from COMSATS University Lahore. With a passion for academia and administration, he dedicated over three years of his career to Superior University, where he served in various capacities, excelling in administration, operations, and management roles. During his tenure at Superior University, Muhammad Haseeb Shakil showcased exemplary skills in streamlining administrative processes, optimizing operations, and contributing to the overall efficiency of the institution. His commitment to excellence and his ability to navigate the complexities of educational administration earned him recognition and respect among his peers. Beyond his administrative responsibilities, he is also a prolific writer, with a notable portfolio of more than five publications and six blogs. His contributions to the academic and literary spheres reflect his dedication to sharing knowledge and insights with a wider audience. His combination of academic qualifications, professional experience, and a rich body of written work underscores his multifaceted talents. His journey in the field of Management Sciences has not only enriched his own professional growth but has also positively impacted the institutions and individuals he has been associated with.

Mishal Tayyab is a dynamic and accomplished Research Scholar at the School of Media Sciences at Superior University Lahore, bringing a wealth of experience and expertise to the academic realm. With a passion for media and communication, she has devoted more than five years to the industry, showcasing her talents in various roles, including that of a Radio Jockey (RJ). Having embarked on her journey in the media landscape, Mishal quickly made a mark with her distinctive voice and captivating on-air presence. Her years as an RJ allowed her to connect with diverse audiences, honing her communication skills and gaining insights into the nuances of effective storytelling. Transitioning into academia, She's now focuses on research at the School of Media Sciences, contributing to the scholarly exploration of media-related topics. Her commitment to advancing knowledge in the field is evident in her pursuit of academic excellence, bridging the gap between practical experience and theoretical understanding. Her dual experience, both as a media professional and a dedicated researcher, positions her as a valuable asset to the academic community. Her ability to blend real-world insights with scholarly pursuits reflects a commitment to holistic understanding and continual growth in the ever-evolving field of media. As a Research Scholar, She continues to make meaningful contributions to the School of Media Sciences, fostering an environment of intellectual curiosity and innovation. Her journey stands as a testament to the seamless integration of hands-on experience and academic rigor in the pursuit of knowledge and excellence.

Index

www.ingramcontent.com/pod-product-compliance
Lightning Source LLC
LaVergne TN
LVHW060003031026
849161LV00025B/1354